DATA STRUCTURES
made simple

(The Complete Text Book for B.E.(Comp. Sc.), MCA, PGDCA and IT Related Examinations of Leading Universities including Distance Learning Education Programme)

by

Satish Jain
B.Sc., B.E.(IISc), M.E.(IISc), M.Tech.(IIT Kanpur),
Wing Commander (Retd.)
Professor of Information Technology,
Institute of Information Technology & Management
GGS Indraprastha University, Delhi.

Shashi Singh
Advance Diploma (IT), M.C.A.

www.bpbonline.com

REPRINT 2025
FIRST EDITION 2006

ISBN-10: 81-8333-122-X
ISBN-13: 978-81-8333-122-7

LIMITS OF LIABILITY AND DISCLAIMER OF WARRANTY

Distributors:

BPB PUBLICATIONS
20, Ansari Road, Darya Ganj
New Delhi-110002
Ph: 23254990 / 23254991

DECCAN AGENCIES
4-3-329, Bank Street,
Hyderabad-500195
Ph: 24756967 / 24756400

MICRO MEDIA
Shop No. 5, Mahendra Chambers,
150 DN Rd. Next to Capital Cinema,
V.T. (C.S.T.) Station, MUMBAI-400 001
Ph: 22078296 / 22078297

Published by Manish Jain for BPB Publications, 20 Ansari Road, Darya Ganj, New Delhi-110002 and Printed by him at Manipal Technologies, Manipal

www.bpbonline.com

Dedicated to

Sri Raja Rajeshwari and Mata Sharda Devi
Goddesses who bless Immense Power of Knowledge

ACKNOWLEDGEMENTS

We gratefully acknowledge the contribution made by the following persons in bringing out the book in this form:

- Mrs. Anita Rajdev
  B.Com., Advance Diploma (IT)
- Ms. Vineeta Pillai
  B.Sc (Hons.), Advance Diploma (IT), M.Sc.(IT)
- Mr. Shashank Jain
  B.E. (Delhi College of Engineering)
- Dr. Madhulika Jain

PREFACE

The objective of this book is to meet the growing needs of Computer Science, Engineering and IT students to lay their hands on a text book that explains Data Structures, a highly technical subject, in a very simple way. The concepts of linked lists, stacks, queues, trees, graphs etc. are brought out in this book in easy-to-understand language as well as by giving many figures, examples and algorithms. It is felt that most of the books available in the market do not cover the syllabus for Data Structures comprehensively. The syllabus for this paper is very vast and needs a thorough understanding of concepts and their implementation correctly. For this reason, we have pressed into service all our practical experience in teaching as well as in academic field, in organizing and explaining complex topics in simple manner so as to meet the needs of all streams of students.

We have made this book user friendly by adding a comprehensive glossary of technical terms and an index at the end of the book. These sections may be very handy for understanding as well as locating page numbers of major topics discussed in this book. The glossary of technical terms will be specially helpful to a reader in answering objective type of questions.

A special feature throughout this book is that the salient and crucial information has been encapsulated within two parallel horizontal lines with a (☞) mark to capture the attention of the reader, to the basic concepts.

This book has come out in this form due to the untiring efforts by Ms. Geetha Iyer Diploma Computer science, in formatting and drawing illustrations for the book in a very short span of time.

We shall feel obliged if the readers send us their critical opinion of the presentation, readability and coverage in this book and to mail their suggestions, if any, to improve the subject matter.

7th May, 2006 Authors

AI...OTHER TITLES OF INTEREST

Rise of Generative AI & ChatGPT
ISBN: 9789355517982

Think AI
ISBN: 9789355513199

Modern Marketing Using AI
ISBN: 9789391030216

The **AI Dilemma**
ISBN: 9788194837787

The Today & Future of
WSN, AI and IOT
ISBN: 9789389845167

Essentials of
Deep Learning and AI
ISBN: 9789391030353

AI & ML - Powering the Agents of **Automation**
ISBN: 9789388511636

Practical Mathematics
for **AI & Deep Learning**
ISBN: 9789355511935

Microsoft Azure AI:
A Beginner's Guide
ISBN: 9789355510518

Cloud Native AI & Machine Learning on AWS
ISBN: 9789355513267

Intelligent Reliability Analysis
Using **MATLAB & AI**
ISBN: 9789390684656

Up and Running **Google AutoML** and **AI Platform**
ISBN: 9789388511926

Pythonic AI
ISBN: 9789355515919

Learn AI with **Python**
ISBN: 9789391392611

Hyperautomation with
Generative AI
ISBN: 9789355518590

Learning Google Cloud Vertex AI
ISBN: 9789355515353

USEFUL TIPS FOR THE EXAMINEE

Dear Reader,

Every examination has its peculiarities and the best results are often obtained by identifying that particular feature and working with the help of right strategies, which in turn can be adopted by correctly analysing the question paper.

The authors have tried to present an effective aid to guide you to analyse the question paper and consequently help to chalk out your own effective plan of action.

The instructions given on the first page of the question paper in an examination should always be read *very* carefully.

How to avoid mistakes?

After having given an initial reading to all the questions, first attempt only those questions about which you are very ***sure*** regarding the correct answer. It is while taking a second go at the questions, that you answer the remaining ones, always making sure that you spend only a *limited* amount of time on each one of them.

While answering to objective questions, the time limit should be strictly kept in mind and every effort must be made to complete all the questions by keeping the answers brief and to the point. Remember you can also resort to making a sketch/diagram in your answer wherever possible, instead of describing it in words, because "a thousand words can be effectively expressed by a small diagram." As the number of questions are normally more for an average student, this precious time saved, enables you to have a wider coverage of the paper.

While attempting the descriptive type of questions, keep a check on the length of your answers and keep in mind the time frame available for answering the remaining questions.

The last stage, being the revision stage, you should save at least 5 to 10 minutes to revise all your answers. Try to find the gross errors, like units of measurement, or wrong question number for a specific answer etc., which do happen because of the inherent tension of the examination.

How to prepare for the examination?

This book has covered the syllabus on Data Structures in an easy to understand manner. But you must learn Chapter 1 thoroughly since it deals with the fundamental of problem solving techniques. For other Chapters also, it is advised that in addition to this book, you may refer to other books available in the library. This will enable you to broaden the horizon of your knowledge.

Last, but not the least, you should simulate examination conditions by conducting a demo examination, taking any of the question papers appeared in previous examinations, attempting to complete the answers within the stipulated time. After a day or two, evaluate your answers and if any doubts still persist, clarify them immediately from a good text book available in the library. This way, you will be sure about the subject and will have confidence while answering the actual question paper in an examination.

WISH YOU A GRAND SUCCESS in the examination, and a very bright future in the fields of IT and Computer Science.

Authors

CONTENTS

DATA STRUCTURES

Chapter 3. Arrays 56

CHAPTER 1

Algorithms (Analysis and Design)

1.1 PROBLEM SOLVING

In order to solve a problem using computer, one needs to write step by step solution first. This may be done by writing simple instructions for each operation. There might be a number of methods to solve the problem and hence solutions will differ from person to person. However, in all cases, basic steps for solving a problem would remain the same. These steps are:

a. Formulating the problem and deciding the data types to be entered.
b. Identifying the steps of computation that are necessary for getting the solution.
c. Identifying decision points *i.e.,* under what circumstances a particular operation is to be performed and when not to be carried out.
d. Finding the result and verifying the values.

1.1.1 Procedure for Problem Solving

Problem solving is simply writing the basic steps and putting them in correct sequence to find the result.

☞ *Problem solving is a logical process of breaking down the problem into smaller parts each of which can be solved step by step to obtain the final solution.*

Though, every problem may be unique in itself, yet the procedures for solving such problems are similar. The procedure for solving a problem involves six steps. These steps should be understood thoroughly and practiced effectively. Using these steps, our problem solving capability will improve with time.

Six basic steps in solving a problem are:

1. First, spend some time in understanding the problem. In this step, you are not required to use a computer. Instead, you should try to answer the question namely, what is expected and how to get it. This means, try to formulate a problem correctly.
2. Construct a list of *variables* that are needed to find the solution of the problem.
3. Decide the layout for the output.
4. Select a programming method best suited to solve the problem and then only carryout the coding, using a suitable programming language.
5. Test the program. Select test data so that each part of the program would be checked for correctness.

6. Finally use data validation steps to guard against processing of wrongly inputted data.

All these six steps are further elaborated in the following sections.

Step 1. Understanding the Problem

Read each *statement* given in the problem carefully, so that you can answer the first question "What is expected by solving the problem?" Do not start drawing a flowchart or decision table straight away. Instead, read each statement of the problem slowly and carefully, by understanding the *keywords*. Use paper and pencil to solve the problem manually for some test data. Let us understand this point by solving the problem given in Example 1.

Example 1 Accept a value M and find the sum of first M even integers.

Solution The solution of this problem requires you to take an input value, say a number 6 is given as the value of M. Then, you should get the sum of first 6 even integers. In the first step, you should be able to answer the following two questions:

"What are the first 6 even integers?"

These are 2, 4, 6, 8, 10, and 12.

"What is their sum?"

The sum is 42. Hence, the solution is to be so made that the sum of first 6 even integers comes out to be 42.

Step 2. Construction of the List of Variables

In this step, you should think in advance the number of variables along with the names of the variables. The names chosen for the variables should be an aid to memory. For example, in the case of the problem stated in step 1 above, the variables may be, I, SUM and COUNT as given below.

1. Generate even integers 2, 4, 6,...(I)
2. Total the sum of even integers 2 + 4 + 6 + ... (SUM)
3. Count the number of even integers, i.e. 1, 2, 3,... (COUNT)

Thus, it is clear that we need to use the above three variables and one more variable "M" whose value will be inputted by the user of the program from the keyboard. Finally, the four variables for this problem would be:

M	to be entered by the user.
I	to generate even integers.
COUNT	to keep a track of the number of even integers that have been summed.
SUM	An accumulator that will hold the current total value of even integers.

Step 3. Output Design

Many a times, the 'output' format is specified in the problem itself, but sometimes, it may not be so. If the output format is not specified, we must keep in mind that the output report should be *easily* understandable by a reader. The headings should not cause any doubt or confusion in the mind of a reader.

In the solution of Example 1, the output format could be as follows:

No. of first even integers	Total sum
6	42

You should keep one more point in mind. The programs and the solution to a problem are for other people (teachers, supervisors, contractors, etc). They will appreciate you only if they can understand the results and analyse them. Hence, the output format should have the following characteristics:

a. Attractive,
b. Easy to read and
c. Self-explanatory.

Step 4. Program Development

You should now draw a flowchart for the procedure that you have just made in steps 1, 2 and 3. Standard symbols should be used for drawing a flowchart. If a problem is complex, you should divide it into several simpler parts. Then, draw a flowchart for each part separately and combine them together using connectors.

A flowchart for the problem in Example 1 is drawn as shown in Figure 1.1.

Now write the code in the prescribed high level language to translate the flowchart into a program.

Step 5. Testing the Program

You should give a *dry* run to the developed program that translates the flowchart of step 4. This means by giving known values to the variables and by checking the result and thus comparing results with manually calculated values. Test values are so selected that each part of a flowchart is tested and the program is free from any logical errors.

Step 6. Validating the Program

It is quite likely that the user of your program may enter values, which are not expected by the program. Such values should be rejected by the procedure drawn by you. This is known as validation of data. For example, in the problem of Example 1, in step 1 we may give some upper limit to the value of "M" and state that "M" should be an *integer* value. Such types of checks can be included to validation a program.

1.1.2 Problem Definition and use of Examples for Problem Solving

Let us take another example of a problem faced in day-to-day life. Suppose you want to reach your college computer laboratory at 8 AM. You would lay out a plan to get ready by 7 AM, then take a bus/rikshaw and reach at the gate of your college. Then climb up the stairs to reach the computer science laboratory. For all these movements, you will note the time taken for each part. If due to some reason, you are unable to get ready by 7 AM and you already know that it takes one hour to reach from house to college by bus/rikshaw, then you will take a faster means of transportation. You may take an autorikshaw or a taxi. Thus, a very simple problem of reaching the computer laboratory of your college by 8 AM will need several steps for solution. Each step is to be accurately defined/marked so that no guess work is

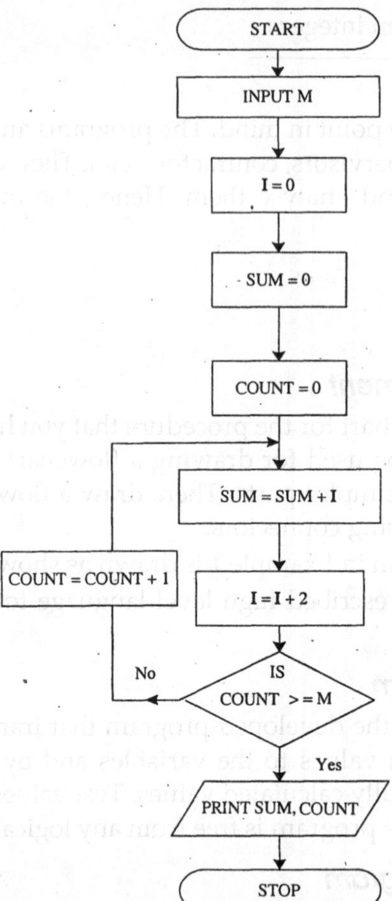

Figure 1.1 Flowchart for solving problem in Example 1

necessary. You can thus represent the solution of this problem in three steps as shown in Figure 1.2.

In Figure 1.2, steps 1, 2 and 3 appear to be very simple. In actual practice when you have to give instructions to a person, who is going for the first time, it may not be so easy. For example, you have to define the word "READY" precisely so that he knows exactly what he has to do by 7AM to get READY. Similarly, in step 2, you may have to clearly specify the bus route number, the bus stop to board the bus, the place to get down from the bus, etc. You may also like to tell that a bus is not to be boarded, if it is overcrowded. The word "overcrowded" needs to be exactly defined. Finally, step 3 needs further elaboration about the room number and floor number; where the computer laboratory is located and how to reach there.

You can explain all this to a person who does not know any thing about the computer laboratory, provided you *know* it correctly. In the same way, you can solve a problem on a computer, if you know exactly what the problem is and how to solve it *manually*.

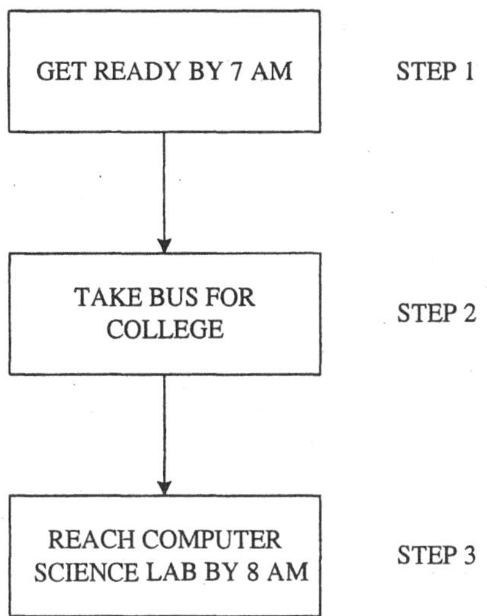

Figure 1.2 Step by step solution to reach college computer science laboratory (LAB)

1.2 TOP-DOWN AND BOTTOM-UP APPROACHES TO ALGORITHM DESIGN

1.2.1 Top-Down Approach of Problem Solving

Top-down design is the technique of breaking down a problem into various sub tasks needed to be performed. Each of these tasks is further broken down into separate *subtasks*, and so on till each subtask is sufficiently simple to be written as a self contained module or procedure. The entire solution of the problem will then consist of a series of simple modules and joining them together will make the complete task of solving the complex problem.

In top-down design, we initially describe the problem we are working with at the highest or most general level. The description of the problem at this level will usually be concerned with what must be done – not how it must be done. The description will be in terms of higher-level operations. We must take all of the operations at this level and individually break them down into simpler steps that begin to describe how to accomplish the tasks. If these simple steps can be represented as acceptable algorithmic steps, we need not split them any further. If that is not the case, then we split each of these second level operations individually into still simpler steps. This stepwise refinement continues until each of the original top-level operations have been described in terms of acceptable shortest (primitive) statements.

The top-down approach, starting at the general levels to gain an understanding of the system and gradually moving down to levels of greater detail, is done in the analysis stage. In the process of moving from top to bottom, each component is exploded into more and more details.

Thus, the problem at hand is analysed or broken down into major components, each of which is again broken down if necessary.

☞ *Top-down process involves working from the most general form, down to the most specific form.*

The design of modules is reflected in an hierarchy chart such as the one shown in Figure 1.3. The purpose of the procedure *Main* is to co-ordinate the three branch operations e.g. *Get, Process* and *Put* routines. These three routines communicate only through *Main*. Similarly, *Sub1* and *Sub2*, can communicate only through the *Process* routine.

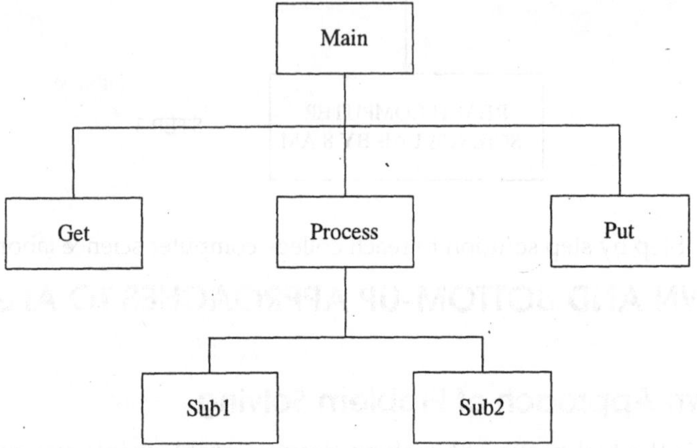

Figure 1.3 Top down modular design

☞ *Using the top-down approach, attention is first focussed on global aspects of the overall system. As the design progresses, the system is decomposed into subsystems and more consideration is given to specific issues.*

Advantages of Top-down approach

a. This approach allows analyst to remain "on top of" a problem and view the developing solution in the context. The solution always proceeds from the highest level to the lowest level. With other techniques, we may find ourselves bogged down with very low-level decisions at a very early stage. It will be difficult to make such decisions if it is not clear as to how they may affect the overall solution of a problem.

b. This would be a very good way to delay decisions on problems whose solution may not be readily available. At each stage in the development, the individual operation will be split up into a number of elementary steps.

c. By dividing the problem into a number of subproblems, it is easier to share problem development. For example, one person may solve one part of the problem and the other person may solve another part of the problem.

d. Since the program may have bugs and the debugging time grows quickly when the program is long, it will be easier to debug a long program which is divided into a number of smaller segments or parts. The top-down development process specifies a solution in terms of a group of smaller, individual subtasks. These smaller tasks would become the ideal units of program for testing and debugging.

   If we add a new piece of code, say "p" to the overall program "P", and an error condition occurs, we can definitely state that the error must be either in "p" itself or in the interface between "p" and "P", because "P" has been previously checked and certified to be correct.

☞ *By testing a program broken into smaller pieces, we greatly simplify the time consuming debugging process. In addition, we will have the satisfaction of knowing that everything we have coded so far is correct.*

---

e. Another advantage of top-down development process is that it becomes an ideal structure for managing and implementing a program using a team of programmers. A senior programmer can be made responsible for the design of a high-level task and its decomposition into subtasks. Each of such subtasks can then be "given out" to a junior programmer who works under the direction of the senior staff. Since software projects are carried out by teams of two or more programmers, this top-down characteristic helps in faster completion of the solution of the complex problem.

☞ *In summary, top-down method is a program design technique that analyses a problem in terms of more elementary subtasks. Through the technique of stepwise splitting, we expand and define each of the separate subtasks until the problem is solved completely. Each subtask is tested and verified before it is expanded further.*

In addition to above the following are three more advantages:

a. Increased comprehension of the problem.
b. Unnecessary lower-level detail are removed.
c. Reduced debugging time.

1.2.2 Bottom-up Approach of Problem Solving

When faced with a large and complex problem, it may be difficult to see how the *whole* thing can be solved. It may be easier to solve parts of the problem individually, taking the easier aspects first and thereby gaining the insight and experience to tackle the more difficult tasks, and finally join each of the solutions together to form the complete solution. This is called a bottom-up approach.

This approach suffers from the *disadvantage* that the parts of the solutions or programs may not fit together easily. There may be a lack of consistency among modules, and thus, more re-programming may have to be carried out. Hence, this approach is not very much favoured.

1.3 USE OF ALGORITHMS IN PROBLEM SOLVING

A set of instructions which describes the steps to be followed to carry out an activity is called an *algorithm* or *procedure* for solving a problem. If the algorithm is written in a language that the computer can understand, then such a set of instructions is called a *program*.

The task of writing a computer program involves going through several stages. So programming requires more than just writing programs. This also requires writing algorithms, as well as testing the program to locate all types of errors.

We can view an algorithm as a way to solve a problem or in other words, as a set of directions, that tell us exactly how to go about for getting the desired results. For example, we can use following steps or actions to reach the office by 10 AM.

Action

1. Get ready by 8 AM.
2. Take breakfast
3. Board the chartered bus at 9 AM.
4. Reach office at 10 AM.

We can thus, define an *algorithm* as an ordered sequence of well-stated and effective operations that, when executed, will produce the results.

By "ordered sequence" we mean that after the completion of each step in the algorithm, the next step is clearly defined. We must know exactly where to look for the next instruction. The ordering could, for example, be specified by writing a number to the steps with the positive integers and following the sequencing rule.

☞ *An algorithm must always have one clearly understood starting point and one or more clearly understood ending points.*

The starting point can be implied – we usually assume that we are to start at step 1 – or it can be stated explicitly (one step may be labeled START). More than one starting point would create confusion about where to start, violating the ordering condition just stated.

It is perfectly acceptable to identify one or more of the steps in the algorithms as *terminators* – steps that, when executed, end the execution of the entire algorithm. However, regardless of which section we execute, we wish to stop after completing that section.

The outline, given in Figure 1.4, contains a single clearly identified starting point (step 1) and three clearly defined terminators (steps 5, 8, and 11). The set of steps executed will always be either (1, 2, 3, 4, 5), or (1, 2, 6, 7, 8), or (1, 2, 9, 10, 11).

1. START
2. Make a decision that divides the problem into three possible cases:

Case 1		Case 2		Case 3	
3.	______	6.	______	9.	______
4.	______	7.	______	10.	______
5.	STOP	8.	STOP	11.	STOP

Figure 1.4 Outline for solving a problem

The existence of one or more terminators, however, is insufficient to guarantee that execution will eventually stop.

Another fundamental characteristic of algorithms is that each individual operation must be both "effective" and "well defined". By "effective" we mean that some formal method must exist for carrying out that operation and also getting an answer. For example:

a. compute n × (n + 1),
b. determine if *x* is even,
c. wait for one hour and 10 minutes,
d. take the square root to a maximum of three decimal place accuracy.

are all effective operations, and could be easily carried out.

But look at the following statements:

e. Compute n ÷ 0 i.e. divide n by zero.
f. Determine the largest prime number.
g. Write the exact value for the square root of 2.
h. Wait for –1 hour.

The above stated steps are not effective. They either cannot be evaluated or we have no idea how to go about answering them.

Each individual operation must be "well defined" — which means, that they are clearly understandable and without an iota of confusion to the person or machine that is executing the algorithm. A basic question about algorithm concerns the type of well-defined operations we are allowed to write at each step. That is, what are the building blocks from which we can compose an algorithm? These building blocks, are also called *primitives*.

For example:

MIX *x* INTO *y*
MEASURE *x* units OF ingredient
STIR *x*
COOK *x* AT *y*°c for *z* minutes
COOK *x* UNTIL temperature = 100°c

The statements whose meaning is clear to most people would be more realistic examples of cooking *primitives*. However, even these simple statements may not be acceptable *primitives* if there is any *confusion* or *uncertainty* about their meaning . For example, does COOK mean bake, boil, fry, or grill?

1.3.1 Developing an Algorithm

The process of developing an algorithm to solve a specific problem is a trial–and–error process that may need numerous attempts. Programmers will make some initial attempt at a solution and review it to test its correctness. The errors they discover will usually lead to insertions, deletions, or modifications in the existing algorithm. It may need scrapping the old one and beginning a new solution.

1.3.2 Characteristics of Algorithmic Language

Some characteristics of the algorithm language are given below:

a. By a judicious choice of algorithmic language primitives, we can ensure that the final algorithm will be closely related to the desired programming language. Thus, it will facilitating the next step of translating the algorithm into that language progam.

b. We will however be bogged down in the restrictive syntax of a specific language. An algorithmic language should be viewed as a set of guidelines for building procedures but not as a rigid set of rules. There will not be any rules for punctuation, spelling, vocabulary, or use of synonyms.

c. The representation of algorithms in our algorithmic language, along with a judicious use of indentation, will clearly indicate the relationships among various statements and thus allow us to gain a better picture of the overall organization and structure of the solution of the problem.

Example 2

Write an algorithm to find the sum of the first k integers, 1, 2, ..., k. The value of k will be an external input to the algorithm. (Be sure to handle the illegal situation of k <= 0.)

```
BEGIN
  read k
  if k <= 0
  then
     write "illegal value for k"
     END
  else
     set i to 1
     set sum to 0
     repeat k times
        add i to sum
        increment i by 1
     end of the repeat loop
     write "the sum of the first", k, "integers is", sum
END
```

Example 3

Develop an algorithm to solve quadratic equations of the form $ax^2 + bx + c = 0$ using the quadratic formula:

$$\text{Roots} = \frac{-b \pm \sqrt{b^2 - 4ac}}{2a}$$

Your algorithm should handle the regular cases as well as the special cases of:

a. a double root if ($b^2 - 4ac = 0$),

b. complex root if ($b^2 - 4ac < 0$),

c. a nonquadratic equation ($a = 0$),

d. an illegal equation if ($a = 0, b = 0$).

Solution

```
BEGIN
  read a, b, c
  if a = 0 and b = 0
  then write ''illegal equation, cannot solve''
  else
    if a = 0 then
      set root to - c/b
      write ''linear equation, the one root is'', root
    else
      set discriminant to b^2 - 4ac
    if discriminant < 0 then
      write ''roots are complex, cannot be solved''
    else
```

set root1 to $\dfrac{-b + \sqrt{discriminant}}{2a}$

set root2 to $\dfrac{-b - \sqrt{discriminant}}{2a}$

```
  write ''answers are'' , root1, root2
END
```

1.4 DESIGN OF ALGORITHMS

In designing algorithms we need methods to separate bad algorithms from good ones. This is because there are usually more than one possible ways to solve a problem. It is for us to decide which method will prove the most effective for the solutions of that problem.

An algorithm is clearly specified set of simple instructions to be followed to solve a problem. Once an algorithm is given for a problem and decided to be correct, another important step would be to determine how much time or space, the algorithm will require.

Each of the algorithms will involve a particular data structure. Accordingly, we may not always to able to use the most efficient algorithm, since the choice of data structure depends on many things, including the type of data and the frequency with which various operations on data are applied. The choice of data structure may involve time-space tradeoff, i.e. by increasing the amount of space for storing the data, one may be able to reduce the time needed for processing the data or vice versa.

☞ *Once the data structure is chosen for a particular application, program is written by the set of logical instructions that manipulate the related data items. Thus, a study of data structure is also a study of the algorithms that control them.*

Certain qualities can be identified as desirable traits in all such algorithms.

First, the algorithm must be expressed in a fashion that is completely free of *ambiguity*. The method we use to express algorithm must be formed to avoid the impercision inherent in a natural language. The algorithm should be flexible enough to allow us to focus on problem-oriented issues.

Second, algorithms should be *efficient*. They should not unnecessarily use memory locations nor should they require an excessive number of logical operations. To analyze the efficiency of an algorithm, we will have to describe numerically the memory and logical operations that they may require.

Third, algorithm should be *concise* and *compact* to facilitate verification of their correction. Verification involves observing the performance of the algorithm with a carefully selected set of test cases. These test cases should attempt to cover all of the exceptional circumstances likely to be encountered by the algorithm.

1.4.1 How to Design an Algorithm?

Algorithm design is a creative activity. The first step in designing an algorithm is to produce a clear specification of the problem. For designing any algorithm, some important things should be considered. These are run-time, space and simplicity of algorithm. In some cases, input data may also be decide in designing an algorithm.

Some common approaches for designing algorithms are:

- **Greedy Algorithm:** The greedy algorithm works in steps. In each step this algorithm selects the best available option until all options finish. This approach is widely used in many places for designing algorithm. For example, the *shortest path algorithm* (discussed in Chapter 8).
- **Divide and Conquer:** Divide and conquer is a design strategy which is well known for breaking down the efficiency barriers. When the method is applied, it often leads to a large improvement in time complexity. In divide and conquer, the big problem is divided into same type of smaller problems and we design the algorithm to combine the implementation of these smaller problems for implementing bigger problem. For example, in *quick sort* (discussed in Chapter 7), we divide initial list into several smaller lists, after sorting those smaller lists, we combine them and get the final list sorted.
- **Non-recursive algorithm:** A set of instructions that perform a logical operation can be grouped together as a function. If a function calls itself, then it is called as *direct recursion*. If a function calls another function, which in turn invokes the calling function, then the technique is called as *indirect recursion*. The recursion is very powerful technique which is supported by programming language C.
- **Randomized algorithm:** In randomized algorithm, we use the feature of random number instead of a fixed number. Performance of some algorithm depends upon the input data. It gives different results with different input data.
- **Backtrack algorithm:** An algorithm technique to find solutions by trying one of several choices. If the choice proves incorrect, computation backtracks or restarts at the point of choice and tries another choice. A backtracking algorithm is to write a function or procedure which traverses the solution space. For example, *game tree*.

- **Modular programming approach:** In industry and commerce, the problems that are to be solved with the help of computer needs thousands or even more number of lines of code. The importance of splitting a problem into a series of self contained modules then becomes important. A module should not exceed about 100 or so lines and should preferably be short enough to be on a single page. Since module is small, it is simpler to understand it as a unit of code. It is therefore, easier to test and debug a shorter module especially if its purpose is clearly defined and documented. In a very large project, several programmers may be working on a single problem. Using modular approach, each programmer can be given a specific set of modules to work on. This enables the whole program to be completed soon.

As soon as one can write an algorithm, it is necessary to learn how to analyze an algorithm. The analysis of an algorithm provides information that gives us a general idea of how long an algorithm will take for solving a problem.

To judge an algorithm, there are many criteria. Some of them are as follows:

- It must work correctly under various conditions.
- It must solve the problem according to the given specification.
- It must be clearly written following the top-down or bottom up strategy.
- It must make efficient use of time and resources available.
- It must be sufficiently documented so that anybody can understand its implementation.
- It must be easy to modify, if required.
- It should not be dependent on being run on a particular type of computer.

1.5 IMPLEMENTATION OF ALGORITHM

After spelling out completely and precisely the requirements for each tasks and sub-tasks (function), it is time to code them into our programming language (say C, C++ or Java etc.). Just as we design from the top down, we should code from the top down. Once the specification at the top levels are complete and precise, we should code the subprograms at these levels and test them appropriately.

1.6 VERIFICATION OF ALGORITHM

Algorithm verification is a proof that the algorithm will accomplish its task. This kind of proof is formulated by looking at the specifications for the subprograms and then arguing that these specifications combine properly to accomplish the task of the whole algorithm.

Verification of algorithm would consist of determining the quality of the output received. In other words, it is a process of measuring the performance of the program with any laid down standards. The feedback so obtained, then sets the basis for making necessary changes in the already designed algorithm specifications. Algorithm verification should precede coding of the programme.

1.7 EFFICIENCY ANALYSIS OF ALGORITHMS

An algorithm analysis provides information that gives us an idea of how long an algorithm will take for solving a problem. For comparing the performance of two algorithms, we have to estimate the time taken to solve the same problem using each algorithm for a set of N input-values. For example, we might determine the number of comparisons a searching algorithm does to find a value in a list of N values. Similarly, we might determine the number of arithmetic operations an algorithm performs to add two matrices of size N * N. A number of algorithms might be able to solve a problem successfully yet the analysis of algorithm gives us the scientific reason to determine which algorithm should be chosen to solve the problem most efficiently.

☞ *The performance of algorithms can be judged by criteria such as whether it satisfies the original specification of task, whether the code is readable. These factors affect the computing time and main memory requirements of the machine.*

1.7.1 Space Complexity

Space complexity of a program is the amount of main memory in a computer. It needs to run for completion. The space needed by a program is the sum of the following components:

a. Fixed part that includes space for the code, space for simple variables and fixed size component variables as well as, space for constants etc.
b. Variable part that consists of the space needed by component variables whose size is dependent on the particular problem instance being solved, and the stack space used by recursive procedures.

1.7.2 Time Complexity

Time complexity of a program is the amount of computer time it needs to run a program to completion. Suppose, space is fixed for one algorithm then only run time will be considered for obtaining the complexity of algorithm. The time complexity may give time for:

a. Best case
b. Worst case
c. Average case

Best Case

Most of the algorithms behave in *best case*. In this case, algorithm searches the elements in first time itself. For example, in linear search, if it finds the element at first time itself then it behaves as best case. Best case takes shortest time to execute, as it causes the algorithms to do the least amount of work.

Worst Case

In *worst case*, we find the element of time at the end or the total time taken when searching of elements fails. This could involve comparing the key to each list value for a total of N comparisons. For example, in linear search, suppose the element for which algorithm is searching, is the last element of an array or the element is not available in array then algorithm behaves as worst case.

Average Case

Analysing the average case behaviour of an algorithm is more complex than best case and worst case. Here, we take the probability with the list of data items Average case of algorithm should be the average number of steps but since data can be at any place, so finding exact behaviour of algorithm is difficult. As the volume of data increases, average case of algorithm behaves like worst case algorithm.

1.7.3 Frequency Count

To make an analysis machine independent it can be assumed that every statement will take the same constant amount of time for its execution. Hence, the determination of time complexity of a given program is the summing of the frequency counts of all the statements of that program. The time complexity can also be expressed to represent only the order of magnitude represented by the frequency counts. One such notation for frequency count is Order notation ('O' notation).

'O Notation'

'O' notation is used to measure the performance of any algorithm. Performance of an algorithm depends upon the volume of input data. 'O' notation is used to define the order of the growth for an algorithm.

We write O(1) to mean a computing time that is a constant i.e. when we get data in first time itself. For example, in hash table,

O(n) is called linear, when all the elements of the linear list will be traversed. For example, the best case while using bubble sort method.

$O(n^2)$ is called quadratic, when all the completed list will be traversed for each element. For example, the worst case of bubble sort method.

O(log n) is when we divide linear list to half each time and traverse the middle element. For example, method used in binary searching.

O(n log n) is when we divide list half each time and traverse that half portion. For example, best case of quick sort of an algorithm will take O(log n) time. This method is faster than O(n). However, O(n log n) is better than $O(n^2)$ but not as good as O(n).

1.8 SAMPLE ALGORITHMS

Some examples of algorithms are given in the following sub-sections.

1.8.1 Exchanging the Value of Two Variables

Exchanging the value of two variables means interchanging their values. We can clearly understand this by an example.

Suppose we have two variables *x* and *y*. Our aim is to swap or interchange the value of *x* and *y*.

The original values of *x* and *y* are:

11	58
x	y

After swapping the result should be:

58	11
x	y

To do so, we need one temporary variable, i.e. *t*. First, copy the value of *x* into *t*, i.e.

11	→	11
x		t

then copy the value of *y* into *x*, i.e.

58	→	58
y		x

copy the value of *t* into *y* i.e.

11	→	11
t		y

At last, we shall get the new values in *x* and *y* as seen below:

58	11
x	y

We find that the value of *x* and *y* have now been interchanged as desired.

Algorithm

1. Begin
2. Get the values of variables *x* and *y*.
3. Assign the value of *x* to *t*.
4. Assign the value of *y* to *x*. So *x* has the original value of *y* now in place of the original value of *x*.
5. Assign the value of *t* to *y*.
6. Show the values of *x* and *y*.
7. Stop

1.8.2 Summation of a Set of Numbers

Summation of a set of numbers is like adding numbers given in a series. To add a set of numbers manually, we are used to start adding the digits in the right most column. For example:

```
 782
 222
 565
-----
 ...9
-----
```

When using computer, we must design an algorithm to perform this task by a different approach. Computer can add two numbers at a time and return the sum of two numbers.

So to add n numbers, we initialize the variable location S, where we are going to store the Sum, by the assignment $S = 0$. Now, we first do the following:

$S = S + a_1$ where a_1 is the first number

then we do $S = S + a_2$ (The new value of S contains $a_1 + a_2$)

then $S = S + a_3$ (The new value of S contains $a_1 + a_2 + a_3$)

and so on till $S = S + a_n$

Here, we are repeating the same process again and again. The only difference is that the values of a and S changes their values with each step.

Algorithm

1. Begin
2. Read n numbers to be summed.
3. Initialize sum as 0.
4. Initialize 'count' as 1.
5. While 'count' is less than or equal to n, i.e. numbers to be added, repeatedly do:
   a. Read the number at position 'count', i.e. when count is 1 read 1st number, when count is 2, read second number and so on.
   b. Update the current sum by adding to it the number read.
   c. Add 1 to 'count'.
6. Write the sum of n numbers. (After the number at n^{th} count has been added, the control will shift to step 7.)
7. Stop.

1.8.3 Decimal Base to Binary Base Conversion

Before doing such a conversion, we need to know definition of decimal number system and binary number system.

Decimal Number System

It is the set of numbers having base 10. Since a decimal number system uses 10 digits from 0 to 9, it has a base 10. The decimal number system is also called base 10 system. For example, 6598, 75, 100567 etc. are examples of decimal numbers.

Binary Number System

Binary means 2. The set of numbers having base 2 is called binary number system.

Binary numbers consist of only two digits, i.e. 0 and 1. Each one of these is also called bit, a short form of **bi**nary digi**t**.

☞ *For storing a binary number, the electronic elements of a computer need to have only two stable states. The output of such electronic circuits at any time is either high or low. These states represent 1 and 0 respectively. High is represented by 1 and low is represented by 0.*

A computer can directly understand only binary number system. But we use data in the form of decimal digits. All such numbers are converted to binary codes within the computer because computers can operate using binary numbers only.

Conversion of Decimal Number to Binary Number

To convert a decimal number to a binary number, the decimal number is divided by 2 successively. The quotient and remainders are noted down at each stage. The Quotient of the preceding stage is divided by 2 at the next stage. The process is repeated until the quotient becomes zero. Now write the remainders to right hand side (R.H.S) of the previous remainder to get a set of digits. To make binary equivalent, put the remainders in reverse order. For example, the binary representation of the decimal number 13 is shown below:

	Quotient	Remainder	
$13 \div 2 =$	6	1	↑ LSB
$6 \div 2 =$	3	0	
$3 \div 2 =$	1	1	
$1 \div 2 =$	0	1	MSB

MSB = Most Significant Bit
LSB = Least Significant Bit

So binary representation of $(13)_{10}$ will be $(1101)_2$.

Algorithm

1. Begin
2. Get the decimal number whose binary equivalent we want.
3. Divide the decimal number by 2.
4. Write the remainder.
5. Quotient of previous stage become the dividend and again divide it by 2 at next stage.
6. Write the remainder to right hand side (R.H.S) of previous remainder.
7. Repeat the process successively till quotient is zero.
8. The set of digits formed by the remainders at different stages, when placed in the reverse order, will form the binary equivalent of the decimal number.
9. Stop.

1.8.4 Reversing Digits of an Integer Number

Reversing digits basically means changing the digits order backwards. For example:

Input	3 5 6 8
Result	8 6 5 3 (Each digit placed in the reverse)

To do so, we divide the number by 10 and print the remainder.

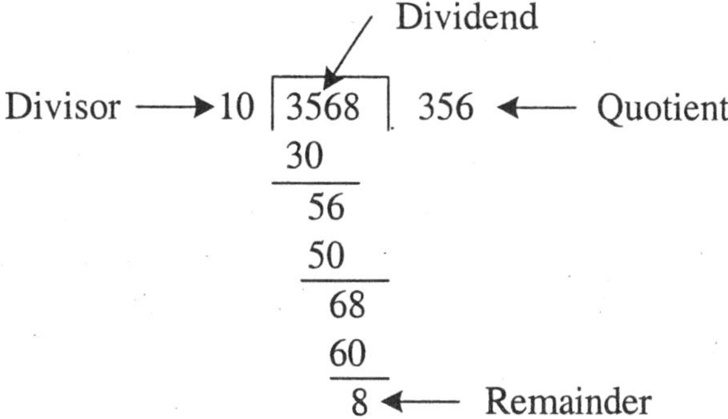

We can get the remainder by mod() function

r = 3568 mod (10)
  = 8

Now remove 8 from the original integer. So we next get 356 (number to be reversed) again

r = 356 mod (10)
  = 6

Successively, we find out the remainders until the dividend is less than 10. Now place the digits of the remainders in the reverse.

Therefore, we can use the integer division by 10 to remove the right most digit from the number being reversed and construct the reversed integer by writing the extracted digits to the right hand side of the current reversed number representation. At last, when the dividend is less than 10, then add it to the right side of the current reversed number representation.

Number to be Changed	**Reversed-digits Number**
3568	8
356	86
35	865
3 (i.e. less than 10)	8653

Algorithm

1. Begin
2. Get positive integer number to be reversed.
3. While the integer number being reversed is greater than 10 repeatedly do:
   a. Extract the right most digit of the number to be reversed by remainder function, i.e. function mod().
   b. Construct the reversed integer by writing the extracted digit to right hand side of the current reversed number.

4. Write the integer (dividend which is less than 10) to the R.H.S of the reversed number.
5. Stop

1.8.5 GCD (Greatest Common Divisor) of Two Numbers

The greatest number which is a common factor of two or more given numbers is called GCD (Greatest Common Divisor).

How to find GCD

Suppose two numbers are given. Now, divide the greater number by the smaller one. Next, divide the divisor by the remainder. Go on repeating the process of dividing the preceding divisor by the remainder last obtained, till the remainder zero is obtained. Then, the last divisor is the required GCD of the given numbers. Suppose, we want to find GCD of 136 and 170, then

Say, $a = 136$
$b = 170$

Greater number is b i.e. 170; so b will be dividend.
Smaller number is a, i.e. 136; so a will be divisor.

```
                          ┌──── Dividend
                          ▼
Divisor ──►  136 | 170 | 1
                   136
                   ───
                    34 ◄── Remainder
```

Remainder i.e. 34 is now divisor

```
                          ┌──── Dividend
                          ▼
Divisor ──►   34 | 136 | 4
                   136
                   ───
                     0 ◄── Remainder
```

Therefore, the greatest common divisor (GCD) is 34.

Algorithm

1. Begin
2. Get 1st and 2nd (non-zero) integers, i.e. a, and b.
3. Check which integer is larger.
4. Get the remainder by dividing the greater integer by the smaller integer.
5. Make smaller integer be dividend and get the remainder.
6. Let remainder be the divisor.
7. Repeat step 4, 5, and 6 until a zero remainder is obtained. Now, the last divisor is the GCD.
8. Stop

1.8.6 Test whether the Given Number is a Prime Number!

The natural number 1 has only one factor. Except 1, every decimal number has two or more factors. For example, 2 has two factors 1 and 2, the number 3 has the factors 1 and 3. The number 4 has three factors 1, 2 and 4, the number 5 has two factors 1 and 5. The positive numbers which have only two factors i.e. 1 and that number itself are called prime numbers. The example of prime numbers are 2, 3, 5, 7, 11, 13, 17, etc.

☞ ***Prime numbers** are any of the positive integer numbers greater than 1, each divisible only by itself and by 1. Thus, 2, 3, 5 ,7,....... etc. are prime numbers.*

Our aim here is to find the prime numbers. A Greek mathematician Erotosthenes who lived in the 3rd century BC gave a very simple method for finding a prime number. The method is known as "*Sieve method*". Suppose we have to find all the prime numbers in the range of 1 to 20. To find the prime number, follow the steps:

1. Strike out 1 because it is not a prime number.
2. Encircle 2 and strike out all the multiples of 2, i.e. 4, 6, 8, 10, 12, ... 20.

   ~~1~~ ② 3 ~~4~~ 5 ~~6~~ 7 ~~8~~ 9 ~~10~~
   11 ~~12~~ 13 ~~14~~ 15 ~~16~~ 17 ~~18~~ 19 ~~20~~

3. Encircle 3 and strike out all the multiples of 3.

   ② ③ 5 7 ~~9~~ 11 13 ~~15~~ 17 19

We continue the process of encircling and striking till every number in list is either encircled or struck out.

② ③ ⑤ ⑦ ⑪ ⑬ ⑰ ⑲

All the circled number are thus prime numbers and the numbers that are struck out except 1 are composite numbers. This method is given as an algorithm below.

Algorithm

1. Begin
2. Get the number which we want to check whether it is prime or not.
3. Set value of divisor to 2.
4. Divide the number by divisor (i.e. 2 first)
   If remainder is zero, then the given number is not prime, else the process is to be continued.
5. Increment divisor by 1, divide the number by the incremented divisor and check if remainder is zero. Keep repeating the process till either the remainder becomes zero or until divisor is equal to the number itself. If remainder becomes zero at any stage, the number is not prime else it is prime if carried to last stage, till incremented divisor is the number itself.
6. Stop.

1.8.7 Organize Numbers in Order (Sorting)

Sorting of numbers means to arrange a given set of numbers in ascending or in descending order. To sort the data, selection-sort is the method popularly used. To sort data in ascending order, we do the following:

1. Place the values in the form of one dimensional array as shown in Figure 1.5(a) below:

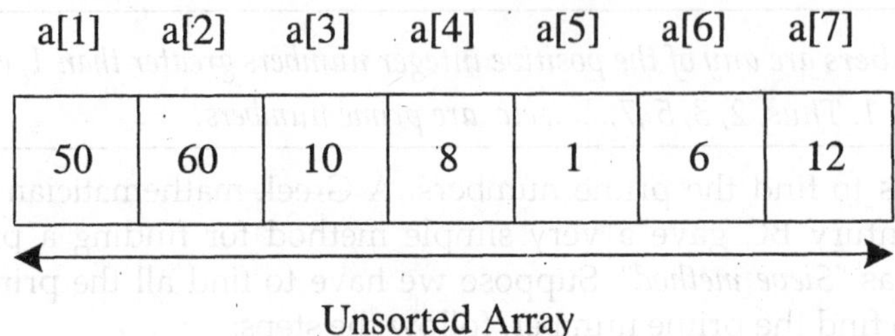

Figure 1.5(a)

2. Find the smallest value and place it as first item in the array. At the same time, move the value of the first location of the array to the location where smallest value was stored. It means interchange the value of *a*[5] with *a*[1] using algorithm given in Section 1.8.1. Current values will be as show in Figure 1.5(b):

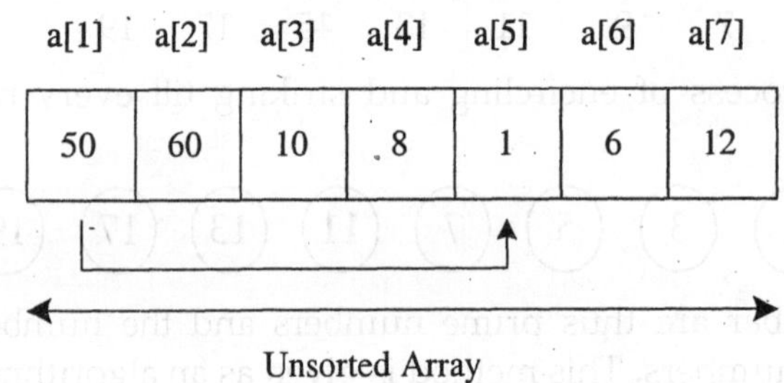

Figure 1.5(b)

3. Now *a*[1] element has the smallest value. See Figure 1.5(c).

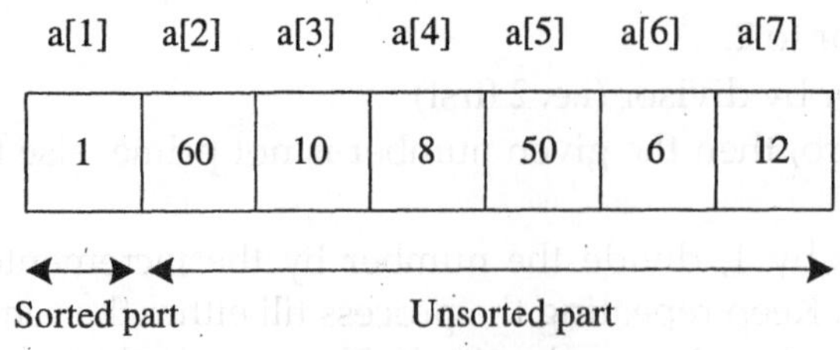

Figure 1.5(c)

Now compare element of *a*[2] with other element in the unsorted array. We get the array as seen in Figure 1.5(d).

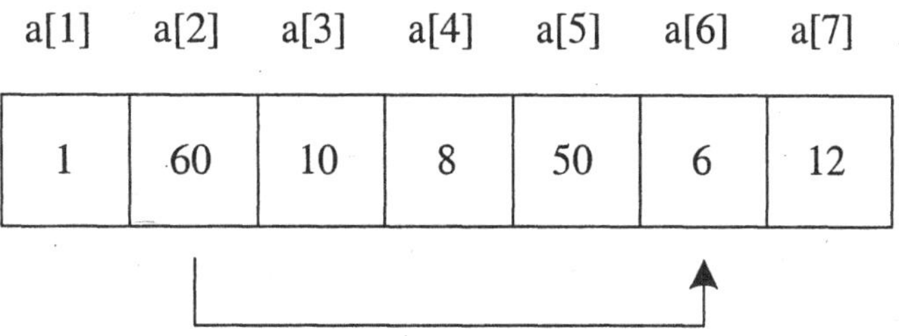

Figure 1.5(d)

Swap the value of $a[2]$ and $a[6]$ with the help of temporary variable, *temp*. See Figure 1.5(e).

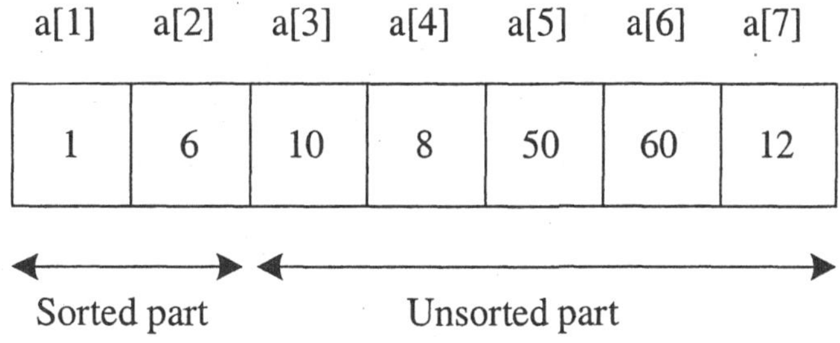

Figure 1.5(e)

Repeat the above steps to get the 3rd element, then 4th, and so on. See Figure 1.5(f).

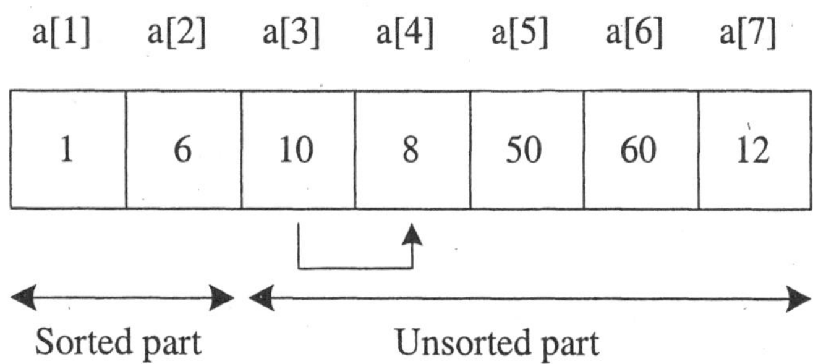

Note that we need to process the unsorted array only $(n - 1)$ times. The last element of the array would now be in the ascending order.

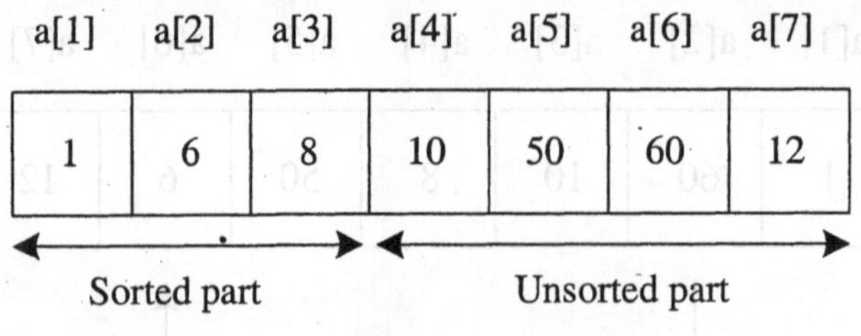

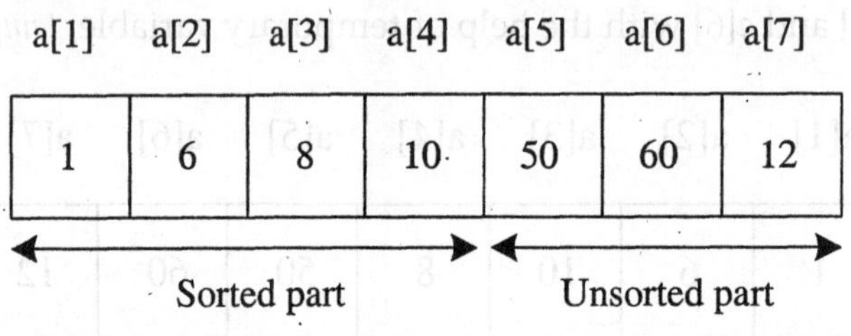

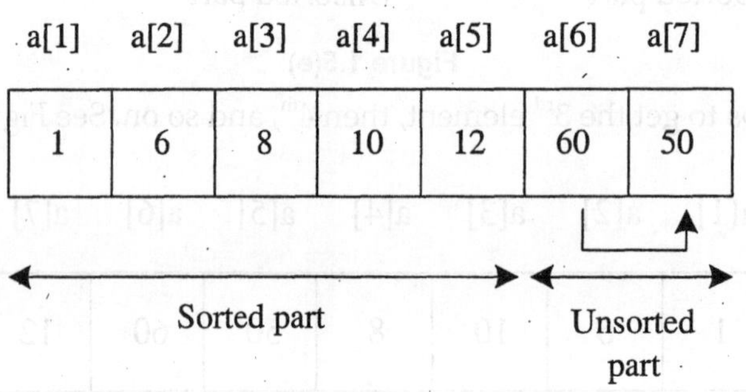

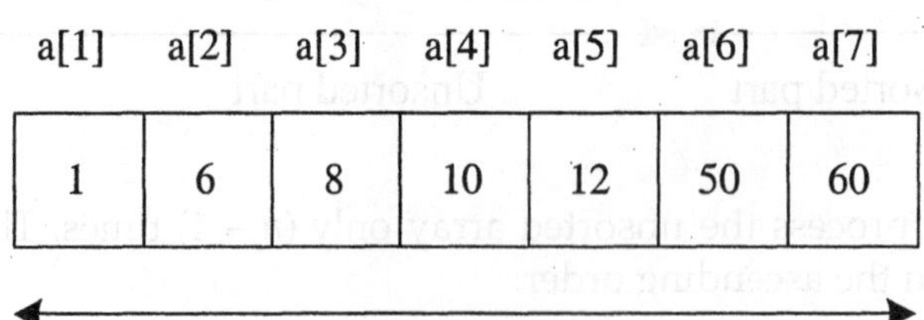

Sorted Array

Figure 1.5(f)

Algorithm

1. Begin
2. Read numbers and store them in an array of *n* elements i.e. size of array *a* is *n* with elements as *a*[1], *a*[2], *a*[3], ..., *a*[*n*].
3. Find the smallest element within unsorted array.
4. Exchange i.e. swap smallest value of the array element and store it in 1st element of the unsorted part of array.
5. Repeat steps 3 and 4 until all the elements in the array are arranged in the ascending order.
6. Stop

1.8.8 Find the Square Root of an Integer Number

Before understanding square root, we must know what we mean by squaring a number. To square a number is to multiply the number by itself. For example:

$1^2 = 1 \times 1$

$= 1$

$2^2 = 2 \times 2$

$= 4$

$3^2 = 3 \times 3$

$= 9$

However, one of the two equal factors of a number is the *square root* of that number.

Let us read some more examples to understand square-root.

$1^2 = 1 \times 1 = 1$ The square root of 1 is 1.

$2^2 = 2 \times 2 = 4$ The square root of 4 is 2.

$3^2 = 3 \times 3 = 9$ The square root of 9 is 3.

Therefore, if we have to find the square root of 49 then we will see "what number multiplied by itself will give 49". Certainly $7 \times 7 = 49$. But (-7×-7) is also 49.

So, ± 7 is the square root of 49.

☞ *A square root of a given number **n** is that natural number which when multiplied by itself gives **n**.*

We can say that if *a* is the square root of *b* then *b* is the square of *a*. For example,

$\sqrt{49} = \pm 7$ (±7 is square-root of 49; 49 is square of +- 7)

$\sqrt{64} = 8$ (±8 is square-root of 64; 64 is square of +- 8)

Algorithm

1. Place bar over every pair of digits starting with the right hand side (R.H.S). The number of bars indicates the number of digits in the square root.

$$\overline{5}\,\overline{29}$$

2. Find the largest square root for the first pair that is less than or equal to the first pair. Take the square root of this number as divisor and get quotient. Put the quotient above the period. Subtract the product and bring down the next pair of digits to the right of the remainder.

	2
2	$\overline{5}\,\overline{29}$
	4
	129

3. Double the quotient as it appears and enter it with a blank on the right for the next digit, as the next possible divisor.

	23
2	$\overline{5}\,\overline{29}$
	4
43	129

4. Guess a possible digit to fill the blank and also to become the new digit in the quotient. Enter this digit in both places. Multiply the new digit in the quotient and the new divisor. Subtract and bring down the next period.

	23
2	$\overline{5}\,\overline{29}$
	4
43	129
	129
	0

5. Repeat steps 3 and 4 till the last pair has been used and the remainder comes to zero.

1.8.9 Factorial of a Given Number

The product of all positive integers from 1 to n is called the 'factorial n' or 'n factorial'. It is denoted by $n!$. For example,

$$5! = 1\times2\times3\times4\times5$$

$$= 120$$

$$n! = 1\times2\times3.....(n-2)\times(n-1)\times n$$

where n is a positive integer.

☞ *It may be noted that $0! = 1$, which means factorial zero is equal to 1.*

Let us take an example. Suppose we want to find out the value of factorial 5.

Initially assign the value of $i = 1$ and *factorial* = 1

So method will be to successively go on increasing the value of i by 1 and keep updating the value of *factorial* by multiplying the current value of i by the value of factorial till the incremented value of i equals to the number desired for finding the factorial.

Thus, factorial = previous value of factorial × i,

i.e. start with $i = 1$, giving factorial 1 = 1 × 1

Now increment the value of i by 1, giving updated

factorial 2 = 1 × 2
= 2

Again increase the value of i by 1, giving

factorial 3 = 2 × 3
= 6

Increment the value of i until the value of i becomes 5 and corresponding value of factorial is obtained.

To summarize, the factorial will be calculated in the following way:

factorial 1 = 1 × 1 = 1
factorial 2 = 1 × 2 = 2
factorial 3 = 2 × 3 = 6
factorial 4 = 6 × 4 = 24
factorial 5 = 24 × 5 = 120

So 5! = 120

Algorithm

1. Begin
2. Get the number of which the factorial is to be calculated i.e. n.
3. Assign the value of $i = 1$ and factorial = 1.
4. Calculate factorial n = factorial (n-1) × i
5. Increment the value of i by 1, i.e. $i = i + 1$.
6. Repeat steps 4 and 5 till step 4 has been executed with the value of $i = n$.
7. Write the value of factorial.
8. Stop.

1.8.10 Fibonacci Sequence

In a Fibonacci sequence, the previous two numbers are added to generate the next Fibonacci number. For example:

$f_1 = 1$ (1st number $\in$ *the Fibonacci series*)

$f_2 = 2$ (2nd in the Fibonacci series)

$f_3 = f_2 + f_1 = 2 + 1 = 3$

$f_4 = f_3 + f_2 = 3 + 2 = 5$

$f_5 = f_4 + f_3 = 5 + 3 = 8$, and so on.

f_1	f_2	f_3	f_4	f_5	f_6	f_7 ....
1	2	3	5	8	13	21 ....

To get next fibonacci number, we have to do sum of previous two numbers in the series.

Algorithm

1. Assign $sum = 0, A = 0, B = 1, i = 1$
2. Get the number of terms up to which you want to generate the Fibonacci number, i.e. n.
3. Add A and B to get next Fibonacci number.
4. Assign the value of B to A i.e $A = B$.
5. Assign the value of sum to B i.e. $sum = B$.
6. Write the value of sum to get next Fibonacci number in the series.
7. Increment i with 1 i.e. $i = i + 1$ and repeat step 3, 4, 5, 6 with the last value of $i = n$ (n is a number of terms up to which we want to generate Fibonacci number series.)
8. Stop

1.8.11 Evaluate 'sin (x)' as Sum of a Series

We know that

$$\text{Sin}\,x = \frac{x}{1!} - \frac{x^3}{3!} + \frac{x^5}{5!} - \frac{x^7}{7!} + \frac{x^9}{9!}$$

Where x is in radians.

Understanding the problem

1. Read X
2. Keep accumulating a product of integers (PRODUCT) in such a way that PRODUCT is first 1,
   then $1 \times 2 \times 3$,
   then $1 \times 2 \times 3 \times 4 \times 5$, and so on.
   Product serves as the denominator in terms of the formula.
3. Accumulate the terms:

   $$\frac{X}{\text{PRODUCT}}, \frac{X^3}{\text{PRODUCT}}, \frac{X^5}{\text{PRODUCT}}, \ldots$$
4. Compute $X^1, X^3, X^5 \ldots$ through the use of X^i where i is initially set to 1 and incremented by 2's to obtain X and odd power of X.
5. Generate the oscillating sequence of terms

$X, \ -X^3, \ +X^5, \ -X^7, + \ldots.$

To do that, we note that $(X)^1$, $(-X)^3$, $(X)^5$, $(-X)^7$ gives rise to X, $-X^3$, X^5, $-X^7$.

Hence we use −1 as successive multiplier to generate successive terms of the sequence from their magnitude.

The algorithm is given below :

Algorithm

1. Read x in radians.
2. Read n where 'n' is the number of terms of series which we may like to add-up to get desired precision of sum.
3. For Ist term,

   sum = x
   product = 1 (variable 'product' used for denominator)
   num = x (variable 'num' used for numerator)
   power = 1
4. For next term,

   num = num × $(-x^2)$
   power = power + 2
   product = product × (power − 1) × power
   next_term = num/product
5. Then,

   sum = sum + next_term
6. Repeat step 4 and 5, looping 'n − 1' times to get the sum of first 'n' terms of the series.
7. Print sum
8. Stop

1.8.12 Reverse the Order of Elements of an Array

Reverse order of elements means value of 1st position of the array is exchanged with last element of the array, 2nd element of array is exchanged with '2nd last' and so on.

For example, see Figure 1.6(a).

a[1]	a[2]	a[3]	a[4]	a[5]
1	3	4	8	9

Before Reverse

Figure 1.6(a)

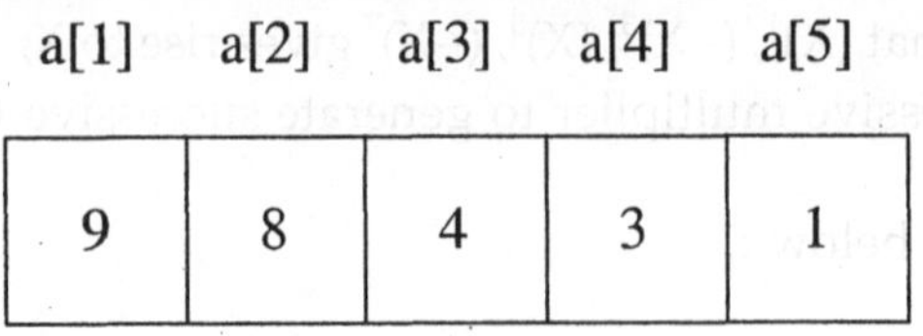

After Reverse

Figure 1.6(b)

Here,

$a[1] \Leftrightarrow a[5]$ (Swap element 5 value with element 1 value)

$a[2] \Leftrightarrow a[4]$

$a[3] \Leftrightarrow a[3]$

Here, we can see the suffixes/subscripts on left hand side are in increasing order and the suffixes/subscripts on right hand side are in decreasing order. (See Figure 1.6(b)).

For determining the reverse-array subscript values, we can use the formula $[n - i + 1]$ where 'n' is total number of elements an 'i' is the subscript of the element of original aıray.

$n - i + 1$

$5 - 1 + 1 = 5$

$5 - 2 + 1 = 4$

$5 - 3 + 1 = 3$

Swapping the values of that elements in the array would thus be reversed.

To exchange the values of the elements of the array, we need one temporary variable. Then we do the swapping as given below:

$\therefore$ $\text{temp} = a[i]$

$a[i] = a[n - i + 1]$

$a[n - i + 1] = \text{temp}$

Algorithm

1. Begin
2. Get the values and store them in an array with elements $a[1], a[2], a[3], a[4], \ldots\ldots, a[n]$ where n is the number of elements.
3. Compute r, the number of exchange needed to reverse the array. r = integer value of 1/2.
4. Exchange the ith element with $[n - i + 1]$ using

   $\text{temp} = a[i]$

   $a[i] = a[n - i + 1]$

   $a[n - i + 1] = \text{temp}$
5. Carry step 4, r times increasing i by 1.

6. Print the reversed array elements $a[1], a[2], a[3], a[4], \ldots\ldots, a[n]$.
7. Stop

1.8.13 Find Largest Number in an Array

Largest number means the number which is greater than all other numbers in the array elements. Another number(s) in the set may be equal to this number, but can not be greater than this number. For example, in the following array:

Array	10	11	15	19	2
	a[1]	**a[2]**	**a[3]**	**a[4]**	**a[5]**

we find that the number 19 is the largest number in the array.

For small set of numbers stored in the array, it is easy to find largest number, but finding the largest value from thousands of numbers stored in the array may take long time. But using following logic, we can get the answer in a short time.

Logic

Assign the value of the first element of the array to variable *temp*, then compare the value of *temp* to those of other elements in the array in order, one by one. If any element value is greater than *temp* then put that value in *temp* and continue comparison.

For the array shown above value of *temp* = 10 taken from first element of the array.

Compare value in *temp* to 2nd element value of the array. Here, 11 is greater than 10, so delete the original value of *temp* and write down the 2nd number i.e. 11 in *temp*. We keep comparing the 3rd element value with the new *temp* value. The procedure will be continued till all the elements in the array have been examined. In the end, we will get the largest value in the *temp* variable.

Algorithm

1. Begin
2. Get the value of element in an array and store them in the array elements a[1], a[2]..... a[n] where *n* is the number of elements.
3. Set temporary variable and assign the value of 1st array element a[1] to *temp*.
4. Compare *temp* with the next element a[2] of the array.
5. If the element is having greater value than *temp*, assign that value to *temp*.
6. Repeat steps 4 and 5 till last element a[n] of the array is encountered.
7. Final value of *temp* is the largest value stored in the array.
8. Stop

1.8.14 Solve a Quadratic Equation and Compute its Real Roots

Compute the real roots of a quadratic equation:

ax² + bx + c = 0

Algorithm

1. Read the values of the coefficients X2, X and constant quantity, i.e., the value of A, B and C and store them in the memory.
2. If A = 0 and B = 0 then print "No root exists" and stop. Else continue.
3. If A = 0 and B = 0 is not equal to 0 then root X1 = C/B. Write the value of root and also write "Linear Equation" and stop. Else Continue.
4. Compute (B^2–4AC) and set $D^2 = B^2–4AC$.
5. If D = 0, then compute Root X1 = Root X2 = (–B/2A), write of Root X1 and Root X2 and stop. Else Continue.
6. If D < 0, then write "Roots are not real" and stop. Else continue.
7. If D > 0, then calculate
   Root X1 = (–B + B^2 – 4AC)/(2A)
   Root X1 = (–B – B^2 –4AC)/(2A)
8. Write values of Root X1, Root X2 and stop.

1.8.15 Multiplication of Two Matrices

Arthur Kelley was the first person to introduce the concept of matrix. Latęr on, the study of matrix was utilized to solve different types of linear equation problems.

How to form a Matrix

$$\left.\begin{array}{l}8x + 5y = 2\\ 6x + y = 3\end{array}\right\}$$

is a system of two linear equations. Arrange the coefficient of *x* and *y* in the following way:

$$\begin{bmatrix}8 & 5\\ 6 & 1\end{bmatrix}$$

[8 5] in the top horizontal line is called 1st row.
[6 1] in the 2nd horizontal line is called 2nd row.

$\begin{bmatrix}8\\ 6\end{bmatrix}$ is called 1st column.

$\begin{bmatrix}5\\ 1\end{bmatrix}$ is called 2nd column.

A matrix is a two-dimensional array having *m* rows and *n* columns. So we have *m* × *n* positions. Each row consists of *m* elements and each column consists of *n* elements.

Matrix Multiplication

Figure 1.7 shows the elements of a 3×3 matrix .

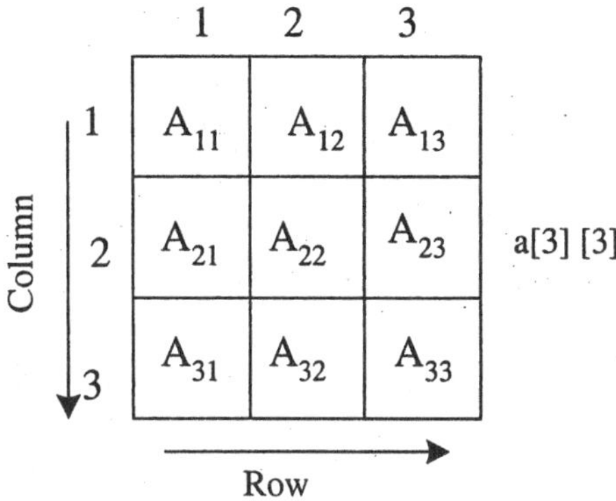

A(i, j) where i = 1, 2, 3 and j = 1, 2, 3

Figure 1.7

Let $A = A_{ij}, i = 1, 2, \ldots, m;$

$j = 1, 2, \ldots, n$

Let $B = B_{jk}, j = 1, 2, \ldots, n;$

$k = 1, 2, \ldots, p$

The product AB of matrices A and B will have i rows and k columns

The two matrices A $(m \times n)$ and B $(n \times p)$ are such that the number of rows of B is same as the number of columns of A. Then the product of these two matrices can be carried out and it is defined as:

$C = AB = C_{ik}$, where i changes from $1, \ldots m$ and

$k = 1, \ldots p$

Thus, $C_{ik} = a_{i1}b_{1k} + a_{i2}b_{2k} + \ldots. + a_{in}b_{nk}$

C_{ik} is obtained by multiplying the values/elements in the ith row of A with the corresponding values/ elements in the kth column of B and then adding them.

☞ *The matrix* ***A*** *is said to be compatible for multiplication with the matrix* ***B****, if the number of columns of* ***A*** *is equal to the number of rows of* ***B****.*

It should be noted that there can be matrices which are not compatible for multiplication and in that case we say that the multiplication of matrices is not defined.

For example, if

$$A = \begin{bmatrix} 5 & 8 & 9 \\ 6 & 9 & 5 \end{bmatrix} \quad B = \begin{bmatrix} 5 & 5 \\ 4 & 8 \\ 7 & 9 \\ 6 & 8 \end{bmatrix}$$

Here, A is a matrix of size 2×3 i.e. 2 rows and 3 columns.

B is a matrix of size 4×2 i.e. 4 rows and 2 columns.

We know that for obtaining the product of two matrices, the number of columns of the matrix *A* must be equal to the number of rows of matrix *B*.

But, *A* has 3 columns and *B* has 4 rows, so *A* and *B* are not compatible for multiplication.

Let us take an example where the multiplication of matrices is defined.

$$A = \begin{bmatrix} 0 & 2 & 3 \\ 1 & 3 & 1 \\ 2 & 5 & 2 \end{bmatrix} \quad B = \begin{bmatrix} 1 & 0 \\ 0 & 2 \\ 2 & 2 \end{bmatrix}, \text{ then}$$

Here A and B are compatible. The product is as follows:

$$A \times B = \begin{bmatrix} 0\times1+2\times0+3\times2 & 0\times0+2\times2+3\times2 \\ 1\times1+3\times0+1\times2 & 1\times0+3\times2+1\times2 \\ 2\times1+5\times0+2\times2 & 2\times0+5\times2+2\times2 \end{bmatrix}$$

$$= \begin{bmatrix} 6 & 10 \\ 3 & 8 \\ 6 & 14 \end{bmatrix}$$

Here 6 is the value of the element lying in the 1st row and 1st column of the *product matrix* ($A \times B$). This is the sum of the products of the corresponding elements of 1st row of *A* with 1st column of *B*.

Algorithm

1. Get 1st and 2nd matrix.
2. Check if number of columns of 1st matrix is equal to the number of rows in 2nd matrix. Then matrices are compatible for multiplication. Otherwise, product is not possible.
3. If matrices are compatible then find the sum of the product of corresponding element of each row of *A* with the corresponding element of each column of *B* and sum the element and equate it to the corresponding position of the product matrix.

1.8.16 Evaluate the Salesman's Wage

Suppose a salesman earns a basic wage of Rs. 1000 in a week. He also earns a commission of 25% of the value of all the goods he sells. If he sells more than Rs. 1000 of goods in any week, he receives a bonus of Rs. 50. Write the algorithm.

Algorithm

1. Input Salesman's name and the value of the goods sold.
2. Calculate the total wage. If the value of goods sold is less than or equal to Rs. 1000, then
   wage = 1000 + 25% of value
3. If value of goods sold is greater than Rs. 10000, then
   wage = 1000 + 25% of value + 50
4. Print the total wage.

DESCRIPTIVE QUESTIONS

Q. No. 1 Define algorithm and write characteristics of an algorithm.

Ans to Q. 1 Algorithm is a set of instructions which describes the steps to be followed to get the solution of a problem.

Characteristics of algorithm

Algorithm should have the following characteristics:

a. Each and every instruction should be precise and unambiguous.
b. Each instruction should be such that it can be performed in a finite time.
c. One or more instructions should not be repeated infinitely. This ensures that the algorithm will ultimately terminate.
d. After performing the instructions, that is, after the algorithm terminates, the desired results must be obtained.

Q. No. 2 Write an algorithm to convert a number of base 10 to a number of base 2.

Ans to Q. 2

a. Begin
b. Get the decimal number whose binary equivalent we want
c. Divide the decimal number by 2
d. Write the remainder.
e. Quotient of previous stage become the dividend and again divide it by 2 at next stage.
f. Write the remainder to R.H.S (right hand side) of previous remainder.
g. Repeat the process successively till quotient is zero.
h. The set of digits formed by the remainders we get at different stages, when will form the binary equivalent of the decimal number.
i. Stop

Q. No. 3 Write short note on following:

a. Greedy Algorithm
b. Non-recursive algorithm
c. Modular programming approach

Ans to Q.3 [*Refer section 1.4.1*]

Q. No. 4 What do you mean by Top down design? What are its advantages.

Ans to Q. 4 [*Refer section 1.2*]

Q. No. 5 What do you understand by bottom-up approach of problem solving.

Ans to Q. 5 *[Refer section 1.2.2]*

EXERCISE

Multiple Choice

1. A natural number 1 is also a
   - a. prime number
   - b. real number
   - c. integer number
   - d. none of the above
2. Prime number is a number
   - a. divisible by 1
   - b. divisible by 1 and by itself
   - c. divisible by 1 and by itself except the number 1
   - d. none of the above
3. Swapping of two numbers is done by
   - a. direct by interchanging their values with each others
   - b. storing the value of one in a temp variable and shifting the value of the other into the first and then copying the value of temp to the other
   - c. transfer one number to other number without storing any number in the temp variable
   - d. none of the above
4. Sorting an array in the ascending order of numbers is the process of
   - a. putting the largest number first and smallest in the last
   - b. putting the smallest number first and the largest number in the last
   - c. putting the numbers in any way you desire
   - d. None of the above
5. GCD of two numbers is
   - a. the smallest number which is a common factor of the given numbers
   - b. the largest number which is a common factor of two given numbers
   - c. 1 is the GCD for all numbers
   - d. none of the above
6. Product of matrices A $(m \times n)$ and B $(n \times p)$ will be matrix C with row and columns as
   - a. m and p
   - b. n and p
   - c. p and n
   - d. none of the above
7. The product of all natural numbers from 1 to n is called
   - a. n!
   - b. $n \times n$
   - c. n^n
   - d. none of the above

8. In analysis of algorithm, approximate relationship between the size of the job and the amount of work required to do it is expressed by using-

a. order of magnitude b. central tendency

c. differential equation d. None of these

9. Which is better computing time (in analysis of algorithm)?

a. O(N) b. $O(N^2)$

c. O(log N) d. None of these

10. Modular programming uses-

a. only top-down method b. only bottom-up method

c. both a & b d. None of these

Key to Multiple Choice Questions

1. c	2. c	3. b	4. b	5. b
6. a	7. a	8. a	9. c	10. c

TEST PAPER

Note: Answer all questions.

1. What is an Algorithm? Why it is necessary to write an algorithm before program coding? Write an algorithm to sort an array in the descending order.
2. Write an algorithm to get the value of Cos(x) given as the following series:

$$\text{Cos}(x) = x - \frac{x^3}{3!} + \frac{x^5}{5!} - \frac{x^7}{7!} \ldots\ldots\ldots$$

3. Write an algorithm that reads a year and determines whether it is a leap year or not.
4. Write an algorithm which computes the roots of a quadratic equation.
5. What do you understand by the term problem definition? Explain it with an example.
6. What, according to you, are the basic steps that needs to be followed to solve a problem using computer?
7. Describe top-down and bottom-up approaches for solving a problem. Which one is the better method and why?
8. Explain, giving examples, the difference between recursive and non-recursive algorithms.

CHAPTER 2

Data Representation (Basic Concepts)

2.1 ABSTRACT DATA TYPE (ADT)

Different types of data are: (a) numeric, (b) alphanumeric (character), (c) date (d) logical (true/false). Programming languages allow creation and manipulation of such data types. When data is assigned a particular type, it can only be manipulated according to the rules used in the particular language of that data type. For example, alphanumeric data cannot be processed for mathematical calculations. The digits within numeric data cannot be separated. In 'C' language *int, float, char, double* etc are available as various kinds of data types. We need to divide data into various types to work with complex objects with ease.

There are two reasons for creating distinctions among different data types. These are:

a. The computer programming language compiler translates a program into object code (0 and 1 form or machine language form) would be able to use appropriate internal representation for manipulating each data type.

b. A programmer while designing programs can use proper operators to operate on each type of data.

A useful tool for specifying the logical properties of any data type is the **abstract data type or ADT**. We already know, that a data type is a collection of values and set of operations that can be performed on those values. Such collections and all such operations form a mathematical construct that can be implemented using a particular data structure[1]. An abstract data type is a data structure and collection of functions and procedures which can operate on that type of data structure.

Thus, an abstract data type (ADT) is a way of looking at the data arrangement (structure) focusing on what ADT does, and ignoring how it does. An abstract data type can be defined as a data type whose properties are specified independent of any particular implementation. *Stacks* and *queues* can be considered as examples of abstract data types. They can be implemented using either arrays or linked lists.

☞ *An abstract data type simplifies program design by allowing you to focus on the essentials of a data structure, without worrying about its implementation.*

---

[1]Organization of data and the relationship among its members is called a data structure.

The meaning of abstract data type is further extended when it is applied to data structure like stacks and queues. An object of any class in Object Oriented Programming (OOPs), means the data and the operations that can be performed on it. Thus, the fundamentals of how data would be stored is not invisible to the user. Users do not know how the member functions work.

For example, in the case of the stack, the user knows that push() and pop() functions exist and does not know, how they are implemented. The user need not know how push() and pop() work, or whether data is stored in the form of an array, a linked list, or tree.

ADT concept is a very useful aid in the software design process for computers.

While designing any software program the following are needed:

a. Identification of data objects needed by the program i.e. creation of Abstract Data Types – ADT.

b. Specification of algorithms and their design strategies.

For example, suppose we are designing a scheduling system for a college. Typical data objects might include students, courses and faculty. Typical operations (algorithms) might include adding a course to the list of courses (inserting), searching for courses taught by a specific faculty member(searching).

As the abstract data types and algorithm specifications are programming language independent, we can postpone implementation decision. For example, we might decide that the student data object should include name, roll_no, age, sex and marks. However, we would not yet pick a specific implementation method for the list of students. There are several data structures to represent the list of students namely as, arrays, linked lists, trees etc. The advantages of deferring their implementation issues are:

a. We can analyse a system that could be implemented in several programming languages.

b. We can select the most efficient implementation among chosen languages.

☞ *Essentially, abstract data type is a kind of abstract collection of data elements and functions, where we are not concerned how the associated functions will be implemented.*

2.2 FUNDAMENTAL AND DERIVED DATA TYPES

Programming Language 'C' supports a wide variety of data types and a programmer can select the type of data appropriate to the needs of the application. However, storage representation and machine instructions to manipulate each data type may differ form microprocessor used in the machine. 'C' supports the following classes of data types:

a. Fundamental or Primary data types

b. Derived or Secondary data types

Programming language 'C' supports the following fundamental data types:

char holds one character.

int an integer

float a single precision[2] floating point fractional number
double a double precision floating point fractional number

The bytes occupied by each of these types of data as well as the names assigned to them are given in Table 2.1.

Table 2.1 Typical range and memory size in bytes of basic data types

Type	Range		Bytes	Represents
	From	*To*		
char/short	–128	127	1	characters
unsigned char	0	255	1	characters
int	–32,768	32,767	2	whole numbers
unsigned int	0	65,535	2	whole numbers
long	–2,147,438,648	2,147,438,647	4	whole numbers
unsigned long	0	4,294,967,295	4	whole numbers
float	3.4×10^{-38}	3.4×10^{38}	4	fractional numbers
double	1.7×10^{-306}	1.7×10^{306}	8	fractional numbers
long double	3.4×10^{-4932}	3.4×10^{4932}	10	fractional numbers

Some of these data types may be modified by keywords *short, long, signed* and *unsigned* to take specific range of data values. The modifier *short* and *long* specify the amount of storage allocation to fundamental data type they modify. The modifiers *signed* and *unsigned* specify whether the most significant bit represents a sign bit or not. Figure 2.1 shows these data types as they would appear in a computer's memory. A character variable occupies one byte of memory in which the character constant such as 'b' or 'x' can be stored. The type name for a character is *char, int* is another type of numerical variable and stores positive or negative integers.

☞ *The data type int should not be used to hold fractions or real numbers.*

To store fraction, we need a floating point type representation of data i.e *float*. It occupies memory size of four bytes. It can hold numbers in the range from 3.4×10^{-38} to $3.4\ 10^{38}$ along with seven digits after decimal.

A *double* data type can store a floating point value with greater accuracy than a *float* type. *Double* data type occupies eight bytes of memory and can hold numbers from 1.7×10^{-306} to 1.7×10^{306} with 15 digits of after decimal.

Every variable holding data needs to be declared before it is used in a program. A declaration provides the compiler with information about how many bytes in the memory should be allocated for that variable and how those bytes would be interpreted.

[2]Precision means how many digits can be used in the decimal part of the number.

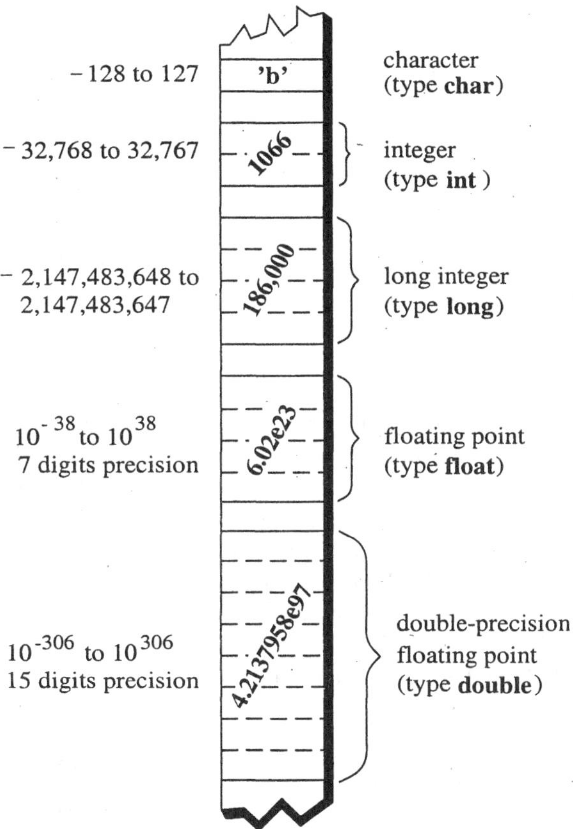

Figure 2.1 Pictorial presentation of different forms of data types and memory in bytes occupied by them

☞ *A variable must be declared by specifying the data type it will store.*

A variable declaration in 'C' consists of a data type followed by one or more variable names, ending with a semicolon (;).

The general format of the variable declaration is:

```
data_type identifier 1,2,...n
```

For example to declare j as an integer, we write :

```
int j;
```

We can also declare variables that have the same data type in a single line of declaration by separating variable names with commas. For example, we can declare j and k in a single line as:

```
int j,k;
```

This is the same for the declaration of *j* and *k* as:

```
int j;
int k;
```

It is a good programming practice to group together the declarations for the same data types for easy reference. For example:

```
int j,k;
float x,y,z;
```

☞ *The word **int** and **float** are reserved words in 'C' language. They specify the integer data type and real data type. These should not be used as variable names.*

A few examples of declarations of the variables are given in Table 2.2.

Table 2.2 Examples of variable declaration

Variable declaration	Remarks
int i = 0, j = 1;	Variables *i* and *j* are declared as integer variables. The variables *i* and *j* are initialized with values 0 and 1 respectively.
float basic_pay;	Variable *basic_pay* is a floating point type with a real value or values containing decimal fractions.
char a;	Variable *a* is a character variable that stores one character.
double theta;	Variable *theta* is a double precision variable that stores single double precision floating point number.

2.2.1 Declaring Different Types of Data

Signed and Unsigned Integers

In Programming Language 'C', a *short int* takes two bytes of memory and a *long int* takes four bytes of main memory. To declare j as a short int and k as a long int, we need to write:

```
short int j;
long int k;
```

If we want to declare an integer variable to be non-negative (positive) only, then we use the unsigned qualifier, as given below:

```
unsigned int k;
unsigned short m;
unsigned long n;
```

☞ *If you need to store integer values smaller than –32,768 or greater than 32,767, you should use **long int**. If you need to store integer values in the range –32767 and 32767, then you can use **short int**. This helps in reducing the size of main memory used for storing data.*

Characters

A variable declared as *char* can be used to hold either characters or numerals. But mathematical operators do not operate on character variables declared by *char* For instance, after making the declaration:

```
char c;
```

we can make either of the following assignments:

```
c = 'A';
```

or

```
c = 65;
```

Note that character constants are enclosed in single quotes. The quotes tell the compiler to get the numeric code (ASCII code value) of the character.

☞ *In the ASCII character code, characters are placed alphabetically. For example, ASCII code value of an uppercase 'A' is 65, 'B' is 66,... 'Z' is 90. ASCII code value of lowercase letters, i.e. 'a' starts at 97 and runs through 122. The char data type should only be used for storing character value in the variable.*

When selecting a data type to represent variable in a program, we first consider the likely range of values that variable may be made to hold. For example, if a variable is to hold the *Age* of a Student, then an *int* type will be more than sufficient. However, if the variable is to hold, the population of India, then the integer data type will be too small, and a *long int* data type should be used.

☞ *Unsigned variables are useful if we know in advance that there will never be a negative value for that variable. For example, the number of students in a class can never be less than zero, so an unsigned variable should be used. In this case, if you enter negative value, it will not be accepted by the program.*

Any variable which is likely to hold decimal fractions or which is required to handle very large numbers should be declared of the type *float*. For programs dealing with astronomy, the *long double* data type would be necessary to deal with very large numerical values to meet the requirements.

Example 1

What would be the appropriate data types to store the following:

a. Someone's height in meters

b. An exclamation mark (!)

c. The number of students in university

Solution

The selected data types should be as follows:

a. A *float*, because the height may contain a decimal fraction.

b. A *char*, because exclamations mark (!) is an ASCII character.

c. An *int*, or more appropriately, an *unsigned int*, because there will never be a negative number of students in the university.

Several other data types can be derived from these fundamental data types. Such data types are known as *derived* or *secondary* data types. C supports derived data types such as pointers, arrays and struct. A pointer is like any other data type in C. In fact, C allows the programmer to reference the location of objects as well as the contents of those locations. For example, if *x* is declared as an integer, &x refers to the location that has been set aside to contain *x*. &x is called a *pointer*. It is possible to declare a variable whose data type is a pointer and whose possible values are memory locations. For example, the declarations

```
int *pi;
float *pf;
char *pc;
```

declare three pointer variables. *pi* is a pointer to an integer, *pf* is a pointer to a float number, and *pc* is a pointer to a character. The asterisk indicates that the values of the variable being declared are pointers to values of type specified in the declaration.

Array is a collection of elements of the same basic data type. *struct* is a collection of elements of various data types.

☞ *In addition to above data types C++ also supports class data type. Class is a collection of elements of various data types.*

2.3 REPRESENTATION

To represent abstract data type, we use combinations of primitive data types. Abstract data type can be created using structures or classes. For example, a most commonly used abstract data type stack can be represented using structure data type as follows:-

```
struct stack
  {
  int top;
  int items[100];
  };
```

Classes are used in C++ to represent abstract data types, while structures can be used in both C and C++.

2.4 PRIMITIVE DATA STRUCTURES

"Data" is the name given to raw facts e.g. numbers of items sold by a business or the numerical values used in some mathematical calculation.

When "data" has been processed into a *more useful* or *intelligible form* (e.g. by a computer) it is called "information" e.g. "AJAY", 48" is data "the examination result for Mr Ajay is 48% and a pass" is information.

When individual data items are arranged or organised together as one unit then we call such an organised collection of data as *data structure.*

We have already discussed four fundamental data types such as *int, float, char* and *double.* These fundamental data types are also called primitive data types. Other data structures can be built from one or more primitive data structure.

Data structures are classified into following two categories.

- Linear data structure
- Non linear data structure

In the linear data structures processing of data items is possible in linear function, i.e. data can be processed one by one sequentially. The linear data structures are *Arrays, Linked list, Stack* and *Queues*.

Data structure is said to be non-linear if its elements do not form a sequence, i.e. where insertion and deletion is not possible in a linear fashion. The non linear data structures are *Trees* and *Graphs*.

2.4.1 Arrays

An array is a collection of two or more adjacent memory locations containing same type of data. These memory locations are called array elements which are given a particular symbolic name. (See Figure 2.2). Arrays elements are accessed using their index number that begins from zero. Array is a static data type since the size should be specified at the declaration point. Arrays do not lead to efficient memory management. Large amount of memory is wasted because estimated maximum memory has to be allocated for storing an array, even if only a very small fraction of the allocated memory is actually used. Arrays are useful when:

- The amount of data is reasonably small.
- Arrays are static[3] data structure. So, the amount of data is predictable in advance.
- There is a need for linear access of data using loops.

Advantage

- Very fast access if index is known.
- Insertion and deletion can be done randomly at any location, be it the start, some where at the middle or at the end.

Disadvantage

- Slow search facility.
- Fixed size i.e. static in nature.
- Insertion and deletion operation requires movement of large amount of data, so it is time consuming and inefficient.

Array x

	x [0]	x [1]	x [2]	x [3]	x [4]
int x[5];	12	14	8	17	3

Figure 2.2 An array of size 5 containin

[3] Static means they have a fixed (pre-specified) size.

2.4.2 Linked List

A linked list is the chain of data items connected by pointers and each item contains a pointer to the address of next item. (See Figure 2.3). Structure (struct) is the most appropriate data structure to represent linked list.

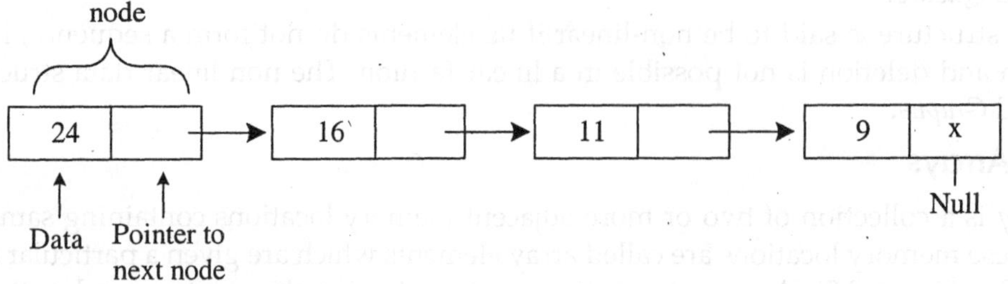

Figure 2.3 A linked list containing integers

Linked list are useful when

- The amount of data to be stored cannot be predicted in advance since it is a dynamic data type.
- Data will frequently be inserted or deleted.

A linked list obtains whatever storage it needs as new items are added, so it can expand to fill all of the available memory; there is no need to fill "holes" during deletion, as in arrays.

Linked lists overcomes the disadvantages of array and offer flexibility in programs. But linked list suffer from one major drawback. The search time for a node containing a certain piece of information is directly proportional to the size of the list even if the list is sorted. Thus the larger the size of the linked list, the greater is the search time.

Types of linked list are:

(a) Singly linked list
(b) Doubly linked list
(c) Circular linked list

In a *singly linked list* each node contains data and a single link which attaches it to the next node in the list.

In *doubly linked list* each node contains data and two links one to the previous node and one to the next node.

In a *circular linked list* the last node, instead of pointing to Null, points to the starting node.

Advantage

- Quick insertion
- Quick deletion
- Insertion and deletion operations in a linked list are much easier compared to those in an array, because these operations can be handled efficiently without having to reconstruct the list.

Disadvantage

- Slow Search

2.4.3 Stack

A stack is a data structure similar to an array but in this elements are added to and removed only from one end of the list called the **top** (See Figure 2.4). In other words, stack provides the information in the reverse of the entry order, so it is called the Last-In-First-Out (LIFO) list.

A stack is implemented as an array or a linked list. The array implementation is efficient because the most recently inserted item is placed at the end of the array, where it is also easy to delete it. *Stack overflow*[4] can occur, but it is not likely if the array is reasonably sized, because stacks may contain huge amount of data.

☞ *If the stack will contain a lot of data and the amount cannot be predicted accurately in advance a linked list is better choice than an array. A linked list is efficient because items can be inserted and deleted quickly from the head of the list. "Stack overflow" cannot occur unless the entire memory is full.*

A stack is useful when you want access only to the last data item inserted as it is a Last-In-First-Out (LIFO) structure.

Insertion sequence A, B, C, D, E

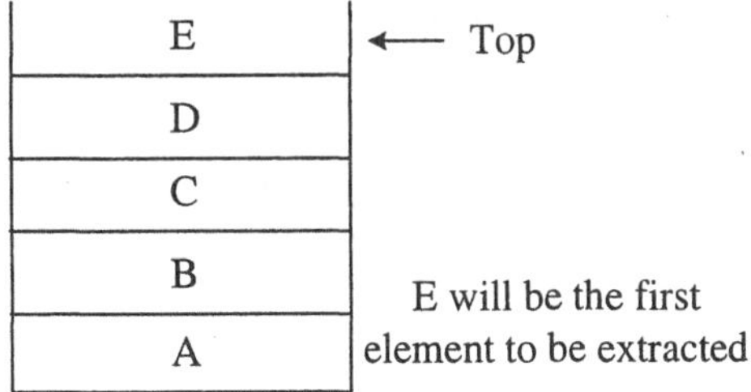

Figure 2.4 A stack

Advantage

- Provides last-in-first-out access.

Disadvantage

- Slow access to other items.

2.4.4 Queue

A queue is a data structure with the restriction that entries can be added or removed at either end but not in the middle. A single-ended queue permits addition on one end, usually through the queue head (front) and deletion from other end, the tail (rear). Queue is also called First-In-First-Out (FIFO) list. (See Figure 2.5)

A queue is used when you want access only to the first data item inserted as it is a first-in-first-out (FIFO) structure.

Like stacks, queues can be implemented as arrays or linked lists. Both are efficient.

[4] Attempt to push elements to the stack beyond its maximum capacity is known as stack overflow.

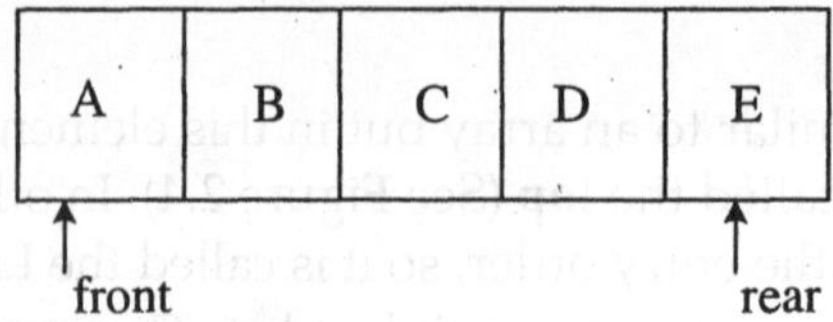

Figure 2.5 A Queue

Advantage

- Provides first-in-first-out access.

Disadvantage

- Slow access to other items.

2.4.5 Tree

The data structures that we have seen so far such as *arrays, linked lists, stacks* and *queues* are linear data structures as against *trees*. Tree data structure is non-linear data structure. A tree is a data structure that represents hierarchical relationships between individual data items.

Figure 2.6 is an example of a tree structure representing student record.

A tree consists of a collection of nodes which are connected by directed arcs. A tree contains a unique first element known as the *root,* which is shown at the top of the tree structure. Here *student* is the root node. The nodes Name, Address and Course, which are directly connected to the root node, are the child nodes of the parent node *student*. A link between a parent and its child is called a branch in a tree structure. A node with no children is called a *leaf* node. In Figure 2.6, Address is a leaf node. LName, MName, FName, Course A, Course B, and Course C are also leaf nodes.

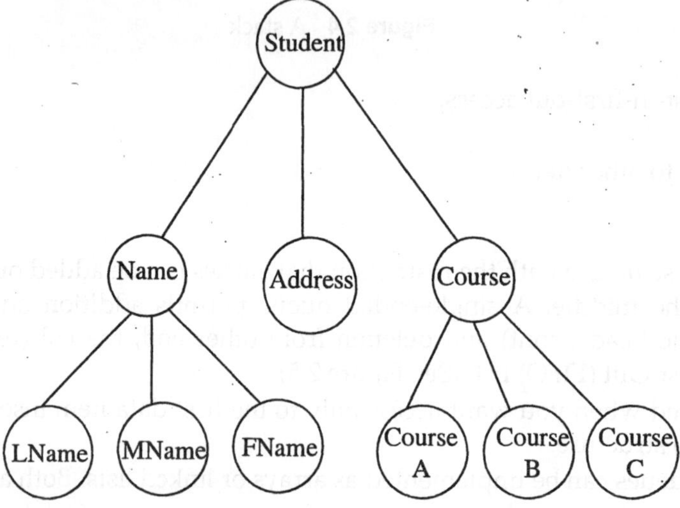

Figure 2.6 A tree structure representing a student's record

Tree is a very flexible and powerful data structure that can be used for a wide variety of applications. For example, the history of a family representing information about ancestors and descendents can be organized into the tree structure.

A tree consists of a collection of nodes which are connected by one or more pointers to the other tree nodes. Although the nodes in a general tree may contain any number of pointers to the other tree nodes. A large number of data structures have at the most two pointers to the other tree nodes. This type of a tree is called a *binary tree.*

A binary tree is the first structure to consider when arrays and linked lists prove too slow. A tree provides fast insertion, searching and deletion. You can also find the minimum and maximum number quickly and you can traverse a range of items very fast.

Advantage

- Quick search, insertion and deletion if tree remains balanced.
- Easy to understand from the graphical view.

Disadvantage

- Needs unnecessary traversal in order to reach a particular node.

2.4.6 Graphs

Data structure tree provides a very useful way of representing relationships in which hierarchy exists. If we remove the restriction that each node may be pointed to by at the most one node, then we come across another data structure called *graphs.*

Thus, the tree structure is a special kind of graph in which the relationship between parent and child is hierarchical. A graph, on the other hand, is a structure that represent a less restrictive relationship between data items. A common example of a graph is a collection of cities and the roads between them; two cities are related, if there is a route between them. Their relationship is not hierarchical because traffic on the routes between cities can flow in either direction. Graphs are frequently applied in diverse areas such as artifical intelligence, cybernetics, chemical structure of crystals, transportation networks, electrical circuitry, and the analysis of programming languages.

☞ *A graph is defined as a set of nodes or vertices and a set of lines or edges or arcs that connect the two vertices. Graphs represents many to many relationship between nodes.*

Graphs are of two types:

- Undirected
- Directed

In an undirected graph (Figure 2.7), an edge between two nodes is not directionally oriented. Thus, in an undirected graph, if AG (A to G) is an edge, so is GA.

In a directed graph or digraph, the edges between nodes are directionally oriented. In the directed graph of Figure 2.8, AB is an edge and not BA. Thus, there are directed edges from A to B, B to C, C to D and D to E. The directed edge is also called an *arc.*

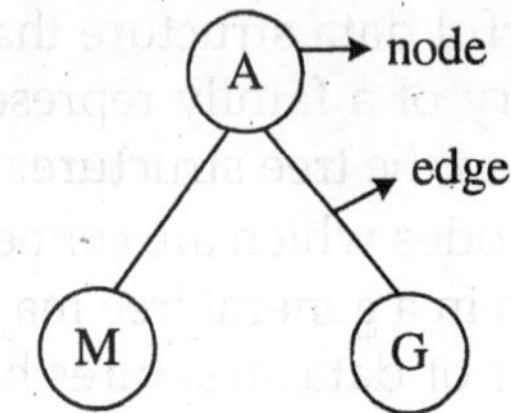

Figure 2.7 Undirected graph

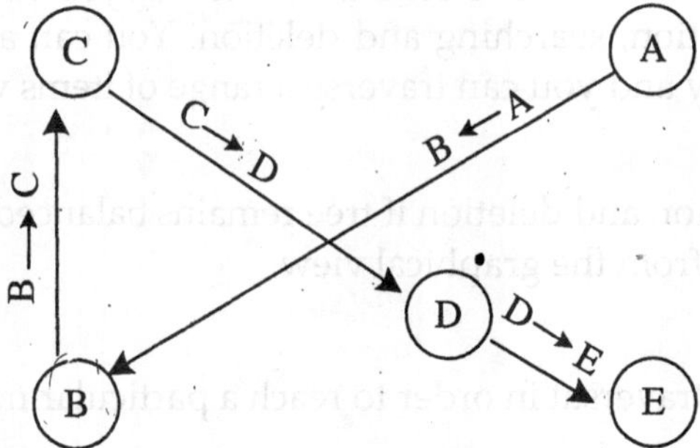

Figure 2.8 A directed graph

Advantage

- Graphs are data structures which have wide ranging applications in real life, like analysis of electrical circuits, finding shortest routes, statistical analysis etc.
- A directed graph is a natural way of describing, representing and analyzing complex projects which consists of many interrelated activities.

2.5 SYMBOL TABLE

Dictionaries are found in many application, including the spelling checker, the thesaurus, the data dictionary found in database management applications and the symbol table generated by loaders, assemblers and compilers. In computer science, we generally use the term symbol table rather than dictionary to refer to the ADT. Part of a compiler that keeps record of names of variable and their associated attributes or values is known as *symbol table*.

Generally, we want to perform the following operations on a symbol table.

- Determine of a particular name in the table.
- Retrieve the attributes of that name.
- Modify the attributes of that name
- Insert a new name and its attributes.
- Delete a name and its attributes.

2.6 RECURSION

The programming language C lets you divide your program into smaller pieces called *functions*. Using functions, your program becomes easier to understand and to debug or test. In addition, the functions you create for one program can often be used by another. As your programs execute, one function may call another, which calls another, which may, in turn, call several other functions–each function to perform a specific operation. C even lets a function call itself.

☞ *A recursive function is a function that calls itself to perform a specific operation. The process of a function calling itself is known as recursion.*

Indirect recursion occurs when one function calls another function that then calls the first function. For example, recursion can be used to calculate the factorial of a number.

0! = 1

n! = n(n-1)!

where n! is defined in terms of (n-1)! which in turn defined in terms of (n-2)! and so on till we reach 0! which is explicitly defined to have a value 1.

The program in Figure 2.9 creates the recursive function *factorial* and then uses the function to return the factorial values for the values 1 through 5.

```
#include <stdio.h>
int factorial(int value)
{
    if(value == 1)
    return(1);
    else
    return(value *factorial(value-1));
}
void main(void)
{
    int i;
    for (i = 1; i <= 5; i++)
    printf("The factorial of %d is %d\n", i, factorial(i));
}
```

Figure 2.9 Calculating factorial of a number using recursion

As you can see, the function factorial, returns a result that is based on the result of the function itself.

The program below, uses recursion to compute the sum of integers from 1 to *n*.

```
int sum(n)
int n;
{
   if (n <= 1)
      return n;
   else
      return (n + sum(n-1));
}
```

It is useful to step through the function, observing what value gets returned with each call. If we pass the function, a value=5, the call trace is shown in Figure 2.10.

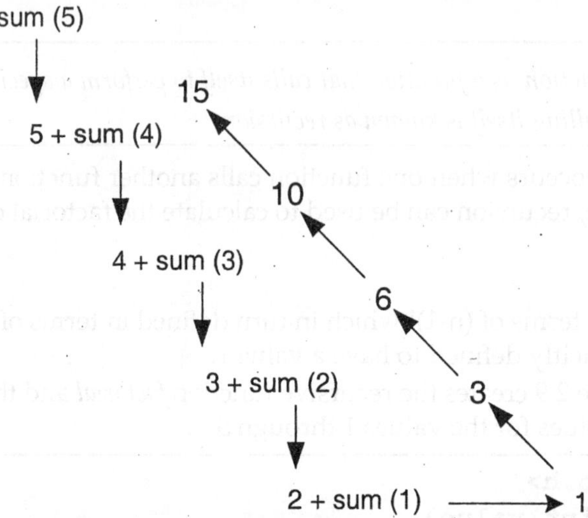

Figure 2.10 Recursion call trace of sum() function when argument is 5

2.6.1 The Tower of Hanoi

The Towers of Hanoi is a well known game for children played with three poles and a number of different sized disks. Each disk has a hole in the center, allowing it to be stacked around any of the poles. Initially the disks are stacked on the leftmost pole in the order of decreasing size i.e. the largest on the bottom and the smallest on the top.

☞ *The objective of the game is to transfer the disks from the leftmost pole to the right most pole, without ever placing a larger disk on top of a small disk.*

Only one disk may be moved at a time, and each disk must always be placed around one of the poles. The problem can be solved in recursive manner:

a. Move the top $n - 1$ disks from the left pole to the center pole.
b. Move the nth disk (the largest disk) to the right pole.
c. Move the $n - 1$ disks on the center pole to the right pole.

DESCRIPTIVE QUESTIONS

Q. No. 1 Differentiate between Abstract Data type and primitive data structures?

Ans to Q. 1 [*Refer to Section 2.1 and 2.4*]

Q. No. 2 What are the advantages of linked list implementation over arrays?

Ans to Q. 2 [*Refer to Section 2.4.2*]

Q. No. 3 Try to represent the linked list and stack data structure using *struct* data structure.

Ans to Q. 3 [*Refer to Section 2.3*]

Q. No. 4 Compare stacks with queues

Ans to Q. 4 [*Refer to Section 2.4.3 and 2.4.4*]

Q. No. 5 Explain the term recursion with an example. Is the recursion is efficient?

Ans to Q. 5 Recursion is a programming technique in which function calls itself. For example, factorial of a number is calculated recursively.

Is recursion efficient?

Calling a function involves certain overheads. Control must be transferred from the location of the call to the beginning of the function. In addition, the arguments to the function and the address to which the function should return, must be pushed into an internal stack, so that the function can access the argument values and know where to return.

Another inefficiency is that memory is used to store all the intermediate arguments and returns values on the system's internal stack. This might cause problems if there is a large amount of data leading to stack overflow.

Recursion is usually used because it simplifies a problem conceptually, not because its inherently more efficient.

EXERCISE

Multiple Choice

1. Data structure
   a. may be helpful to develop efficient algorithms in different phases of data processing.
   b. need not give relationship between data items.
   c. is programming language dependent
   d. None of the above
2. Which is not true?
   a. abstract data type is the useful tool for specifying the logical properties of data type.
   b. while defining an abstract datatype as a mathematical concept, the space and efficiency is not a major concern.
   c. Every abstract data type can be implemented using any programming language
   d. None of the above
3. A data structure, in which a element is added and removed only from one end is known as:-

a. Queue
b. Stack
c. Array
d. None of these

4. Queue
   a. can be created by setting up an ordinary contiguous array to hold the items
   b. can take care of delete operation automatically
   c. need a one pointer to handle addition and deletion of an item.
   d. None of the above.

5. Structured data type made up of finite collection of ordered elements, all of which are of the same data type is-
   a. Record
   b. Array
   c. File
   d. None of these

6. Implementation of list in a dynamic fashion is
   a. to call upon the system to allocate and free storage may not be time consuming
   b. a set of nodes is not reserved in advance for use.
   c. the address computation is complex.
   d. None of above

7. Memory allocation at the runtime is known as
   a. static memory allocation
   b. dynamic memory allocation
   c. paging
   d. None of the above

8. Memory allocation at the compile time is known as
   a. static memory allocation
   b. dynamic memory allocation
   c. paging
   d. None of the above

9. Most appropriate data structure in C to represent linked list is
   a. array
   b. struct
   c. union
   d. None of the above

10. Part of a compiler that keeps record of names of variables and their associated attributes/values is known as a-
   a. parser
   b. symbol table
   c. lexical analyzer
   d. None of these

Key to Multiple Choice Questions

1.	a	2.	c	3.	b	4.	a	5.	b
6.	b	7.	b	8.	a	9.	b	10.	b

TEST PAPER

Note: Answer all questions.

1. What do you mean by Abstract data type? How will you represent abstract data type?
2. Explain stack and queue with an example.
3. What is symbol table?
4. What is graph? Explain two different types of graph.
5. Write short note on the Tower of Hanoi.

CHAPTER 3

Arrays

3.1 INTRODUCTION

An array is a collection of similar data types or elements, addressed by a common name. By similar data type we mean that all the elements in the array must be of same type. For example, an array may contain all integers or all characters but do not contain both in the same array.

In terms of PC memory, an *array* is a collection of two or more adjacent memory locations containing the same type of data. These adjacent memory locations are called array elements. An array is given a particular symbolic name. For example, if we want to store salary of 6 employees, then we have two options. The *first* one is to construct 6 variables to store salary of 6 different employees i.e each variable containing one employee's salary. The *second* option is to construct just one variable which is capable of holding all the 6 employees salary in its different elements. This option uses as *array* variable say, *salary*.

Figure 3.1 shows the individual variables and a single array of memory locations with a common name. The individual variables would be like individual folders in a file cabinet whereas an array is like a single folder with many leaves and kept at one place.

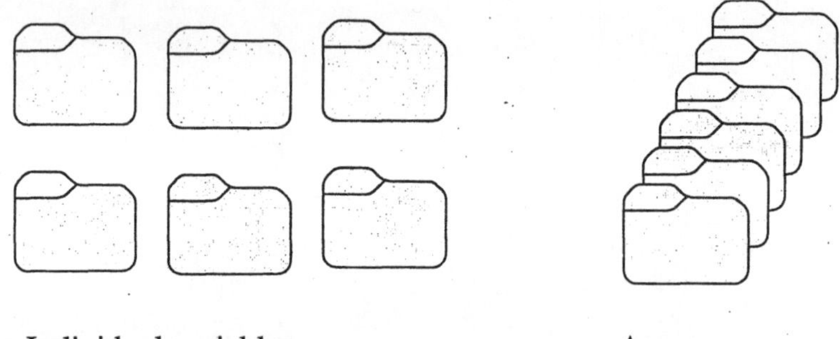

Individual variables An array

Figure 3.1 Illustration of individual variables and an array of 6 elements

3.2 REPRESENTATION OF AN ARRAY

To create an array, we need to declare both the name of the array and the number of cells or elements i.e. the size of this array.

The declaration of an array x in a programming language 'C' is as follows:

```
double x[8];
```

This declaration instructs the compiler of 'C' language to associate eight memory cells with the variable name *x*. These memory cells storing different values will be adjacent to each other. The *double* here indicates the precision of numerical values, held by each of the array elements.

☞ *When you declare an array, the brackets along with the variable such as x[8], indicates to the compiler that we are declaring an array and the compiler sets aside a block of memory large enough to hold the entire array. In this case, it keeps the size to 8 memory locations.*

In order to manipulate data stored in the array, we reference each element of the array by specifying the array *name* say *x* and the element desired using a *subscript*, say 7.

A subscript is a number in brackets that follows an array's name. This number identifies the index of an individual element of the array. For example, the variable *x*[0] may be used to reference the initial or 0th element of the array *x*, *x*[1] the next element, and finally *x*[7] the last element. The integer enclosed in brackets is the array subscript, and its value must be in the range from zero to a number one less than the number of memory cells in the array. In 'C' language, the lower bound (smallest index of the array) is always 0 and the upper bound (the highest index of the array) is one less than *n* i.e (n-1), where *n* is the number of elements of the array.

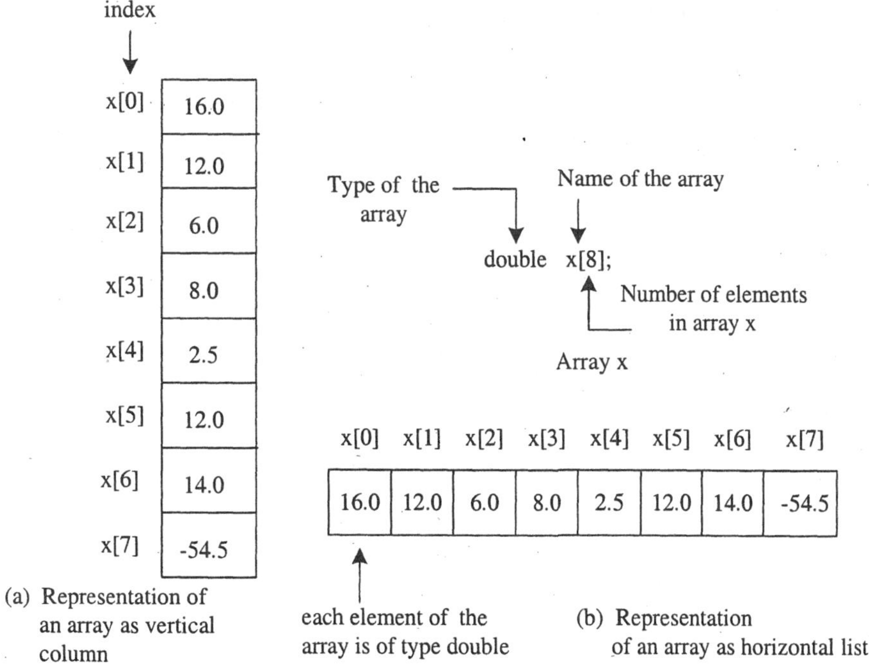

Figure 3.2 Representation of an array *x* containing 8 adjacent memory locations in a computer

☞ *The subscript of an array is also called an index. The index set consist of integers 0, 1, 2, 3 ... etc.*

Let *x* be the array shown in Figure 3.2. The first element is *x*[0], the second element of the array is *x*[1] and finally *x*[7] is the last element of the array *x* of size 8, thus using 8 memory locations of a computer we can store 8 values.

☞ *Remember that array elements starts with 0 not by 1. Also remember that the last element is one less than the number of elements in the declaration of array. For example, an array with 10 elements will have subscripts numbered from 0 to 9 elements i.e. x(0) ..... x(9).*

3.2.1 Declaration of more than One Array

Declaration of one or more arrays can be made in 'C' language by a single statement as given below:

```
double cal[5], pin[6];
int factors[12], n, sal;
```

In the above statements, *cal*[5] and *pin*[6] are two arrays with five and six elements respectively. Each array stores numerical data with *double* precession. The array *factors*[12] with 12 elements, can store the data of type integer. In addition, individual memory cells will be allocated for storing integer data in the variables say *n* and *sal* in the above method of declaration. Another method for declaring an array is as follows:

```
#define num_readings 20
double gauge[num_readings];
int time[num_readings];
```

Above declaration allocates storage for two arrays of numerals. The array *gauge*[] can hold 20 elements of numerical data type double precission and array *time*[] can hold 20 elements of numerical data type integer.

Array Initialization

A variable can be initialized as we declare it. For example, in the following statement:

```
int sum = 0;
```

An array can also be initialized (given initial values to all the elements) at the time of declaration. For example, in the following statement 25-element array named as prime_x[25] is initialized with twenty five prime numbers:

```
int prime_x[25] = {2, 3, 5, 7, 11, 13, 17, 19, 23, 29, 31, 37, 41, 43,
47, 53, 59, 61, 67, 71, 73, 79, 83, 89, 97};
```

The arrays sex[2] and name[6] are initialized storing *character* data type.

```
char sex[2] = ['m','f'];
char name[6]=['s', 'h','a','s','h','i'];
```

☞ *The first element is always placed in the 0th place. The array size may be omitted if the array is initialized while giving it a definition.*

Some other examples for declarations for arrays with initial values are given below:

```
char vowels[] = {'A','E','I','O','U'};
int age[] = {16, 21, 19, 1, 5};
```

In the above two cases, note that 'C' compiler assumes that the array size is equal to the number of elements enclosed in the curly braces. Thus, in above statements, size of the array is assumed to be 5.

3.2.2 Difference between Array Subscript and Array Element

Understanding the distinction between an array *subscript* value and an array *element* value is essential. The explanation is based on Figure 3.2. The subscript variable *i* references a particular element of the array by x[i]. If i has the value 0, the subscript value is 0, and x[0] is referenced . The element value of x[0] in this case is 16.0. If i has the value 2, the subscript value is 2, and the element value of x[2] is 6.0. If i has the value 8, the subscript value is 7 but we cannot predict the element value of x[8] because the subscript value is out of allowable range (as the range is from 0 to 7 and not 8).

3.3 MULTIDIMENSIONAL ARRAYS

Multidimensional arrays are declared in 'C' language in the same manner as one dimensional array, except that a separate pair of square brackets are required for each additional dimension of the array. Thus, a two dimensional array will require two pairs of square brackets. A two-dimensional array, having two subscripts, is suitable for processing a table having rows and columns. For this purpose, we use two subscripts enclosed in square brackets. The first subscript designates the *row* and the second subscript designates the *column*.

To declare a two-dimensional array, the first value we specify indicates the number of rows and the second value specify the number of columns.

For example:

```
int x[3][5];
```

is the declaration of two dimensional array *x* which has 3 rows and 5 columns. It stores integer data in each element. A two dimensional array is best visualized as a table consisting of rows and columns. Figure 3.3 shows such an array with 3 rows starting with rows 0 and ending with row 2. Also the number of columns are 5 starting with 0 and ending with column 4. Each of the cells in this two-dimensional array can take an integer value because we have declared the array *x* to be of integer type. The array can be declared of any other type much similar to the type of variables. But each element of the array can store that type of data value only. To refer a specific array element, we must specify the corresponding row and column numbers.

☞ *Note that two dimensional arrays are stored in a row-column format, where the first index gives the row numbers and second index indicates the column numbers.*

To access an element of the array shown in Figure 3.3, we need to specify two indices say for example, x[i] [j], where i is the row number and j is the column number. For example, to access the shaded element in Figure 3.3, we have to specify x[1][2].

☞ *All arrays, no matter how many dimensions they have, are stored sequentially in the memory of a computer.*

	Column 0	Column 1	Column 2	Column 3	Column 4
Row 0					
Row 1			X[1][2]		
Row 2					

Figure 3.3 An array with 3 rows and 5 columns

Similarly,

Array with 3 Dimensions

```
char x[3][4][5];
```

is the declaration of an array *x* that *x* has 3 dimensions. The first dimension has 3-elements. The second dimension has 4-elements. The third dimension has 5 elements. Thus, the array *x* in this declaration is of 3 dimensions where the values in each of the brackets represent the number of elements contained. Hence, there are a total of $3 \times 4 \times 5$ i.e. 60 elements each storing character type of data in the array *x*.

3.3.1 Initializing a Two Dimensional Array

To initialize two dimensional array, we should enclose each row in braces. To store the elements of an array shown in Figure 3.4, we can make the following declaration:

```
int magic[5][5] = { {17, 24, 1, 8, 15},
                    {23, 5, 7, 14, 16},
                    {4, 6, 13, 20,22},
                    {10, 12, 19, 21, 3},
                    {11, 18, 25, 2, 9}
                    };
```

The stored values are seen in Figure 3.4.

	0	1	2	3	4
0	17	24	1	8	15
1	23	5	7	14	16
2	4	6	13	20	22
3	10	12	19	21	3
4	11	18	25	2	9

Figure 3.4 Pictorial representation of 5 x 5 integer array named magic

While initializing, each row with values enclosed with in braces, and the numbers entered are less than the number of elements declared in the array, then the balance of the elements will take zero as initial value.

☞ *If there are insufficient initialisers, then the extra elements are initialized to zero.*

Consider the following array:
For example,

```
int examp[5][3] = {  {1, 2, 3,
                      {4},
                      {5, 6, 7
                   };
```

This declares the array *examp* with five rows and three columns. However, values for all the elements is not given. Pictorially, this declaration produces the array, as seen below. This declaration takes the values for the elements not initialized in the declaration to contain zero value.

Columns →

Rows ↓

1	2	3
4	0	0
5	6	7
0	0	0
0	0	0

☞ *Initialization values must be separated by a comma, even when there are braces enclosing them.*

In case we do not include the inner brackets and declare array as follows:

```
int examp[5][3] =    { 1, 2, 3,
                        4,
                        5, 6, 7
                     };
```

The result will be as shown in Figure 3.4(a) the values stored in the array will be as follows:

Columns →

Rows ↓

	0	1	2
0	1	2	3
1	4	0	0
2	5	6	7
3	0	0	0
4	0	0	0

Figure 3.4(a) Array declared with seven initial values only

It is obvious that the initialization in this case is very misleading. Hence to enhance readability and clarity, you should always enclose each row of initialisers in its own set of braces.

☞ *Do not use comma to separate subscripts while programming in 'C'. This notation has a very different meaning because comma is an operator in 'C'. Thus, int x[2,3]; is wrong declaration. The correct declaration is x[2][3];.*

3.3.2 Matrix Representation of Two Dimensional Array

An array with two dimension array is also called a *matrix*. A two dimensional array can be represented as [A_{ij}] where *i* is the number of rows and *j* is the number of columns.

Even though the elements of two dimensional array are represented as a matrix yet the values are stored in adjacent memory locations in computer like a one dimensional array. The values of the elements may be stored row-by-row (row major order) or column by column (column major order). The choice of the arrangement is not with the user and would depend on the programming language and the type of compiler for the high level language.

Let *x* be the two dimensional array. The array *x* may be stored in the memory in one of the following two ways.

- Row major order (row by row)
- Column major order (column by column)

Figure 3.5 shows the row major representation of an array, of the type *int marks[3][5];* where *marks* is the name of the array with 3 rows and 5 columns.

	Column 0	Column 1	Column 2	Column 3	Column 4
Row 0					
Row 1			X[1][2]		
Row 2					

Figure 3.5 Row major representation of two dimensional array int marks[3][5]

3.4 SEQUENTIAL ALLOCATION AND ADDRESS CALCULATION

Consider the following array declaration:

```
long LongArray[5];
```

When the compiler sees this declaration, it sets aside enough memory locations to hold 5 elements as declared in the statement above. Because each long integer requires 4 bytes of memory location, this declaration sets aside 20 contiguous bytes of memory, as illustrated in Figure 3.6.

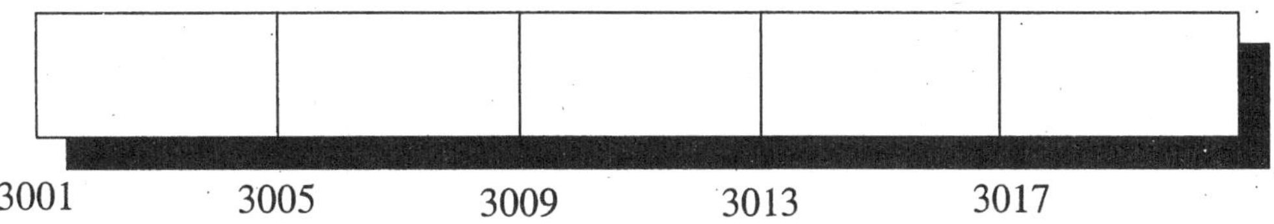

Figure 3.6 The array *LongArray* as stored in main memory of PC

Note that the address of each subsequent element of the array is as follows:

`address of previous element + number of bytes occupied by the data type`

For example, if an array storing integer data begins at location 4002, then the elements arr[1] and arr[5] would be present at locations 4004 and 4012, respectively. This is because each integer element will occupy 2 bytes of memory. Similarly, if a character array begins at location 4002, then the elements arr[1] and arr[5] would be present at locations 4003 and 4007, respectively. This is because each character element will occupy only 1 byte of memory.

Note that if the array is not initialized, all the elements present in it would be containing garbage values. Whatever be the initial values, all the array elements would always be present in contiguous memory locations as seen in Figure 3.7.

Suppose we have an array

```
float arr[] = {24.24, 34.5, 12.0, 44.666, 56.10, 17.0};
```

Figure 3.7 shows how this array is stored in memory

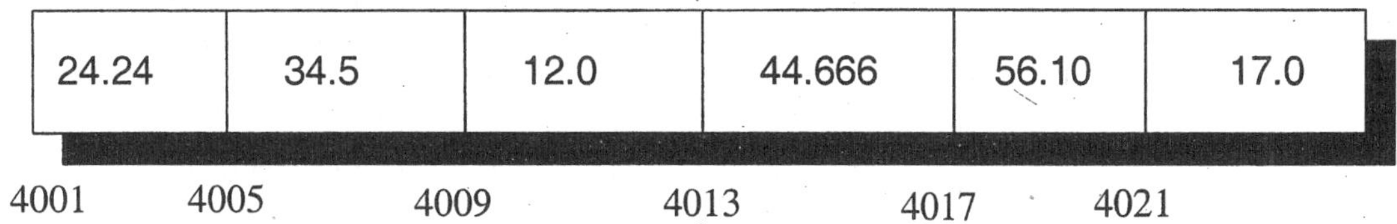

Figure 3.7 The array *arr* storing float data and located in memory of a PC

3.4.1 Address Calculation of Array Element using Column/Row Major Ordering

Knowing the base address or the address where the first element of the array will be stored, we can then calculate the address of any element of the array having m rows and n columns.

The address of the Ith row and J^{th} column element i.e. A(I, J), when the arrangement of array *A* is row wise, will be calculated as follows:

`Address of the element A(I, J) = BA + (I – 1) × n + (J – 1)`

where BA is the base address from where the storing of elements in the memory will start. The I and J are the row^{th} number and $column^{th}$ number of the element stored in the memory. Thus, if the address of the element A(4, 3) is to be found, then we are trying to locate the address of the element in the 4th row and 3rd column.

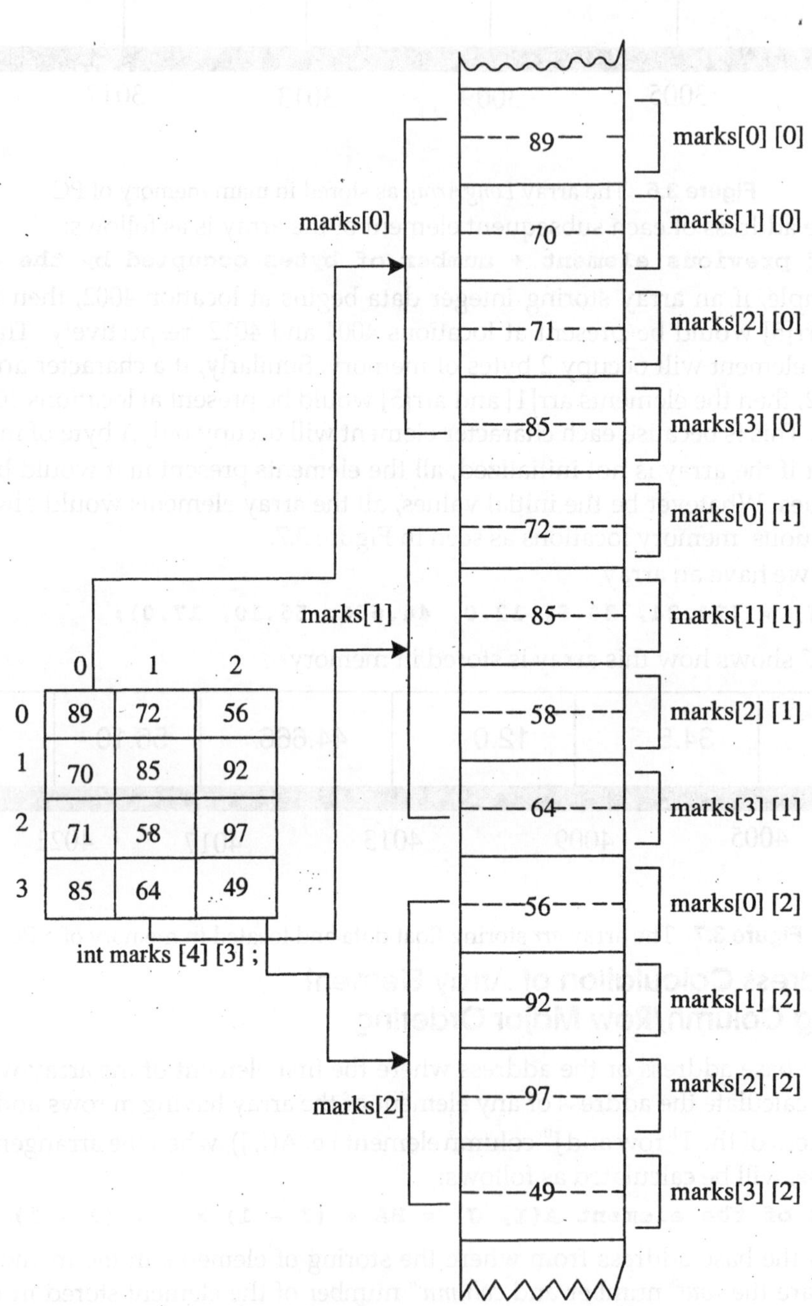

Figure 3.8 Column major representation of a two dimensional array stored in memory of PC

Similarly, the address of the element A(I, J) when the arrangement of A is columnwise can be calculated as follows:

Address of the element A(I, J) = BA + (J − 1) × m + (I − 1)

where BA is the base address from where the storing of elements in the memory will start. The I and J are the *row*th number and *column*th number of the element stored in the memory.

When each of the elements of the array occupy *w* words, then the address of the element A(I, J) for the *row major* arrangement is given by:

Address of the element A(I, J) = BA + w × [(I − 1) × n + (J − 1)]

where BA is the base address and w is the number of words that each element occupies. Similarly, when each of the elements of the array occupy w words, then the address of the element A(I,J) for column major arrangement is given by:

Address of the element A(I, J) = BA + w × [(J − 1) × m + (I − 1)]

where BA is the base address and w is the number of words that each element occupies.

Example 1

Let A be a 4 × 5 array with the base address BA = 42. Find the address of the element A(4,3) when the storage is row major. (See Figure 3.9).

We use the following formula for row wise:

Address of the element A(I,J) = BA + (I − 1) × n + (J − 1)

Here BA = 42, I = 4, J = 3, and n = 5

So the address of the element A(4, 3) is

= BA + (I − 1) × n + (J − 1)

= 42 + (4 − 1) × (5) + (3 − 1)

= 59

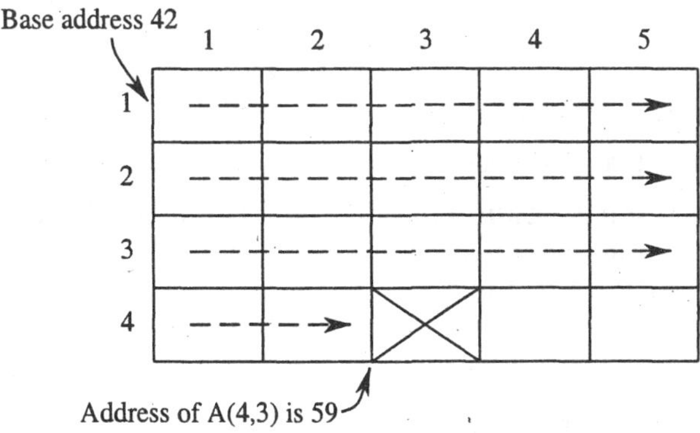

Figure 3.9 Address of the element A(4,3)

Example 2

Let A be a 5 × 6 array with base address BA = 2146. If each element of the array occupies 3 words, find the address of A(3, 5) when the arrangement is (i) row major and (ii) column major.

When the arrangement is row major The formula for finding the address of the element A(3, 5) when the arrangement is row major and each element occupies 3 words, with the base address as 2146 is given by:

$$A(I, J) = BA + w \times [(I - 1)\, n \times + (J - 1)]$$

Substituting the values, we get

$$= 2146 + 3 \times [(3 - 1) \times 6 + (5 - 1)]$$
$$= 2194$$

See Figure 3.9(a).

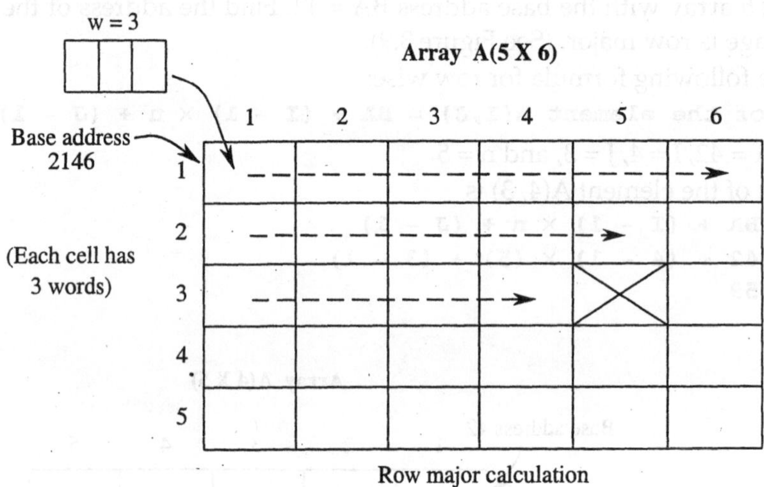

Figure 3.9(a) Address of the element A(3,5) with 3 words in each element

When the arrangement is column major The formula for finding the address of the element A(3, 5) when the arrangement is column major and each element occupies 3 words, with the base address as 2146, is given by:

$$A(I, J) = BA + w \times [(J - 1) \times m + (I - 1)]$$

Substituting the values, we get:

$$= 2146 + 3 \times [\,(5 - 1) \times 5 + (3 - 1)]$$
$$= 2212$$

See Figure 3.9(b).

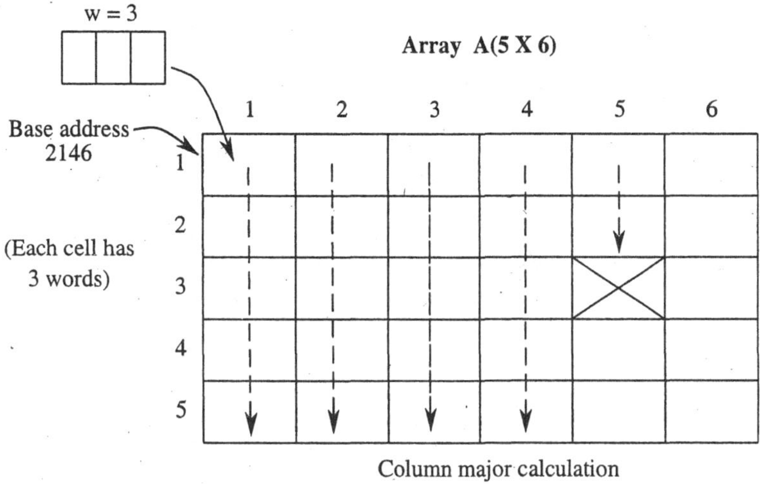

Figure 3.9(b) Address of the element A(3,5) with 3 words in each element and arranged column major

Example 3

An array A is kept row wise. If the address of A(2, 2) is 107 and that of A(4, 5) is 122, find the address of A(3, 3).

Using the formula for the address of A(2, 2), and A(4, 5) row wise, we get

Let there be y number of rows, then

$$BA + (2 - 1)\,y + (2 - 1) = 107$$

or

$$BA + y = 106 \quad \text{..................} \quad (1)$$

Similarly, for the element A(4, 5) the address is:

$$BA + (4 - 1)\,y + (5 - 1) = 122$$

or

$$BA + 3y = 118 \quad \text{.........................} \quad (2)$$

Solving equations 1 and 2, we get:

y = 6 and BA = 110

Knowing the values of y and BA, we can calculate the address of A(3,3) by using the formula for row major. Thus the address of A(3,3) is:

$= 100 + 2y + 2$

$= 114$

3.5 OPERATIONS ON ARRAYS

The operations that can be performed on linear structure i.e. arrays are:

a. Traversal – *Processing* each element in the array or list.

b. Search – *Finding* the location of the element with a given value with a given key.

c. Insertion – *Adding* a new element to the list.

d. Deletion – *Removing* an element from the list.

e. Sorting – *Arranging* the element in some type of order, ascending or descending.

f. Reversing – Reversing the elements of an array.

g. Merging – *Combining* two lists or arrays to give a single list or array.

3.5.1 Traversal

Traversal is the act of processing each element of the array one after the other. Suppose we have an array X that is collection of integer data type in the computer's memory. If we visit each and every element in X, then this process of visiting is called *traversing*. The traversal algorithm for a linear array is given in Figures 3.10 and 3.11.

Algorithm for traversal of an array using while loop

Let the linear array be LA with lower bound LB and upper bound UB. The smallest element of an array's index is called its *lower bound* and in programming language C it is always 0, and the highest element is called its *upper bound*. The number of elements in the array is called its range. The algorithm given in Figure 3.10 traverses LA applying an operation PROCESS to each element of LA.

Algorithm for traversal of an array using for loop

Let the linear array be LA with lower bound LB and upper bound UB. The algorithm in Figure 3.11 traverses LA applying an operation PROCESS to each element of LA.

```
Step 1   [Initialize counter] Set K := LB
Step 2   Repeat steps 3 and 4 while K <= UB
Step 3   Apply PROCESS to LA[K]
Step 4   Set K := K + 1
         [End of loop in step 2]
Step 5   Exit
```

Figure 3.10 Algorithm for traversing a linear array using while loop.

```
Step 1   [Initialize counter] Set K := LB
Step 2   Repeat steps 3 for K := LB to UB
Step 3   Apply PROCESS to LA[K]
         [End of loop in step 2]
Step 5   Exit
```

Figure 3.11 Algorithm for traversing an array linearly using *for* loop

3.5.2 Search

To locate a particular item or element in an array is called *search*. Suppose a specific (*Info*) information is to be located in an array then *Searching* refers to the operation of finding the location of *Info* in an array and displaying the appropriate message. The search is said to be successful, if *Info* appears in the array else it is known as unsuccessful search.

We will consider two search techniques for finding a specific item from a large amount of data elements. These techniques are:

- Linear Search
- Binary Search

Both these search techiques are discussed in detail in Chapter 7.

3.5.3 Insertion and Deletion

Insertion means adding a new element to an array. *Deletion* means removing an element form an array.

Let X be a collection of data elements in the memory of the computer. *Inserting* means the operation of adding another element to the collection of X. Similarly, *deleting* means the operation of removing *one* of the elements from X.

It is important to note that you can insert an element at the "end" of the linear array provided there is a memory space available in the linear array.

If we want to insert an element in the middle of the array, then we have to first *move* elements of the array *downward*, to the new locations to accommodate the new element and keep the order of these elements of the array.

Similarly, deleting an element located at the "end" of an array will cause no difficulty. But if we want to delete an element of an array somewhere in between the array, then we shall require that each element be *moved* one location *upward* in order to "fill up" the gap created due to deletion of the element in the array.

To understand it further, let us look at the array NAME given in Figure 3.12 (a), (b), (c), (d).

NAME is an array. In Figure 3.12 (a), it consists of 4 elements, having the contents i.e. the names in alphabetic order. When a new name VINAY is to be inserted, it occupies the

Element Number	NAME	Element Number	NAME	Element Number	NAME	Element Number	NAME
1	BABU	1	BABU	1	BABU	1	BABU
2	DEV	2	DEV	2	DEV	2	JANAK
3	JANAK	3	JANAK	3	JANAK	3	SHIVA
4	SHIVA	4	SHIVA	4	SHIVA	4	TILAK
5		5	VINAY	5	TILAK	5	VINAY
6				6	VINAY		
	(a)		(b)		(c)		(d)

Figure 3.12 Illustration of insertion and deletion in an array

location 5 in the memory as seen in part(b) of this figure. There is no disturbance for other elements. But if we have to add TILAK as shown in Figure 3.12(c), then VINAY is to be shifted to the location 6 and then TILAK is inserted at position 5 to maintain the alphabetic order of the names. Similarly, if we have to remove DEV from the array, then we have to move other names i.e. JANAK, SHIVA, TILAK and VINAY, one element upward as shown in Figure 3.12(d).

Algorithm shown in Figure 3.13 inserts a data element ITEM into the Kth position in a linear array, LA[] with N elements. The first four steps will create space in LA[] by successively moving each element downward one location each from the Kth position. Note the following points while moving each element downwards.

Each element is moved in the reverse order i.e. first LA[N], then LA[N – 1] and last LA[K]. This will avoid deletion of data.

The step no. 5 inserts ITEM into the array in the space just created. The number of elements N in the array LA[] will be increased by one value.

Insertion in an array

Insertion is the process of adding a new element to the array. The algorithm shown in Figure 3.13 inserts a data element ITEM into the array LA[] at the Kth position. We assume that the array LA[] has N elements.

```
INSERT(LA,N,K,ITEM)
Step 1  Set J:= N (initialize the counter)
Step 2  Repeat steps 3 and 4 while J >= K
Step 3  Set LA[J + 1]:= LA[J]
        (move the jth element down)
Step 4  Set J:= J - 1 (decrease the counter)
        [End of loop in step 2]
Step 5  Set LA[K]:= ITEM (copy ITEM to Kth element of array LA)
Step 6  Set N:= N + 1
Step 7  Exit
```

Figure 3.13 Algorithm for inserting an element ITEM into the array LA[] at the Kth position

Deletion in an array

Deletion is the process of removing an element from the array. The algorithm shown in Figure 3.14 deletes the Kth element from the linear array LA[] and assigns it to a variable ITEM.

```
Delete (LA, N, K, ITEM)
1.  Set ITEM: = LA[K]
2.  Repeat for K = K to N - 1;
    Set LA[J]: = LA[J+1]
    [End of loop]
3.  Set N: = N - 1
    [Reset the number N of elements in La]
4.  Exit
```

Figure 3.14 Algorithm for deleting an element from the linear array LA and assigning it to a variable ITEM

3.5.4 Sorting

Sorting is the process of arranging data items in a particular order (ascending or descending). Arrays are convenient for storing many forms of data, because they allow the access of the entry using its index. Here, we shall look at several methods of sorting data held in one-dimensional arrays. Although the data can be of any type which is not in the order—that is, any type of data for which relations such as "greater than" and "less than" make sense. Basically, we will assume that we are sorting numerical data.

The first group of sorting methods we would look into consist of sequential methods. They keep scanning through the data elements from one end to the other, moving entries that are out of order into correct position. They are conceptually simpler and easy to program, and for small amount of data they are very effective.

However, they become slow for large amount of data. We will therefore also examine a type of *binary sort* that provides a greater degree of speed over the sequential sort, specially when number of elements to be sorted are very large.

3.5.5 Reversing of Elements

The process reverses the elements of an array. For example, suppose elements of array are:

11 22 33 44 55

Then after reversing the elements, array will contain elements as:

55 44 33 22 11

Let us now see a program that enables us to perform these operations in an array.

```
#include <stdio.h>
#include <conio.h>

#define MAX 5

void insert (int *, int pos, int num);/* Function to insert elements */
void del ( int *, int pos);          /* Function to delete elements */
void rev ( int *);                   /* Function to reverse elements */
void dis ( int *);                   /* Function to display elements */
void sear ( int *, int num);         /* Function to search elements */

void main()
{
   int arr[5];

   clrscr();

   insert (arr, 1, 11);
   insert (arr, 2, 22);
   insert (arr, 3, 33);
   insert (arr, 4, 44);
   insert (arr, 5, 55);
```

(*Contd...*)

```
   printf ( "\n Elements of Array are: ");
   dis ( arr);

   del ( arr, 2);
   del ( arr, 4);
   printf ( "\n\nAfter deletion elements are: ");
   dis ( arr );

   insert ( arr, 2, 222);
   insert ( arr, 4, 444);

   printf ( "\n\nAfter insertion elements are: ");
   dis ( arr );
   rev ( arr );
   printf ("\n\nAfter reversing elements are: ");
   dis ( arr );
   sear (arr, 222);
   sear (arr, 888);

   getch();
}
/* inserts an element num at given position pos*/
void insert ( int *arr, int pos, int num)

{
   /* shift elements to right */
   int i;
   for (i = MAX - 1 ; i >= pos ; i--)
      arr[i] = arr[i -1];
   arr[i] = num;
}
/* deletes an element from the given position pos */
void del ( int *arr, int pos)
{
   /* skip to the desired position */
   int i;
   for (i = pos ; i < MAX ; i++)
      arr[i - 1] = arr[i];
   arr[i - 1] = 0;
}

/* reverses the entire array */
void rev ( int *arr)
{
   int i;
   for (i = 0; i < MAX/2; i++)
   {
      int temp = arr[i];
```

(Contd...)

```
        arr[i] = arr[MAX - 1 - i];
        arr[MAX - 1 - i] = temp ;
    }
}

/* searches array for a given element num */
void sear ( int *arr, int num)
{
    /* Traverse the array */
    int i;
    for (i = 0 ; i < MAX ; i++)
    {
        if ( arr[i] ==  num)
        {
            printf ( "\n\n The element %d is present at %dth position.",
                        num, i + 1) ;
            return;
        }
    }
    if (i == MAX)
        printf ("\n\n The element %d is not present in the array.", num);
}

/* displays the contents of a array */
    void dis ( int *arr)
{
    /* traverse the entire array */
    int i;
    printf ( "\n");
    for ( i = 0 ; i < MAX; i++)
        printf ("%d\t", arr[i]);
}
```

RUN

```
Elements of Array are:
11   22   33   44   55

After deletion, elements are:
11   33   44  0   0

After insertion, elements are:
11   222   33   444   44

After reversing elements are"
44   444   33   222   11

The element 222 is present at 4th position.
The element 888 is not present in the array.
```

3.5.6 Merging

Merging is the technique for combining several sorted lists (arrays) into a single sorted list (array). This method is used for combining large sized arrays of data or files held on the disk or magnetic tapes. All that is required in this method is the sequential access of the entries in the array or list.

Imagine two sorted arrays. They need not be of the same size. Let us say array *A* has 4 elements and array *B* has 6 elements. They are to be merged into an array C that should have 10 empty cells. Figure 3.15(a) and (b) illustrate the procedure.

☞ *Merging two sorted arrays A and B creates a third array C, that contains all the elements of A and B, with contents arranged in sorted order. See Figure 3.15. If the arrays A and B are unsorted, then first sort them and then merge.*

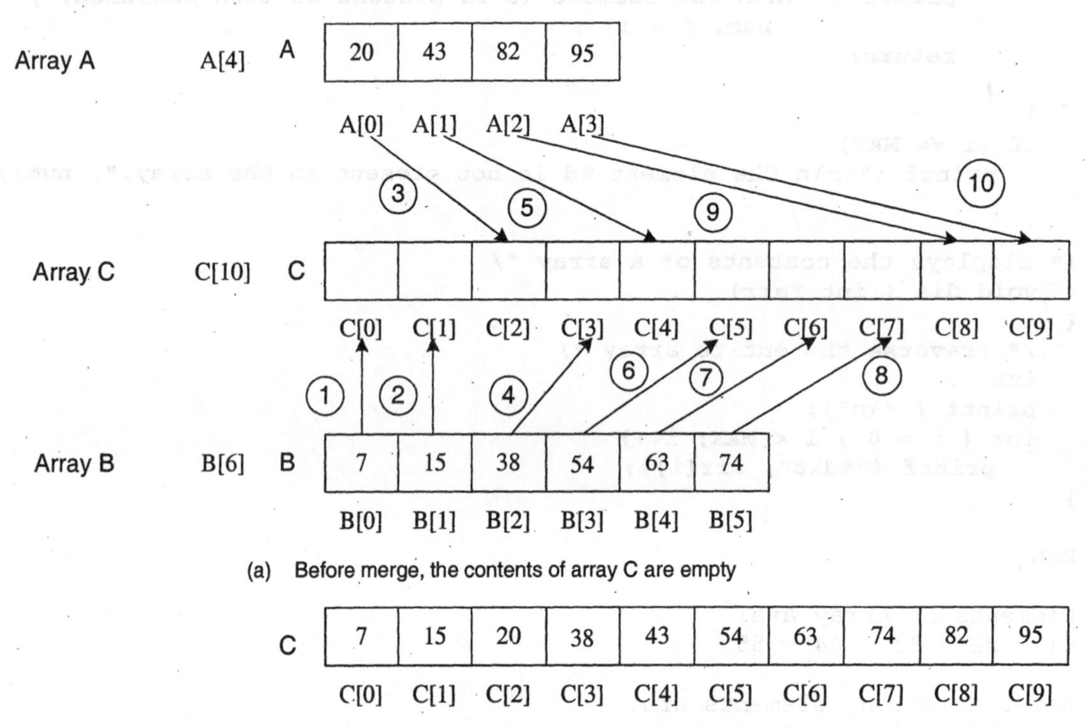

(a) Before merge, the contents of array C are empty

(b) After merging, the contents of array C are in ascending order

Figure 3.15 Merging two arrays

Example 4

Write a program to read two sorted arrays of dimensions m and n, respectively. The program should merge them together and print the merged array of size m + n. (See Figure 3.16)

3.6 VECTOR

'Vectors' and 'matrices' are mathematical terms which refer to collections of numbers which are analogous, respectively, to linear and two dimensional arrays. That is, an n-element vector *V* in a list of *n* numbers usually given in the form:

$$V = (V_1, V_2, V_3, \ldots\ldots, V_n)$$

where as an m × n matrix A is an array of m · n numbers arranged in *m* rows and *n* columns as follows:

$$A = \begin{pmatrix} A_{11} & A_{12} & . & . & . & A_{1n} \\ A_{21} & A_{22} & . & . & . & A_{2n} \\ . & . & . & . & . & . \\ A_{m1} & A_{m2} & . & . & . & A_{mn} \end{pmatrix}$$

☞ *In algebra, a vector is a single dimensional matrix.*

```
/* Program for Simple Merge */
#include<stdio.h>
main()
{
  int a[50],n,b[50],m,c[50],k,l,i,j;
  printf("Enter  number of elements for matrix A\n");
  scanf("%d",&n);
  printf("%d",n);
  printf("\n");
  for(i=0;i<n;i++)
  {
  printf("\nEnter contents of the array elements in sorted
            form %d:",i+1);
  scanf("%d",&a[i]);
  printf("%d",a[i]);
  }
  printf("\n");
  printf("Enter number of elements for matrix B\n");
  scanf("%d",&m);
  printf("%d",m);
  printf("\n");
  for(i=0;i<m;i++)
```

(Contd...)

```
 {
   printf("\nEnter contents of the array elements in sorted form
            %d:",i+1);
    scanf("%d",&b[i]);
    printf("%d",b[i]);
  }
  printf("\n");
/* Merge Sort */
  i = 0;
  j = 0;
  k = 0;
  while((i<n) &&(j<m))
   if(a[i] < b[j]) {
   c[k] = a[i];
   i++;
   k++;
   }
   else
   if(a[i]>b[j])
   {
   c[k] = b[j];
   j++;
   k++;
   }
   else {
   c[k] = a[i];
   i++;
   j++;
   k++;
   }
  if(i<n){
   for(l=i;l<n;l++){
   c[k] = a[i];
   i++;
   k++;
   }
  }
  else
  if(j<m){
  for(l=j;l<m;l++){
  c[k]  = b[j];
  j++;
```

(Contd...)

```
  k++;
  }
  }
  printf("\nMerged Array C :\n");
  for(i=0;i<k;i++)
    printf("%5d",c[i]);
    printf("\n");
return 0;
}
```

RUN

```
Enter number of elements for matrix A
3
3
Enter contents of the array elements in sorted form 1 : 11
11
Enter contents of the array element in sorted form 2 : 33
33
Enter contents of the array element in sorted form 3 : 55
55
Enter number of elements for matrix B
3
3
Enter contents of the array element in sorted form 1 : 22
22
Enter contents of the array element in sorted form 2 : 44
44
Enter contents of the array element in sorted form 3 : 88
88
Merged Array C:
11   22   33   44   55   88
```

Figure 3.16 Merging two arrays

Example 5

Program in Figure 3.17 is written for finding the largest and the smallest element in a vector or single dimensional array.

```
/* Finding the largest and smallest element in a vector*/
#include<stdio.h>
main()

{
   int i, n;
   float a[50], large, small;
   printf ("\nEnter the size of vector:");
   scanf ("%d", &n);
   printf("%d\n", n);
   printf("\n \nEnter vector elements : \n");
   for (i = 0; i < n; i++)
      scanf("%f", &a[i]);
   for (i = 0; i < n; i++)
      printf("%8.2f", a[i]);
   printf ("\n");
   /* Initialistation */
   large = a[0];
   small = a[0];
   /* Finding largest and smallest elements */
   for (i = 1; i < n; i++)
   {
      if (a[i] > large)
         large = a[i];
      else if (a[i] < small)
         small = a[i];
   }
   printf ("\nLargest element in vector is %8.2f\n", large);
   printf("\nSmallest element in vector is %8.2f\n", small);
}
```

RUN

```
Enter the size of vector : 5
5
Enter vector elements:
33.01
55.02
11.03
88.04
44.01
33.01   55.02    11.03    88.04   44.01
Largest element in vector is 88.00
Smallest element in vector is 11.03
```

Figure 3.17 Program and the output of example 5 for finding the largest and smallest elements in a vector

Example 6

Program in Figure 3.18 is written for finding second largest and second smallest element in the vector or single dimensional array.

```
/* Finding the second largest and smallest element in a vector*/
#include <stdio.h>
main()
{
   int i, j, k, n, num;
   float a[50], b[50], temp;

   printf ("Enter size of vector:");
   scanf ("%d", &n);
   printf("%d\n", n);
   num = n;
   printf("\n Enter vector elements : \n");
   for (i = 0; i < n; i++)
   {
      scanf("%f", &a[i]);
      b[i] = a[i];
   }
   for (i = 0; i < n; i++)
      printf("%8.2f", a[i]);
   printf ("\n");
/* copying vector A to B without duplicates */
   for (i = 0; i < n - 1; i++)
      for (j = i + 1; j < n; j++)
   {
      if (b[i] == b[j])
      {
      for (k = j; k < n - 1; k++)
         b[k] = b[k+1];
      n = n - 1;
      j = j - 1;
      }
   }
/* sorting vector B without duplicates */
for (i = 0; i < n - 1; i++)
   for (j = i + 1; j < n; j++)
      {
      if (b[i] > b[j])
            {
      /* swapping */
      temp = b[i];
```

(Contd...)

```
        b[i] = b[j];
        b[j] = temp;
        }
    }
    printf ("\n Vector A sorted and without duplicates :\n");
    for (i = 0; i < n; i++)
        printf("%8.2f", b[i]);
    printf ("\n");
    printf ("\nSecond largest element : %8.2f\n", b[n - 2]);
    printf ("\nSecond smallest element : %8.2f\n", b[1]);
}
RUN

Enter size of vector : 5
5
Enter vector elements:
55
88
44
77
11
55.00   88.00   44.00   77.00   11.00
Vector A sorted and without duplicates:
11.00   44.00   55.00   77.00   88.00
Second largest element: 77.00
Second smallest element: 44.00
```

Figure 3.18 Program and the output for finding the second largest and second smallest element in a vector

Example 7

Program and its output for deleting duplicate values in a vector is given in Figure 3.19.

```
/* Deleting duplicates in a vector */

#include <stdio.h>
main()

{
    int i,j,k,n, num, flag = 0;
    float a[50];

    printf("Enter size of vector :");
    scanf("%d", &n);
    printf("%d\n", n);
    num = n;
```

(*Contd...*)

```
    printf("\nEnter vector elements :\n");
    for (i = 0; i < n; i++)
       scanf("%f", &a[i]);
    for (i = 0; i < n; i++)
       printf ("%6.2f", a[i]);
    printf ("\n");
    /* removing duplicates */
    for (i = 0; i < n - 1; i++)
       for (j = i + 1; j < n; j++)
       {
       if (a[i] == a[j])
    {
       n = n - 1;
       for (k = j; k < n; k++)
          a[k] = a[k+1];
       flag = 1;
       j = j - 1;
       }
    }
    /* use of IF and ELSE statement */
    if (flag == 0)
       printf ("\nNo duplicates found in vector \n");
    else
    {
       printf ("\nVector has %d duplicates \n\n", num - n);
       printf ("Vector after deleting duplicates : \n");
       printf ("\nNo duplicates found in vector \n");
    else
    {
       printf ("\nVector has %d duplicates \n\n", num - n);
       printf ("Vector after deleting duplicates : \n");
       for (i = 0; i < n; i++)
          printf("%6.2f", a[i]);
       printf ("\n");
    }
}
```

RUN

```
Enter size of vector: 5
5
Enter vector elements:
12
16
```

(Contd...)

```
17
11
16
12.00     16.00    17.00    11.00    16.00
vector has 1 duplicates
vector after deleting duplicates:
12.00    16.00    17.00    11.00
```

Figure 3.19 Program and the output for deleting duplicates in a vector

3.7 APPLICATION OF ARRAYS

A two dimensional array can be represented as $[A_{ij}]$ where *i* is the number of row and *j* is the number of columns.

3.7.1 Addition and Subtraction of the Two (Arrays Matrices)

Let A and B are two matrices of the same order. Then their sum, A + B is defined as another matrix, each element of which is summation of the corresponding elements of A and B. For example, if we have:

$$A = \begin{vmatrix} 9 & 8 \\ 7 & 5 \end{vmatrix}$$

$$B = \begin{vmatrix} 2 & 4 \\ 3 & 4 \end{vmatrix}$$

then,

$$A + B = \begin{vmatrix} 9+2 & 8+4 \\ 7+3 & 5+4 \end{vmatrix}$$

$$\text{or} \quad A + B = \begin{vmatrix} 11 & 12 \\ 10 & 9 \end{vmatrix}$$

i.e. If $A = [a_{ij}]$ and $B = [b_{ij}]$ then $A + B = [a_{ij}] + [b_{ij}]$

Similarly, the subtraction

$$A - B = [a_{ij}] - [b_{ij}]$$

Example 8

Write a program to read two matrices each of size m × n. It should then print the contents of each matrix and thereafter performs the following operations on the two matrices

(a) Prints the sum of the two matrices,

(b) Prints the difference of two matrices.

The program and its output are shown in Figure 3.20.

```
/*Program to add and subtract two matrices*/
#include<stdio.h>
main()
{
  int a[10][10],b[10][10],c[10][10],d[10][10],i,j,m,n,p,q;
  printf("Enter row & column of A matrix\n");
  scanf("%d %d",&n,&m);
  printf("%d %d\n",n,m);
  printf("Enter row & column of B matrix\n");
  scanf("%d %d",&p,&q);
  printf("%d %d\n",p,q);
/* Check if matrices can be added */
  if((n == p) && (m==q))
  {
     printf("Matrices can be added\n");
     printf("Input matrix A\n");
     for(i=0;i<n;++i)
     for(j=0;j<m;++j)
     scanf("%d",&a[i][j]);
/* Print - A matrix */
     for(i= 0;i<n;++i)
     {
        for(j=0;j<m;++j)
        printf("%5d",a[i][j]);
        printf("\n");
     }
     printf("Input matrix B\n");
     for(i=0;i<n;++i)
     for(j=0;j<m;++j)
     scanf("%d",&b[i][j]);
/* Print - B matrix */
     for(i=0;i<n;++i)
     {
        for(j=0;j<m;++j)
        printf("%5d",b[i][j]);
        printf("\n");
     }
/* Addition of A and B matrices */
     for(i=0;i<n;++i)
     for(j=0;j<m;++j)
     c[i][j] = a[i][j] + b[i][j];
     printf("Sum of A and B matrices :\n");
     for(i=0;i<n;++i)
     {
```

(Contd...)

```
        for(j=0;j<m;++j)
        printf("%5d",c[i][j]);
        printf("\n");
      }
/* Subtraction of A and B matrices */
      for(i=0;i<n;++i)
      for(j=0;j<m;++j)
        d[i][j] = a[i][j] - b[i][j];
        printf("Subtraction of matrix A and B\n");
        for(i=0;i<n;++i)
        {
          for(j=0;j<m;++j)
          printf("%5d",d[i][j]);
          printf("\n");
        }
  }
  else
    printf("Matrices cannot be added or subtracted\n");
}

RUN

Enter row & column of A matrix
2
2
  2 2
Enter row & column of B matrix
2
2
  2 2
Matrices can be added
Input matrix A
9
8
7
5
9 8
7 5
Input matrix B
2
4
3
4
```

(Contd...)

```
2  4
3  4
Sum of A and B matrices:
11  12
10  9
Subtraction of matrix A and B
7  4
4  1
```

Figure 3.20 Program and the output to add and subtract two matrices

3.7.2 Multiplication of Two Matrices

Two matrices A and B can be multiplied if matrix A is having the dimension (i, j) and B is of the dimension (j, k). Which means, the number of rows in A is equal to the number of columns in B. This is an important condition for multiplication.

☞ *The product of two matrices A and B is possible if number of rows in A is equal to the number of columns in B.*

For example, if A is having 3 rows and 3 columns and B also has 3 rows and 3 columns, as given below:

$$A = \begin{vmatrix} 1 & 2 & 3 \\ 4 & 5 & 6 \\ 7 & 8 & 9 \end{vmatrix}$$

$$B = \begin{vmatrix} 1 & 2 & 3 \\ 4 & 5 & 6 \\ 7 & 8 & 9 \end{vmatrix}$$

Multiplying row of first matrix and column of second matrix, A × B = C is given by

$$A \times B = \begin{vmatrix} 1\times1+2\times4+3\times7 & 1\times2+2\times5+3\times8 & 1\times3+2\times6+3\times9 \\ 4\times1+5\times4+6\times7 & 4\times2+5\times5+6\times8 & 4\times3+5\times6+6\times9 \\ 7\times1+8\times4+9\times7 & 7\times2+8\times5+9\times8 & 7\times3+8\times6+9\times9 \end{vmatrix}$$

$$\text{or} \quad C = \begin{vmatrix} 1+8+21 & 2+10+24 & 3+12+27 \\ 4+20+42 & 8+25+48 & 12+30+54 \\ 7+32+63 & 14+40+72 & 21+48+81 \end{vmatrix}$$

$$C = \begin{vmatrix} 30 & 36 & 42 \\ 66 & 81 & 96 \\ 102 & 126 & 150 \end{vmatrix}$$

3.7.3 Transpose of a Matrix

A *transpose* of a 2 dimensional array or a matrix is obtained by interchanging the rows with corresponding columns. The transpose of matrix A is denoted by A^T. If matrix A is an $m \times n$ then after transposing it we will get an $n \times m$ matrix which is the transpose of matrix A and represented as A^T. For example:

$$A = \begin{vmatrix} 1 & 2 & 3 & 4 \\ 5 & 6 & 7 & 8 \\ 9 & 6 & 7 & 8 \end{vmatrix}$$

Then transpose of matrix A is:

$$A^T = \begin{vmatrix} 1 & 5 & 9 \\ 2 & 6 & 6 \\ 3 & 7 & 7 \\ 4 & 8 & 8 \end{vmatrix}$$

Example 9

Program for transposing a matrix is given in Figure 3.21.

```
/* Program to transpose a matrix */
#include <stdio.h>
main()
{
   int mat1[20] [20],  mat2[20] [20], i,  j,  m,  n;
   printf("Enter row & column of matrix (1 to 20, 1 to 20) : ");
   scanf("%d %d", &m, &n);
   printf("Enter %d elements of matrix\n", m *n);
   for (i = 1;  i < m+1;  i++)
       for (j = 1; j < n+1; j++)
       scanf("%d", &mat1[i] [j]);
       printf("\n\t Original matrix  \n");
       for (i = 1; i < m+1; i++)
       {
           for (j = 1; j < n+1;  j++)
           printf("%7d", mat1[i][j]);
           printf("\n");
       }
       for(i = 1;  i < n+1;  i++)
       for (j = 1; j < m + 1; j++)
           mat2[i][j] = mat1[j][i];
           printf("\n\t Transpose of matrix  \n");
       for (i = 1;  i < n + 1; i++)
       {
```

(Contd...)

```
            for (j = 1; j < m + 1; j++)
            printf("%7d", mat2[i][j]);
            printf("\n");
      }
}

RUN
Enter row and column of matrix (1 to 20, 1 to 20): 3 3
Enter 9 elements of matrix
1 2 3 4 5 6 7 8 9
Original matrix
      1  2  3
      4  5  6
      7  8  9

Transpose of matrix
      1  4  7
      2  5  8
      3  6  9
```

Figure 3.21 Program and the output for transpose of a matrix

3.8 STRINGS AS AN ARRAY OF CHARACTERS

Strings of characters are a form of data used in programming for storing and manipulating text, such as words, names and sentences. In programming language C, a string is not a formal data type but it is an array of type *char*. A character can be a single letter, numeral, punctuation mark, or other such symbol or a special character like %, @, ! etc. A string is any sequence of all these different types of characters.

For example "Hello Computer" is a string and is stored in memory using the ASCII codes of the characters. Each character is represented by eight bits (1 or zero) and stored in the memory of the computer as a matrix of two dimensions. Thus, a string of 10 characters is stored as a matrix of 10 × 8 size. Where 10 is the number of rows and 8 is the ASCII bits corresponding to each character. In a simple way, the string is represented using character form in Figure 3.22.

☞ *A string is a series of characters, terminated by a null character. Null character is a character with a numeric value of zero and it is represented by '\0' in C.*

3.8.1 String Variables

Variables of type *char* can hold a single character. You also need a way to store strings, which are sequence of characters. For example, person's name and address are character strings. There is no special data type for strings. Programming language C handles strings as array of characters.

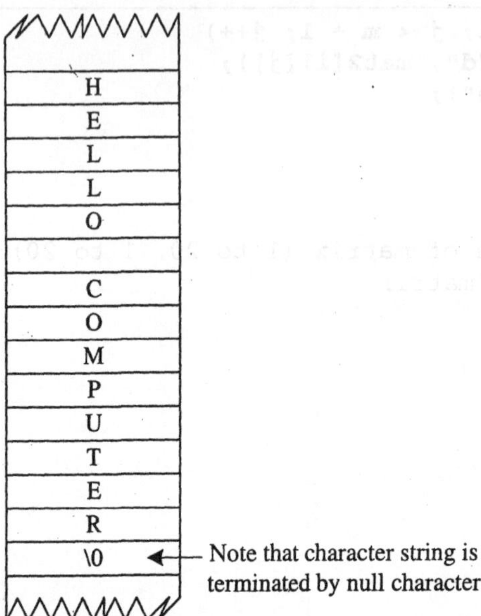

Figure 3.22 String representation of "Hello Computer" in memory

Before a string is read, some space in the computer's memory must be set aside for storing it. Since string is a series of characters, therefore a series of bytes (representing each character in ASCII code) must be set aside for them.

An array of characters representing a string is defined as follows:

```
char array_name[size];
```

☞ *Size of an array must be an integer value.*

For example:

```
char fname[15];
```

Here, array **fname** is defined which reserves 15 bytes of memory for storing maximum of 14 characters. If the maximum size of the string to be read is 14 characters, then the array declared should be at least one number more than the maximum size of the string read. In this case, it should be 15 characters. The last character in the case of array of string is used to store null character (namely\0). The null character indicates that the last character is the end of the string.

☞ *String variables are used to hold text data, which comprises of letters, numerals, punctuation marks, and other symbols.*

Example 10

The program shown in Figure 3.23 reads a string of characters from the keyboard and prints out a part of long phrase.

As the program is run, you will observe that the string *Shashi* is printed on the screen even if the input was given as *Shashi Singh*. The reason is that the blank character between the two words *Shashi Singh* gives a signal to compiler that the string is complete after the word *Shashi*.

```
/* Reading a string of characters from the keyboard and printing it */
#include<stdio.h>
main ()
{
    char fname[15];
    printf("Enter the firstname:  ");
    scanf("%s", fname);
    printf("Greetings, %s", fname);
}

RUN
Enter the firstname: Shashi Singh
Greetings, Shashi
```

Figure 3.23 Reading data from keyboard and printing part of the string

☞ *If the length of the string read is of a size greater than 15 characters in the program shown in Figure 3.23, then the existing characters would be overwritten. Hence, the size of the array should be sufficient to store the longest expected size of the string, so that whole of the string can be printed or retrieved, if needed.*

3.8.2 Initializing a String of Characters

To store a string in memory, you need to declare the array of the type *char*. For example,

```
char feline[] = {'c','a','t','\0'};
```

You can also have a simpler choice by giving the following declaration:

```
char feline[] = "cat";
```

☞ *Note that the string cat is surrounded by double quotes (" "). We do not need to insert the null character '\0' in second method of declaration. Using the string format, this null character '\0' will be inserted automatically.*

Example 11

The program shown in Figure 3.24 is a variation of the program given in Example 10.

```
/* Reading a string and printing it */
/* showing string initialization */
#include<stdio.h>
main()
{
  static char salute[] = "Greeting, ";
  char name[80];
  puts ("Enter your name: ");
  gets (name);
  puts (salute);
  puts (name);
}

RUN

Enter your name:
Shashi Singh
Greeting,
Shashi Singh
```

Figure 3.24 Reading a string from the keyboard and printing it completely

The output of the program in Example 11 will be similar to that in Example 10. But the string "Greeting" is included in the array declaration. The puts() function can then print it out using the array address as an argument.

Example 12

Write a program to input a name. The characters used in the name should then return their corresponding ASCII values of the characters in the string. The program and its output is shown in Figure 3.25.

```
#include<stdio.h>
#include<conio.h>
main()
{
 int i;
 char str[10];
 printf("Enter the string: ");
 scanf("%s", &str);
  for(i=0; str[i] !='\0'; i++)
   {
    printf(" %c = %d  ", str[i],
         str[i]);
      }
```

(Contd...)

```
        getch();
      return  0;
}

RUN

Enter the string: Apple
A = 65  p = 112  p = 112  l = 108
e = 101
```

Figure 3.25 Printing ASCII code of entered string

3.8.3 Array of Strings

Similar to two-dimensional arrays, we can also declare an array of strings. A string is stored as an array, therefore, an array of string is really an array of arrays, or a multi-dimensional array. The program shown in Figure 3.26 demonstrates the use of an array of strings.

```
/* Program for comparing a word entered from keyboard to the set of
words stored as database */
#include<stdio.h>
#include<string.h>
#define MAX 5
#define LEN 40
main ()
{
int dex;
int enter = 0;
char name[LEN];
static char list[MAX][LEN] =  { "Kartik", "Neelam", "Augustin",
                                "Francis", "Gautam" };
printf("\n Please enter your name:  ");
gets(name);
for (dex = 0; dex < MAX; dex++)
    if (strcmp(&list[dex][0],name) == 0)
       enter =1;
     if (enter == 1)
      { printf("\n");
        puts(name);
        printf("you may enter please.");
      }
    else
    {
    printf("\n");
```

(Contd...)

```
  puts(name);
  printf("sorry!  You are not allowed to enter.");
  }
}

RUN

Please enter your name:  Neelam
Neelam
you may enter please.
```

Figure 3.26 Using array of strings for comparing a word with the set of words in the database

Example 13

This program asks you to type your name. When you do, it checks your name against a master list to see if you are permitted to enter or not. It then displays the message accordingly.

You will notice in the program shown in Figure 3.26, that we used a function *strcmp* which is available in the header file *string.h*. Accordingly, string.h file is included in the beginning of the program. This function will compare the string entered from the keyboard with the strings already available in the program and if the comparison is true, then the permission to enter will be displayed otherwise not.

☞ *The C standard library includes a number of functions that manipulate strings. strcmp is one such function.*

3.9 STRING MANIPULATION

A file *string.h* available in 'C' library has several built-in functions, such as strlen(), strcat(), strcpy(), strcmp(), etc. for string manipulation. To use these functions, the header file *string.h* must be included at the beginning of a program as shown below:

```
#include<string.h>
```

3.9.1 String Length (strlen())

The function *strlen()* is used to find the length of the string or the number of characters in a given string, excluding the end-of-string character (null). The program in Example 14 demonstrates the use of this function.

Example 14

Program to demonstrate use of strlen() function is shown in Figure 3.27. Here the length of the string includes any special or blank characters also.

```
/* Program for demonstration of strlen() function */
#include <stdio.h>
#include <string.h>
void main()
  {
     char name[25];
     int nch;
     printf("\n Enter name");
     gets(name);
     nch = strlen(name);
     printf("Length of the string name = %d \n", nch);
  }

RUN

Enter name: Vivek
Length of the string name = 5
```

Figure 3.27 Demonstration of the use of the function strlen()

3.9.2 String Concatenation (strcat())

The strcat() function concatenates (joins or places together) the two strings resulting in a single string. It takes the two arguments, which are the destination and source strings. The destination and source strings are concatenated and the resultant string is stored in the destination (first) string. For example,

if s_1 = "LAKHAN"
  s_2 = "LAL"
  then $s_1 + s_2$ = "LAKHANLAL"

Example 15

Figure 3.28 shows the program that concatenates two strings resulting in a single string.

```
/* Program to concatenate two strings */
#include <stdio.h>
#include <string.h>
main()
 {
  char s1[15], s2[15];
  printf("\n Enter first name s1 :");
  gets(s1);
  printf("\n Enter last name s2:");
  gets(s2);
```

(Contd...)

```
  strcat(s1, s2);
   puts(s1);
  }

RUN

Enter first name s1 : LAKHAN
Enter second name s2 : LAL
LAKHANLAL
```

Figure 3.28 Program for concatenating two strings

3.9.3 String Copy (strcpy())

The strcpy() function copies the contents of one string to another i.e source string is copied to destination string.

`strcpy(s1,s2)` copies string s2 to string s1

Example 16

The program in Figure 3.29 copies the contents of string str1 to another string str2.

```
/* Program that copies contents of one string to another */
     #include <stdio.h>
     #include <string.h>
     main()
     {
       char str1[15], str2[15];
       printf ("Enter a string str1 to be copied into str2  : ");
       gets(str1);
       strcpy(str2, str1);
       puts(str2);
      }
RUN
Enter a string str1 to be copied into str2: Computer
Computer
```

Figure 3.29 Copying one string to another

3.9.4 String Comparison (strcmp())

The string strcmp() function compares two strings, character by character. It accepts any two strings as parameters and returns an integer value, which gives the comparison of two strings.

☞ *Two strings are equal if their contents are identical or exactly the same.*

When we compare two strings s1, s2 using strcmp as:

`strcmp(s1,s2)`

If s1 < s2	/* If the first string s1 is less than the second string, it returns -1 */
If s2 == s1	/* If both are identical it returns 0 */
If s1 > s2	/* If the first string s1 is greater than s2 the second string it returns 1 */

3.10 PATTERN MATCHING

A string is usually defined as a sequence of characters. Using strings we can perform operations such as reading a string or printing it out, appending two strings together or copying a string. Comparing strings, inserting a substring into a string, removing a substring from a string or finding a pattern in a string.

Pattern matching is the problem of finding whether or not a given string pattern *P* appears in a string text *S* we assume that the length of *P* does not exceed the length of *S*. For example, Let us take a pattern for matching *P* = "Kumar", in a given string text *S* = "Vivek Kumar Singh".

Now we want to find whether string *P* is in string *S* or not and also what is the starting position of *P* in *S*. Here, the length of *P* should be less than or equal to *S*.

Many string searching algorithms have been developed till date. However, the performance of these algorithms depends on the nature of the string and the pattern to be searched.

3.10.1 First Pattern Matching Algorithm

In the first pattern matching algorithm the string *S* in which the pattern string is to be searched is scanned character by character. Each character is compared to each and every character of the pattern string *P*. This process continues till either there is no mismatch or the pattern string *P* is not exhausted. If a match is found then the index of the character *S* from which the comparison began is returned as the position where the pattern string *P* is found. However, if there is mismatch then the next character of the string *S* is considered and there onwards again it is compared with the characters of the pattern string *P*. The process ends either when a match is found or when the number of character in the string *S* that remain to be scanned is less than the total number of characters in the pattern string *P*. The first pattern matching algorithm is given in Figure 3.30.

Observe that algorithm shown in Figure 3.30 contains two loops, one inside the other. Outer loop will be for the text in which we have to search the pattern and inner loop will be for matching the pattern.

3.11 WHAT IS A FUNCTION?

A *function* is a routine, or set of instructions, that performs a specific task. It can be processed independently and called by another function. When the program passes control to a function, the function performs that task and *returns* control to the instruction following the *calling* function or program instruction. The function may perform a stand-alone task, such as intializing a set of variables, or it may accepts values (arguments) from the calling instruction, process them and pass the results back to calling program.

```
(Pattern matching) P and S are strings with lengths A and B, respec-
tively, and are stored as arrays with one character per element. This
algorithm finds the Index of P in S.
1.   [Initialize] set k = 1 and MAX = B - A+1
2.   Repeat steps 3 to 5 while K <= MAX
3.        Repeat for L = 1 to A [Tests each character of P]
               If P[L] != S[K+L-1], then go to
               step 5
          [End of inner loop]
4.        [Success] Set Index = K, and Exit.
5.   Set K = K+1
     [End of step 2 outer loop]
6.   [Unsuccess] set Index = 0
7.   Exit
```

Figure 3.30 Pattern matching algorithm

☞ *The most important reason to use functions is to make program writing easier. Another reason of using a function is to reduce the size of the program and to make program more readable and understandable.*

A function can be thought as a "blackbox" to which one or more input values are passed and output values are then calculated by the function automatically. Figure 3.31 illustrates the sequence for the call to a function *sqrt*. The value of *x*, that is 16, is the input, and the function result or output is the square root of 16.0, i.e. 4 (See Figure 3.31).

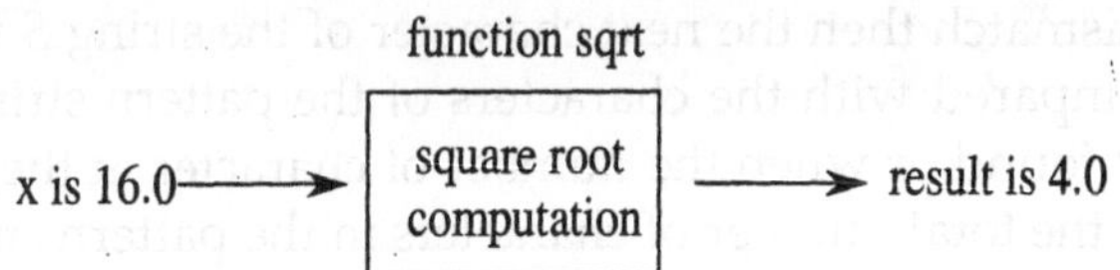

Figure 3.31 Function *sqrt* as a "Black Box"

Suppose you want to calculate total marks of various students in a class. If you write a program without using function, you have to write the same code again and again to calculate total marks. But if you use a function say *Total*, then you need not write the code again and again. Instead, you can jump to the section of code that calculates *Total* marks and come back to normal program flow when you have finished. (See Figure 3.32)

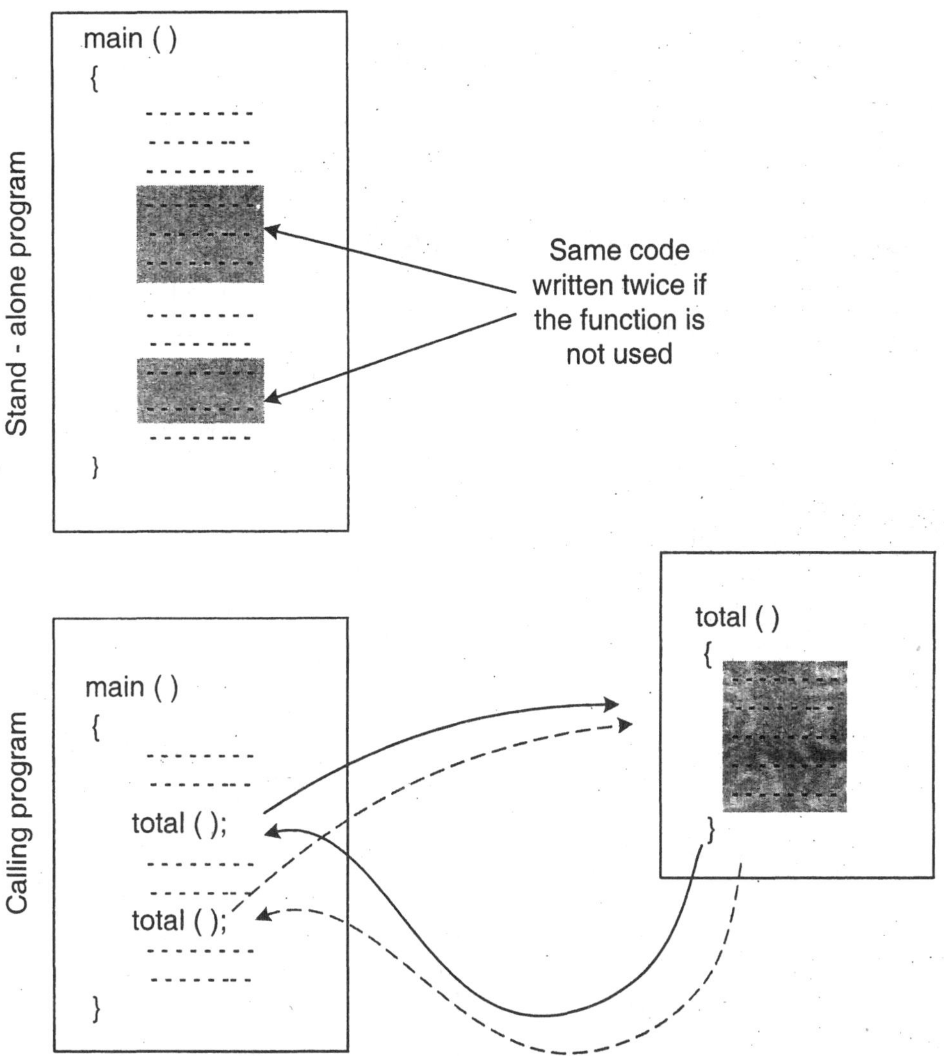

Figure 3.32 Program with and without using function total()

3.12 ADVANTAGES OF USING FUNCTIONS IN A PROGRAM

The following are some advantages of using the concept of functions.

a. The complexity of the entire program can be divided into simple subtasks and then function subprograms can be written for each subtasks (modular programming).

b. The subprograms (which are in the form of functions) are easier to write, understand and debug.

c. A function can be shared by other programs by compiling this function separately and loading and linking them together.

d. In C, a function can call itself again. It is called a *recursive function*. Many calculations can be done easily using recursive functions such as calculation of *factorial* of a number, etc. In such a case, function can call itself.

e. Reduction in size of program due to program code of a function can be used again and again, by calling it.

f. A library of functions can be designed and tested for use by every programmer.

3.13 CALLING FUNCTIONS USING ARRAYS

Before we can understand calling functions with arrays, we need to learn how does a compiler stores a variable and an array and also how, each one is addressed. Imagine an integer variable *num* with a value of 37. Suppose it is initialized as:

```
int num = 37;
```

Figure 3.33 shows how this variable would look in the main memory of a PC.

There are four things to know about the variable. These are:

a. The name of the variable (say *num*)
b. The magnitude or value of the variable (say *37*)
c. The address of the variable where it is stored in the main memory of the computer (say *1202* as illustrated in Figure 3.33)
d. The name of the address which is *&num* (See Figure 3.33).

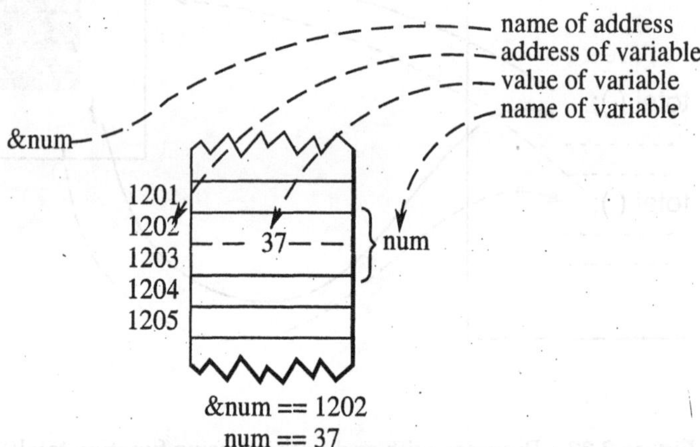

Figure 3.33 Address and value of variable *num* in the memory

A similar representation is also available in the case of an array when stored in the main memory of the PC. An array is referred to by its address, which is represented by the name of the array, used without subscripts. Figure 3.34 illustrates the array list[], which for the purpose of explanation is stored at the address 1200.

There are four important points to be observed in Figure 3.34 These are:

a. The values of the individual elements in the array (say *64*)

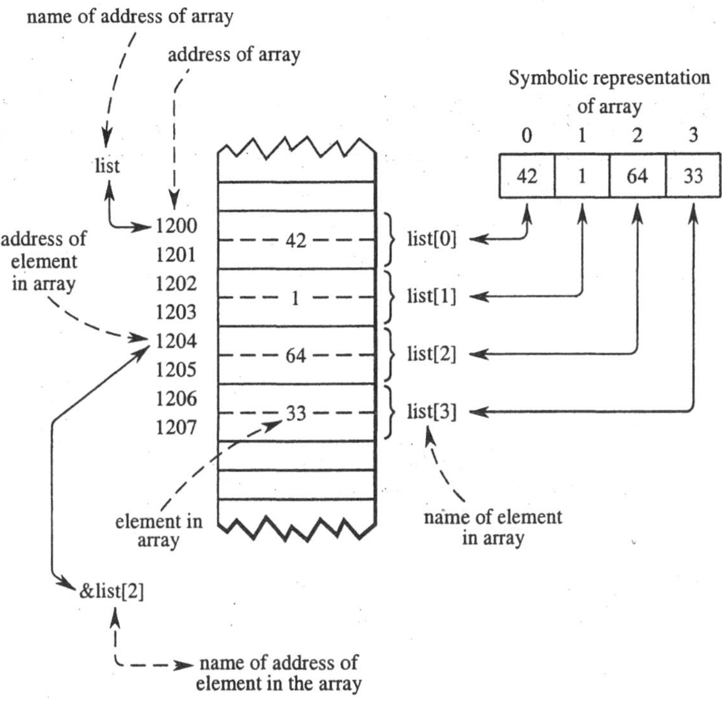

Figure 3.34 Address and elements of an array *list[]* as stored in the memory of the computer

☞ *The name for example, list, in the case of an array refers to an address but would refer to a value if list were a simple variable.*

b. The names of these elements (say *list[2]*)
c. The address of the array (say *1200*)
d. The name of this address (*list*)

3.13.1 Address of things versus things

You must realize that passing the address of *something* is not the same as passing the value in *it*. When a simple variable *name* is used as an argument passed to a function, the function takes the value corresponding to this variable *name* and installs it as a new variable in a memory location created by the function for that purpose.

Since arrays can be of very large size, the designers of C have determined that it would be better to have only one copy of an array no matter how many functions want to access it. So, instead of passing the *values* in the array, only the address of the array is passed. The function then can use the address to access the original array. This process is shown in Figure 3.35.

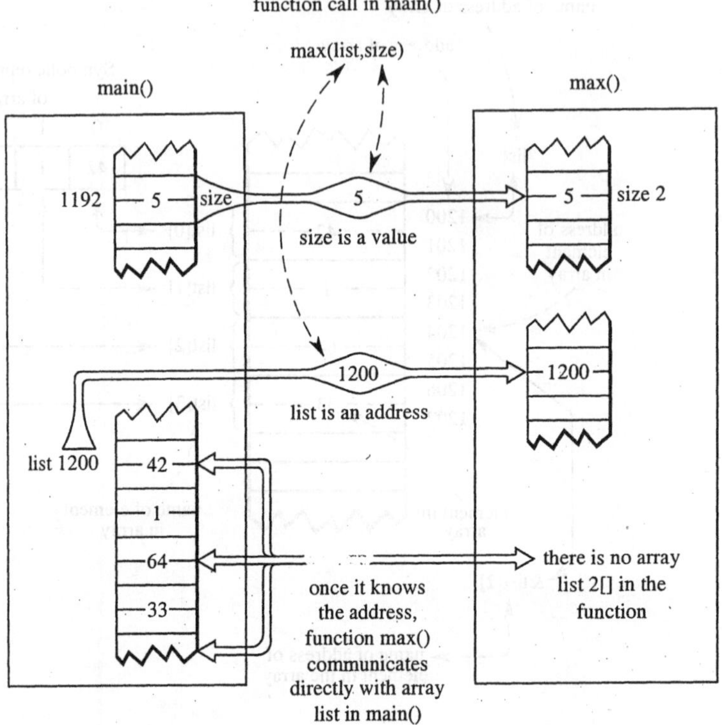

Figure 3.35 Passing a value and an array address to a function

☞ *Passing an array name to a function does not create a new copy o, ray.*

3.14 WHAT IS A POINTER?

A *pointer* is a variable that holds the memory *address* of another variable (rather than data). The storage and retrieval of data using the memory address of a variable (i.e. a pointer) is *faster* than that of using variable.

A pointer provides a way of accessing a variable without referring to the name of the variable directly. To declare and refer to a pointer type variable, C provides two special unary operators namely, * and &.

When variables are declared, compiler allocates memory to each variable. Number of bytes occupied by each variable varies with respect to the *type* of the variables. For example, integer variable occupies *two* bytes of memory, float occupies *four* bytes and character occupies *one* byte of memory.

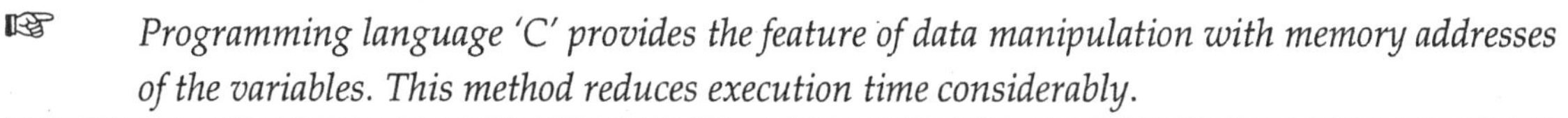

☞ *Programming language 'C' provides the feature of data manipulation with memory addresses of the variables. This method reduces execution time considerably.*

☞ *Data manipulation with variable memory address is possible with the special data type called pointers.*

Pointers are regarded by most users as one of the difficult topics in 'C'. There are several reasons for this:

- First the concept behind pointers – indirection operator namely * may be new for many programmers, since it was not used in languages such as BASIC or Pascal.
- Secondly, the symbols used for pointer notation in 'C' are not as clear as they might be; for example, the same symbol is used for two different but related purposes. An asterisk (*) used as an indirection operator, is also the unary operator. The former operates on only one variable such as *px. However, asterisk (*) is used for multiplication which is binary operator, operating on two variables, e.g. `a*b`.

When you declare a variable in a C program, the compiler sets aside a memory location with a unique address to store that variable. The compiler associates that address with the variable's name. When your program uses this variable name, it automatically accesses the proper memory location.

a. A variable named *rate* is declared and initialized to 100. The compiler has set aside memory at address 2004 for this variable and has associated the name *rate* with the address 2004. (See Figure 3.36)

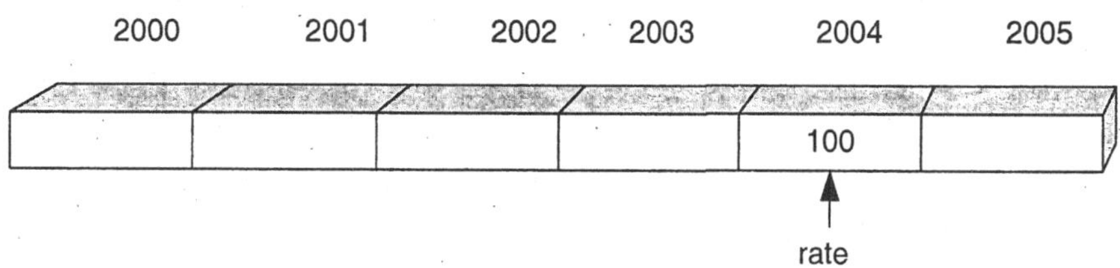

Figure 3.36 A variable *rate* is stored and initialized at a specific memory address

b. The first step is to declare a variable to hold the address of *rate*. Let the name be **`p_rate`**, for example. At the time of declaration, **`p_rate`** is uninitialised. Memory has been allocated for **`p_rate`**, but its value is not specified, as shown in Figure 3.37.

c. The next step is to store the address of the variable *rate* in the variable *p_rate*. Because *p_rate* now contains the address of rate, it indicates the location where *rate* is stored in memory. This is shown in Figure 3.38.

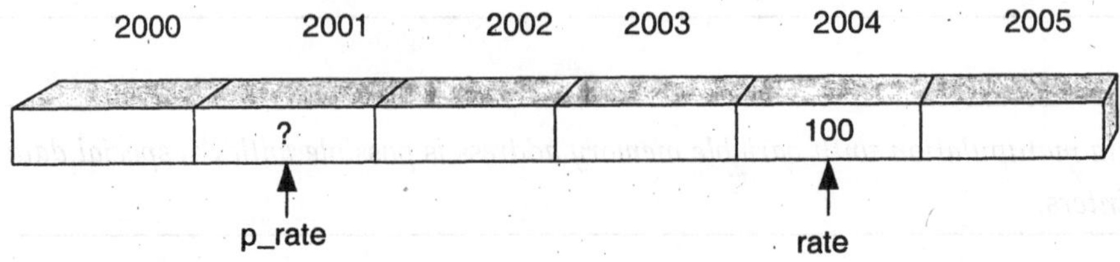

Figure 3.37 Memory storage space has been allocated for the variable `p_rate`

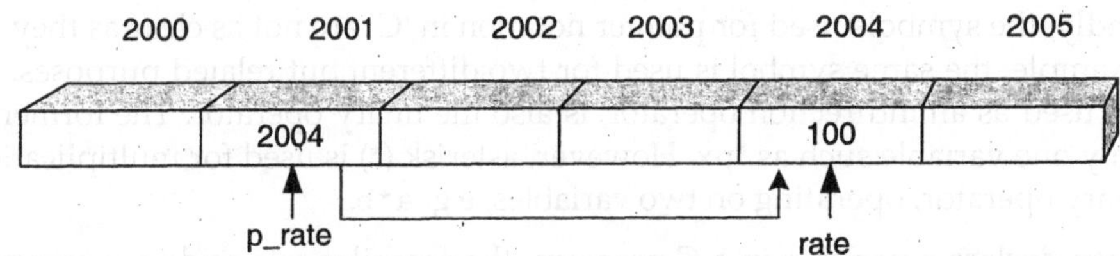

Figure 3.38 The variable `p_rate` contains address (2004) of variable *rate* and is therefore a pointer to *rate*

3.14.1 Why use Pointers?

Pointers are essential because of the following reasons:

1. Passing arguments to functions by address when the modification of *formal* arguments are to be reflected on *actual* arguments.
2. Passing arrays and strings more conveniently from one function to another.
3. Manipulating arrays more easily by moving pointers to them instead of moving the arrays themselves.
4. Creating complex data structure, such as linked lists and binary tree, where one data structure must contain references to other data structures.
5. Communicating information about memory as in the function *malloc()* which returns the location of free memory by using a pointer.

3.14.2 Address of (&) and Dereferencing Operators (*)

All the variables defined in a program (including pointer variables) reside at specific addresses in the main memory of a computer. It is possible to obtain the address of a variable in the main memory by using the & (ampersand) operator.

Let us see the following declaration:

```
int x = 2;
```

The above declaration tells the compiler of 'C' language, to perform the following actions:

1. Reserve space in the main memory to hold an integer value.
2. Associate the name x with this memory location.
3. Store the value 2 at this location. (See Figure 3.39)

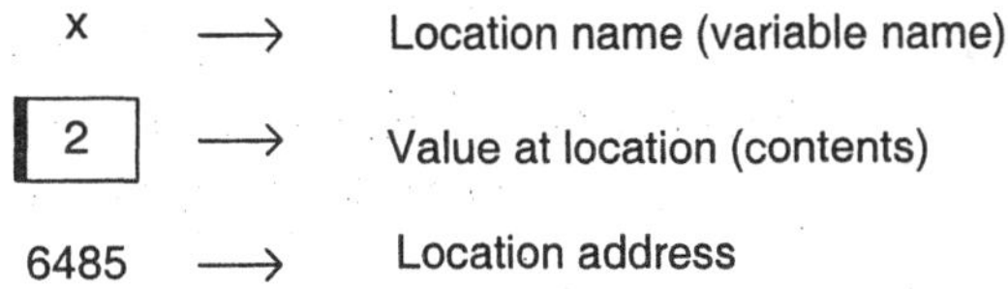

Figure 3.39 Memory address of the variable x

To get the address of an integer variable, it has to be used with unary operator '&' preceding the variable name. The memory address for the variable x holding the value 2 is 6485.

Example 17

Program in Figure 3.40 explains the pointer operator (&). The output from the program shows that the address corresponding to x is 6485. Thus the address of x is given by &x and it is 6485.

```
/* program using pointer operator (&) */
   #include<stdio.h>
main()
{
   int x = 2;
   printf("\n Address of x = %u", &x);
   printf("\n Value at address x = %u",
              x);
}

RUN

Address of x = 6485
Value at address x = 2
```

Figure 3.40 Program to explain the pointer operator &

☞ *%u (unsigned) format string is used to print the location (address) in main memory of the computer where the variable is stored.*

The other pointer operator available in C is the character '*' and this * is called "value at address" operator. It returns the value stored at a particular address. The "value at address" operator is also called *indirection* or *dereferencing* operator.

Example 18

Program in Figure 3.41 explains the pointer operators (&) and (*).

```
#include <stdio.h>
main()
{
 int x = 2;
 printf("\n Address of x = %u", &x);
 printf("\n Value at address x = %d", x);
 printf("\n Value of x = %d", *(&x));
}

RUN

Address of x = 6485
Value at address x = 2
Value of x = 2
```

Figure 3.41 Program showing address and value stored at that address

☞ *Printing the values of* ***(&x)** *is same as printing the value x, i.e. it will print the value present in that address.*

Accessing the contents of a variable by using the variable name is called *direct access*. The following statement in Figure 3.41, is the example of direct access

```
printf("\n Value at address x = %d," x);
```

Accessing the contents of a variable by using a pointer to the variable is called *indirect access* or *indirection*. The following statement, in Figure 3.41, is an example of indirection.

```
printf("\n Value of x = %d", *(&x));
```

3.15 DECLARATION OF POINTER TYPE VARIABLES

A pointer is defined as a variable used to store memory address. It is similar to any other variable and must be declared before it can be used. Just like an integer variable can hold any integers each pointer variable can hold only address of the pointer to a specific data type, such as int, char, float, double, etc.

A pointer declaration takes the following form:

```
typename *ptrname;
```

where *typename* is any of 'C' language variable types and it indicates the type of the variable that the pointer points to. The (*) asterisk is the indirection operator, and it indicates that *ptrname* is a pointer to *typename* and not a variable of type typename. For example,

```
int *ptr_i;        ptr_i is a pointer to an integer
float *ptr_f;      ptr_f is a pointer to a float
```

All the above pointer variables reside at specific addresses. The address of a variable can be assigned to a pointer variable as follows:

```
ptr_i = &age;
```

where the variable *age* is of integer type.

```
ptr_f = &marks;
```

where the variable *marks* is of float type.

We have already seen &x returns the address of x.

You can store this address in a variable. The variable which stores an address, is declared as a *pointer* variable.

Thus, the variable *y* in Figure 3.42 should be declared as follows:

```
int *y;
```

Thus, *int *y* would mean that *y* is a pointer to an integer. The asterisk(*) prefixed to the variable name indicates that *y* is a pointer variable. The data type *int* tells that *y* can point to any integer data type item, stored in the memory. The format for declaration is shown in Figure 3.42.

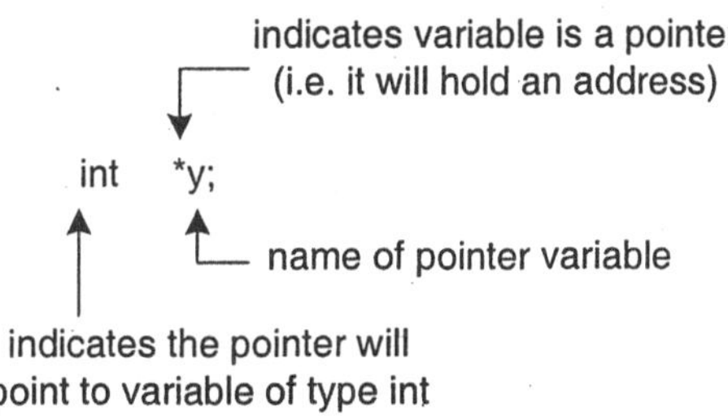

Figure 3.42 Format of pointer declaration

If we write:

```
Y = &x; // assigns the address of x to y
```

then address 6485 which is the address where the variable x is lying in the main memory is now stored in the variable y.

Example 19

The program given in Figure 3.43 demonstrates the relationships, among the (*) and (&) operators.

☞ *Note that the asterisk * (indirection operator), is a unary operator i.e it operates on one variable (such as y in *y). Thus, the compiler cannot confuse it with the same symbol used for multiplication, which is a binary operator, operating on two variables such as a*b where * operates on variables a and b.*

```
#include<stdio.h>
main()
{
 int x = 2;
 int *y;
 y = &x;
 printf("\n Address of x = %u", &x);
```

(Contd...)

```
printf("\n Address of x = %u", y);
printf("\n Address of y = %u", &y);
printf("\n Value of y = %d", y);
printf("\n Value of x = %d", x);
printf("\n Value of x = %d", *(&x));
printf("\n Value of x = %d", *y);
}
RUN

Address of x = 6485
Address of x = 6485
Address of y = 3276
Value of y = 6485
Value of x = 2
Value of x = 2
Value of x = 2
```

Figure 3.43 Program demonstrating the relationships

☞ *The results in your program shown in Figure 3.43 may be different because of memory location.*

Study the following statements to understand further the concept of pointer.

```
int a = 20;
int b,x,y;
int *pa, *pb, *px;
pa = &a;
x = *pa;
b = x+a;
pb = &b;
px = &x;
y = *pa + *Pb;
```

Consider that the memory location address of $a = 100$ and $b = 102$.

Now we can find out *pa, x, b, pb, *pb,* and **px + *Pb*

```
pa will be 100
x will be 20
b will be 40
pb will be 102
*pb will be 40
*px + *pb will have a value 60
```

3.16 ARRAYS AND POINTERS

An array in programming language 'C' can be declared as follows:

```
int value[5] = {2,4,6,5,9};
```

which means that the variable *value* is an array of integers and it has five components namely, value[0], value[1], value[2], value[3] and value[4]. The array may be stored in consecutive addresses in memory locations as shown below:

name	address	contents
value [0]	2000	2
value [1]	2002	4
value [2]	2004	6
value [3]	2006	5
value [4]	2008	9

Suppose we write:

```
int *ptr
ptr = &value[0]
```

it will display result

```
ptr = 2000;
```

If we write

```
ptr = value;
```

then also it will display 2000. This is because in 'C' language, the name of an array variable is taken as the address of its zeroth component.

The pointer variable *ptr* is also an address. So the declaration, & value[0] and *ptr* is same because both hold the addresses. Thus, we can write:

```
ptr = &value[0];
```

i.e the address of the zeroth element is assigned to a pointer variable *ptr*. If the pointer is incremented to next data element, then the following is true:

```
ptr++ == value[1];
```

Likewise, array subscripts are defined in terms of pointer arithmetic.

`value[i]` is same as `*((value) + i)` and it is same as `*(& (value) [0] + (i))`

3.16.1 Arrays of Pointers

As there are arrays of integers, or arrays of floats, similarly there can be an array of pointers also. As the pointer variable contains an address, an array of pointers is a collection of addresses. The most common use of an array of pointers is with strings. The start of the string is indicated by a pointer to the first character (a pointer to array type char), and the end of the string is marked by a null character. By declaring and initialising an array of pointers to type *char*, we can access and manipulate a large sized string using the pointer array. Each element in the array points to a different string, and by looping through the array, we can access each one of them in turn. Consider the following declaration:

```
char *ar_of_P[5];
```

the variable ar_of_P[] is an array of pointers of 5 elements pointing to character. This is because the array element operator[] has higher precedence than the dereferencing operator *.

☞ *Array of pointers are frequently used to access arrays of strings, because it allows more efficient use of available main memory.*

The most common use of array of pointers is to hold character strings. For example, the following declaration creates an array, named weekdays, that contains pointers to character strings.

```
char *weekdays[7] = {"Sunday", "Monday", "Tuesday", "Wednesday",
                     "Thursday", "Friday", "Saturday"};
```

If you examine the array's type from right to left, you will note that the array contains seven elements. The asterisk before the variable name specifies a pointer.

☞ *When you declare an array of character strings, the 'C' compiler does not append a NULL entry to indicate the end of the array as it does for character strings.*

Example 20

A program to display the contents of pointer using an array of pointers is given in Figure 3.44.

```
#include <stdio.h>
main()
{
  char *ptr[3]
  ptr[0] = "Rani";
  ptr[1] = "Shiv";
  ptr[2] = "Ram";
  printf("The content of pointer 1 = %s \n", ptr[0]);
  printf("The content of pointer 2 = %s \n", ptr[1]);
  printf("The content of pointer 3 = %s \n", ptr[2]);
}

RUN

The content of pointer 1 = Rani
The content of pointer 2 = Shiv
The content of pointer 3 = Ram
```

Figure 3.44 Contents of the array of pointers displayed

3.17 DYNAMIC REPRESENTATION OF A TWO-DIMENSIONAL ARRAY

Single dimensional array can be represented in terms of the pointer (the array name) and an offset (the subscript). Similarly, a multidimensional array can also be represented with an equivalent pointer notation. A two dimensional array, is actually a collection of one-dimensional arrays. Therefore, we can define a two dimensional array as a pointer to a group of contiguous one-dimensional arrays. A two dimensional array declaration can be written as follows:

```
data-type (*ptvar) [expression2];
```

instead of writing

```
data type array[expression1]
[expression2];
```

where, *data-type* refers to the type of data in the array. Moreover, *ptvar* is the name of the pointer variable, array is the corresponding array name, and *expression*1, *expression*2 are positive valued integer expressions that indicate the maximum number of array elements associated with each subscript.

For example, suppose *x* represents a two-dimensional integer array having 10 rows and 20 columns. Then, we can declare *x* as:

```
int (*x) [20];
```

rather than

```
int x[10][20];
```

In the first method of declaration, *x* is defined to be a pointer to a group of contiguous, one-dimensional 20-elements of an integer array. Thus, *x* points to the first 20-element array, which is actually the first row (row 0) of the original two dimensional array. Similarly, (*x*+1) points to the second 20-elements array, which is the second row (row 1) of the original two-dimensional array, and so on. (See Figure 3.45)

To access the item in row 2 and column 5, we can write either of the following:

```
x[2][5]
```

or

```
*(*(x+2) + 5)
```

Note that (x+2) is a pointer to row 2. Therefore, the object of this pointer, *(x+2), refers to the entire row. Since row 2 is a one-dimensional array, *(x+2) is actually a pointer to the first element in row 2. We now add 5 to this pointer. Hence, (*(x+2) + 5) is a pointer to element 5 (the sixth element) in row 2. *(*(x+2) + 5), therefore refers to the item in column 5 of row 2, which is x[2][5].

3.18 DATA TYPE STRUCTURE

The data type *structure* consists of a number of data items grouped together— but unlike arrays, each data item in the group need not be of the same *type*. Thus, for example, a structure may contain employee's data encompassing employee's_name, employee's_number, salary, and any other relevant information about the employee. A structure can hold as many of these items as we need. Only limitation is the main memory size of a computer. Figure 3.46

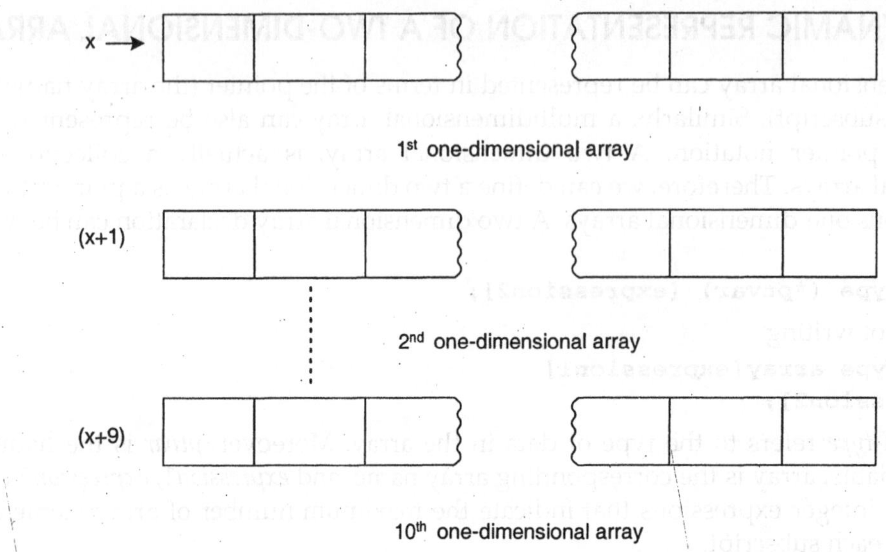

Figure 3.45 Representation of two-dimensional array having 10 rows and 20 column.

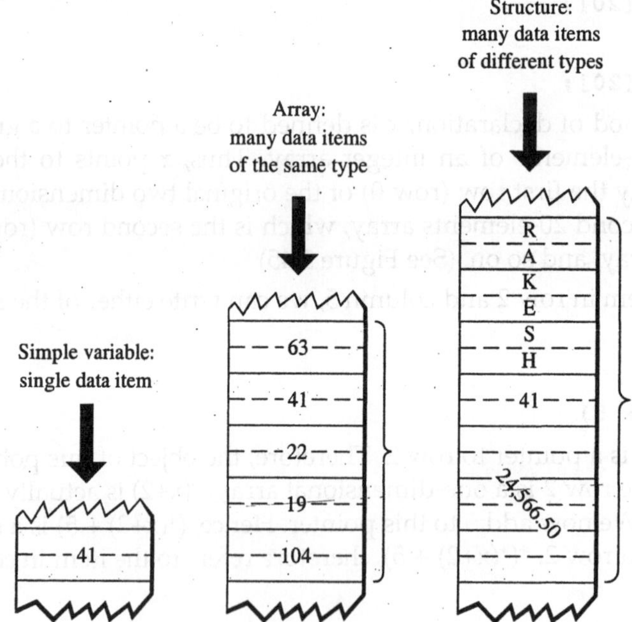

Figure 3.46 Depiction of simple variable, array and structure

shows the differences between a simple variable, an array and a structure variable. Simple variable holds one integer data value. The array holds many integers values. It is the structure that can hold data of various types such as integers, float, and char type.

3.19 ARRAY OF STRUCTURE

The real power in using structure comes when you use an array of structures. By maintaining an array-of-structures, a database of information can be manipulated for a wide range of items.

An array-of-structures is defined as follows:

```
struct personnel
{
  char name[25];
  int numb;
  float height;
};
struct personnel emp[MAXNUMB];
```

In order to declare an array-of-structures, we use the following statement after the declaration of the structure *personnel*:

```
struct personnel emp[MAXNUMB];
```

An array-of-structure creates space in the main memory for storing data and accessing data of a maximum number of employees given by the variable MAXNUMB.

☞ *The above statement sets space equal to as many as MAXNUMB times of a single structure personnel and assigns this much total memory space to the structure of type personnel.*

Figure 3.47 shows conceptually the array-of-structures as stored in the main memory of a computer.

☞ *When working with an array-of-structures, be aware about the memory limitations of the computer system you are programming on. If main memory is not sufficient, the machine may hang up.*

3.19.1 Initialization of an Array of Structures

An array of structures can be initialized in the same way as an array of data in 'C'.

☞ *The only syntactic difference between referencing a structure member versus an array-of-structures member is the use of the subscript. The array elements can be accessed with the help of a loop.*

Example 21

Program demonstrating initialization of array of structures is shown in Figure 3.48.

☞ *The program (shows in Figure 3.48) initializes the data immediately after the declaration of the array of structures.*

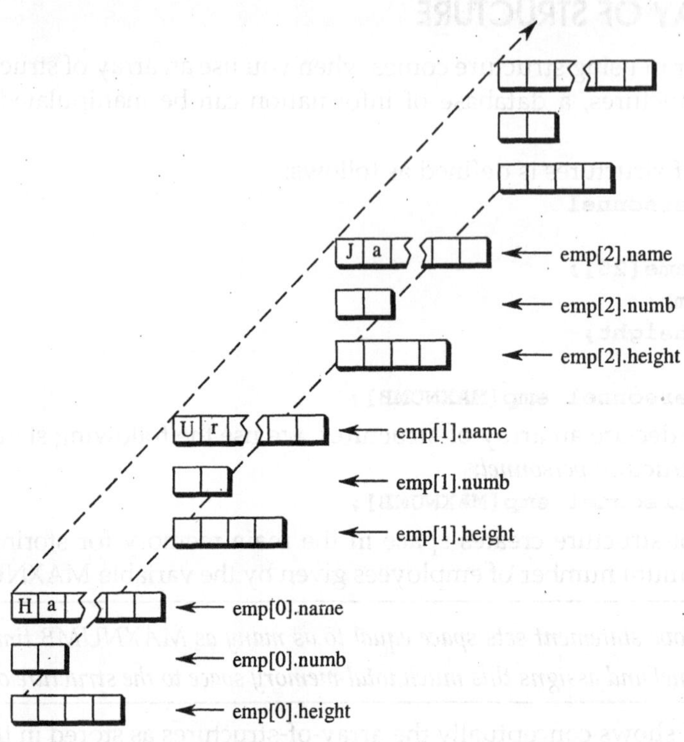

Figure 3.47 Array-of-structures emp[] conceptually stored in the memory of a computer

```
/* Program demonstrating array of structures initialization */
#include<stdio.h>
 struct data /* definition of data structure */
 {
   int numb;  /* employee number */
   int sal;    /* employee salary */
 };
struct data emp[2] = {
        {111,4000 },    /* initializing data for emp1*/
        {222,5000 }     /* initializing data for emp2 */
          };
main()
{
  printf( "\nList of Employees");
  printf( "\nEmployee1 number = %d",emp[0].numb);
  printf( "\nEmployee1 salary = %d",emp[0].sal);
```

(Contd...)

```
  printf( "\nEmployee2 number = %d",emp[1].numb);
  printf( "\nEmployee2 salary = %d",emp[1].sal);
}

RUN

List of Employees
Employee1 number = 111

Employee1 salary = 4000

Employee2 number = 222

Employee2 salary = 5000
```

Figure 3.48 Program demonstrating initialization of an array-of-structures

Example 22

Program shown in Figure 3.49 demonstrates the use of array member name[20] which is of the type character. Note that while initializing the structure, the character data is placed within the double quotes (" "). The program demonstrates an array within a structure.

```
/* Program demonstrating array within a structure */
#include<stdio.h>
#define MAX 2
void main(void)
{
 struct data /* definition of data structure */
 {
   char name[20]; /* employee name */
   int numb;  /* employee number */
   int sal;    /* employee salary */
 };
 struct data emp[MAX] = {
    {"Purvasha",111,4000 }, /* initializing data for emp1*/
    {"Yatin",222,5000 }  /* initializing data for emp2 */
   };
 printf( "\nList of Employees");
 printf( "\nEmployee1 name = %s ",emp[0].name);
 printf( "\nEmployee1 number = %d ",emp[0].numb);
 printf( "\nEmployee1 salary = %d",emp[0].sal);
 printf( "\nEmployee2 name = %s"  ,emp[1].name);
```

(Contd...)

```
 printf( "\nEmployee2 number = %d ",emp[1].numb);
 printf( "\nEmployee2 salary = %d" ,emp[1].sal);
}
RUN
List of Employees
Employee1 name = Purvasha

Employee1 number = 111

Employee1 salary = 4000

Employee2 name = Yatin

Employee2 number = 222

Employee2 salary = 5000
```

Figure 3.49 Program demonstrating initialization of structure containing an array

Example 23

The program shown in Figure 3.50 is rewritten using *for* loop to demonstrate array within a structure.

```
/* Program demonstrating array within a structure */
#include<stdio.h>
#define MAX 2
main()
{
  struct data /* definition of data structure */
  {
    char name[20]; /* employee name */
    int numb;  /* employee number */
    int sal;    /* employee salary */
  };
  struct data emp[MAX] = {
   {"Purvasha",111,4000 },/* initializing data for emp1*/
   {"Yatin",222,5000 }/* initializing data for emp2 */
    };
  int i;
  for (i = 0; i<= MAX-1; i++)
  {
    printf("\nData of Employee %d ", i + 1);
    printf("\nEmployee name :  %s", emp[i].name);
    printf("\nEmployee number : %03d ",emp[i].numb);
```

(Contd...)

```
    printf("\nEmployee salary : %03d ",emp[i].sal);
  }
}

RUN

Data of Employee 1

Employee name: Purvasha

Employee number: 111

Employee salary: 4000

Data of Employee 2

Employee name: Yatin

Employee number: 222

Employee salary: 5000
```

Figure 3.50 Program demonstrating initialization of structure containing an array

Example 24

While initializing an array-of-structures, if the data items are not sufficient for all the members, then the initial value of all *such* members is assumed to be zero. For example, in the program shown in Figure 3.51, the value of MAX is three. It means that there are three employees for whom the data should be given. But the data given are only for two employees, therefore, the data for the third employee is assumed to be zero.

3.20 MEMORY ALLOCATION

The memory allocation may be classified as *static allocation* and *dynamic allocation*. In static allocation, the size of the memory may be required for the calculation that must be defined before loading and executing the program, whereas in dynamic allocation, the required memory size is allocated while program is being executed.

There are four dynamic memory allocation functions. These functions are:

a. malloc()
b. calloc()
c. realloc()
d. free()

```
/* Program demonstrating arrays within a structure and containing
insufficient data */
#include<stdio.h>
#define MAX 3
main()
{
  struct data /* definition of data structure */
  {
    char name[20]; /* employee name */
    int numb;       /* employee number */
    int sal;        /* employee salary */
  };
  struct data emp[MAX] = {

    {"Purvasha",111,4000 }, /* initializing data for emp1*/
    {"Yatin",222,5000 }  /* initializing data for emp2 */
                 };
  int i;
  for (i = 0; i<= MAX-1; i++)
  {
    printf("\nData of Employee %d ", i + 1);
    printf("\nEmployee name :  %s", emp[i].name);
    printf("\nEmployee number : %03d ",emp[i].numb);
    printf("\nEmployee salary : %03d ",emp[i].sal);
  }
}
```

RUN

```
Data of Employee 1

Employee name: Purvasha

Employee number: 111

Employee salary: 4000

Data of Employee 2

Employee name: Yatin

Employee number: 222
```

(Contd...)

```
Employee salary: 5000

Data of Employee 3

Employee name:

Employee number: 000

Employee salary: 000
```

Figure 3.51 Program demonstrating initialization of structures containing insufficient data

3.20.1 malloc()

The function *malloc()* allocates a specified number of bytes in main memory. The allocated region is not filled with zero. The starting address is returned if the function is successful. A zero is returned if the function fails to allocate memory. To assign sufficient memory for x, we can make use of the library function malloc(), as follows:

```
x = malloc(10 *size of(int))
```

This function reserves a block of memory whose size (in bytes) is equivalent to the size of an integer.

3.20.2 calloc()

This is similar to the function malloc(), but initializes the allocated byte to zero. This function also allows you to allocate memory for more than one object at a time. The starting address of the area is returned if the function is successful. A zero is returned if the function's attempt to get a block of memory fails.

The general declaration of the calloc() function is:

```
char *calloc(elements, element_size)
unsigned int element;
unsigned int element_size;
```

3.20.3 realloc()

The realloc() function is used to change the size of the previously allocated block of memory.

The general format of the realloc() function is:

```
char *realloc(oldblock, size)
char *oldblock;
unsigned int size;
```

3.20.4 free()

The free() function frees up memory that was previously allocated with malloc(), calloc(), or realloc()

The general format of free() function is:

```
int free(pointer)
char *pointer;
```

3.21 REPRESENTATION OF SPARSE MATRICES

Matrices with relatively high proportion of zero entries are called *sparse matrices*. The natural method of representing matrices in memory of a computer as two-dimensional arrays may not be suitable for sparse matrices. This is because one may save space by storing only those entries, which may be non-zero. For example, the matrix shown below has only 10 non zero elements out of 42 elements.

$$M[6]\,[7] = \begin{bmatrix} 0 & 0 & 5 & 0 & 10 & 0 & 0 \\ 3 & 0 & 0 & 8 & 9 & 0 & 3 \\ 11 & 0 & 0 & 0 & 0 & 0 & 0 \\ 0 & 0 & 13 & 0 & 0 & 0 & 0 \\ 0 & 0 & 0 & 0 & 0 & 0 & 0 \\ 0 & 0 & 0 & 4 & 0 & 0 & 6 \end{bmatrix}$$

The 10 nonzero elements are with their values are as follows:

M [1] [3] = 5
M [1] [5] = 10
M [2] [1] = 3
M [2] [4] = 8
M [2] [5] = 9
M [2] [7] = 3
M [3] [1] = 11
M [4] [3] = 13
M [6] [4] = 4
M [6] [7] = 6

One of the basic method for storing such a sparse matrix is to store only non-zero elements in a one dimensional array and keep the identity of each array element with row and column indices as shown in Figure 3.52.

Index	Row	Column	Non-zero element value
1	1	3	5
2	1	5	10
3	2	1	3
4	2	4	8
5	2	5	9
6	2	7	3
7	3	1	11
8	4	3	13
9	6	4	4
10	6	7	6

Figure 3.52 Sequential representation of sparse matrix

Example 25

A program along with output is given in Figure 3.53 for matrix represented as sparse matrix.

```
#include <stdio.h>

main()

{
   void spr();
   void dis();
   void dis_sp();
   int a[10][10];
   int sp[20][3];
   int i,j,k,m,n;

   printf ("Please enter size of matrix A(m n)\n");
   scanf ("%d %d", &m, &n);
   printf ("%d X %d\n", m, n);
   printf ("\nEnter %d elements of sparse matrix A\n", m*n);
   for (i = 0; i < m; i++)
      for (j = 0; j < n; j++)
      {
         printf ("a[%2d][%2d] = ", i, j);
         scanf ("%d", &a[i][j]);
      }
   printf ("\n");
   spr (a,m,n,sp);
   printf ("\nMatrix A is \n");
   dis (a,m,n);
   printf ("\nSparse Matrix representation of A is:\n");
   dis_sp (sp, sp[0][2]+1);
   printf ("\n");
}
/* Transforming a matrix to sparse matrix */
void spr (x, y, z, ss)
int x[10][10], ss[20][3];
int y, z;
{
   int i,j,k,c;
   k = 1;
   c = 0;
   for (i = 0; i < y; i++)
   {
      for (j = 0; j < z; j++)
   {
```

(Contd...)

```
    /* Transfer every non-zero entry to sparse matrix */
    if (x[i][j] !=0)
    {
       ss[k][0] = i; /* store row number */
       ss[k][1] = j; /* store column number */
       ss[k][2] = x[i][j];
       k++;
       c++;
    }
  }
  }
  /* update first row of spare matrix */
  ss[0][0] = y;
  ss[0][1] = z;
  ss[0][2] = c;
  return;
}

/* Function to display ordinary matrix */

void dis (a,b,c)
int a[10][10], b, c;
{
  int i,j,k;
  for (i = 0; i < b; i++)
  {
    for (j = 0; j < c; j++)
      printf ("%5d", a[i][j]);
    printf ("\n");
  }
}

/* Function to display sparse matrix */

  void dis_sp (s, b)
  int s[20][3], b;
{
  int i,j,k;
  for (i = 0; i < b; i++)
  {
    for (j = 0; j < 3; j++)
      printf ("%5d", s[i][j]);
    printf ("\n");
  }
}
```

(*Contd...*)

```
RUN

Please enter size of matrix A(m  n)
4
3
4 x 3
Enter 12 elements of sparse matrix A
a[0][0] = 1
a[0][1] = 5
a[0][2] = 0
a[1][0] = 0
a[1][1] = 3
a[1][2] = 0
a[2][0] = 0
a[2][1] = 4
a[2][2] = 0
a[3][0] = 0
a[3][1] = 8
a[3][2] = 5

Matrix A is

1  5  0
0  3  0
0  4  0
0  8  5

Sparse matrix representation of A is:
4  3  6
0  0  1
0  1  5
1  1  3
2  1  4
3  1  8
3  2  5
```

Figure 3.53 Output of example 25 representation of matrix as sparse matrix. The top row 4 3 6 shows the number of rows, columns and non zero elements number

Let the size of matrix A is 3 × 3 i.e. m1 = 3, and n1 = 3.
Elements of sparse matrix A are:
a[0] [0] = 1
a[0] [1] = 0
a[0] [2] = 0
a[1] [0] = 1
a[1] [1] = 2

a[1] [2] = 3
a[2] [0] = 0
a[2] [1] = 0
a[2] [2] = 0
Matrix A of the order 3 × 3 is as follows:
1 0 0
1 2 3
0 0 0

Sparse matrix representation of A (order 5 × 3) is:
3 3 4
0 0 1
1 0 1
1 1 2
1 2 3

The size of matrix B(m2, n2) is 3 × 3
Elements of sparse matrix B is
b[0] [0] = 1
b[0] [1] = 0
b[0] [2] = 0
b[1] [0] = 0
b[1] [1] = 0
b[1] [2] = 2
b[2] [0] = 1
b[2] [1] = 0
b[2] [2] = 0

Matrix B of order 3 × 3 is
1 0 0
0 0 2
1 0 0

Sparse matrix representation of B (order 4 × 3) is
3 3 3
0 0 1
1 2 2
2 0 1

Sum of the matrices is:
3 3 5
0 0 2
1 0 1
1 1 2
1 2 5
2 0 1

Example 26

Program and its output for adding sparse matrix is given in Figure 3.54.

```
/* Sparse matrix addition */

#include <stdio.h>
main()
{
   void sparse();
   void sum();
   void write_mat();
   void write_sparse();
   int a[10][10], b[10][10];
   int sp1[20][3], sp2[20][3], sp3[20][3];
   int i,j,k,m1,n1,m2,n2;
   printf("Please enter size of matrix A (m1 n1) ");
   scanf ("%d %d", &m1, &n1);
   printf ("\nEnter %d elements of sparse matrix A\n", m1*n1);
   for (i = 0; i < m1; i++)
      for (j = 0; j < n1; j++)
      {
         printf ("a[%2d] [%2d] = ", i, j);
         scanf ("%d", &a[i][j]);
      }
   sparse (a, m1, n1, sp1);
   printf ("\nMatrix A of Order %d x %d is :\n", m1, n1);
   write_mat (a, m1, n1);
   printf ("\n");
   printf ("Sparse Matrix representation A (Order %d x %d) is:\n",
          sp1[0][2]+ 1,3);
   write_sparse (sp1, sp1[0][2]+1);
   printf ("\nEnter size of matrix B (m2, n2) ");
   scanf ("%d %d", &m2, &n2);
      if (m1 == m2 && n1 == n2)
   {
      printf ("\nEnter %d elements of sparse matrix B\n", m2*n2);
      for (i = 0; i < m2; i++)
         for (j = 0; j < n2; j++)
         {
            printf ("b[%2d][%2d] = ",i, j);
            scanf ("%d", &b[i][j]);
         }
      sparse (b, m2, n2, sp2);
      printf ("\nMatrix B of Order %d x %d is :\n", m2, n2);
```

(Contd...)

```
        write_mat (b, m2, n2);
        printf ("\n");
        printf ("Sparse Matrix representation of B(Order %dx%d) is:\n",
            sp2[0][2]+1,3);
        write_sparse (sp2, sp2[0][2]+1);
        /* Invoking function sum */
        sum (sp1, sp2, sp3);
        printf ("\nSum of the matrices (Order %d x %d) is:\n",
                sp3[0][2]+1,3);
        write_sparse (sp3, sp3[0][2]+1);
    }
    else
        printf("Matrices not of same order. Addition not possible. \n");
}
/* Function to represent matrix in sparse form */
    void sparse (x, y, z, ss)
    int x[10][10], ss[20][3];
    int y, z;
{
    int i,j,k,c;
    k = 1;
    c = 0;
    for (i = 0; i < y; i++)
    {
        for (j = 0; j < z; j++)
        {
            if (x[i][j])
            {
                ss[k][0] = i;
                ss[k][1] = j;
                ss[k][2] = x[i][j];
                k++;
                c++;
            }
        }
    }
    ss[0][0] = y;
    ss[0][1] = z;
    ss[0][2] = c;
    return;
}
```

(Contd...)

```
/* Function adds two sparse matrices A and B */

void sum (a,b,c)
int a[20][3], b[20][3], c[20][3];
{
   int i,j,k, m, r1, r2;
   i = j = k = 1;
   r1 = a[0][2];
   r2 = b[0][2];
   while (i <= r1 && j <= r2)
   {
      if (a[i][0] == b[j][0])
      {
/* if the elements are in the same row */
   if (a[i][1] == b[j][1])
   {
      /* if the elements are in the same column */
      c[k][0] = a[i][0];
      c[k][1] = a[i][1];
      c[k][2] = a[i][2]+b[j][2];
      i++;
      j++;
      k++;
   }
   else
      if (a[i][1] < b[j][1])
      {
      /* if the elements of the first matrix is in a preceding column */
         c[k][0] = a[i][0];
         c[k][1] = a[i][1];
         c[k][2] = a[i][2];
         i++;
         k++;
      }
      else
      {
         c[k][0] = b[j][0];
         c[k][1] = b[j][1];
         c[k][2] = b[j][2];
         j++;
         k++;
      }
   }
```

(Contd...)

```
else
   if (a[i][0] < b[j][0])
   {
   /* if element of the first matrix is in a preceding row */
      c[k][0] = a[i][0];
      c[k][1] = a[i][1];
      c[k][2] = a[i][2];
      i++;
      k++;
   }
   else
   {
   /* element of the first matrix is in a following row */
      c[k][0] = b[j][0];
      c[k][1] = b[j][1];
      c[k][2] = b[j][2];
      j++;
      k++;
   }
}
/* end of while loop */
/* if any elements are left */
if (i < r1 + 1)
   /* if elements are remaining in the first matrix */
   for (m = i; m < r1 + 1; m++)
   {
      c[k][0] = a[m][0];
      c[k][1] = a[m][1];
      c[k][2] = a[m][2];
      k++;
   }
   else
      if (j < r2+1)
         /* if elements are remaining in the second matrix */
         for (m = j; m < r2+1; m++)
         {
            c[k][0] = b[m][0];
            c[k][1] = b[m][1];
            c[k][2] = b[m][2];
            k++;
         }
```

(Contd...)

```
      c[0][0] = a[0][0];
      c[0][1] = a[0][1];
      c[0][2] = k - 1;
      return;
   }
   /* Function displays a matrix */
   void write_mat (a,b,c)
   int a[10][10], b, c;
   {
      int i,j,k;
      for (i = 0; i < b; i++)
      {
         for (j = 0; j < c; j++)
            printf ("%4d", a[i][j]);
         printf ("\n");
      }
      return;
   }
/* Function displays a sparse matrix */

   void write_sparse (s,b)
   int s[20][3], b;
   {
      int i,j,k;
      for (i = 0; i < b; i++)
      {
         for (j = 0; j < 3; j++)
            printf ("%4d", s[i][j]);
         printf ("\n");
      }
      return;
   }
```

RUN

```
Please enter size of matrix A(m1 n1) 3 3
Enter 9 elements of sparse matrix A
a[0][0] = 1
a[0][1] = 0
a[0][2] = 0
a[1][0] = 0
a[1][1] = 2
a[1][2] = 1
```

(Contd...)

```
a[2][0] = 0
a[2][1] = 0
a[2][2] = 0

Matrix A of order 3 × 3 is:
 1  0  0
 0  2  1
 0  0  0

Sparse matrix representation of A(order 4 × 3) is:
   3  3  3
   0  0  1
   1  1  2
   1  2  1

Enter size of matrix B(m2, n2) 3 3

Enter 9 elements of sparse matrix B

b[0][0] = 1
b[0][1] = 0
b[0][2] = 0
b[1][0] = 0
b[1][1] = 3
b[1][2] = 0
b[2][0] = 0
b[2][1] = 2
b[2][2] = 4

Matrix B of order 3 × 3 is:
 1  0  0
 0  3  0
 0  2  4

Sparse matrix representation of (Order 5 × 3) is:
 3  3  4
 0  0  1
 1  1  3
 2  1  2
 2  2  4

Sum of the matrices (order 6 × 3) is:
 3  3  5
 0  0  2
 1  1  5
 1  2  1
 2  1  2
 2  2  4
```

Figure 3.54 Program and the output of Example 26 for adding sparse matrix

3.21.1 3-tuple Method

A common way of representing non-zero elements of a sparse matrix is the 3-tuple forms. Now we will see the 3-tuple method for presenting sparse matrix.

As the name implies, every non-zero entry of sparse matrix is represented by three tuples. First tuple represents row, second for column and third for the actual value of the non-zero elements of matrix. Let us take a matrix of size 4 x 5.

$$M[4]\,[5] = \begin{bmatrix} 0 & 8 & 6 & 0 & 2 \\ 9 & 0 & 0 & 3 & 0 \\ 0 & 3 & 0 & 0 & 0 \\ 6 & 0 & 0 & 0 & 7 \end{bmatrix}$$

We have to represent the matrix in 3-tuple representation of sparse matrix. Here total number of rows is 4, number of column is 5 and non zero entries are 8. So the sparse matrix will be

M =	No of rows (4)	No of columns (5)	Non-zero entries (8)
	1	2	8
	1	3	6
	1	5	2
	2	1	9
	2	4	3
	3	2	3
	4	1	6
	4	5	7

It is a row major 3-tuple presentation. So elements are coming sequentially on the basis of row. Suppose we want to represent column major 3-tuple sparse matrix then it will be as shown below.

M =	No of columns (5)	No of rows (4)	Non zero entries (8)
	1	2	9
	1	4	6
	2	1	8
	2	3	3
	3	1	5
	4	2	3
	5	1	2
	5	4	7

DESCRIPTIVE QUESTIONS

Q. No. 1 Write a program to read the values for the elements of a one dimensional array of integers and then sorts it in the ascending order, i.e. minimum to maximum.

Ans to Q. 1

```
/* Program for Question No. 1 */
#include<stdio.h>
main()
{
   int a[100];
   int i,j,n,temp,evensum;
   evensum = 0;
   printf("How many numbers are in the array ?\n");
   scanf("%d",&n);
   printf("Enter the elements : \n");
   for(i = 0; i<=n-1; ++i)
   {
      scanf("%d",&a[i]);
   }
   printf("Contents of the array(unsored form\n" );
   for (i = 0; i<=n-1; ++i)
   {
      printf("%d\t",a[i]);
   }
   printf("\n");
   for(i = 0;i<= n-1;++i)
   {
      for(j = 0;j<=n-1;++j)
      if (a[i] < a[j])
      {
         temp = a[i];
         a[i] = a[j];
         a[j] = temp;
      }
   }
   printf("Contents of the array(sorted form)\n");
   for(i=0;i<=n-1;++i)
   {
      printf("%d\t ",a[i]);
   }
   return 0;
}
```

Q. No. 2 Write a program to read a matrix of size M × N. It then calculates the sum of the values contained in the elements row wise as well as column wise, and then prints them.

Ans to Q. 2

```
/* Program for Question No. 2 to print row and column wise
total */
#include<stdio.h>
main()
{
  int a[10][10],i,j,m,n;
  printf("Enter row and column of matrix A\n");
  scanf("%d %d",&n,&m);
  printf("%d %d\n",n,m);
  printf("Enter elements of matrix A\n");
  for(i=1;i<n+1;++i)
     for(j=1;j<m+1;++j)
        scanf("%d",&a[i][j]);
/* Printing Row total */
  for(i=1;i<n+1;++i)
  {
     a[i][m+1] = 0;
     for(j = 1;j<m+1;++j)
     {
        a[i][m+1] = a[i][m+1] + a[i][j];
     }
  }
/* Printing Column total */
  for(j = 1;j<m+1;++j)
  {
     a[n+1][j] = 0;
     for(i=1;i<n+1;++i)
     {
        a[n+1][j] = a[n+1][j] + a[i][j];
     }
  }
  for(i=1;i<n+1;++i)
  {
     for(j=1;j<m+2;++j)
     printf("%5d",a[i][j]);
     printf("\n");
  }
  i = n +1;
  for(j = 1;j<m+1;++j)
  printf("%5d",a[i][j]);
  printf("\n");
  return 0;
}
```

Q. No. 3

a. Write a program to input a string and the search character. If the character is found then it should display message "Character is found" otherwise it displays "Character is not found".

b. Write a program to read a string and print how many words are stored in the string.

c. Write a program to print encrypted character (i.e some other character in place of the character that is inputted).

Ans to Q.3(a)

```
/* Program for Question No 3(a) */
#include<stdio.h>
#include<conio.h>
main()
   {
   int i, f;
   char s[10], c;
   printf("\n Enter the string  ");
   scanf("%s", &s);
    printf("\n Enter the character to be searched: ");
   fflush(stdin); /* the fflush() function empties
         the buffer associated with specified stream.*/
   scanf("%c", &c);
   for(i=0; s[i] != '\0'; i++)
      {   if (s[i] ==  c)
        {
         printf("Character is found");
         f = 0;
         break;
         }
       else
        f = 1;
       }
          if (f==1)
         {
        printf("Character not found");
         }
        getch();
        return 0;
   }
```

Ans to Q.3(b)

```
/* Program for Question No. 3(b) */
#include<stdio.h>
main()
{
   char strg[80];
   int words = 1;
   int i;
   puts("Enter a string (max. 79 character)");
   gets(strg);
   for(i=0; strg[i] != '\0'; i++)
   {
   if(strg[i] == ' ')
   words++;
   }
   printf("The no. of words are  %d  ", words);
   printf("\n");
   return 0;
}
```

Ans to Q.3(c)

```
/* Program for Question No. 3(c) */
#include<stdio.h>
main()
{
  char string [80], i = 0;
  printf("Enter String: ");
  gets(string);
  while (string[i])
  {
     printf("Encrypted Character");
     putchar(255 - string[i]);
     printf("Original Character");
     putchar(string[i]);
     i++;
  } return 0;
}
```

Q. No. 4 Write a program which prints the number of vowels in the word, entered from the keyboard.

Ans to Q. 4

```
/* Program for Question No. 4 to print number of vowels */
#include<stdio.h>
main()
{
  int i,v = 0;
  char word[30];
  printf("\n Please enter a word\n");
  scanf("%s", word);
  i = 0;
  while (i < 30 && word[i] != '\0')
  {
     switch(word[i])
     {
        case 'a': case 'A':
        case 'e': case 'E':
        case 'i': case 'I':
        case 'o': case 'O':
        case 'u': case 'U':
        v++;
        break;
     }
     i++;
     }
  printf("\n Number of vowels = %d\n", v);
  return 0;
}
```

Q. No. 5

a. Write a program to read a string of words and then it prints out, each word in the reverse order.
For example if the input string is:
Computer Science
Then the output should be shown as:
ecneicS retupmoC

b. Write a program to read a string of characters of the maximum size of 25 characters and then it finds the total number of words in the string.

Ans to Q. 5(a)

```
/* Program for Question No. 5(a) */
#include<stdio.h>
#include<string.h>
main()
{
  char st[255],c;
  int i,n;
/*Accept a string*/
  printf("Enter a string :");
  gets(st);
/*Find the length of a string*/
  n = strlen(st);
/*Printing the string in reverse order*/
  for(i=n-1;i>=0;i--)
    printf("%c",st[i]);
    return 0;
 }
```

Ans to Q. 5(b)

```
/* Program for Question No. 5(b) */
 #include<stdio.h>
 main()
 {
    char line[80],ch;
    int i,words;
    i=words=0;
    printf("\nEnter line of string: \n");
    gets(line);
    printf("%s",line);
    while((ch=(line[i++])) != '\0')
    {
      if (ch == ' ')
      ++words;
    }
    ++words;
    printf("\n\nTotal number of words = %d\n",words);
    return 0;
}
```

EXERCISE

Multiple Choice

1. Elements of an array are accessed by-
   a. accessing function in built-in data structure
   b. mathematical function
   c. index
   d. None of these.
2. Array is-
   a. linear data structure
   b. non-linear data structure
   c. complex data structure
   d. None of these.
3. Row-major order in two dimensional array refers to-
   a. all elements of a row are stored in memory in sequence followed by next row in sequence and so on
   b. all elements of a row are stored in memory in sequence followed by next column in sequence and so on
   c. all elements of a column are stored in memory in sequence followed by next column in sequence and so on
   d. None of these.
4. A data structure, in which an element is added and removed only from one end, is known as-
   a. queue
   b. stack
   c. array
   d. None of these.
5. String concatenation means:
   a. combining two strings
   b. extracting a substring out of a string
   c. partitioning a string into two strings
   d. None of these.
6. A sparse matrix is better represented using a/an:
   a. array
   b. binary tree
   c. multi-linked list
   d. stack.
7. Row major ordering of a rectangular array means:
   a. columns are stored before rows
   b. rows are stored in a sequence starting from the first element
   c. greatest element of each row is stored first in memory
   d. None of the above.
8. A is an array of size $m \times n$, stored in the row major order. If the address of the first element in the array is M, the address of the element A(i,j) (A(0,0) is the first element of the array and each element occupies one location in memory) is

a. M + (i-j)*m + j-1
b. M + i*m + j
c. M + (j-1)*m + i-1
d. M + (i-1)*n + j-1

9. Array is a collection of

a. identical data objects
b. different data object
c. Both a and b
d. None of these.

10. When one dimensional character array of unspecified length is assigned an initial value, then

a. an arbitrary character is automatically added to the end of the string
b. '\0' is added at the end of the string
c. length of the string is added to the end of the string
d. None of the above

Key to Multiple Choice Questions

1.	c	2.	a	3.	a	4.	b	5.	a
6.	c	7.	b	8.	d	9.	a	10.	b

TEST PAPER

Note: Answer all questions.

1. Define arrays. Explain how they simplify programming with suitable examples.
2. Discuss in detail the implementation of two dimension arrays in memory.
3. Discuss the use of arrays and how they initialized at the time of declaration?
4. In what way does an array differ from an ordinary variable?
5. What do you mean by subscripts? How they are written?
6. What is pointers? why we use pointers?
7. Differentiate between malloc() and calloc().

CHAPTER 4

Linked Lists

4.1 INTRODUCTION TO LINKED LISTS

We are all familiar with the dynamics of waiting in a long queue. When some one cuts into the middle of the queue, then everyone behind that person has to move back. When someone in the middle of the line decides to leave the line, the reverse effect occurs; everyone behind the departed person has to move ahead one slot. It is possible to draw an analogy between people waiting in a line and data items stored next to each other in computer memory. If the data items are arranged in some type of order and it becomes necessary to insert into or delete from the middle, a considerable amount of data movement is involved. This data movement would require computer time and thus decrease efficiency. So, the linked list data structure is used to eliminate the movement of data items if a new data item is inserted or deleted from the middle of a list.

A linked list is an ordered list of data items. Typical examples of ordered lists are alphabetical lists of names in a telephone directory, a master payroll file containing information about employees in ascending order of Employee_code etc. Although using arrays, small ordered lists can be implemented with ease but maintenance of longer ordered lists in this type of contiguous storage structure becomes complex. It is so because of the number of data items that must be moved for each operation for additions or deletions. For example if, in a large company, the master list of employees arranged in ascending order of Employee_code is updated frequently by insertions and deletions, then the array data structure would take lot of time to update.

☞ *A linked list is a structure that minimizes data movement for insertions and deletions in an ordered list.*

A *link list* is a collection of records of the same data type, and all such records are connected through pointers (a variable which holds a memory address). Each record in a linked list has a *pointer* field pointing to the next record in the list. The pointer field in the last record of the list is assigned the null[1] value. A pointer variable is used to point to the first record in the list. The pointer system in the linked list structure eliminates the need for complete movement of data in memory. Thus, insertions, deletions of data items in the list takes lesser time than in the case of an array.

☞ *A linked list maintains data items in logical order rather than in a physical order.*

---

[1] A value that can be assigned to a pointer variable but the variable is empty, is called *null*.

☞ *A linked list is the chain of nodes or data items connected by pointers and each node contains a pointer pointing to the address of next node or data item.*

Diagrammatic representation of a linked list is shown in Figure 4.1.

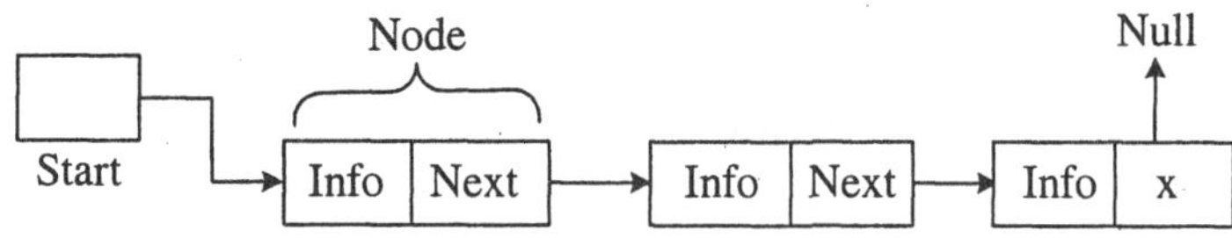

Figure 4.1 Diagrammatic representation of a linked list

The linked list contains a pointer variable called *Start*, which contains the address of the first node in the list. Each node has two parts, an *Info* part and a *Next* pointer. The *Info* part contains information which may be an integer, a character, a string etc., and *Next* contains the information for pointer to which it points to the next node. Pointer contains the address of the next node in the list. If *Next* has the value null(x), then it is the last record. This only tells us that we have reached the end of the list. An Example of linked list is given below.

Suppose a hospital ward contains twelve beds, out of which six are occupied as shown in Figure 4.2(a). This figure gives the Bed number, name of the patients and pointers. The pointer gives the bed number of the patient whose name will follow alphabetically. The "FIRST NAME" is a variable that stores the address (bed number) of the first patient in the list.

Here, you should note that you need the address of the first record only, in order to follow your way through the entire list. A special 'x' character is used as the Null pointer of the last record in the list.

In Figure 4.2(a) the variable 'FIRST NAME' contains the address of bed no. 6. This is linked to 5 where the patient's name KUMAR alphabetically follows the name of GYAN in the list. Pointer for bed no. 3 is occupied by MOHAN whose name is alphabetically followed by that of KUMAR.

In case, a new patient named AJAY comes and occupies bed no. 9, then the linked list will be modified and it will look as shown in Figure 4.2(b).

Here AJAY is the first name alphabetically, therefore the variable FIRST NAME will get a value 9 and the pointers will change as shown in Figure 4.2(b). The sign 'x' represents the end of the list. Similarly the empty beds list is linked by the pointers pointing to 8, 9, 10, 11 and 12 bed numbers in Figure 4.2(b).

The empty beds list is started by the variable named FIRST EMPTY and links to empty beds by pointers pointing to 7, 8, 10, 11, 12 in Figure 4.2(b). The sign x represents the end of the lists.

FIRST NAME = 6		
FIRST EMPTY = 7		
Bed Number	**Name of Patient occupying the Bed**	**Pointer to next Bed**
1	RAM	2
2	SHYAM	x
3	MOHAN	4
4	RAGHU	1
5	KUMAR	3
6	GYAN	5
7		8
8		9
9		10
10		11
11		12
12		x

Figure 4.2(a) Initial linked list

FIRST NAME = 9		
FIRST EMPTY = 7		
Bed Number	**Name of Patient occupying the Bed**	**Pointer to next Bed**
1	RAM	2
2	SHYAM	x
3	MOHAN	4
4	RAGHU	1
5	KUMAR	3
6	GYAN	5
7		8
8		10
9	AJAY	6
10		11
11		12
12		x

Figure 4.2(b) Modified linked list after patient AJAY occupied bed 9

The following program segment illustrates the linear linked list in the programming language 'C'.

```
struct node
  {
    int value;
    struct node *next;
  };
struct node *a, *b, *c;
  a → value = 2;
  b → value = 3;
```

```
c → value = 4;
a → next = b;
b → next = c;
c → next = null;
```

The above program segment can be represented in a linked list structure as seen in Figure 4.3.

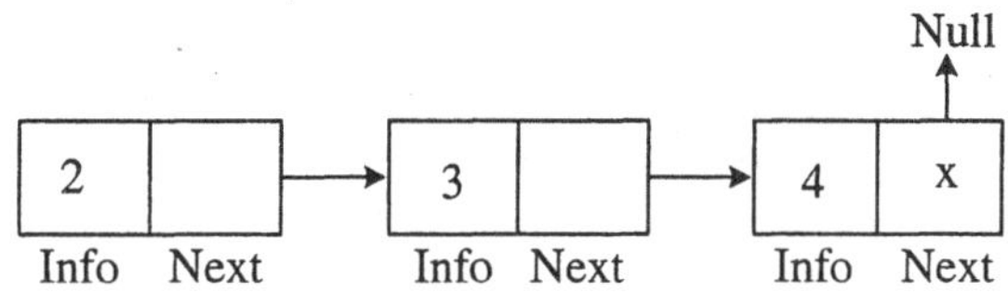

Figure 4.3 Pictorial representation of linked list

4.2 REPRESENTATION OF LINKED LISTS IN COMPUTER MEMORY

Let LIST be a linked list. First of all LIST will need two linear arrays. These are named as INFO and LINK arrays.

INFO[K] and LINK[K] contain the information part and the next pointer field respectively.

LIST will also require a variable name such as START - which contains the location of the beginning of the list, and a Next point sentinel - denoted by a NULL - which indicates the end of the list. The NULL will be chosen as '0' or 'x' as shown in Figure 4.4.

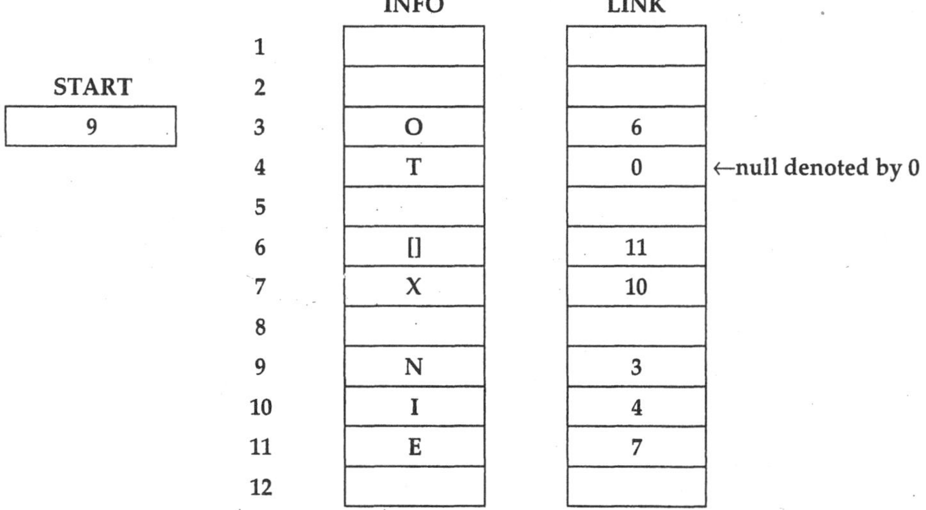

Figure 4.4 Linked list in memory

The linked list indicates that the nodes of a list need not occupy adjacent elements in the array INFO and LINK , and that more than one list may be maintained in the same linear array INFO and LINK. However, each list must have its own pointer variable giving the location of its first node.

Figure 4.4 shows linked list where each node of the list contains a single character. We can obtain the actual list of characters, or, in other words, the string, as follows.
START = 9, so INFO [9] = N is the first character
LINK [9] = 3, so INFO [3] = O is the second character
LINK [3] = 6, so INFO [6] = (blank) is the third character
LINK [6] = 11, so INFO [11] = E is the fourth character
LINK [11] = 7, so INFO [7] = X is the fifth character
LINK [7] = 10, so INFO [10] = I is the sixth character
LINK [10] = 4, so INFO [4] = T is the seventh character.
LINK [4] = 0, is the Null value, so the list has ended.
In other words NO EXIT **is the character string stored in the linked list.**

In Figure 4.5, START has a value 5. We can trace the alphabetic list of patients by traversing through the linked list containing Bed Number, Patient and the Next pointer. Start and Avail are the variables containing the bed numbers of the patients. Start contains the bed number occupied by the first patient in the alphabetic order. Avail is the first empty bed. 'x' symbol indicate Null pointers. Also the first available bed is 6. We can also trace the list of empty beds (Avail List).

Start: 5 → Bed 5
Avail: 6 → Bed 6

Bed Number	Patient	Next
1	Kanti	7
2	Abhay	5
3	Dev	11
4	Mohan	12
5	Ajay	3
6		10
7	Lal Singh	4
8	Gyan	1
9	Suresh	x
10		x
11	Fateh Singh	8
12	Narendra	9

Figure 4.5 Physical representation of linked list

4.2.1 Advantages and Disadvantages of Linked List

Advantages of linked list

a. It is not necessary to know in advance the number of elements to be stored in the list and therefore, need not allocate memory beforehand. Memory can be allocated as and when necessary. i.e. it facilitates dynamic memory allocation. By this technique memory is allocated and released to the system during the execution of a program (at run time) rather than fixed in advance. The mechanism to allocate memory dynamically is provided by the standard 'C' library function *malloc()*.

b. In a linked list, insertions and deletions can be handled efficiently without fixing the size of the memory in advance.

c. An important advantage of linked lists over arrays is that the linked list uses exactly as much memory as it needs, and can be made to expand to fill all available memory locations if needed. The size of an array is fixed when it is created.

Disadvantages

Disadvantages of linked list are:

a. The traversal is sequential i.e to reach at node 7, it is required to first traverse node 1 to 6. Therefore it does not support random access.

b. Increased overhead for storing pointers for linking the data items.

4.3 TYPES OF LINKED LIST

There are three types of linked lists.

(a) Singly linked list

(b) Doubly linked list

(c) Circular linked list

4.3.1 Singly Linked List

In this type of linked list, each node contains two fields i.e. data and a link pointing to the next node in the list (See Figure 4.6(a)). Consider singly linked list representation, seen in Figure 5.6(a).

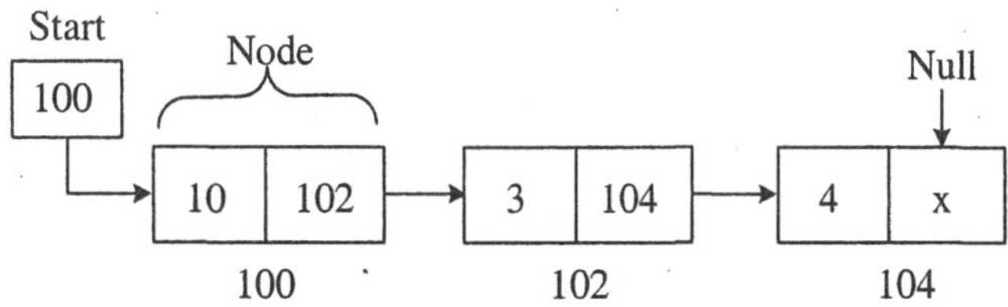

Figure 4.6(a) Singly linked list

The first node in the list is pointed by a Start pointer. The last node in the list has a link pointer field containing a x or Null, indicating "end of list". 10, 3, and 4 are the data items and the links are represented by arrows. The Item and the link pointer combined together are called *node*.

4.3.2 Doubly Linked List

In this type of linked list, each node contains data and two links, one link pointing to the previous node and one link pointing to the next node (See Figure 4.6(b)). Suppose we are in the middle of a linked list and we want to do some operation with the previous node, then we have no way to go to pervious node. It means, we will again traverse from starting node. So, this is a drawback of singly linked list. However, doubly linked list can be traversed forward as well as backward.

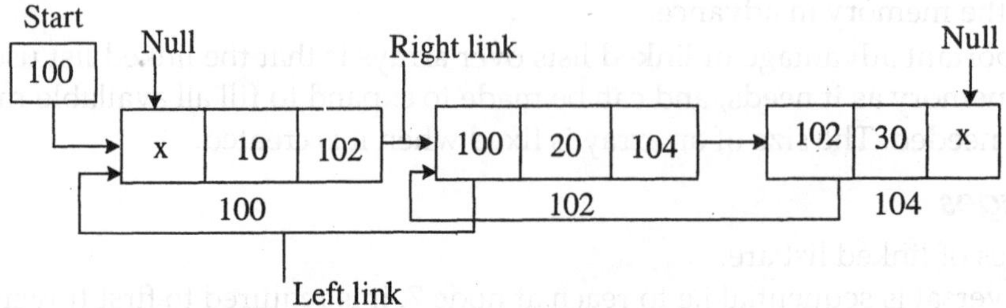

Figure 4.6(b) Doubly linked list

In the doubly linked list shown in Figure 4.6(b), 10, 20, 30 are the values of the data fields and the links are represented by forward arrows or arrows in the reverse direction. In each node, there are two links, one representing the address of the previous item and the other that of the next item. Null i.e.(x) represents the Null pointer. In doubly linked list, two Null pointers (x) are maintained. When traversing the list from left to right, it identifies the end of the list when *node → next* is Null. Likewise, when traversing the list from right to left, the end of the list is indicated when *node → previous* is Null.

The structure node in 'C' language for doubly linked list will be as:

```
struct node
  {
      struct node *prev;
      int info;
      struct node *next;
  }
```

Here *struct node *prev* is a pointer to pointing to previous node and it will contain the address of previous node and **next* will contain the address of next node in the list. So we can traverse in both directions forward as well as backward at any time.

Sometimes, it may be advantageous to keep an extra node in the front of the list. This node does not represent an item in the list but may contain some global information about an entire list. For example, number of nodes in the list. Such a node is called a header node. A doubly linked list may be either linear or circular and it may or may not contain a header node.

In doubly linked list, the cost of an extra link, adds to the space requirement and thus doubles the cost for insertions and deletions because there are no more pointers to fix. On the other hand, it simplifies deletions, because you do not have to refer to a key using a pointer to the previous cell.

4.3.3 Circular Linked List

One of the short comings of a linear singly linked list is that having reached to the last node in the list, we cannot go back to the previous node unless the address is available. Also to reach the first node after reaching the end, there will be a need to traverse the whole list backward if pointers are available. Suppose we make a small change in the structure of a list so that the next address field of the last node in the list is not null, but it is the address of the first node of the list. Then we have a *circular* list (See Figure 4.6(c)). In such a structure, we can reach any node from any other node in the list by moving from one end to other end.

☞ *Circular linked lists are the linked lists which are obtained by linking the last node of the linked list to the first node of the list as seen in Figure 4.6(c).*

In a circular linked list, the last node does not contain the NULL pointer. Instead it contains the pointer of the first node.

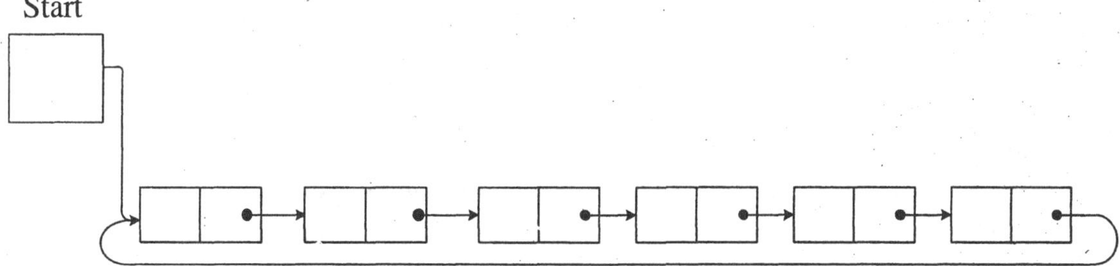

Figure 4.6(c) Circular linked list

Advantages Circular Linked List

Circular linked list has following advantages:

a. Each node in a circular list can be accessed from any node. It means that the circular list can be traversed starting from any node.

b. While deleting a particular node, we just need the address of the node prior to the node to be deleted. So, we have to first traverse through out the linked list to reach to this address and then delete the node next to this address. But in a circular list, we can reach directly to this address and hence reduce the effect of traversing from the begining.

Disadvantages of Circular Linked List

a. In a circular linked list, an infinite loop may be caused while traversing it. It can occur specially when care is not taken to detect the end of the circular list.

b. One way of avoiding the infinite loop condition is to place a header node at the beginning of a circular linked list. This header node does not contain any information. It only contains the address of the next node. Figure 4.7 illustrates this. In circular header linked list, the last node points to the node at the beginning of the list.

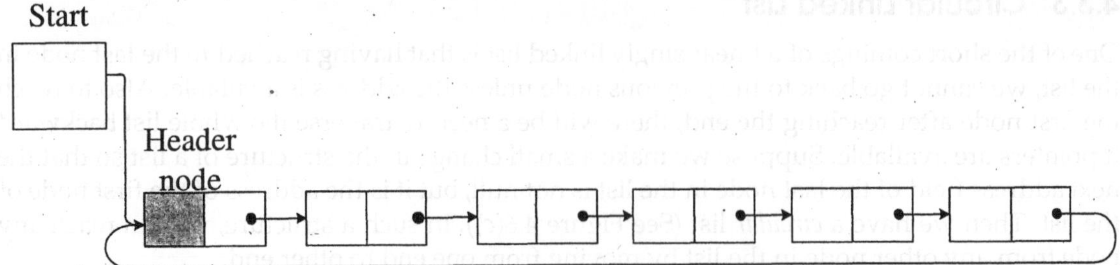

Figure 4.7 Circular header list

4.4 IMPLEMENTATION OF LINKED LIST

To implement a linked list following steps are carried out.

a. Allocate memory for storage during run-time, which is also known as dynamic allocation of memory. By this technique, memory is allocated and released to the system during the execution of a program (at run time) rather than being fixed when the program is compiled. The mechanism to allocate memory dynamically is provided by the standard function *malloc()* in 'C' programming language.

   The syntax of malloc() function is:

```
char * malloc   (unsigned size-of- memory-to-be-allocated)
```

   A program which uses this function must include the header file malloc.h.

b. Dividing the main memory into two parts i.e. data and link. The first part of node contains the data and the second part is a pointer (link) which contains the address of the next node.

c. Releasing the memory to operating system when it is not needed. Library function *free()* in 'C' language is used to return the memory space to the system, which is not needed for the program execution.

4.5 OPERATIONS PERFORMED ON LINKED LIST

Following operations can be performed on the linked list.

a. Creation of the linked list
b. Insertion of nodes
c. Traversal of the linked list
d. Search a specific node in the linked list
e. Deletion of a node in the linked list

4.5.1 Insertion of a Node in a Linked List

Insertion of a node in a linked list involves adding a new node to an existing linked list. You can add a node in the beginning, at the end or in the middle of the existing linked list.

Insertion of a node at the beginning of a linked list

To insert a node at the beginning of a linked list, (See Figure 4.8) do the following:

a. A pointer called *New* will be used to point to, i.e. store the address of the node which contains the *New* node to be inserted. This node is created by a function called *getnode()* which accepts the *New* data and stores it in the *Info* part of the node. The function also sets the pointer *Next* of the new node to Null.

b. The address at which the *New* node is inserted should be created as an arbitrary address.

If the New Info to be inserted at the beginning say A114, it would have to be positioned as shown in Figure 4.9. This Figure shows the linked list with the new node linked at the address 193. The dotted line represent the link to be established.

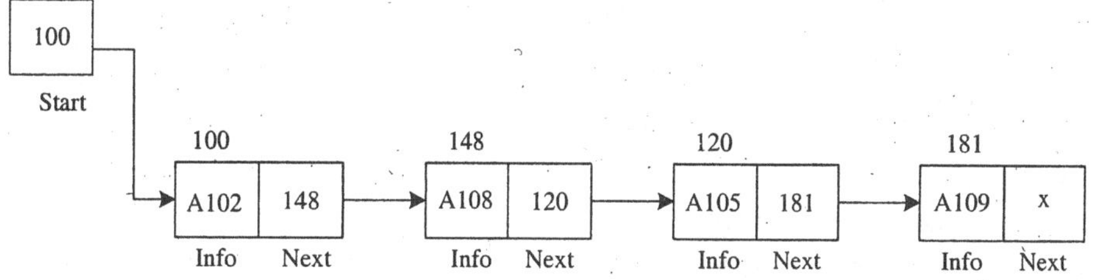

Figure 4.8 An existing linked list

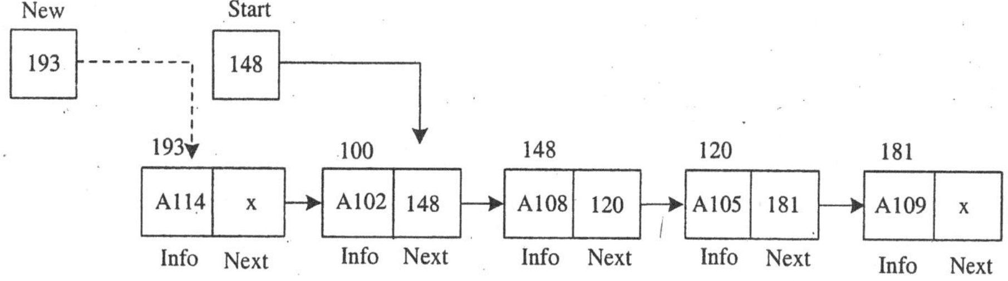

Figure 4.9 Inserting at the beginning of the linked list

In order to insert the new node at the beginning of the list, do the following:

a. New node is to be linked to the current first node in the list, i.e. its pointer Next would store the address of the first node (the address currently stored in Start).

This is done by the instruction:

```
New -> Next = Start;
```

b. Further, after the insertion of the new node at the beginning of the list, the address at the beginning of the list is no longer the same. As a result, Start would have to be updated so that it stores the address of the current first node (which is 193 instead of 100). (See Figure 4.10)

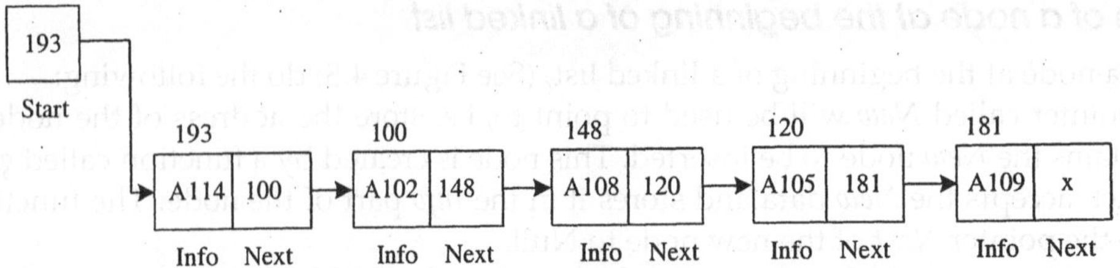

Figure 4.10 Linked list after insertion

This is done by the instruction:

```
Start = New;
```

Note that the insertion of new node is done only at the beginning of the list, i.e. node is not inserted in the middle of the list or in any particular position.

Suppose the linked list is not a sorted in any order and the new node is to be inserted in the linked list at any place. Then, the easiest place would be at the beginning of the linked list. The algorithm will be as follows:

```
INSERT (Start, data)
1.    Allocate memory to NEW
2.    Set New → Info = data
3.    New → Next = Start
4.    Start = New
5.    Return     Start
```

Explanation

New is a pointer which points to the node where the new node is to be inserted.

```
New → Info = data
```

Start points to the first element of linked list. For insertion at the beginning, we assign the value of start to the Next part of the inserted node as:

```
New → Next = Start
```

Now inserted node points to the next node which was before insertion the first node of the linked list. Now, after insertion the inserted node is the first node of the linked list.

So *Start* will be reassigned as

```
Start = New
```

Now *Start* will point to the inserted node which is first node of the linked list.

Insertion in the Middle of the list

Some times, we might want to insert a node at specific locations in a list. For example, if we want to create a linked list that contains the sorted names, and if a new name is to be inserted, it needs to be placed at proper position to maintain its sorted alphabetic order. To insert a node at a specific location in a list, the program will normally track the starting node, current node and the previous node. To achieve this, we scan the list from the beginning and move up to the desired node where we want to insert the new node. Here we create a new node and insert it into the list and restructure the complete list.

Let LIST be a linked list with successive Node A and Node B, as seen in Figure 4.11.

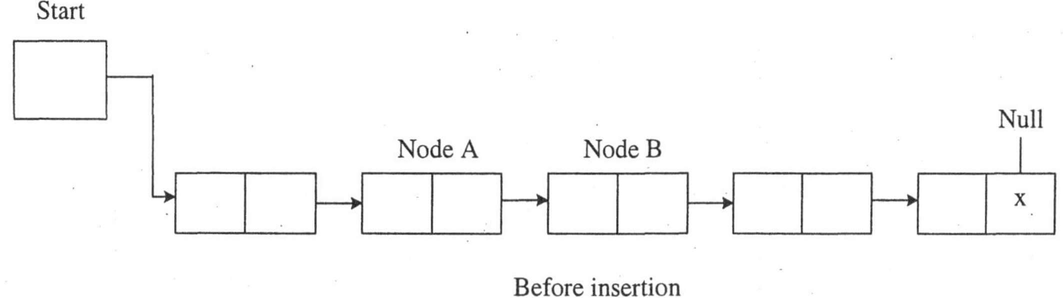

Figure 4.11 Linked list before insertion a node

Suppose a node N is to be inserted into the list between nodes A and B. The diagram with inserted node N is shown in Figure 4.12.

Here, we find that the Node A points to Node N, and Node N points to Node B, to which A was pointing previously.

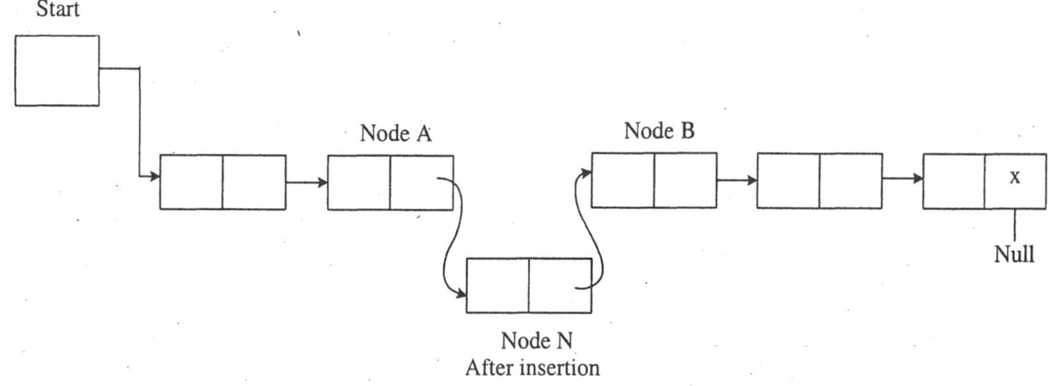

Figure 4.12 After insertion

Example 1

Consider the alphabetic list of patients in a ward as shown in Figure 4.13. Suppose patient HAMEED is admitted to the ward. You will observe the following:

a. HAMEED is put in bed 10, the first available bed.

b. HAMEED should be inserted into the list between GHANSHYAM and KRISHAN.

Observe that Bed[10] is the first available bed, Bed[2] is the next available bed, and bed[6] is the last available bed. Hence bed[6] has the null pointer in its next pointer field; that is, Link[6] = 0.

The three changes in the pointer fields are as follows:

1. LINK(8) = 10 [Now GHANSHYAM points to HAMEED]
2. LINK(10) = 1 [Now HAMEED points to KRISHAN]
3. AVAIL = 2 [Now AVAIL points to the next available bed]

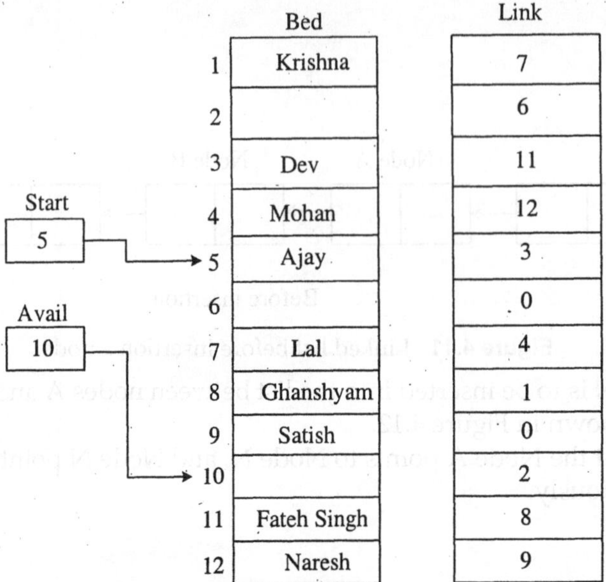

Figure 4.13 Linked list for insertion

The Algorithm for insertion of a node at specific location will be as follows:

```
INSERT (node_before, node_after, data)
1.    Allocate memory to New
2.    Set New → Info = data
3.    Set New → Next = node_after
4.    Set Node_before → Next = New
```

If the pointers to node_before and node_after are not available, then we need to traverse the linked list using Start to search the node_before for the insertion of New. After reaching at node_before following code will be used.

```
New → next = node_before → next
node_before → next = New
```

Insertion at the End of linked list

Insertion at the end means attaching a new node at the end of the linked list which means, adding with the last node. The implementation will be as follows:

1. Reach the last node by traversing the list from Start.
2. Link the last node with the New node containing data.
3. Set the pointer field of New to Null since, it has become the last node now.

The algorithm to insert the node at the end of the linked list is as follows:

```
1.    Allocate memory to New
2.    Set New → info = data
3.    Set New → next = Null
4.    Reach Nodelast
5.    Set Nodelast → next = New
```

Insertion in doubly linked list

Inserting a node into a doubly linked list, or deleting a node from it, is a much easier task because we do not have to search the list sequentially to locate the preceding node. For performing insertion operation in doubly linked list we need to perform the following steps:

1. Get a new node and set its fields.
2. If the linked list is empty, insert the node in the list and update the previous and the next pointers of the list.
3. If the node tobe inserted is at the front of the list, insert the node and update the previous pointer of the list.
4. Insert the node in the list at desired location.

☞ *To insert a node after a given node, we need to change four pointers rather than two pointers as in the case of singly linked list.*

4.5.2 Creation of a Linked List

Creation of a linked list is basically a special case of insertion, i.e. insertion into an empty list.

If the value of *Start* is equal to *Null*, it implies that *Start* does not store the address of any node. This means that there are no nodes in the list. Hence, the list does not exist and has to be created.

Creation of the list will involve creation of the first node in the list and this is done by:

a. Creating the *New* node.
b. Storing the address of the *New* node in *Start*.

Now that the list exists, *New* nodes can be inserted in it using the logic discussed for insertion.

☞ *Note that Start must be initialised to Null at the time of declaration, before the insertion function is invoked for the first time.*

A list can also be created in a sorted order. In this type of the list, the nodes are inserted based on the order of their Info (data). The nodes with smaller Info values precede the nodes with larger values of Info part of the node. This is known as a *sorted linked list*. (See Figure 4.14)

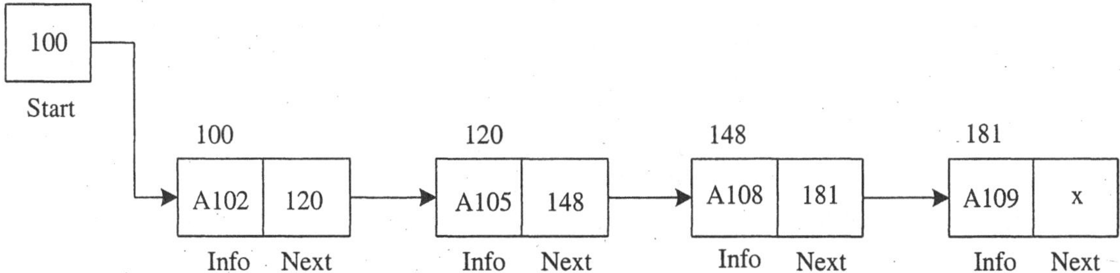

Figure 4.14 A Linked list sorted in the ascending order of Info values

Inserting a node in a sorted linked list between two nodes makes it necessary for us to know the addresses of the two nodes in order to establish the links between them and the new node to be inserted.

Hence assuming that the new Info is A107, we would need:

a. A pointer called (*Ptr*) positioned at the node with Info A108 to establish a link between the nodes with Info A107 and A108. The purpose of *Ptr* would be to point to the node before which the new node has to be inserted.

b. Another pointer (called *Prev*) positioned at the node with Info A105 to establish a link between the nodes with Info A105 and A107. The purpose of *Prev* would be to point to the node after which the *New* node has to be inserted.

This positioning can be achieved by advancing the pointer *Ptr* from the beginning of the list till it reaches the first node with Info greater than the *New* Info to be inserted. The pointer *Prev* is made to trail (follow) *Ptr* so that it points to the node just before the node that *Ptr* points to.

☞ *The nodes in the list are sorted logically with respect to the values stored in the Info in the nodes. The physical order of the nodes (address in memory) may not be in the sorted order since memory is allocated randomly and not contiguously.*

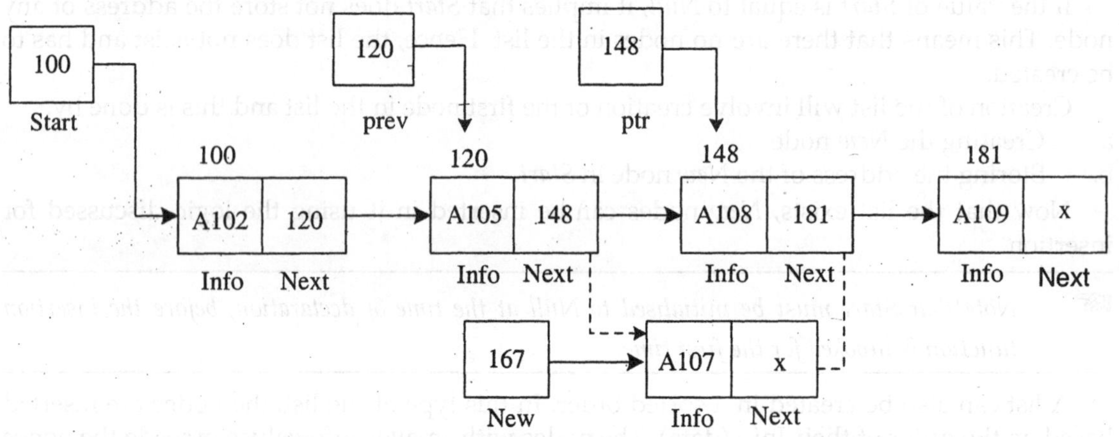

Figure 4.15 Inserting in the middle of a sorted linked list

Using the logic to insert a node in a sorted linked list, Figure 4.15 displays the list with *Prev* and *Ptr* positioned. It also shows the position at which the New node, which has info 167 will be inserted maintaining the sorted order of the list.

After positioning *Prev* and *Ptr*, all that is left is to link them up with New, which is done by:

```
prev->next = New;
New->next = ptr;
```

As a result, the final list with the new node inserted into the list will be as seen in Figure 4.16.

All other types of linked lists can be implemented in the same way. i.e.

Doubly linked list:

When the first node will be created both the pointer fields will be having Null and their values will change as the list will grow.

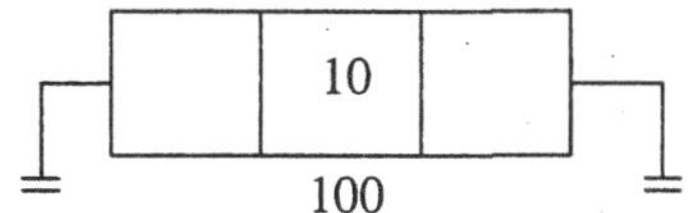

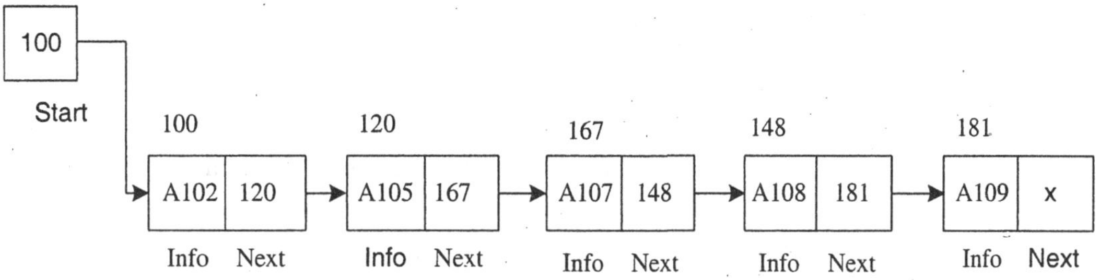

Figure 4.16 Sorted linked list after inserting a node in the middle of the list

Circular linked list:

The first node will be pointing to itself and as the linked list will grow, the last node will continue to point the Start node i.e. the first node.

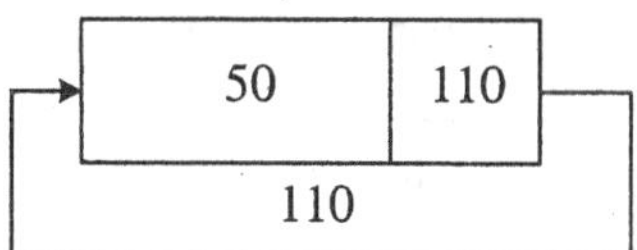

4.5.3 Traversal in a Linked List

Traversal of a linked list means to traverse each node of the list, and visiting each node exactly once. Assuming that we need to process the linked list and print the *Info* part of each node. Then, the logic for traversal would be:

1. Set *Ptr* to *Start*.
2. Repeat steps 3 and 4 until *Ptr* is not equal to Null.
3. Print the *Info* part of each node to which *Ptr* is pointing currently.
4. Advance the pointer *Ptr* so that it points to the next node.
5. End

The process can be depicted graphically as shown in Figure 4.17 and Figure 4.18.

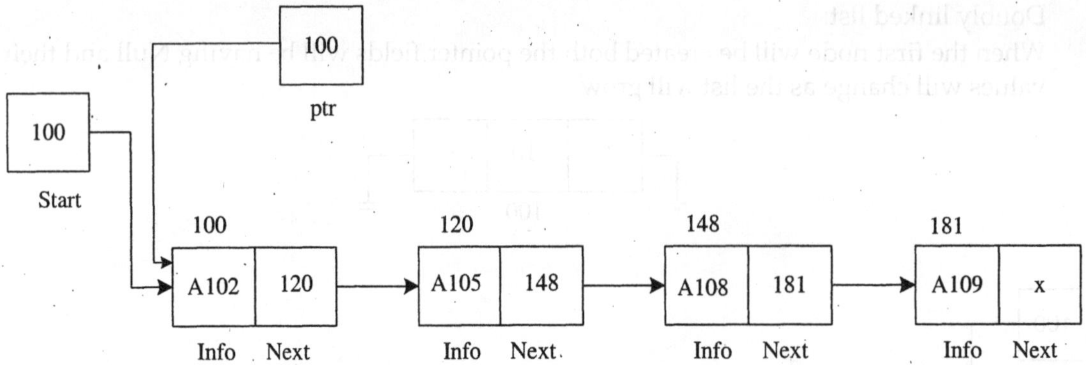

Figure 4.17 Initial values of Start and Ptr in Traversal algorithm

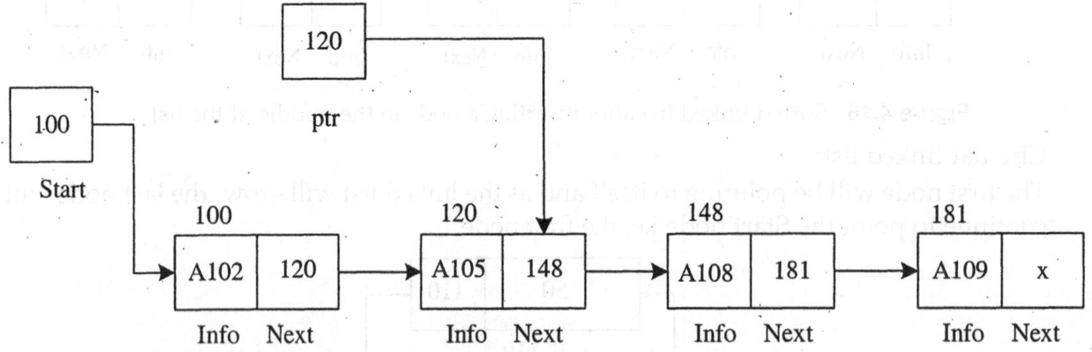

Figure 4.18 Values of Start and Ptr after execution of step 4 in traversal algorithm

The logic for traversal can easily be translated into the following 'C' Programming Language function named as traverse():

```
traverse()
{
    struct node *ptr;
    ptr = start; /* make ptr point to the beginning of the list */
    while (ptr)
    {
        printf("The current item is %s", ptr->item_no);
        ptr = ptr->next;
    }
}
```

Here *ptr* is a *pointer* variable and *start* is a pointer, which points to the first element of the linked list. Initially we assign the value of *start* to *ptr*. So that *ptr* points to the first element of the linked list. i.e.

```
ptr = start;
```

The condition:

```
while (ptr)
```

actually translates to:

(ptr is true)

which in 'C' language means:

```
(if ptr is non zero)
```

The values NULL and '\0' are treated as zero values.

Hence, the condition (ptr != NULL) can be written as (ptr).

For processing the next element we assign the address of next element to the *ptr* by the statement:

```
ptr = ptr → next
```

Now *ptr* has address of the next node to be processed. We can traverse each node of linked list using this assignment statement until *ptr* has Null value which means the of last node.

Example 2

Following procedure can be used to find the number of elements NUM in a linked list.

Algorithm

Count (Link, Start, Num)

1. Set Num := 0 [initialize the counter]
2. Set Ptr := Start (initialize the Pointer]
3. Repeat Steps 4 to 5 While Ptr != Null
4. Set Num := Num + 1 [increase Num by 1]
5. Set Ptr := Link [Ptr] [update pointer]
   [End of Step 3 loop]
6. Return.

Traversal in doubly Linked List

In a linear linked list structure, traversing is possible only in one direction. Some times it is required to traverse the list in any direction, forward or backward. This increases the performance and efficiency of algorithms. Traversing a doubly linked list means processing each and every node either in forward or backward directions or in both the directions i.e the program can traverse the list from left to right or right to left. Therefore, two Null pointers are maintained. The doubly linked list can be traversed as:

```
while (ptr != Null)
  ptr = ptr → next;
```

where *ptr* is a pointer variable, and *next* is the address of the node either in the forward direction or in the backward directions.

4.5.4 Searching in a Linked List

Searching means to locate a node in a linked list containing the desired value in the Info part of the node. Suppose we have a linked list and we have to search the element 72. Whether the element 72 is present in the given linked list or not and if it is present, then at which node location it is present.

For searching the element, we need to traverse the linked list and while traversing, we will compare the *info* part of each node with the desired value, which is say 72. The following steps are carried out to search in the linked list.

1. Set *Ptr* to *Start*.
2. Input the Info part of the Node (Item_No) to be searched.
3. While Ptr != Null do steps 4 and 5.
4. Compare the Item_No of the node to which *Ptr* is pointing out currently, with the given Item_No and, if they are the same, exit from loop and go to step 6. *else*
5. Set *Ptr* to the *Next* Node to which Ptr is pointing to, currently.
6. Report that the given Item_No exists in the list. In case, Ptr != Null (i.e. if the loop was exited from step 4) then search is successful. Else it does not exist in case Ptr = Null (i.e. if the loop was not exited from step 4, but stopped because there was no match).

Example 3

Consider a case where we are interested to find the code number of an employee (say XXX) in the linked list and give him 10% increase in salary. The procedure will be to search the node containing employee code xxx and then do the process of raising salary by 10% .

```
1.    Read XXX
2.    Call Search (Info,Link,Start,XXX,Loc)
3.    IF Loc != Null then
      Set Salary[Loc] := Salary[Loc] + 0.1 * Salary[Loc]
      Else
         Write XXX not in the file
      End if
      Return
```

Complete Algorithm will be as follows:

Increment (Info, Link, Start, Loc, XXX)

(List is the Linked List in the memory of the computer. This algorithm finds the location Loc of the node where employee code XXX first appears in the list or sets Loc = Null)

```
1.    Set Ptr := Start
2.    Repeat step 3 while Ptr != Null
3.    If XXX = Info[Ptr]
         Then set Loc := Ptr
              Set Salary[Loc] = Salary[Loc] + 0.1 * Salary[Loc]
              Else
              Set Ptr := Link[Ptr] (Pointer now points to the next node).
      End if
      End of Step 2 loop.
4.    (Search is unsuccessful) Set Loc = Null
5.    Exit.
```

4.5.5 Deletion of a Node from a Linked List

Deletion of a node is an important operation on a linked list.
Deletion of a node is carried out in two steps; viz.

a. Logical deletion of the node, which involves pointer shuffling in order to remove the links which attach it to the list, and
b. Physical deletion of the node by using the function *free()* to release the memory occupied by it.

The deletion operation is classified into following three categories.

- Deletion of first node of the linked list
- Deletion of desired node of the linked list
- Deletion of last node of the linked list

Deletion of First Node

If the node to be deleted is the first node in the linked list, then we are required to make the start equal to the next node address in place of the first node address of the list (See Figure 4.19). The dashed arrow (--->) in the Figure 4.19 shows that start should point to the next node (which is 102) in place of the first node (i.e. node 100) in the list.
For deletion of first node, steps involved are:

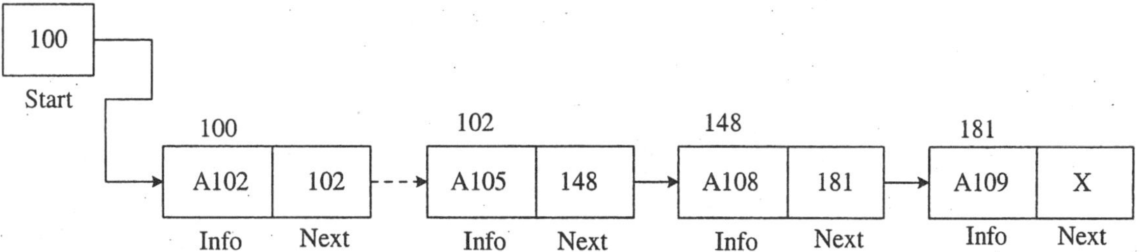

Figure 4.19 Linked list for deletion of node with item A105

1. Make value of Start pointer to be pointing to the second node in the linked list.
2. Free the space associated with first node.
3. Operating system collects the free space of the memory and use it with available free space.

So, the whole process for deletion of first element of the linked list will be as follows:

```
temp = start;
start = start → next;
free (temp);
```

Initially, *start* points to the first element of the linked list. Because the element to be deleted is the first element of the linked list, so we store the value of *start* to *temp* as given below:

```
temp = start;
```

Now *temp* points to the first node which has to be deleted. So, we assign the link (next) value of the node to Start as:

```
start = start → next;
```

Since *start* point to the first element of the linked list, but now, after the above step, start will point to the second element of the linked list. Now, we should free the memory occupied by the previous node, or the node deleted. This is done by the statement:

```
free(temp);
```

Deletion of desired Node from a Linked List

Let us assume that node containing item number A105 is to be deleted from the list. The links in the list would appear as seen in Figure 4.20. Here, the dotted arrows (--->) indicate the node containing the item A105. This is to be deleted.

This can be done by:

a. Traversing the list to find the *Info* in the node to be deleted. The search logic written earlier can be used to return a pointer to the node that is to be deleted. This pointer will be referred to *curr_ptr*.

b. In case the *Info* to be deleted exists in the list, its corresponding node will have to be removed from the list by connecting the previous node to the node after it. Hence a pointer to the node before the node being deleted, will have to be maintained. This pointer will be referred to as *prev*.

Therefore, if the node to be deleted is the node with Info A102, then the pointer to node 120 will now point to node 148. (See Figure 4.20)

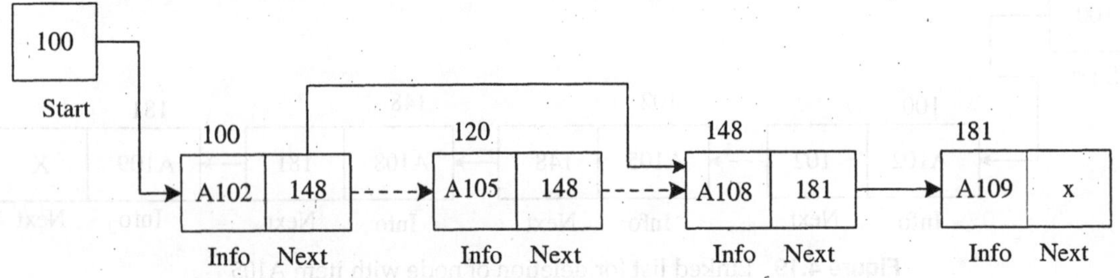

Figure 4.20 Linked list for deletion of node with item A105

With *prev* positioned at the node with Info A102 and *curr_ptr* positioned at the node with Info A105, we can write the instructions:

```
prev->next = curr_ptr->next;
```

Which will store the address of the node with Info A108 in the pointer Next of the node with Info A102. Thus, node with Info A105 will be deleted.

☞ *If the node with Info A102 is to be deleted, the address in Start will have to be changed to the address of the node next to node containing Info A102.*

An important point to note here is that it is not sufficient to delete a node logically. The node has to be deleted physically also. Although logical deletion cuts off the node from the list by breaking the links, the memory is still reserved for the node. Hence, it has to be released to the operating system for future use; thus avoiding clustering up of the memory with unnecessary data. Physical deletion is achieved by the function *free()*.

The syntax is as follows:

```
free(p);
```

where p is the pointer to the memory address to be freed.

Deletion of last node

To delete a node, we need to know the address of the previous node where its address is given in the pointer address. As deleting a node means changing the next pointer of the previous node to point to the node following the node which is to be deleted. If the the node to be deleted is the last node of a linked list, which means next of current node points to null. This node is deleted as follows:

```
tmp = q → next;
q → next = Null;
free (tmp);
```

Here *q* is pointing to the previous node of the node to be deleted. After first statement, *tmp* will point to the node to be deleted. After statement 2, link of previous node will point to Null. Operating system then collects the free space created by deletion of nodes and makes link for currently freed node with available free memory space.

Deletion from doubly linked list

For deleting the node from a doubly linked list, first we traverse the list and compare the current node to be deleted with each element. After finding the element there may be three possibilities.

1. Deletion at the beginning (left most node)
2. Deletion of last node (right most node)
3. Deletion of any desired node

For performing deletion in doubly linked list, we need to perform the following steps:

1. If the list is empty, display "underflow" message.
2. If a single node exists in the list, set both the pointers i.e left and right as Null. Else if the node to be deleted is the first (left most) node, then delete the node and update the left pointer to the value where the current node was pointing to.
3. Else if the node to be deleted is the last (right most) node, then delete the node and update the right pointer to the list. Else delete the node from the desired location from the list.
4. Restore the deleted node to the free list.

4.6 LINKED STACKS AND QUEUES

Figure 4.21 shows linked list representation of stacks and queues. In Figure 4.21(a), we can easily add a node at the *top* or delete a node from the *top* in the linked list representation stack. The operation of adding an element to the front is similar to that of pushing an element onto a stack. In such cases, a new item is added at the immediately accessible node. A stack can be accessed only through its *top* element, and a linked list can be accessed by using the pointer to its first element. Similarly, the operation of removing the first element from a linked list is analogous to popping a stack. In both cases, immediately accessible item is removed from that type of linked list representation. The next item becomes immediately accessible for further processing after deletion of first node. In Figure 4.21(b), we can add a node at the *rear* or deletion can be performed at the *front* because it is the linked list representation of a queue.

Linked list representation of queues are as easy to handle as are linked list representation of stacks. We need two pointers, *front* and *rear* that will point, respectively, to the beginning and the end of the queue. We can insert a new element at the end of the list after the last node which is pointed to by pointer *rear*.

We must take care when we insert an element into an empty queue. Becauase, in this case, we need to adjust the *front* pointer to be the new node. Whenever we remove an element from a queue, we must ensure that the queue is not empty.

If we are deleting the last node, we must make

```
q. rear = null
```

to indicate that the queue is now empty.

The advantage of using linked lists is that the stacks and queues of a program have access to the same free list of nodes. Nodes not used by one stack may be used by another, as long as the total number of nodes in use at any one time is not greater than the total number of nodes available.

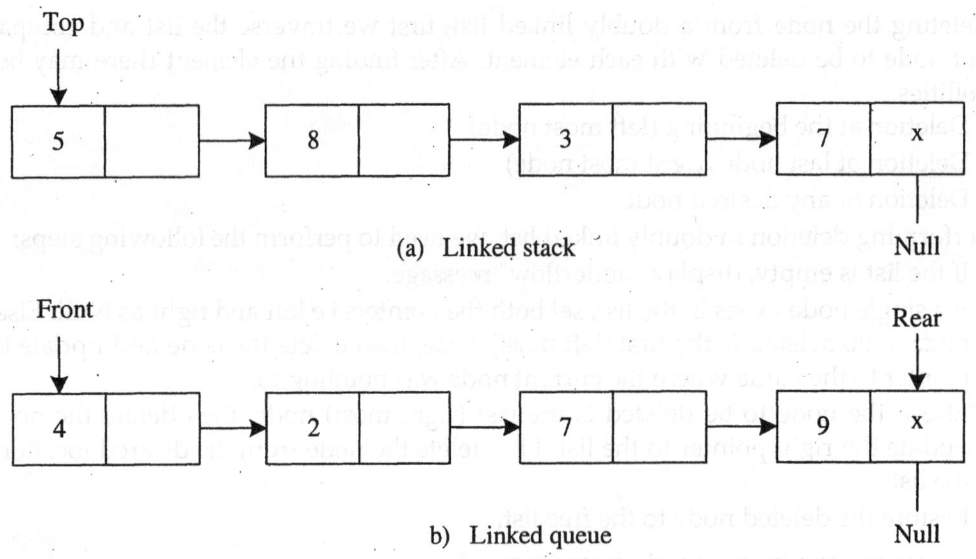

Figure 4.21 Linked stacks and queues

4.7 HEADER LINKED LIST

Header linked list is a linked list which always contains a special node called the header node. Header node is at the beginning of the list. Dummy node placed as the first node of a list is used to simplify linked list processing. It may or may not contain meaningful information. Header node does not represent an item in the list. The *Info* portion of such a header node might be unused (See Figure 4.22(a))

The *Info* portion of such a node could be used to keep global information about the entire list. For example Figure 4.22(b) Illustrates a list in which info portion of the header node contains the number of nodes (excluding the header) in the list. In such a case more work is needed to add or delete an item from the list, since the count in the header node must be adjusted. However, the number of items in the list may be obtained directly from the header node without traversing the entire list.

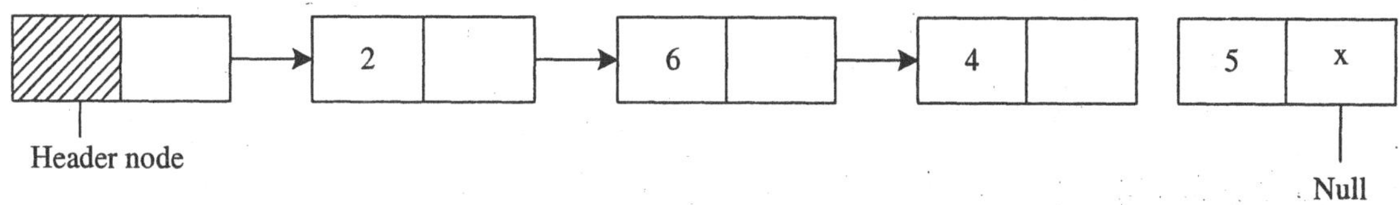

Figure 4.22(a) A Linked list with header node

☞ *The header for a linked list is a pointer variable that locates the beginning of the list.*

Figure 4.22(b) Header node stores information about number of nodes in a linked list

4.8 MANIPULATION OF POLYNOMIAL USING LINKED LIST

A *polynomial* contains series of terms and each term consists of a coefficient and an exponent. For example, let us take a polynomial expression:

$7x^4 + x^3 - 2x + 3$

The above polynomial contains two things namely, *coefficient* and *exponent*, where x is a formed parameter. As in the first term of the polynomial, $7x^4$, coefficient is 7 and exponent is 4.

Polynomials like $7x^4 + x^3 - 2x + 3$ can be represented using a linked list. To achieve this, each node would consist of three elements, namely the coefficient value, the exponent value and a link to the next term.

Let us take the polynomial expression $7x^4 + x^3 - 2x + 3$ and represent it in the following form:

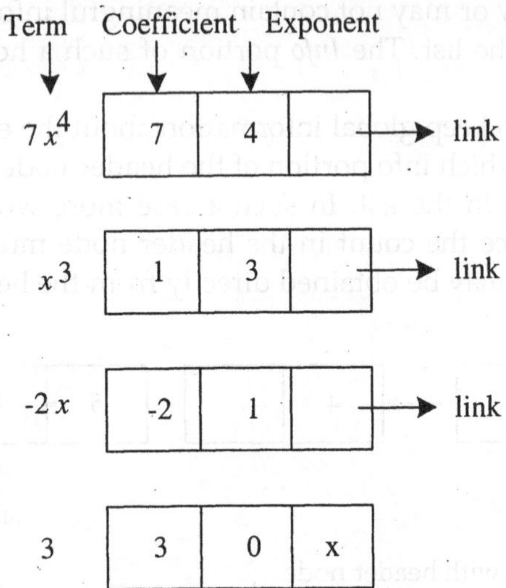

Here 3 is represented as $3x^0$ because $x^0 = 1$.

☞ *We will always store terms of the polynomial in descending order of powers of x. For example, $17x + 3x^2 + 5$ would be stored as $3x^2 + 17x + 5$. This order of power of x is maintained to achieve efficient processing of polynomial.*

We can represent polynomial expression using a single linked list where each node of list will contain the coefficient and exponent of each term of the polynomial expression. So the function for such a data structure for polynomial expression will be:

```
struct node
        {
            int coefficient;
            int exponent;
            struct node *link;
        }
```

To represent polynomial as linked list, we only need to record the co-efficient and exponent values for each term. So the polynomial would look like as shown in Figure 4.23.

☞ *For representing polynomial in memory, using linked list each node must contain three fields.*

After we build a linked list to represent a polynomial, we can use this linked list to perform common polynomial operations such as addition and multiplication etc.

4.8.1 Addition of Two Polynomials

To add two polynomials, we need to traverse the nodes in both the lists term by term. If we find terms with the same exponent in the two polynomials, then we add the coefficients and the result is stored in another third polynomial. If the exponents of two terms are not equal, then the term with larger exponent value is added to the resultant polynomial. When we reach at the end of one of the polynomials, then remaining part of the other polynomial is copied into the third polynomial.

☞ *Do not include terms with zero coefficient in the sum, of the two polynomials.*

Let us consider the addition of two polynomials $6x^4 + 3x^2 + 4x + 5$ and $3x^3 + 2x + 4$. We can visualize this as follows.

$$
\begin{array}{ccccccccc}
6x^4 & & & + & 3x^2 & + & 4x & + & 5 \\
 & + & 3x^3 & & & + & 2x & + & 4 \\
\hline
6x^4 & + & 3x^3 & + & 3x^2 & + & 6x & + & 9 \\
\hline
\end{array}
$$

Step by Step addition of two polynomials

1. Scan both the list i.e list 1 and list 2 one by one till the end of one of them is reached. While doing this traversal the polynomials are compared on term by term basis. i.e. compare the exponent of list 1 nodes with list 2 nodes.
   a. If the exponents of two terms are not equal. i.e if one node has bigger exponent than another node, then add the bigger exponent node in list 3 and scan the next node in bigger exponent node
2. Repeat the process till all the nodes of two the lists are exhausted.

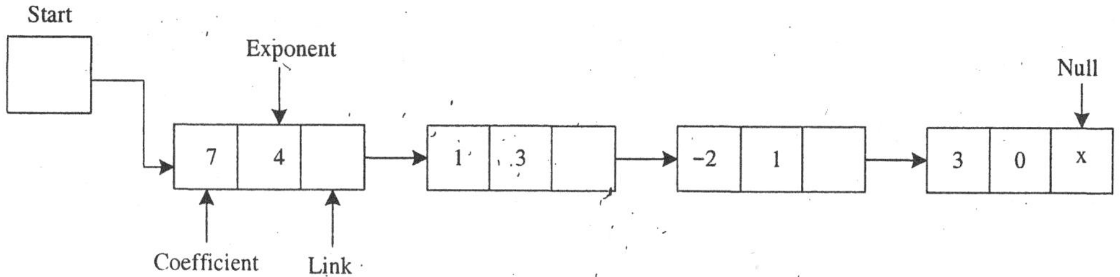

Figure 4.23 Polynomial representation using linked list

3. Add the remaining nodes of unfinished list in the list 3.

We shall take two polynomial expressions show them as linked lists. The resultant sum is represented as linked lists. The resultant sum is represented as linked list 3.

Poly 1: $6x^4 + 3x^2 + 4x + 5$

List 1 Start → | 6 | 4 | | → | 3 | 2 | | → | 4 | 1 | | → | 5 | 0 | x | Null

Poly 2: $3x^3 + 2x + 4$

List 2 Start → | 3 | 3 | | → | 2 | 1 | | → | 4 | 0 | |

As we scan the first node of the two polynomials. we find that the exponent value of first node of List 1 is greater than the exponent value of first node of List 2.

i.e 4 > 3

So we copy the exponent value of first node of the first polynomial into the exponent part of the List 3

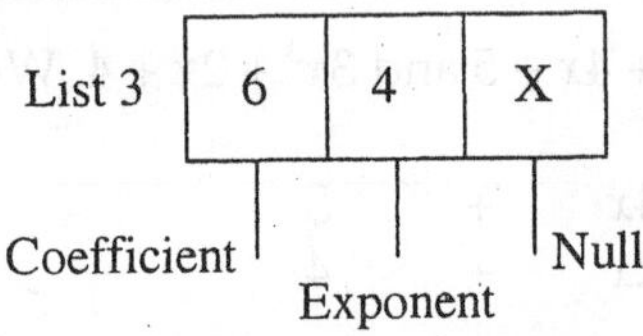

We now consider the second exponent value of first polynomial and the exponent value of the first node of second polynomial.

Compare the exponent values of current node (node 1) of list 2 with exponent value of second node of first polynomial.

i.e. 2 < 3

Hence we add the first node of List 2 into List 3 after the current node. Now List 3 becomes as seen below:

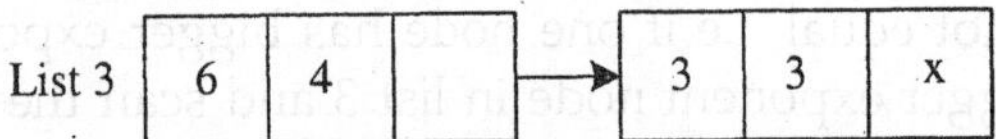

We carry on this comparisons further.

Consider the exponent value of the second node of the first polynomial and compare it with the exponent value of the second node of the second polynomial. Here again, we find 2 > 1.

So, we copy the second node of first polynomial into the List 3 as seen below.

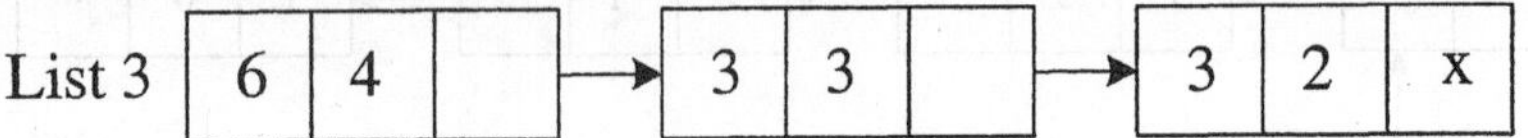

Compare the exponent value of third node in list 1, with the exponent value of current node (node 2) of List 2. We find both are equal i.e each is 1. Hence add their coefficients and copy the result in List 3, as shown below:

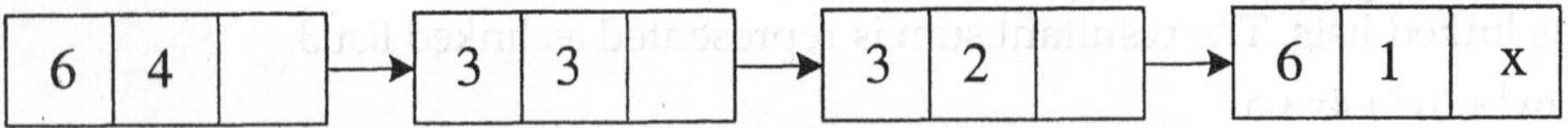

Once again, compare the value of the exponent of current node of List 1 (i.e node 4) with List 2 (node 3). We find both are equal and have value as zero. Hence we add their coefficient and copy the result in List 3.

Thus, final List 3 becomes:

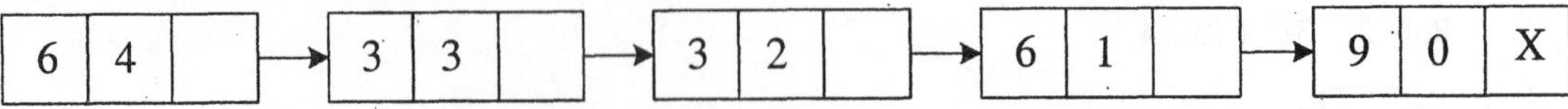

4.9 GARBAGE COLLECTION

Suppose, a part of memory space becomes reusable because a node of a list is deleted or complete list is deleted while processing in a program. We store such space into the free storage list. The operating system of a computer may periodically collect all the deleted memory space onto a free storage list. A technique which does this collection is called *garbage collection*.

Under this method, nodes thar are no longer in use will remain allocated and undetected till available storage has been allocated. A request made for allocation cannot be executed until nodes that were allocated but are no longer in use, are recovered. If a request is made for additional nodes and there are none available, a system routine calls the garbage collector module available in OS. This routine searches through all of the nodes in the system, identifies those that are no longer accessible from an external pointer, and restores such inaccessible nodes to the available pool of memory.

The request for additional nodes is thus fulfilled, with some of the reclaimed nodes. The system continues processing user's requests for more space. When available space is again used up, garbage collector routine is called once more.

Garbage collection usually takes place in two steps. In first step, called *marking phase*, it will sequentially visit all nodes in the memory and mark them which are used in the program. In second step, called *collection phase*, it will collect all unmarked nodes in memory which are allocated but not used in programs and place them in free storage area.

☞ The garbage collection may take place when there is only some minimum amount of space or no space at all left in the free storage list, or when the CPU is idle and has time to do the collection. The garbage collection is invisible to the programmer.

Compaction

Memory management system uses the concept called compaction, which collects all free space blocks and places them at one location as a single free block. Any request for memory allocation will be made from this free block. Memory management system uses some technique for purpose. Following methods for assigning memory are available:

- First Fit method
- Best Fit method
- Worst Fit method

In *First fit* method of memory allocation, the first entry, which has free block equal to or more than required, is allocated. For example

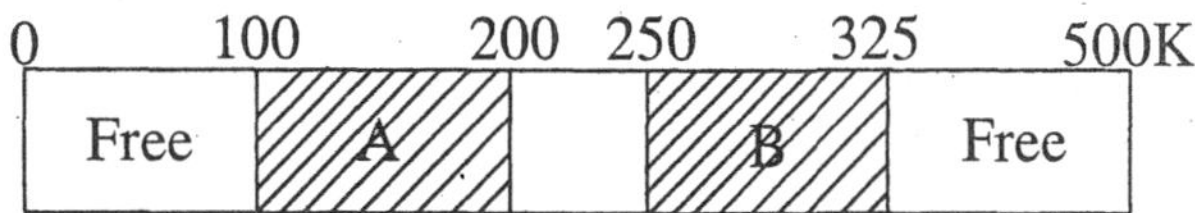

To allocate memory for process C, which require size of 25K in first fit method will be:

0	25	100	200	250	325	500K
C		A		B	Free	

As seen in the figure, above process C is assigned to the first free block of memory. The required size of memory is enough to be allocate for process C.

In *best fit* method of memory allocation, the entry which is smallest, amongst all the entries which are equal or bigger than the required one is chosen. For example, to allocate memory for process C, which require size of 25K in best fit will be as shown below.

0	100	200	225	250	325	500K
Free	A	C	Free	B	Free	

As seen in the figure above, process C is assigned to the smallest free block which is enough to fulfill the request of process C.

In *worst fit* method, the system always allocates a portion of the largest free block in memory. For example, to allocate memory for process C, which requires memory size of 25K in worst fit case will be as shown below:

0	100	200	250	325	350	500K
Free	A	Free	B	C	Free	

As seen in the figure above, process C is assigned memory from the largest available free block.

The reason for choosing a method over the other is dependent on the efficiency of the OS. In each of the methods, the search can be made more efficiently. For example, a true first-fit method, which allocates the block at the lowest memory address first, will be very efficient if the available list is maintained in the order of increasing memory address. On the other hand, if the available list is maintained in the order of increasing size, the best fit search for a block will become more efficient. Finally, if the list is maintained in the order of decreasing size, the worst fit request will require no searching, as the largest size block is always the first available memory on the list.

4.10 GENERALIZED LISTS

We can write the list A as: A = (α_0 .... α_{n-1}) Here A is the name of the list, (α_0 .... α_{n-1}) and n is the length of the list. By convention, all list names are represented by capital letters and atoms are represented by lowercase letters. If ($n \geq 1$), then α_0 is the head of A, and (α_0 .... α_{n-1}) is the tail of A.

Generalized list A is a finite sequence of $n \geq 0$ elements, α_0 .... α_{n-1} where α_1 is either an atom or a list. The elements α_i, $0 \leq i \leq n-1$, that are not atoms are said to be the sublists of A.

Some *examples* of generalized lists are:

1. D = () : the null, or empty list, its length is zero.
2. A = (a (b, c)) : a list of length 2, its first element is the linear list (b, c)

3. B = (A, A, ()) : a list of length three whose first two elements are the list A, and the third element is the null list.
4. C = (a, c) a recursive list of length two, c corresponds to the infinite list c = (a, (a, (a, ...)))

The important consequences of our definition for a list are:

1. List may be shared by other lists as in example 3, where list A makes up two of the sublists of B
2. Lists may be recursive as in example 4.

DESCRIPTIVE QUESTIONS

Q. No. 1 Write a program in 'C', to build a linked list by adding new nodes (a) at the beginning, (b) at the end (c) in the middle of the linked list. Also write a function display() which display all the nodes present in the linked list.

Ans to Q.1 Program to Q1.

```
/* Building a linked list*/
#include <stdio.h>
#include <malloc.h>

/* structure definition */
struct linklist
{
   int item;
   struct linklist *link;
};
struct linklist *p;
main()
{
   p = NULL; /* Last node link is always NULL */
   clrscr();

   /* Function to add the item to the beginning of the
                       linklist*/
   add (10);
   add (20);
   add (30);
   add (40);
   printf("Items added at the begining of the list:\n");

/* Function to display all the items in the linklist */
   display();
   printf("Press any key....");
   getch();
```

(Contd...)

```
/* Function to add item at the end of the linklist */
   printf ("\n\nItem added at the end of list:\n");
   add_end (50);
   display();
   printf("Press any key...");
   getch ();
/* Function to add item at a given location */
   printf ("\n\nItem added in the middle of the list:\n");
   add_item_at_loca (60, 4);
   display();
   printf("Press any key...");
   getch();
}
add_item_at_loca (int item, int loca)
{
   struct linklist *q = (struct linklist*) malloc (sizeof
                              (struct linklist));
   struct linklist *r, *w = p;
   int i = 1;
   q -> item = item;
   q -> link = NULL;
   if (p == NULL)
     p = q;
   else
   {
     while ((w -> link != NULL) && (i != loca))
     {
       i++;
       w = w -> link;
     }
     if(i == loca)
     {
       r = w -> link;
       w -> link = q;
       q -> link = r;
     }
     else
       w -> link = q;
   }
}
```

(Contd...)

```
add_end (int item)
{
    struct linklist *q = (struct linklist.*) malloc (sizeof
                     (struct linklist));
    struct linklist *w = p;
    q -> item = item;
    q -> link = NULL;
    if (p == NULL)
        p = q;
    else
    {
        while (w -> link != NULL)
            w = w -> link;
        w -> link = q;
    }
}
display()
{
    struct linklist *q = p;
    int i = 0;
    while (q != NULL)
    {
        i++;
        printf("\nitem number %d = %d", i, q -> item);
        q = q -> link;
    }
}
add (int item)
{
    struct linklist *q = (struct linklist*) malloc (sizeof
                           (struct linklist));
    q -> item = item;
    q -> link = NULL;
    if(p == NULL)
        p = q;
    else
    {
        q -> link = p;
            p = q;
    }
}
```

Q. No. 2 Add a function delete() to the program in Q.No.1 above, that can delete any node in the linked list.

Ans to Q. 2

```
/* Delete from a linked list */
#include <stdio.h>
#include <malloc.h>

struct linklist
{
   int item;
   struct linklist *link;
};
struct linklist *p;
main()
{
   p = NULL;
   clrscr();
/* Function to add the item to the beginning of the
      linklist */
   add ( 10 );
   add ( 20 );
   add ( 30 );
   add ( 40 );
   printf("Items added at the begining of the list:\n");
/* Function to display all the items in the linklist */
   display();
   printf(" Press any key...");
   getch();
/* Function to delete the item from the linklist */
   deleteitem ( 40 );
   printf ("\n\nItem deleted from the list:\n");
   display();
   printf("Press any key ....");
   getch();
/*Function to add item at the end of the linklist*/
   printf ("\n");
   add_end (50);
   printf("\n\nItem added at the end of list:\n");
   display();
   printf("Press any key...");
   getch();
   printf("\n");
   add_item_at_loca (60, 3);
   printf("\n\nItem added in the middle of the list:\n");
   display();
   printf("Press any key...");
   getch();
}
```

(Contd...)

```
deleteitem (int item)
{
   struct linklist *w, *q = p;
   int i = 0;
   if(p == NULL)
      printf("linklist is empty");
   else
   {
      while(q != NULL)
      {
      i++;
      if (q -> item == item)
      {
         if(i == 1)
         {
            w = q;
            q = q -> link;
            p = q;
            free (w);
            break;
         }
         w = p;
         while (w -> link != q)
            w = w -> link;
         w -> link = q -> link;
         free (q);
         break;
      }
      q = q -> link;
         }
      }
   }
add_item_at_loca(int item, int loca)
{
   struct linklist *q = (struct linklist *) malloc (sizeof
                                 (struct linklist));
   struct linklist *r, *w = p;
   int i = 1;
   q -> item = item;
   q -> link = NULL;
   if(p == NULL)
```

(Contd...)

```
      p = q;
    else
    {
      while ((w -> link != NULL) && (i != loca))
      {
        i++;
        w = w -> link;
      }
    if(i == loca)
    {
      r = w -> link;
      w -> link = q;
      q -> link = r;
    }
    else
      w -> link = q;
}
add_end(int item)
{
    struct linklist *q = (struct linklist *) malloc (sizeof
                                (struct linklist));
    struct linklist *w = p;
    q -> item = item;
    q -> link = NULL;
    if(p == NULL)
      p = q;
    else
    {
      while (w -> link != NULL)
        w = w -> link;
      w -> link = q;
    }
}
display()
{
    struct linklist *q = p;
    int i = 0;
    while(q != NULL)
    {
      i++;
      printf("\nitem number %d = %d", i, q -> item);
      q = q -> link;
    }
}
```

(Contd...)

```
add (int item)
{
struct linklist *q = (struct linklist *) malloc (sizeof
                              (struct linklist));
   q -> item = item;
   q -> link = NULL;
   if(p == NULL)
      p = q;
   else
   {
      q -> link = p;
      p = q;
   }
}
```

Q. No. 3 Write a program to maintain a linked list such that that every element added to the linked list gets inserted at such a place that the linked list is always maintained in ascending order.

Ans to Q. 3

```
/* Insertion in a sorted linked list in ascending order */
#include <stdio.h>
#include <conio.h>
#include <malloc.h>

   struct linklist
   {
      int item;
      struct linklist *link;
   };
   struct linklist *p;

main()
{
   int n;
   p = NULL
   clrscr();
/* Add the item to the beginning of the linked list */
   add( 40 );
   add ( 5 );
   add ( 3 );
   add ( 10 );

/* Display all the items in the linked list */
   display();
/* Insert an item entered through keyboard at a proper
        place */
```

(Contd...)

```
    printf ("\n\nEnter an integer to be added to linked
            list:");
    scanf("%d", &n);
    add ( n );
    display();

    printf("\n\n\n\n\nPress any key to exit...");
    getch();
}

/* Function to display all the items in the linked list */
    display()
    {
       struct linklist *q = p;
       int i = 0;
       while (q != NULL)
       {
          i++;
          printf("\nitem number %d = %d", i, q -> item);
          q = q -> link;
       }
    }
/* Function to add the item to the beginning of the linked
          list */
add (int item)
{
    struct linklist *q = (struct linklist *) malloc (sizeof
            (struct linklist));
    struct linklist *p1;
    int i = 0;
    q -> item = item; /* new node */
    q -> link = NULL; /* link of new node set to NULL */
    if(p == NULL)
       p = q; /* create first node */
    else
    {
       p1 = p; /* loop counter */
       while(p1 != NULL)
       {
          i++;
          if(p1 -> item < item) /* compare new item with
                                   existing */
          {
             if(p1 -> link == NULL)
             {
                p1 -> link = q; /* add second node at the
                                   end */
```

(Contd...)

```
                  break;
               }
               if(p1 -> link -> item >= item)
               {
                  q -> link = p1 -> link; /* add node in the
                                                 middle */
                  p1 -> link = q;
                  break;
               }
            }
            else
            {
               if(i == 1)
               {
                  q -> link = p; /* add second node at the
                                    beginning */
                  p = q;
               }
            }
            p1 = p1 -> link;
         }
      }
   }
```

Q. No. 4 Write a program in 'C' to reverse the order of links in the existing linked list so that the last node becomes the first node and the first node becomes the last.

Ans to Q. 4

```
/* Reversing the links in the linked list */
#include <stdio.h>
#include <conio.h>
#include <malloc.h>

struct linklist
{
   int item;
   struct linklist *link;
};
struct linklist *p;

main()
{
   p = NULL;
   clrscr();
/* Add the item to the beginning of the linked list */
   add ( 1 );
   add ( 2 );
```

(Contd...)

```
   add ( 3 );
   add ( 4 );
   add ( 10 );
   add ( 20 );
   add ( 30 );
   add ( 40 );
/* Display all the items in the linked list */
   printf("\nLinked list as entered:");
   display();
   getch();
/* Reverse the linked list */
   reverse();
   printf("\n\nlinked list after reversing:");
   display();
   printf("\n\n\nPress any key to exit...");
   getch();
}
/* Function to reverse the linked list */
   reverse()
   {
      struct linklist *q = p, *r, *w = NULL;
      int i = 1;
      if(p != NULL)
      {
         while(q != NULL)
         {
            r = (struct linklist*) malloc (sizeof (struct
                     linklist));
            r -> item = q -> item;
            if (i == 1)
               r-> link = w;
            else
               r -> link = w;
            w = r;
            i++;
            q = q -> link;
            free ( p );
            p = q;
         }
         p = w;
      }
      else
         printf("\nLinked list is empty");
   }
```

(Contd...)

```
/* Function to display all the items in the linked list */
   display()
   {
      struct linklist *q = p;
      int i = 0;
      printf("\n");
      while (q != NULL)
      {
         i++;
         printf("\nitem number %d = %d", i, q -> item);
         q = q -> link;
      }
   }
/* Function to add the item to the beginning of the linked
            list */
add (int item)
{
   struct linklist *q = (struct linklist*) malloc (sizeof
                        (struct linklist));
   struct linklist *p1;
   int i = 0;
   q -> item = item;
   q -> link = NULL;
   if(p == NULL)
      p = q;
   else
   {
      q -> link = p;
      p = q;
   }
}
```

Q. No. 5 Write an algorithm for summing two polynomials.

A to Q. 5 In order to add two polynomials we examine their terms starting at nodes pointed to by p and q.

1. while p and q are not null, repeat step 2
2. If powers of the two terms are equal then if the terms do not cancel then insert the sum of the terms into the sum polynomial
   Advance p
   Advance q
   else if the power of the first polynomial > power of the second.
   then insert the term from first polynomial into sum polynomial
   advance p
   else insert the term from second polynomial into sum polynomial
   advance
3. copy remaining terms from the non empty polynomial into sum polynomial.

EXERCISE

Multiple Choice

1. In linked list, a node contains at least-
   a. node address field, data field
   b. node number, data field
   c. next address field, information field.
   d. None of these
2. In linked list, the logical order of elements-
   a. is same as their physical arrangement
   b. is not necessarily equivalent to their physical arrangement
   c. is determined by their physical arrangement.
   d. None of the above
3. Direct or random access of element is not possible in-
   a. linked list b. array
   c. string d. None of the above
4. In liked list, the successive elements-
   a. must occupy contiguous space in memory
   b. need not occupy contiguous space in memory
   c. must not occupy contiguous space in memory.
   d. None of the above.
5. Null pointer is used to tell-
   a. end of linked list
   b. empty pointer field of a structure
   c. the linked list is empty.
   d. All of the above
6. Underflow condition in linked list may occur when attempting to-
   a. insert a new node when their is no free space for it
   b. delete a non-existent node in the list
   c. delete a node in empty list
   d. None of the above
7. Overflow condition in linked list may occur when attempting to-
   a. create a node when free space pool is empty
   b. traverse the nodes when free space pool is empty
   c. create a node when linked list is empty
   d. None of the above
8. Header of a linked list is a special node at the-
   a. end of the linked list b. at middle of the list
   c. beginning of the list d. None of the above

9. Header linked list in which last node points the header node is called-
   a. grounded header list b. circular header list
   c. general header list d. None of the above
10. A technique which collects all deleted space onto free storage list is called-
   a. static memory allocation b. Garbage collection
   b. dynamic memory allocation d. None of the above

Key to Multiple Choice Questions

1.	c	2.	b	3.	a	4.	b	5.	a
6.	c	7.	a	8.	c	9.	b	10.	b

TEST PAPER

Note: Answer all questions.

1. Write a 'C' program to delete a node containing a given information in singly linked list.
2. Write a 'C' program to create a doubly linked list in the ascending order of the information.
3. What are advantages of using linked list structure over arrays structure. Give an example.
4. List different types of linked list data structure. Explain any one of the them in detail.
5. Write short note on Header linked list.

CHAPTER 5

Stacks and Queues

5.1 INTRODUCTION

The linear data structure such as an array or linear list allows us to insert and delete an element at any place, namely either at the beginning or at the end or in the middle of the linear list. It is possible that we need a data structure which takes operation on only one end i.e. either at the beginning or at the end of the list. *Stack* and *Queue* are two such types of data structures which take operation only at the ends or at the beginning of the list. In stacks, insertion and deletion of elements is possible at the *top* end. In queues, insertion is possible only at end known as the *rear* and deletion is possible from the other end, known as *front*.

5.2 REPRESENTATION OF STACKS

A *stack* is a linear data structure. But in this data structure, elements are added to and removed only from one end of the list i.e. top of the stack. Thus, stack provides the information in the reverse of the entry order, so it is called the last-in-first-out (LIFO) list. An example of a stack is the stack of plates that you would have seen in a restaurant (See Figure 5.1). Clean plates are added to the top of the stack of plates. Moreover, user remove plates from the top of the stack. The last plate put in the stack is the first plate removed by the user.

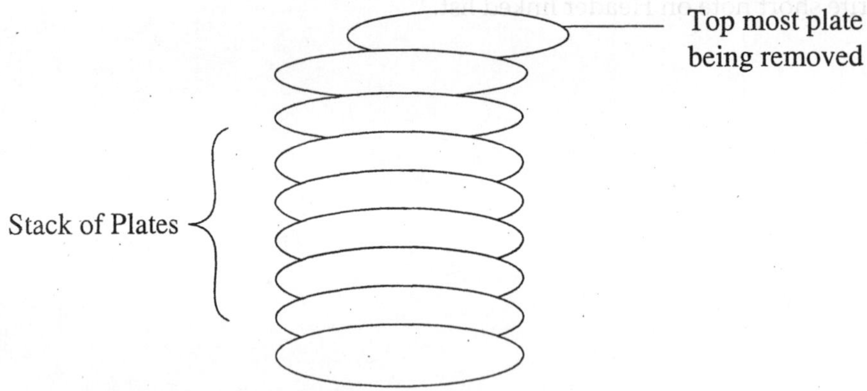

Figure 5.1 Representation of stack of plates

A data structure of linear list in which an element is added or removed only from top end, is called as ***stack.***

In computer field, the operation of removing an entry from a stack is called a *pop* operation. The operation of adding an entry to a stack is called *push* operation.

If the elements are added continuously to a stack, it grows at the top end. (See Figure 5.2(a)) New items are pushed on the top of the stack. On deletion of elements, the stack shrinks as the elements at the top are removed. See Figure 5.2(b) where two items are popped from stack.

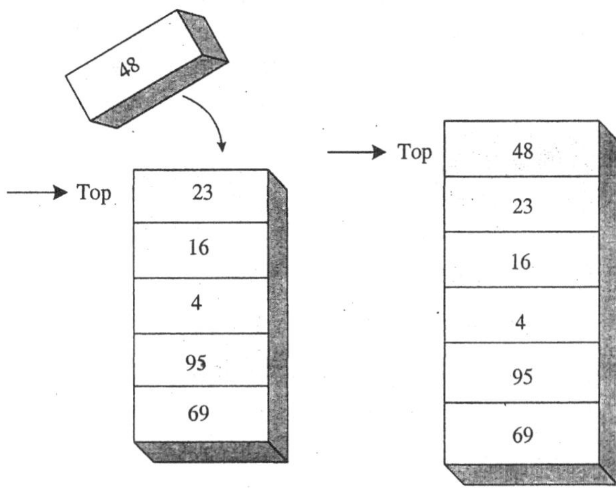

Figure 5.2(a) Pictorial representation of stack after inserting element

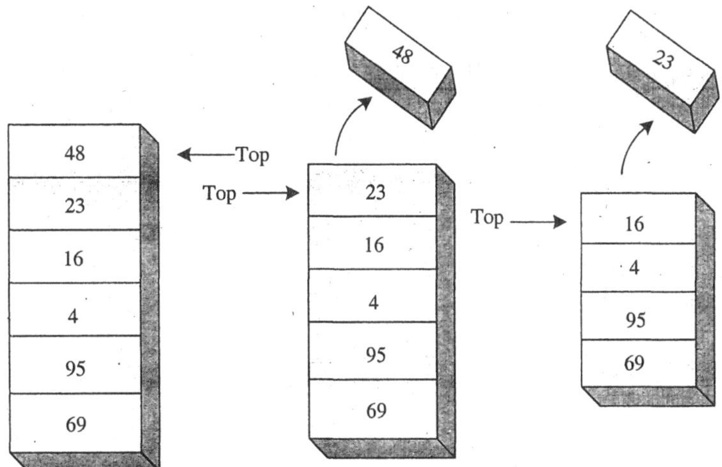

Figure 5.2(b) Pictorial representation of stack after deletion of two elements

5.3 IMPLEMENTATION OF STACK

A stack is a linear list and hence any of the implementation technique used in list may be implemented in the stack. Two common methods of implementations of stacks are:

(a) Array implementation

(b) Linked list implementation

5.3.1 Array Implementation of stack

We can use an array of data elements for implementing it as stack. In array, we push elements one by one from 0th position, 1st position and so on upto n-1th position.

In an array, any element can be added or deleted from any place. However, we push or pop the element from top of the stack only. So the variable which gives us the location of the top element of stack may be called TOP. A variable of data type *int*, called TOP contains the location of the top element of the stack and a variable MAXSTK contains the maximum number of elements that are held by the stack. Stack data structure can be represented in C programming language by the following:

```
struct stack
{
    int items [MAXSTK];
    int top;
};
```

It may be possible that a condition arises when there is no place for adding (push) the element in the stack. This is called *overflow*. So first we should check the value of top with the size of array.

☞ *If the stack is implemented using an array, the maximum number of elements it can accommodate is determined by the dimension of the array. Attempt to push elements to the stack beyond its maximum capacity is known as stack overflow.*

Another possibility arises when there is no element for deleting (poping) from stack. If there is no element available in stack then value of top will be -1, i.e Top = -1 will indicate that the stack is empty. So check the value of top before deleting the element of stack.

Stack underflow occurs when the stack is empty and an attempt is made to delete an element from the stack.

Figure 5.3 illustrates the array representation of stack. Size of MAXSTK = 8. The value of Top is 3, the stack has three elements XXX, YYY and ZZZ. Since MAXSTK = 8, there is room for 5 more items in the stack.

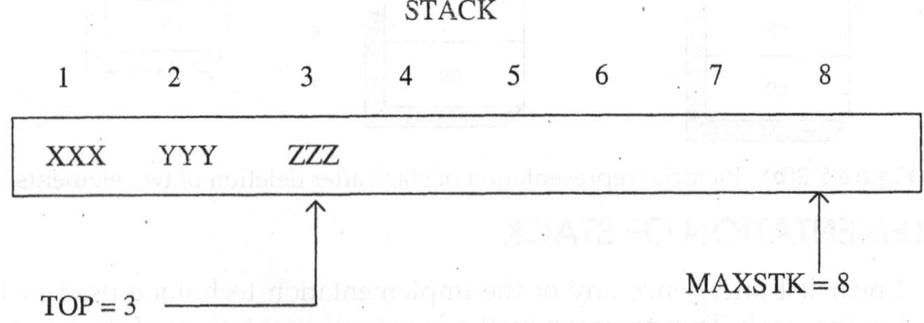

Figure 5.3 Array representation of stack

☞ *Note that top always points to the last added item of stack. After pop operation, it will point to the previous pushed item of stack.*

Following procedure gives the operation of adding (Pushing) an item onto a stack and the operation of removing (Poping) an item from the stack.

Push

PUSH is the operation of adding an element in the stack. In executing this operation, one must first test whether there is a room in the stack for pushing the new Item. An item is always inserted at the top of the stack. If there is no room, then we have the condition known as *overflow*. Figure 5.4 illustrates the algorithm for inserting an ITEM to a stack.

```
BEGIN
PUSH (STACK,TOP,MAXSTK,ITEM)
(This procedure pushes the ITEM onto a stack)
    Step 1. (Is stack already filled?)
            IF TOP = MAXSTK then print stack OVERFLOW and Return
    Step 2. Else Set TOP := TOP + 1 {Increase TOP by 1}
    Step 3. Set STACK [TOP] := ITEM { Insert ITEM in new TOP position}
    Step 4. Return
END
```

Figure 5.4 Algorithm for Push operation on a stack

☞ *Push means to insert an item onto the stack.*

Pop

POP is the operation of deleting the topmost element from the stack.

In executing the POP operation, i.e. removing an item from the stack, we must first test whether there is an element in the stack to be deleted. If not, then we have the condition known as *underflow*. Figure 5.5 gives the algorithm for deleting an ITEM from the stack. After removal of top most information, new value of the pointer Top becomes the previous value of Top i.e. Top = Top - 1 and freed position is allocated to free space.

```
BEGIN
POP (STACK,TOP,ITEM)
(This procedure deletes the TOP element of the STACK and assigns it to
a variable ITEM)
    Step 1. (Is there an Item in STACK for removal?)
            IF TOP = -1 then print UNDERFLOW and Return
    Step 2. Else Set ITEM := STACK [TOP] {assign TOP element to ITEM};
    Step 3. Set TOP := TOP - 1 {Decrease Top by 1}
    Step 4. Return
END
```

Figure 5.5 Algorithm for Pop operation on stack

☞ *The pop operation deletes or removes the top most item from the stack.*

☞ *A stack is empty when it contains no elements. We can indicate this by making TOP as -1.*

Example 1

a. We shall use the procedure PUSH for adding an ITEM WWW on the STACK.

```
Step 1.    Since the TOP = 3 (i.e. not equal to MAXSTK); we transfer the
           control to Step 2.
Step 2.    TOP = 3 + 1 = 4;
Step 3.    STACK [TOP] = STACK [4] = WWW
Step 4.    Return.
```

Figure 5.6 shows the element WWW at the position 4, i.e WWW is now the top element in the stack.

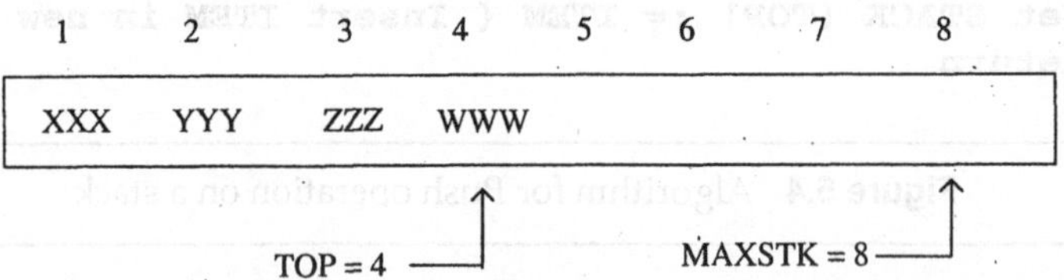

Figure 5.6 Figure shows element WWW is pushed at the position 4

Example 2

We want to remove the TOP element, i.e. WWW from the stack. For this we use the procedure POP as given below:

```
Step 1.    Since TOP = 4, (not equal to -1) Control is transferred to
           Step 2.
Step 2.    ITEM := WWW; {Contents of location 4 i.e TOP is copied to
           variable ITEM}
Step 3.    TOP = TOP - 1 = 4 - 1 = 3
Step 4.    Return.
```

After the POP operation,

STACK [TOP] = STACK [3]

contains ZZZ in the STACK. (See Figure 5.7)

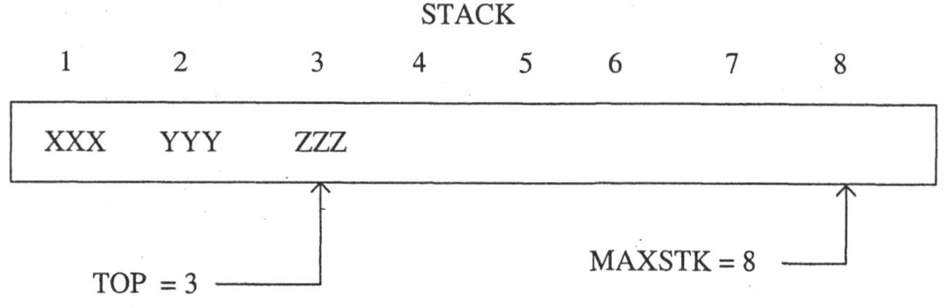

Figure 5.7 Top element ZZZ in the stack after removing WWW

☞ *Any insertion and deletion from location other than the TOP is not possible in a stack. Moreover, procedures such as traversing, searching a stack etc. do not apply in this case.*

Example 3

Consider the stack in Figure 5.7. We will delete item ZZZ.

```
Step 1. Since Top = 3, Control is transferred to step 2.
Step 2. ITEM = ZZZ
Step 3. Top = Top - 1 = 3 - 1 = 2
Step 4. Return
```

Now after pop operation

STACK[TOP] = STACK[2] = YYY is now the top element in the stack.

Example 4

Consider the following stack of characters, where STACK is allocated N = 8 memory cells.

STACK: A, C, D, F, K, ___, ___, ___.

Describe the STACK at the end of each of the following operations. Here POP and PUSH are algorithms for deleting and adding an element to the stack.

a. POP (STACK, ITEM));
b. POP (STACK, ITEM);
c. PUSH (STACK, L);
d. PUSH (STACK, P);
e. POP (STACK, ITEM);
f. PUSH (STACK, R);
g. PUSH (STACK, S);
h. POP (STACK, ITEM);

We know that the POP procedure deletes the top element from the stack. Similarly, the PUSH procedure always adds a new element to the TOP of the stack. Therefore, the stack contents will be as follows after the operation of each sub-paragraph a, b, c, d, e, f, g, and h.

a. STACK : A, C, D, F, ___, ___, ___, ___.
{ K is deleted }
b. STACK : A, C, D, ___, ___, ___, ___, ___.
{ F is deleted }
c. STACK : A, C, D, L, ___, ___, ___, ___.
{ L is pushed in }
d. STACK : A, C, D, L, P, ___, ___, ___.
{ P is pushed in }
e. STACK : A, C, D, L, ___, ___, ___, ___.
{ P is popped off }
f. STACK : A, C, D, L, R, ___, ___, ___.
{ R is pushed in }
g. STACK : A, C, D, L, R, S,___, ___.
{ S is pushed in}
h. STACK : A, C, D, L, R, ___, ___, ___.
{ S is popped off}

Example 5

Suppose STACK is allocated N = 6 memory locations and initially STACK is empty or TOP = -1. Find the output of the following module:

1. Set AAA = 2 and BBB = 5;
2. CALL PUSH (STACK, AAA);
   CALL PUSH (STACK, 4);
   CALL PUSH (STACK, BBB + 2);
   CALL PUSH (STACK, 9);
   CALL PUSH (STACK, AAA + BBB);
3. Repeat while TOP ≠ -1;
   Call POP (STACK, ITEM);
   Write ITEM;
   (End of loop)
4. Return.

☞ *A stack is empty when it contains no elements.*

Step 1. Set AAA = 2 and BBB = 5

Step 2. STACK: 2, 4, 7, 9, 7 (would contain these values)

Step 3. Pops and prints the elements of STACK until the STACK is empty. Since the top element is always popped first, the output would be having numbers in the reverse sequence.

The resultant output is 7, 9, 7, 4, 2

Example 6

Program and the output of stack operation using arrays is shown in Figure 5.8

```
/* Stack operation using arrays */
#include <string.h>
#include <stdio.h>
#define MAX 5
int top, status;
/* function to push elements on to the stack */
void push(stack, item)
int stack[], item;
{
   if (top == (MAX - 1))
       status = 0;
   else
   {
       status = 1;
       ++top;
       stack[top] = item;
   }
}

/* function to pop the elements off the stack */
int pop(stack)
int stack[];
{
   int ret;
   if (top == -1)
   {
       ret = 0;
       status = 0;
   }
   else
   {
       status = 1;
       ret = stack[top];
       --top;
   }
   return ret;
}
/* function to display the elements of the stack */
void display (stack)
int stack[];
{
   int i;
```

(Contd...)

```
   printf("the stack is");
   if (top == -1)
      printf("empty\n");
   else
   {
      printf("\n");
      for (i = top; i >= 0; --i)
         printf("\n_________\n|%5d|\n_________", stack[i]);
   }
   printf("\n");
}
/* main program */
void main()
{
   int stack[MAX], quit,item;
   char c;
   quit = 0;
   top = - 1;
   do
   {
      printf("\nPush / pOp / Quit (P / O / Q)");
      printf("\nEnter choice :");
      do
         c = getchar();
      while (strchr("pPoOqQ", c) == NULL);
      printf(" %c", c);
      switch (c)
      {
      case'p':
      case'P' :
         printf("\nEnter the element to be pushed: ");
         scanf("%d", &item);
         push(stack, item);
         if (status)
         {
            printf("\nAfter pushing ");
            display (stack);
            if (top == (MAX - 1))
            printf("\nThe stack is full.\n");
         }
         else
            printf("\n Stack overflow on push.\n");
```

(Contd...)

```
        break;
        case'o':
        case 'O':
            item = pop(stack);
            if (status)
            {
            printf("\nThe popped item is %d. After popping", item);
            display(stack);
            }
            else
            printf("\nStack underflow on pop.\n");
            break;
        case 'q':
        case 'Q':
            quit = 1;
        }
    } while (!quit);
    printf("\n");
}
```

RUN

```
Push / pOp / Quit ( P / O / Q)
Enter choice : P
Enter the element to be pushed : 15
After pushing the stack is

______
  15
______

Push /pOp / Quit ( P / O / Q)
Enter choice : P
Enter the element to be pushed : 19
After pushing the stack is

______
  19
______

______
  15
______
```

(Contd...)

```
Push /pOp / Quit ( P / O / Q)
Enter choice : P
Enter the element to be pushed : 23
After pushing the stack is

 ______
   23
 ______

 ______
   19
 ______

 ______
   15
 ______

Push /pOp / Quit ( P / O / Q)
Enter choice : P
Enter the element to be pushed : 43
After pushing the stack is

 ______
   43
 ______

 ______
   23
 ______

 ______
   19
 ______

 ______
   15
 ______

Push /pOp / Quit ( P / O / Q)
Enter choice : P
Enter the element to be pushed : 63
After pushing the stack is
```

(Contd...)

```
   ______
     63
   ______


   ______
     43
   ______


   ______
     23
   ______


   ______
     19
   ______


   ______
     15
   ______

The stack is full

Push /pOp / Quit ( P / O / Q)
Enter choice : P
Enter the element to be pushed : 72
Stack overflow on push.

Push /pOp / Quit ( P / O / Q)
Enter choice : O
The popped item is 63. After popping the stack is

   ______
     43
   ______


   ______
     23
   ______


   ______
     19
   ______
```

(Contd...)

```
 ______
   15
 ______

Push /pOp / Quit ( P / O / Q)
Enter choice : O
The popped item is 43. After popping the stack is

 ______
   23
 ______

 ______
   19
 ______

 ______
   15
 ______

Push /pOp / Quit ( P / O / Q)
Enter choice : O
The popped item is 23. After popping the stack is

 ______
   19
 ______

 ______
   15
 ______

Push /pOp / Quit ( P / O / Q)
Enter choice : O
The popped item is 19. After popping the stack is

 ______
   15
 ______

Push /pOp / Quit ( P / O / Q)
Enter choice : O
The popped item is 15. After popping the stack is empty.
```

(Contd...)

```
Push /pOp / Quit ( P / O / Q)
Enter choice : O
Stack underflow on pop.

Push / pOp / Quit ( P / O / Q)
Enter choice O
Stack underflow on pop.

Push /pOp / Quit ( P / O / Q)
Enter choice : Q
```

Figure 5.8 Program in 'C' language for stack operations using arrays

5.3.2 Linked List Implementation of a Stack

A stack can be implemented using an array or linked list. Using an array is more efficient, but we need to declare the size of the array before starting any operation on stack. Suppose, we know that no more than 15 entries will be present in the stack at any time, we can dimension an array **STACK** to take a maximum of 15 entries and assign **STACK(0)** to hold the first (bottom) entry, **STACK(1)** to hold the next entry, and so on. The location of the top of the stack must be known. Thus, another integer variable, **STACK_TOP** is needed to hold the index of the top of the stack. The operation **PUSH on to STACK** can be done by the algorithm shown in Figure 5.9(a). The algorithm for **POP on to STACK** is shown in Figure 5.9(b).

```
BEGIN
   if STACK_TOP < 15
     then
       STACK_TOP ← STACK_TOP + 1
       STACK_TOP(STACK_TOP) ← VAR
     else
       output 'STACK overflow in PUSH operation'
   endif
END
```

Figure 5.9(a) Algorithm for PUSH operation on a STACK

```
BEGIN
   if STACK_TOP > -1   //stack is not empty
     then
       VAR ← STACK(STACK_TOP)
       STACK_TOP ← STACK_TOP - 1
     else
       output 'STACK underflow in POP operation'
   endif
END
```

Figure 5.9(b) Algorithm for POP operation on a STACK

If we implement stack using an array, then we come across situations where an attempt to push an element in the stack may cause overflow. So, we must implement the stack in such a way that the stack can grow to the maximum size limited by the computer's memory.

Arrays have several advantages over linked lists for implementing stacks. Firstly, lesser memory space is used, because pointers do not have to be stored. Furthermore, about half as many operations are needed in the *push* and *pop* operations when arrays are used. The main disadvantage of arrays being used as stack is that their size must be fixed in advance before they are implemented as stacks, i.e the size of the stack cannot be increased or decreased once it is declared at the beginning. Thus, it is necessary to know the maximum size of the stack beforehand if we are using arrays.

This problem can be overcome if we implement a stack using a linked list. In case of a stack using linked list, we shall push and pop nodes from one end of a linked list only. The stack as linked list is represented by a singly connected list. Each node in the linked list contains the data and a pointer that gives location of the next node in the list. (See Figure 5.10)

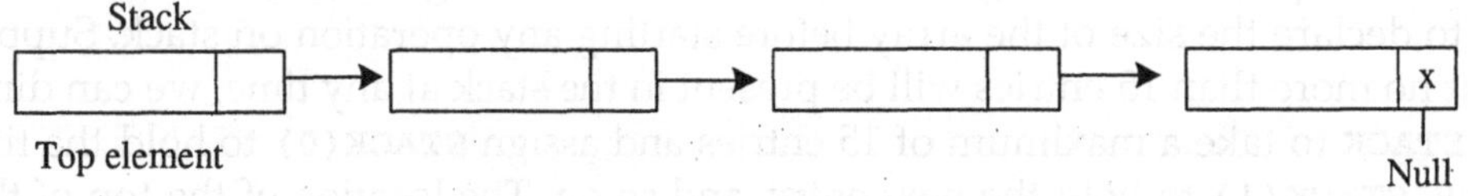

Figure 5.10 Representation of stack as a linked list

Stack can be implemented through linked list using the structure as:

```
struct stack
    {
        int item;
        struct stack *next;
    };
```

For pushing the element on stack, we follow the insertion operation of the linked list. It means, we add the element at the start of the list. Push requests storage for a node and copies the data passed to it into the allocated storage. Finally, it adds the allocated node to the beginning of the linked list and updates the starting pointer of the stack. This is done by the statements:

```
tmp → item = pushed_item;
tmp → next = top;
top = tmp;
```

Here, *top* always points to the first node of the linked list. After statement 3, the latest pushed item will become the first node of linked list. Since stack implementation is through linked list, so we do not check overflow condition.

For *pop* operation on stack, we delete the first element of linked list, because stack is a Last In First Out structure (LIFO). Pop checks whether the stack is empty or not. If it is empty, it returns, otherwise it copies the data at the top of the stack into the variable. It then saves the address of the first node of the stack, so that it can free this node later. Finally, it updates the first address of the stack to point to the second node and free the first node and return to the variable.

```
if (top == NULL)
    printf("stack is empty\n");
else
{
    tmp = top;
    printf("popped item is %d\n", tmp -> item);
    top = top -> next;
    free(tmp);
}
```

First we check for stack empty condition, then we pop the first element of stack. Now top will point to second node of linked list and this will become the first node of linked list.

Example 7

Program and the output of stack's operation using linked list is shown in Figure 5.11.

```
/* Implementation of stack using a linked lists */
#include <stdio.h>
#include <malloc.h>
struct list_element
{
    int item;
    struct list_element *link;
};
typedef struct list_element node;
void main()
{
    node *start;
    int key;
    int ch;
    int menu();
    void create();
    node *push();
    node *pop();
    void display();
    start = NULL;
    do
    {
        ch = menu();
        switch (ch)
        {
        case 1: /* Add element to the top of stack */
            start = push (start);
            printf ("\nStack after Pushing : \n");
            display (start);
            break;
```

(Contd...)

```
        case 2: /* Delete  element from the top of stack */
            start = pop (start);
            break;
        default: /* Terminate */
            printf ("End of computation \n");
        }
    } while (ch !=3);
}
int menu() /* menu function */
{
    int ch;
    do
    {
        printf ("\n\nMain Menu: \n");
        printf (" 1 - Push \n");
        printf (" 2 - Pop \n");
        printf (" 3 - END \n");
        printf ("Please enter your choice (1, 2 or 3) : ");
        scanf ("%d", &ch);
        printf ("%d\n", ch);
        if (ch < 1 || ch > 3)
            printf ("\nInvalid choice - try again\n");
    }
        while (ch < 1 || ch > 3);
    printf ("\n");
    return (ch);
}
void display (record) /* display the linked list */
node *record;
/* Argument points to the current node */
{
    if (record != NULL)
    {
        /* display the data item */
        printf (" -> %d", record -> item);
        /* get the next data item */
        display (record -> link);
    }
    return;
}
/* Add one component to linked list return pointer to the
    beginning of modified list */
node *push (first)
node *first;
/* Argument points to first node */
{
    node *newrecord;/* pointer points to new node */
    int newitem;/* new data item */
```

(Contd...)

```
    printf("New data item ?");
    scanf ("%d", &newitem);
    printf ("%d\n", newitem);
/* allocate space for the new node using malloc */
newrecord = (node *) malloc(sizeof(node));
/* assign the new data item to newrecord -> item */
newrecord -> item = newitem;
/* assign the current pointer to newrecord -> link */
newrecord -> link = first;
/* new pointer becomes the beginning of the list */
first = newrecord;
return (first);
}
node *pop (first)
/* delete one component from linked list */
node *first;
/* return pointer to beginning of modified list */
/* argument points to first node */
{
    node *temp;/* temporary pointer */
    int target;/* data item to be deleted */
    if (first == NULL)
        printf("STACK EMPTY \n");
    else
    {
        printf ("Element deleted is : %d", first -> item);
        /* delete the first node */
        /* mark the node for deletion */
        temp = first -> link;
        /* free space of the target node */
        free (first);
        /* adjust the pointer to the first node */
        first = temp;
        printf ("\nStack after Popping : \n");
        display (first);
    }
    return (first);
}

RUN

Main Menu:
1 - Push
2 - Pop
3 - END
Please enter your choice (1,2 or 3) : 1
```

(Contd...)

```
New data item ? 5

Stack after Pushing :
→ 5

Main Menu:
1 - Push
2 - Pop
3 - END
Please enter your choice (1,2 or 3) : 1

New data item ? 12

Stack after pushing:
→ 12 → 5
Main Menu:
1 - Push
2 - Pop
3 - END
Please enter your choice (1,2 or 3) : 1

New data item ? 26

Stack after pushing:
→ 26 → 12 → 5

Main Menu:
1 - Push
2 - Pop
3 - END

Please enter your choice (1,2 or 3) : 2

Element deleted is : 26

Stack after Popping:
→ 12 → 5

Main Menu:
1 - Push
2 - Pop
3 - END
Please enter your choice (1, 2, or 3) : 2
```

(Contd...)

```
Element deleted is : 12

Stack after Popping:
→ 5

Main Menu:
1 - Push
2 - Pop
3 - END
Please enter your choice (1, 2, or 3) : 2

Element deleted is : 5
Stack after Popping:

Main Menu:
1 - Push
2 - Pop
3 - END
Please enter your choice (1, 2, or 3) : 2

Stack empty

Main Menu:
1 - Push
2 - Pop
3 - END
Please enter your choice (1, 2, or 3) : 3

End of computation
```

Figure 5.11 Program and the output of stacks using linked list

5.4 POLISH NOTATION

There are three ways to represent an arithmetic expression.

Infix A + B (Here the + sign is in between the variables A, B)

Prefix or polish notation + AB (Here the + sign is before the variables A, B)

Postfix or reverse polish notation AB+ (Here the + sign is after the variables A, B)

For most common arithmetic operations, the operator symbol is placed between its two operands namely infix notation. For example:

A + B   C - D   E * F   F/G

Polish notation, named after the polish mathematician Jan Lukasiewicz, refers to the notation in which the operator symbol is placed before its two operands. For example,

+ AB   –CD   *EF   /FG

Reverse polish notation refers to the analogous notation in which the operator symbol is placed after its two operands. For example:

AB+   CD+   EF*   FG/

We, normally write the operators in between the operands. The manner of writing arithmetic expressions with each operator written in between the operands is the *infix notation*. But stack manipulation, i.e performing arithmetic or logical operations on items in a stack, is best done using *postfix notation*.

Stacks can be used to convert an algebraic expression to Postfix notation so that the compiler can use it. For example the expression:

```
((( A/B)^C) * (E - A) * C )
```

is difficult for the machine to know and keep track of the precedence of operations say ^ (raised to the power) and * (multiplication operation).

In order to overcome this difficulty, the solution lies in using the postfix notation technique. It means if we want to carry out (A + B) operation, we write it as AB+ in postfix notation. Similarly, to write (A * B), we denote it as AB* in postfix notation. For this, we use stack for converting the infix notated expression to a postfix notation.

We already know that the order of precedence for the arithmetical operators is as follows:

Symbol	*Precedence*
^	Topmost
*, /	Middle
+, −	Lowest

☞ *Postfix notation is also known as reverse polish notation that places the operators after the operands.*

5.4.1 Conversion of Infix Expression to Postfix Expression

To convert an infix expression to postfix expression, we need to consider the way in which precedences of operations are performed in infix notation. In an infix expression, the operations in parenthesis are performed first. In the postfix string, therefore, we will first write the operands in the parenthesis followed by the operators in between them. Then the other operands are written followed by their respective operators keeping in mind the operator's precedences. For example, the multiplication and division operations are performed before addition and subtraction operations.

For example, if an expression in infix notation is:

$$5 + 4 * 3/1$$

then in postfix notation, it will be expressed as follows:

$$5\,4\,3 * 1 / +$$

Any mathematical expression in the infix notation can be evaluated using stacks as follows:

a. First convert the arithmetic expression into equivalent reverse polish notation (postfix notation).

b. Push the operands into stack in the order in which they appear.

c. Use the two topmost operands for evaluation.
d. The stack is popped and the result of the operation is again pushed into the stack.
e. Finally, only the result of the operation is left on stack top.

To evaluate the postfix expression **4 3 * 1 / 5 +**, we will push these, from left to right, into a stack. First of all 4 is pushed (See Figure 5.12), followed by 3. Now an operator * is encountered. When an operator is encountered, the two topmost operands in the stack are popped. Hence in this case 4 and 3 are popped and multiplied (*). The result is pushed into stack. (see stage 3 in Figure 5.12). The content of stack is 12.

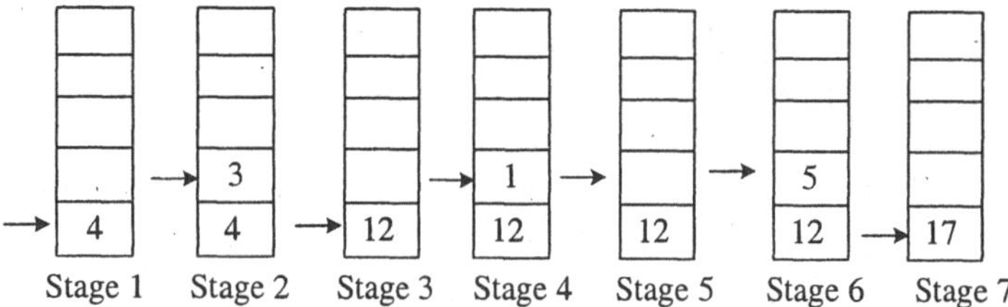

Figure 5.12 Stack contents while evaluating postfix notation expression 4 3 * 1 / 5 +

☞ *Sequence of operands does not change when an expression is converted from infix to postfix.*

Now push 1, then an operator / is encountered. Pop and divide 12 with 1 and push the result back into the stack.

Stack now contains

(12/1) i.e. 12 (see stage 5)

Now 5 is pushed into the stack. Then the operator + is encountered. Pop 12 and 5 and add the two values. Push the result to stack and the stack now contains the result of the arithmetic operation (i.e 17). (see stage 7)

We shall now consider another example. Suppose an infix expression is as follows:

$$(x + y) * [z * (w + v) + s]$$

Now, we try to write its postfix expression. Two sub-expressions in parenthesis are there. These are $(x + y)$ and $(w + v)$. Therefore, the postfix expression will be the following for the two sub expressions in postfix

$$x\ y\ + \qquad w\ v\ +$$

Now in the square brackets $(w + v)$ is multiplied by z. The postfix is then

$$x\ y\ + \quad z\ w\ v\ +\ *$$

The result is then added with s in the square bracket. Hence

$$x\ y\ + \quad z\ w\ v\ +\ *\ s\ +$$

The result of addition is then finally multiplied with $(x + y)$. Hence the postfix string is

$$x\ y\ +\ z\ w\ v\ +\ *\ s\ +\ *$$

Algorithm for converting an expression from infix to postfix or polish notation

To maintain the precedence of the mathematical operators, we follow the following procedure for converting an *infix* notated algebraic expression into *postfix* algebraic expression. The scanning is done from left to right on the algebraic expression.

1. If the encountered symbol is '(', i.e. opening parentheses, it is pushed onto the operator stack.
2. If the symbol is an operand, it goes direct to the output.
3. If the symbol is ')', i.e. closing parentheses, everything from the operator stack down to the first '(' (opening parentheses) encountered is popped off the stack. The operators go to the output as they are popped off the stack. The '(', i.e. the opening parentheses is popped off but does not go to the output.
4. If the symbol is an operator, then we check if the operator on the top of the operator stack is of the same or higher precedence. If the symbol on the top of the operator stack is of equal or higher precedence then the operator on top of the stack is popped off and goes to output. We keep checking in this fashion until we encounter a '(', i.e. the opening parentheses or an operator of lower precedence in the operator stack. When this happens, the current operator is pushed into the stack.
5. When the encountered symbol is a terminating symbol, say a semicolon, it results in everything being popped off the stack.

The above steps are given in the form of an algorithm and shown in Figure 5.13. The algorithm transforms the infix expression Q into its equivalent postfix expression P. The algorithm uses a stack to temporarily hold operators and left parentheses. The postfix expression P will be constructed from left to right using the operands from Q and the operators which are removed from STACK. We begin by pushing a left parenthesis onto STACK

```
It is assumed that Q is written in an infix notation. Find the equiva-
lent postfix expression P.
BEGIN
1.   Push "(" onto STACK, and add ")" to the end of Q.
2.   Scan Q from left to right and repeat Steps 3 to 6 for each
     element of Q until the STACK is empty.
3.   If an operand is encountered, add it to P.
4.   If a left parentheses is encountered, push it onto STACK.
5.   If an operator is encountered, then:
       (a)   Repeatedly pop from STACK and add to P each operator
       (on the top of STACK) which has the same precedence as, or a
       higher precedence than the operator.
       (b)   Add the operator to STACK.
       Endif
6.   If a right parentheses is encountered, then:
       (a)   Repeatedly pop from STACK and add to P each operator (on
             the top of STACK) until a left parentheses is encountered.
       (b)   Remove the left parentheses but do not add it to P
       Endif
       [End of Step 2 loop]
7.   EXIT.
END.
```

Figure 5.13 Algorithm transforming an infix expression to a postfix expression

and adding a right parenthesis at the end of Q. The algorithm is completed when STACK is empty.

Evaluation of an expression in postfix notation

Suppose P is an arithmetic expression written in postfix notation. The algorithm shown in Figure 5.14, evaluates P using STACK to hold operands.

```
BEGIN
1.      Add a right parenthesis ")" at the end of P.
        [This acts as a sentinel.]
2.      Scan P from left to right and repeat Steps 3
        and 4 for each element of P until the sentinel
        ")" is encountered.
3.      If an operand is encountered, put it on STACK.
4.      If an operator is encountered, then:
          (a)   Remove the two top elements of STACK, where A is the
                top element and B is the next-to-top element.
          (b)   Evaluate B operator A
          (c)   Place the result of (b) back on STACK.
          Endif
        [End of Step2 loop]
5.      Set VALUE equal to the top element on STACK.
6.      EXIT
END
```

Figure 5.14 Algorithm to find the VALUE of an arithmetic expression P written in postfix notation

Note that when Step 5 is executed, there should be only one number on STACK.

Example 8

Convert the expression (A/B ^ C) into a postfix notation.

Figure 5.15 illustrates the method of converting the infix expression into a postfix expression using the conversion algorithm.

Step	1	2	3	4	5	6	7
Symbol scanned	(	A	/	B	^	C	)
Operator stack	(	(	/	/	^	^	← Top of Stack
Output		A		B		C	^/

Figure 5.15 Converting (A/B^C) into post fix notation

In Step 1, as we scan the expression from left to right, we encounter opening parenthesis '(' and it is pushed into the stack. In Step 2 the operand 'A' is encountered. This operand 'A' goes to the output. In Step 3, the symbol '/' is encountered. This symbol is pushed into the Stack. In Step 4, the operand 'B' is encountered. This operand 'B' goes to the output. In Step 5, the operator '^' {exponentiation symbol} is encountered. Its precedence is higher than the precedence of '/', which is on the top of the stack. So this operator '^' is pushed into the stack. In Step 6, the operand 'C' is encountered. This goes to the output. In Step 7, the closing parentheses ')' is encountered. This closing parenthesis causes all the contents of the stack to pop off till the opening parentheses '(' is encountered. So the operators '^' and '/' are popped off in this order. Thus, the postfix notation of (A/B^C) is ABC^/.

Example 9

Convert the algebraic expression

```
( ( ( A / B ) ^ C ) * ( E - A ) * C )
```

into its postfix notation.

The expression is converted into a postfix notation with the help of a stack by using the following method:

In Step 1, the opening parentheses '(' is pushed into the operator stack. In Steps 2 and 3, two opening parentheses '(', '(' are pushed into the stack. In Step 4, the operand A goes to the output. In Step 5, the slash sign '/' is pushed into the stack. In Step 6, the operand B goes to the output. In Step 7, the closing parenthesis is encountered. As per point 3 of the procedure when a closing parentheses is encountered, everything from the operator stack down to the first '(' encountered is popped off. So in Step 7, '/' is popped off. In Step 8, the symbol '^' is encountered. It is pushed onto the stack. In Step 9, operand 'C' is encountered. This is sent to the output. In Step 10, a closing parenthesis is encountered. So the contents of the stack are popped off till the next '(' is encountered. Therefore '^' is sent to the output. In Step 11, the symbol '*' is pushed into the Stack. In Step 12, the opening parentheses '(' is pushed into the stack. In Step 13, the operand 'E' is sent to the output. In Step 14, the symbol '-' is pushed into the stack. In Step 15, the operand 'A' is sent to the output. In Step 16, the closing parentheses is encountered.

So the contents of the stack are popped off till the next opening parentheses is encountered. Therefore, the symbol '-' is sent to the output. In Step 17, we have the symbol '*' on the top of the stack. Also the scanned symbol is '*'. As per the point 4 of the procedure which reads:

If the symbol is an operator, then we check if the operator on the top of the operator stack is of the same or higher precedence. If the symbol on the top of the operator stack, is of equal or higher precedence then the operator on top of the stack is popped off and goes to the output.

We keep checking in this fashion until we encounter a '(' or an operator of lower precedence in the operator stack. When this happens, the current operator is pushed into the stack.

So the '*' on the top of the stack is popped off and sent to the output. The scanned '*' is pushed into the stack. In Step 18, the operand 'C' is sent to the output. In Step 19, the symbol encountered is ')'. This means that all the contents of the stack till the opening parentheses '(' is encountered are pushed off. Hence the symbol '*' which is the only content of the stack is sent to the output. Thus, the postfix notation is seen in figure 5.16 and is follows:

A B / C ^ E A - * C *

Step	1	2	3	4	5	6	7	8	9	10	11	12	13	14	15	16	17	18	19
	(	(	(	A	/	B	)	^	C	)	*	(	E	–	A	)	*	C	)
Operator Stack	(	(	(	(	/	/	(	^	^	)	*	(	(	-	-	(	*	*	*
Output				A		B	/		C	^			E		A	-	*	C	*

Figure 5.16 Converting infix to postfix expression using stack

Example 10

Convert the following expressions into reverse polish notation that is postfix notation

a. $A*B+C*D+E*F$

$[Answer{:}AB*CD*+EF*+]$

b. $A*B+A*(B*D+C*E)$

$[Answer{:}BD*CE*+A*AB*+]$

c. $A+B*C*D+E*(F+G)$

$[Answer{:}ABC*D*+EFG+*+]$

d. $\dfrac{A*[B+C*(D+E)]}{F*(G+H)}$

$[Answer{:}ABCDE+*+*FGH+*/]$

Example 11

Convert the following expressions in prefix notation

a. (A + B) * C
Ans : * + ABC

b. A + (B * C)
Ans : + A * BC

c. (A + B)/ (C - D)
Ans : / + AB - CD

5.5 REPRESENTATION OF QUEUES

Queue is a linear data structure in which all insertions take place at one end namely *rear* and deletions takes place at the other end namely *front*.

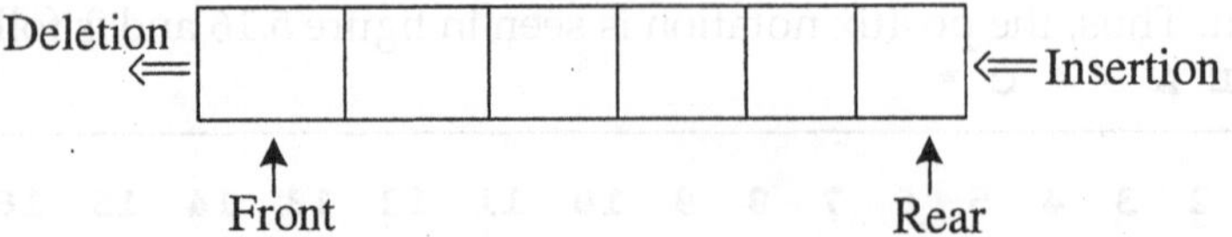

Queues implementation arise in situations where we wish to record information for later use keeping the order in which it was received. As new information is recorded, it is placed at the end or the tail of the queue. When information is needed, it is removed from the front, or head of the queue. For this reason, Queue is called First-In-First-Out list (FIFO) or First-Come-First-Serve (FCFS) list.

A day-to-day example of a queue is the queue where people are waiting in a line at a bank. Here, the first person in the line is the first person to be entertained (See Figure 5.17). In computer field, programs with the same *priority* in time sharing operating systems form a queue for execution.

Figure 5.17 An example of Queue

The terms FRONT and REAR are used to describe a linear list only when it is implemented as a queue.

The first element in a queue will also be the first element out of the queue. In other words, the order in which elements enter a queue is the order in which they leave the queue.

Example 12

In Figure 5.18, there is a queue with four elements.

The element **A** is the FRONT and element **D** is the REAR in part (a) of the diagram. The FRONT and REAR elements of the queues are also the first and last elements of the list. If we delete an element from the list then it is the element **A** which will be deleted first.

This will give us the queue shown in part (b) of Figure 5.18. If we add **E** to the queue, it will be added at the REAR thus showing the addition in part (c) of Figure 5.18. If we eliminate another element from the queue then it will be **B**. If we add **F**, the resulting queue is shown in part (d) of Figure 5.18.

This process of adding and deleting can continue, but while adding an element it is to be added at the REAR and while deleting an element, it is to be deleted from the FRONT. This means that if we have to delete **D**, then **C** is to be deleted first in part (d) of Figure 5.18.

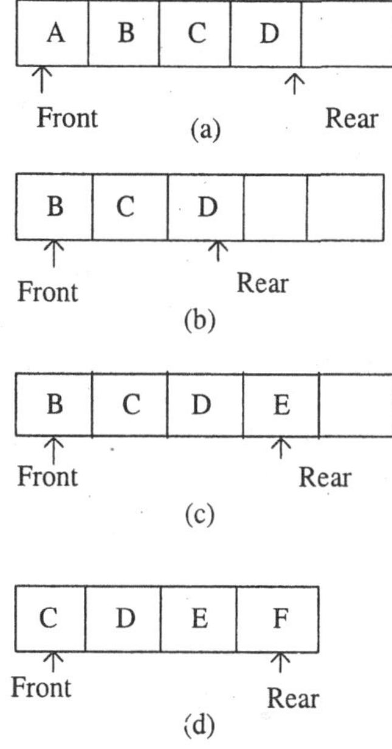

Figure 5.18 Representation of a queue with four elements

5.6 IMPLEMENTATION OF QUEUES

Queues, being a linear data structure can be represented in two ways. These are:

(a) Arrays implementation

(b) Linked list implementation

5.6.1 Array Implementation of Queue

An array is a data structure that can store a fixed number of elements. The size of an array should be fixed before using it. Queue, on the other hand keeps on changing as we remove elements from the front end or add new elements at the rear end. Declaring an array with a maximum size would solve this problem. The maximum size should be large enough for a queue to expand.

Since we want to add an item in a queue at the rear end and delete the item in the queue at the front, so we take two variables *rear* (keeps the status of last added item in queue) and *front* (keeps the status of first item of queue). It may be possible that condition arises when there is no place for adding elements in a queue. This is called *overflow*, so first we check the value of rear with the size of array.

The second possibility arises when there is no element for deleting from queue. If there is no element in a queue then value of front and rear will be -1 or front will be greater than rear. So, we check this condition before deleting the element of queue. Figure 5.19 shows Queue stored in the memory of the computer.

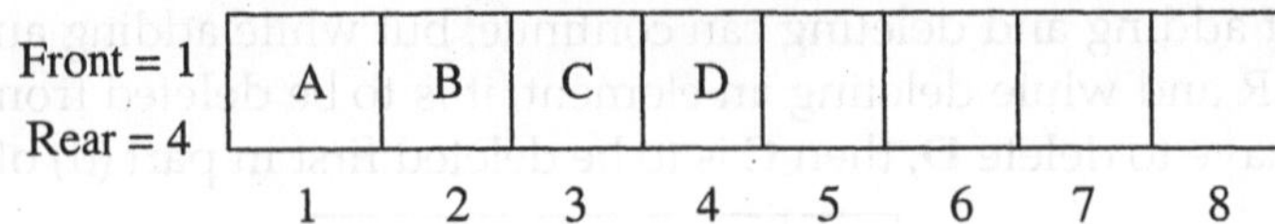

Figure 5.19 Queue stored in the memory of computer

Here, the size of queue is 8. The value of the *front* is 1, means element will be deleted from the 1st position of array. Value of rear is 4, means the element will be added at 5th position of array.

While adding a new element to the queue, first it would be ascertained whether such an addition is possible or not. If the array indexing begins with 0, the maximum number of elements that can be stored in the queue are Maxsize - 1. But, if the first element is numbered as 1, as in Figure 5.19, than the elements that can be stored would be the Maxsize. As in the case of the array in Figure 5.19. The Maxsize = 8. If these many elements are already present in the queue, then the array is reported to be full. For adding the element in a queue, first we check the condition of overflow. Then only, we can add elements. For this, we can use the algorithm:

```
if (rear == Maxsize - 1)
    printf("Queue overflow\n");
else
{
    if front == -1 /* if queue is initially empty */
    front = 0;
    rear = rear + 1;
    que[rear] = item;          /* Add the item in the end */
}
```

Initially let front and rear are both empty and hence given the value -1. After adding first element both will become 0 and after that only rear will increase when we add further elements in the queue.

Before deleting an element from the queue, it is first ascertained whether there are any elements available for deletion. If not, then the queue is reported to be empty. Otherwise, an element is deleted from the array. For deleting the element of the queue, first check the condition of underflow then only delete the elements as follows:

```
if (front == -1 || front > rear)
{
    printf("Queue underflow\n");
    return;
}
else
{
    printf("Element delete from queue is: %d\n", que[front]);
    front = front + 1;
}
```

The sign || is the logical operator OR in programming language 'C'.

Underflow condition can arise in situations when front is -1 or *front* is greater than *rear*. After deleting the element, we increase the *front* value by 1.

Figure 5.20 shows an algorithm for insertion in a queue. Figure 5.21 shows the algorithm for deletion from a queue.

```
    BEGIN
    QINSERT (QUE, N, FRONT, REAR, ITEM)
    (This procedure inserts an item into a straight line queue)
1.  [Is Que already filled?]
    If REAR = N Then Write Overflow and Return
2.  Else [Find a new value of REAR]
3.  If FRONT = NULL Then (Queue is initially empty)
    Set FRONT := 1 and REAR := 1
    Else
    Set REAR := REAR + 1
    End if
3.  Set Que [REAR] := ITEM (This inserts item)
4.  Return
    END
```

Figure 5.20 Algorithm for inserting an ITEM in a straight queue

```
   BEGIN
   QDELETE (QUE, N, FRONT, REAR, ITEM)
   (This procedure deletes an element from a straight queue and
    assigns it to the variable ITEM)
1. [ Is Que already Empty? ]
   If FRONT = NULL Then
   Write Underflow and Return
2. Else set Item := Que [FRONT] { Copy the contents in variable ITEM }
3. [Find new value of FRONT]
   If FRONT = REAR Then
   Set FRONT := NULL and REAR := NULL
   (Que has only one element and so emptied)
   Else Set FRONT = FRONT + 1
   (End of if structure)
4. Return.
    END
```

Figure 5.21 Algorithm for deleting an ITEM from a straight queue

☞ Queues are represented by means of one-way lists or linear arrays.

We shall call this array as QUEUE. It will have two variables:

a. FRONT. This variable contains the location of the front element of the queue to be deleted.

b. REAR. It contains the location of the *rear* element of the queue.

If FRONT = NULL, then it is an indication that the queue is empty.

When an element is deleted from the queue, the value of FRONT is increased by 1, which is carried out by the assignment statement:

```
FRONT := FRONT + 1;
```

Similarly, when an element is added to the queue, the value of REAR is increased by 1 before insertion. This is done by the assignment statement:

```
REAR := REAR + 1;
```

By this method, when the number of insertions have reached N, the last element will occupy the Nth position in the queue or QUEUE(N) will contain the Nth insertion item. But as we go on deleting items, the QUEUE will be getting emptied from the FRONT. This procedure is expensive because the number of elements actually in the queue may not be large but we have to go on inserting the newer elements at the REAR of the queue. Thus, this procedure is modified and the queue so created is known as circular queue. circular queue is discussed in detail later in the chapter.

Example 13

Program in 'C' language and the output for an array implementation of queue is shown in Figure 5.22.

```
/* Array Implementation of a queue */
#include <stdio.h>
#define qsize 5
int front,rear,error,count = 0;
main()
{
   void ins();
   void del();
   void wrique();
   float que[qsize];
   float item;
   int choice;
   rear = 0;
   front = 0;
   printf ("\nQUEUE OPERATIONS :");
   do
   {
      error = 1;
      printf ("\n1 - Insert, 2 - Delete, 3 - Quit : ");
      scanf ("%d", &choice);
      switch (choice)
      {
```

(Contd...)

```
        case 1:
            printf ("\nEnter the item to be inserted : ");
            scanf ("%f", &item);
            ins (que, item);
            if (!error)
                {
                    printf ("\nThe Queue after Insertion :\n");
                    wrique (que);
                    printf ("\n");
                }
                break;
        case 2:
            del (que);
            if ((!error) && (count))
            {
                printf ("\nThe Queue after Deletion :\n");
                wrique (que);
                printf ("\n");
            }
            break;
        case 3:
            if ((!error) && (front))
            {
                printf ("\nThe Final Queue :\n");
                wrique (que);
                printf ("\n");
            }
            break;
        default:
            printf ("\nInvalid Option.\n");
            break;
        }
    } while (choice !=3);
  }
/* function to insert items into a queue */
void ins (qu,item)
float qu[qsize],item;
{
   if (rear < qsize)
   {
       rear++;
       qu[rear] = item;
       if (!front)
```

(Contd...)

```
        rear++;
        qu[rear] = item;
        if (!front)
            front = 1;
        error = 0;
        count++;
    }
    else
    {
        printf ("\nQUEUE OVERFLOW. \n");
        error = 1;
    }
    return;
}
/* function to delete items from a queue */
void del(qu)
float qu[qsize];
{
    float item;
        if (front)
    {
        item = qu[front];
        error = 0;
        count--;
        printf ("\nThe item deleted = %6.2f\n", item);
    if (front == rear)
    {
        front = 0;
        rear = 0;
        printf ("\nThe Queue is EMPTY .\n");
    }
    else
        front++;
    }
    else
    {
        printf ("\nQUEUE UNDERFLOW. \n");
        error = 1;
    }
    return;
}
/* function to display queue items */
void wrique(qu)
float qu[qsize];
{
    int c,k;
    k = 0;
```

(Contd...)

```
   for (c = front; c < rear+1; c++)
   {
       k++;
       if (k > 8)
       {
           k = 1;
           printf ("\n");
       }
       printf("%8.2f",qu[c]);
   }
   return;
}
```

RUN

```
Queue Operations:
1 - Insert, 2 - Delete, 3 - Quit : 1

Enter the element to be inserted: 11.00

The queue after Insertion :
11.00

1 - Insert, 2 - Delete, 3 - Quit : 1

Enter the element to be inserted : 22.00

The Queue after Insertion:
11.00   22.00

1 - Insert, 2 - Delete, 3 - Quit: 1

Enter the element to be inserted : 33.00

The Queue after Insertion:
11.00   22.00   33.00

1 - Insert, 2 - Delete, 3 - Quit: 1

Enter the element to be inserted : 44.00

The Queue after Insertion:
11.00   22.00   33.00   44.00

1 - Insert, 2 - Delete, 3 - Quit: 2
```

(Contd...)

```
The element deleted = 11.00

The queue after Deletion :
22.00    33.00    44.00

1 - Insert, 2 - Delete, 3 - Quit : 2

The element deleted = 22.00

The queue after Deletion:
33.00    44.00

1 - Insert, 2 - Delete, 3 - Quit : 2

The element deleted = 33.00

The queue after Deletion:
44.00

1 - Insert, 2 - Delete, 3 - Quit : 2

The element deleted = 44.00

The Queue is Empty

1 - Insert, 2 - Delete, 3 - Quit : 2

Queue underflow

1 - Insert, 2 - Delete, 3 - Quit : 3
```

Figure 5.22 Program and Output of Example 13 for array implementation of queue

5.6.2 Linked List Implementation of Queue

We can implement Queue using a linked list (See Figure 5.23). Linked lists do not have any restrictions on the number of elements it can hold. Memory space for the elements in a linked list is allocated dynamically, hence linked list can grow as long as there is enough memory available for dynamic allocation. We can also insert a new element at the end of the list after the last node. This is pointed to by the *pointer* Rear. We must also take care when we insert a new element into an empty queue. Then, we need to adjust the Front pointer to be the new node.

Whenever we remove an element from a queue, we must ensure that the queue is not empty.

Suppose queue contains only one element that means:

Front = Rear ≠ Null

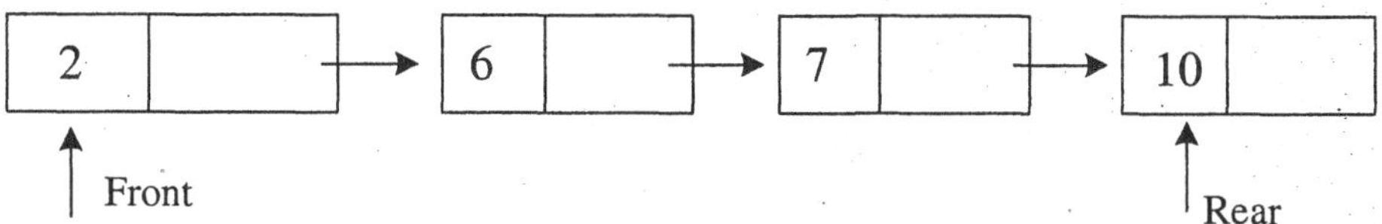

Figure 5.23 Linked list implementation of a Queue

and suppose that the element is removed. In such a case, the Front and Rear pointers are assigned NULL to indicate that the queue is empty.

To implement a queue through linked list, the structure of the node will be, as shown below:

```
struct node
   {
      int item;
      struct node *next;
   }
```

The add operation adds a new element at the rear end of the list. If the element added is the first element, then both *front* and *rear* are made to point to the new node. However, if the element added is not the first element, then only rear is made to point to the new node, whereas front continues to point to the first node in the list. For adding the element in queue we add the element at the end of linked list. Here *front* will point to the first node of linked list and *rear* will point to the last node of the linked list.

Thus, we have in terms of pointers,

```
tmp -> info = added_item;
tmp -> next = NULL;
if (front == NULL) /* If queue is empty */
     front = tmp;
else
     rear -> next = tmp;
     rear = tmp;
```

The delete operation removes an element from the list which is at the front end of the list. Removal of an element from the list actually deletes the node to which front is pointing. After deletion of a node, *front* is made to point to the next node that comes in the list, whereas *rear* continues to point to the last node in the list.

For deleting the element of a queue, we delete the first node of the linked list. Since queue is the First In First Out (FIFO) structure and also, the first node of the linked list will be the first element of the queue. Therefore, we can write the following in 'C'.

```
if(front == NULL)
    printf("Queue underflow\n");
else
{
    tmp = front;
    printf("Deleted element is %d\n", tmp -> info);
```

```
        front = front -> next
        free (tmp);
    }
```

Here front is pointing to the first element of queue. After deleting the element, it will point to the next element of queue.

☞ *Whenever we remove an element from a queue, we must ensure that the queue is not empty.*

Example 14

Program along with output for illustrating implementation of a queue using linked list is shown in Figure 5.24.

```
/* Implementation of Queue using linked list */
#include <stdio.h>
#include <malloc.h>
struct node
   {
   int info;
   struct node *link;
   };
/* function to insert queue elements to a linked list */
   void enqueue(front,rear,i)
   struct node **front, **rear;
   int i;
   {
       struct node *new;
       new = (struct node *) malloc(sizeof(struct node));
       new -> link = NULL;
       new -> info = i;
       if ((*front) == NULL)
       {
           (*front) = new;
           (*rear) = new;
       }
       else
       {
           (*rear) -> link = new;
           (*rear) = new;
       }
   }
```

(Contd...)

```
/* function to delete queue elements from a linked list */
void del_queue(front)
struct node **front;
{
   struct node *temp;
   if ((*front) != NULL)
   {
      temp = *front;
      (*front) = (*front) -> link;
      free(temp);
   }
}
/* function to display the queue elements */
   void display (front)
   struct node *front;
   {
      printf("\nFront -> ");
      while (front != NULL)
      {
         printf("%d -> ",(*front).info);
         front = (*front).link;
      }
      printf("NULL\n");
   }
/* main function */
   main()
   {
      struct node *front = NULL, *rear = NULL;
      int finished = 0,choice;
      do
      {
      printf("\n\nQueue operations : ");
      printf("\n  1) Insert");
      printf("\n  2) Delete");
      printf("\n  3) Quit\nEnter choice :");
      scanf("%d", &choice);
      switch (choice)
      {
         case 1:
            printf("\nEnter the new element : ");
            scanf("%d", &choice);
            enqueue(&front,&rear,choice);
            break;
         case 2:
            del_queue(&front);
            break;
```

(Contd...)

```
        case 3:
            finished = 1;
    }
    printf("\nThe queue is \n");
    display(front);
    if (front == NULL)
        printf("\nThe queue is empty.");
    }
        while (!finished);
        printf("\n\n");
        while (front != NULL)
        {
            rear = front -> link ;
            free (front);
            front = rear;
        }
    }
```

RUN

```
Queue operations:

1) Insert
2) Delete
3) Quit
Enter choice: 1

Enter the new element : 11

The queue is

Front → 11 → NULL

Queue operations:

1) Insert
2) Delete
3) Quit
Enter choice: 1

Enter the new element : 22

The queue is

Front → 11 → 22 → NULL

Queue operations:

1) Insert
2) Delete
3) Quit
Enter choice : 1
```

(Contd...)

```
Enter the new element : 33

The queue is

Front → 11 → 22 → 33 → NULL

Queue operations:

1) Insert
2) Delete
3) Quit
Enter choice : 1

Enter the new element : 44

The queue is

Front → 11 → 22 → 33 → 44 → NULL

Queue operations:

1) Insert
2) Delete
3) Quit
Enter choice : 2

The queue is

Front → 22 → 33 → 44 → NULL

Queue operations:

1) Insert
2) Delete
3) Quit
Enter choice : 2

The queue is

Front → 33 → 44 → NULL

Queue operations:

1) Insert
2) Delete
3) Quit
Enter choice : 2

The queue is

Front → 44 → NULL
```

(Contd...)

```
Queue operations:

1) Insert
2) Delete
3) Quit

Enter choice : 2

The queue is

Front → NULL

The queue is empty.

Queue operations:

1) Insert
2) Delete
3) Quit
Enter choice : 1

Enter the new element : 12

The queue is

Front → 12 → NULL

Queue operations :

1) Insert
2) Delete
3) Quit
Enter choice : 3

The queue is

Front → 12 → NULL
```

Figure 5.24 Program and output of Example 14 implementation of queue using linked list

5.7 CIRCULAR QUEUE

As in a circle, after last element, the first element occurs. So, when circular Queue technique is used to construct a queue, then also the queue is called *circular queue*. In other words, we can say that a queue is called circular when the last element comes just before the first element of the queue. Figure 5.25 illustrates a circular queue.

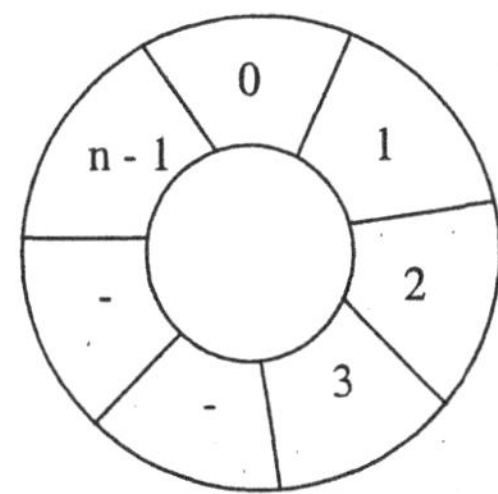

Figure 5.25 Pictorial representation of a circular queue

Here, after n-1th element, 0th element will occur.

> *When the REAR element of an array joins the Front, then the array becomes a circular queue. It means the next location to queue [N] will be queue [Front].*

5.7.1 Array Implementation of a Circular Queue

In order to understand the insertion procedure in a circular queue, let us take the case of a QUEUE which has 5 memory locations as shown in Figure 5.26.

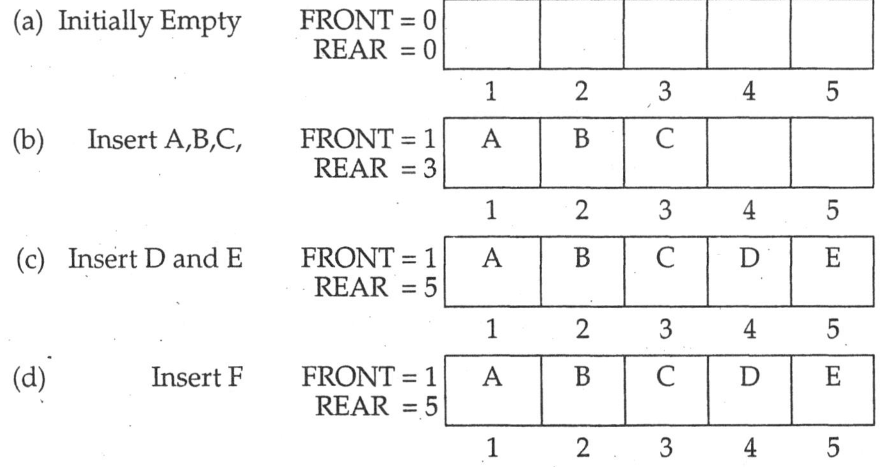

Figure 5.26 Insertion of elements in a circular Queue

In step (a), the queue is empty and therefore values of FRONT as well as REAR = 0. In step (b), the values *A*, *B*, and *C* are inserted in memory locations 1, 2, and 3. In step (c), values *D* and *E* are inserted in memory locations 4 and 5. In step (d), the Queue is full, so the message "overflow" is printed. Figure 5.27 shows the algorithm for insertion in a circular queue.

In order to understand the algorithm for deletion of an item in a Circular Queue, we shall take the case where QUE has 5 memory locations and all are filled. [See Figure 5.28]. To delete the first element, we first take out *A* because queue is first in, first out structure. (See Figure 5.28)

```
     Begin
1.   QINSERT (QUE, N, FRONT, REAR, ITEM)
     (This procedure inserts an item into a circular queue)
     [Is Queue already filled?]
     IF FRONT = 1 AND REAR = N or
2.   IF FRONT = (REAR + 1) Then
     Write OVERFLOW and Return
     Else [to find a new value of REAR]
     If FRONT = NULL Then (Que is initially empty)
     Set FRONT := 1 and REAR := 1
     Else IF REAR = N Then
     Set REAR : = 1
     Else Set REAR : = 1
3.   End if [End of if structure]
4.   Set Que [REAR] := ITEM (This inserts a new item)
     Return.
     End
```

Figure 5.27 Algorithm for inserting in a circular queue

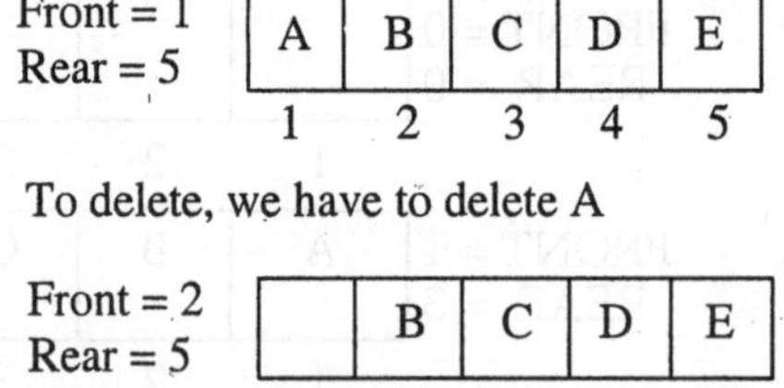

Figure 5.28 Deletion of first element from the circular queue

The algorithm for deletion from a circular queue is shown in Figure 5.29.

```
     Begin
     The following algorithm deletes an element from a circular
     queue.
     QDELETE (QUE, N, FRONT, REAR, ITEM)
     (This procedure deletes an element from a queue and assign it to
     the variable ITEM)
1.   [ Is QUE already empty? ]
     IF FRONT = NULL Then
     Write UNDERFLOW and Return.
2.   Else
     Set ITEM := QUE [FRONT] {Copy the value of QUE[FRONT] in ITEM}
3.   [Find new value of FRONT]
     IF FRONT = REAR Then
     {QUE has only one element to spare}
```

(*Contd...*)

```
        Set FRONT := NULL and REAR := NULL
        Else IF FRONT = N Then
        Set FRONT : = 1
        Else
4.      Set FRONT : = FRONT + 1
        (End of if structure)
        Return.
        End
```

Figure 5.29 Algorithm for deleting an ITEM in a circular queue

Example 15

Figure 5.30 represents an example for implementing an array as a circular queue.

(a) Initially Empty — FRONT = 0, REAR = 0

1	2	3	4	5

(b) A1, B1, C1, are inserted — FRONT = 1, REAR = 3

1	2	3	4	5
A1	B2	C1		

(C) A1 is deleted — FRONT = 2, REAR = 3

1	2	3	4	5
	B1	C1		

(d) D1 and E1 are inserted — FRONT = 2, REAR = 5

1	2	3	4	5
	B1	C1	D1	E1

(e) B1 and C1 are deleted — FRONT = 4, REAR = 5

1	2	3	4	5
			D1	E1

(f) F1 is inserted (because circular Queue) — FRONT = 4, REAR = 1

1	2	3	4	5
F1			D1	E1

(g) D1 is deleted — FRONT = 5, REAR = 1

1	2	3	4	5
F1				E1

(h) G1 and H1 are inserted — FRONT = 5, REAR = 3

1	2	3	4	5
F1	G1	H1		E1

(i) E1 is deleted — FRONT = 1, REAR = 3

1	2	3	4	5
F1	G1	H1		

		1	2	3	4	5
(j) F1 deleted	FRONT = 2 REAR = 3		G1	H1		
(k) K1 is inserted	FRONT = 2 REAR = 4		G1	H1	K1	
(l) G1 and H1 are deleted	FRONT = 4 REAR = 4				K1	
(m) K1 is deleted QUEUE is empty	FRONT = 0 REAR = 0					

Figure 5.30 Array implementation of circular queue

We assume that QUEUE is a circular queue, N = 5 are the memory locations and that the queue always occupies consecutive locations. The queue is empty only when FRONT = REAR = NULL and no element is deleted in such a situation.

5.8 PRIORITY QUEUE

Priority queue is a specialized data structure than a stack or a queue. It is a useful tool in a number of situations. Like an ordinary queue, a priority queue has a *Front* and *Rear*. Items are inserted in the Rear and removed from the Front. However, in a priority queue, items are *ordered* by *key* or *priority value,* so that the item with the lowest key (or in some implementation the highest key) is always at the front. Items are inserted in the proper position to maintain the order or priority.

There are two types of priority queues. These are:

a. *Ascending priority queue*

b. *Descending priority queue*

5.8.1 Ascending Priority Queue

It is a collection of items into which new items can be inserted arbitrarily and from which only the smallest item can be removed first.

5.8.2 Descending Priority Queue

It allows deletion of only the largest item first from the queue.

☞ *The order in which the elements should get added or removed is decided by the priority of the element.*

5.8.3 Rules for Maintaining Priority Queue

Following rules are applied to maintain a priority queue:

a. The elements with a higher priority are processed before any element of lower priority.

b. If there are elements with the same priority, then the element added first in the queue would be processed first.

The real life example of priority queue is the priority for answering the mail received from various places. Every time the postman hands over a letter, you insert it into the file of pending letters according to its priority. If it must be answered immediately, it goes on top, but if it need not be answered immediately, it goes at the end of other mail.

When you have time to answer mail, you start by taking from the top (the front of the queue) thus ensuring that the most important mail is answered first. (See Figure 5.31)

Like stacks and queues, priority queues are also used by programmer as tools for developing systems. In a preemptive multitasking OS, for example, programs may be placed in a priority queue so the highest priority program is the next one to receive a time slice to be executed.

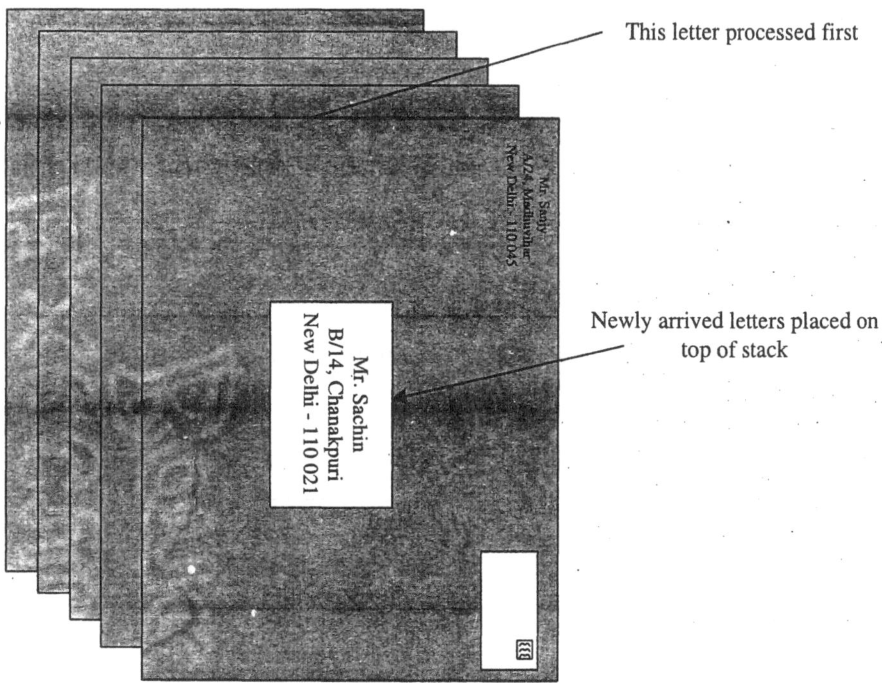

Figure 5.31 Priority queue example

5.9 D-QUEUE

We know that, in stacks, insertions and deletions are done only from one end i.e. LIFO (Last In First Out) but in a queue, insertion is possible from one end, and deletion from the other end i.e FIFO (First In First Out).

D-Queue (Double ended Queue) is a linear list where insertions and deletions can be made at either the head or the tail, but not any where else in the list. (See Figure 5.32).

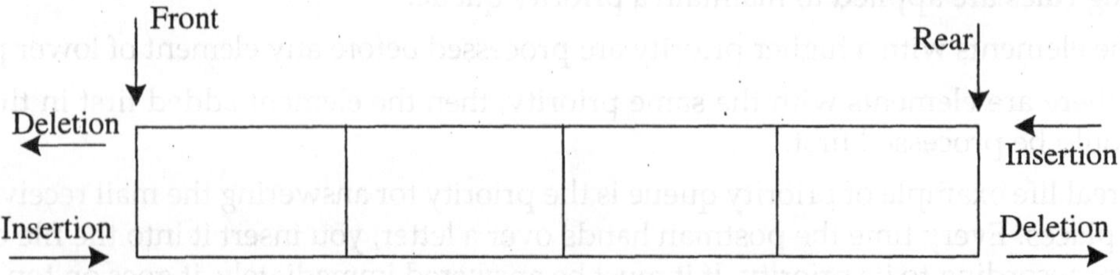

Figure 5.32 Representation of D-Queue

Types of D-Queues are:

1. Input restricted D-Queue
2. Output restricted D-Queue

D-Queue can have different forms such as Input-restricted D-queue, which allows insertions at only one end. But the deletion of elements can be done at both the ends of a queue (See Figure 5.33). Similarly, output restricted D-Queue, allows deletions from only one end, and allows insertion done from both the ends of a D-Queue (See Figure 5.34).

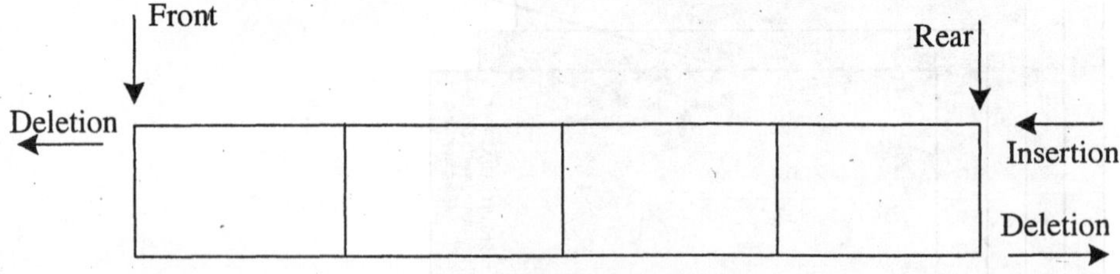

Figure 5.33 Representation of an input-restricted D-Queue

Figure 5.34 Representation of an output restricted D-Queue

5.10 APPLICATIONS OF STACKS AND QUEUES

Following are some of the applications of stacks and queues in computer field.

- Stack is a LIFO structure. It is used for applications where information must be stored and later retrieved in the reverse order.

- Stack can be used to check whether parentheses, braces and brackets are balanced while processing formulas in a computer program.
- Stacks also play a vital role in parsing (analyzing) arithmetic expression such as (2 + 8 * 9). The priority of the multiplication operator over arithmetical operator is maintained.
- While traversing a Binary Tree, a stack is used.
- Micro-processors in a PC uses a stack-based architecture. When a member function is called, its return address and arguments are pushed into the stack and when the function returns the values they are popped off. The stack operations are in-built in a microprocessor.
- The most useful application of queue is the simulation of a real world situation such as people waiting in line at a bank or data packets waiting for transmission over the Internet.
- Queues are frequently used in computer programming and a typical example is the creation of job queue by an operating system (OS).

  If the operating system does not use priorities, then the jobs are processed in the order they enter the system. i.e first come first served basis.

  Queues are also useful in a time sharing computer system where many users share the system simultaneously, such as print queue where printing jobs wait for the printer to be available. Printer maintains a queue of jobs waiting to get the printer. This technique is called *spooling*.
- A queue also stores keystroke of data as you type on the keyboard.
- Another useful application of queue is in the solution of problems involving searching a non-linear collection of states. Queue is used for finding a path using Breadth-First-Search graphs.

DESCRIPTIVE QUESTIONS

Q. No. 1 Define stack. What are the advantages and disadvantages of implementing a stack using an array or a linked list?

Ans to Q. 1 Stack is defined as a list in which we can insert or delete the element only at the top of the stack. It is also called LIFO structure.

A stack is often implemented as an array or a linked list.

The array implementation is efficient because the most recently inserted item is placed at the end of the array, where it is also easy to delete it. Stack overflow can occur, but is not likely if the array is reasonably sized, because stacks seldom contains huge amounts of data.

If the amount of data to be stored can not be predicted accurately in advance, a linked list is a better choice for implementing a stack than an array. A linked list is efficient because data items can be inserted and deleted quickly from the head of the list. Stack overflow can't occur (unless the entire memory is full). A linked list implementation of stack is slightly slower than an array implementation because more memory allocation is needed to create a new link for insertion, and deallocation of the link is necessary at some point following removal of an item from the linked list.

Q. No. 2 Write an algorithm for the following:

a. Push operation on stack.

b. Pop operation on stack.

Ans to Q. 2 *[Refer section 5.3.1]*

Q. No. 3 Convert the following expression into postfix and prefix form

Z = (A + B) * C – D

Ans to Q. 3 The steps for finding the post fix expression for Z are

a. Evaluate A+B and store it as T1

T1 = AB+

b. Evaluate T1*C and store it as T2

T2 = (AB+)*C

= AB+C *

c. Evaluate T2-D and assign the result to Z

Z = T2 - D

= AB + C * D-

For quick evaluation the same may be written as:

Z = (A+B) * C - D

=AB + * C - D

=AB + C* - D

= AB + C * D-

The prefix form for expression Z may be found as under:-

Z = (A + B) * C - D

= + AB * C - D

= * + ABC - D

= - * + ABCD

a. (A - B) * (C/D) + E

= AB - * CD/+E

= AB - CD/*+E

= AB - CD/* E +

b. (A+B) * (C*(D+E)+F)

= AB+ * (C * DE + +F)

= AB+ * (CDE+ * + F)

= AB+ * CDE + * F +

= AB + CDE + * F + *

Q. No. 4 Convert the following into postfix form

a. (A - B) * (C/D) + E

b. (A + B) * (C * (D + E) + F)

Ans to Q. 4 a. (A - B) * (C/D) + E

= AB - * CD/+E

= AB - CD/*+E

= AB - CD/* E +

b. (A+B) * (C*(D+E)+F)
= AB+ * (C * DE + +F)
= AB+ * (CDE+ * + F)
= AB+ * CDE + * F +
= AB + CDE + * F + *

Q. No. 5 Write an algorithm for evaluation of postfix expression.

1. Let the postfix expression be p.
2. Repeat steps 3 through 9
   while there are more symbols in p
3. Let S be the next symbol in p.
4. If S is an operand or constant goto step 5
   If S is an operator go to step 6
5. Push S to stack goto step 2
6. U = pop(stack)
7. V = pop(stack)
8. R = Result when operator S operates on V and U.
9. Push R on stack go to step 2
   {end while}
10. Pop result from stack and display

EXERCISE

Multiple Choice

1. A data structure, in which a element is added and removed only from one end, is known

a. queue b. stack
c. array d. None of these

2. Stack is

a. static data structure b. dynamic data structure
c. in built data structure d. None of these

3. Stack cannot be used to

a. evaluate an arithmetic expression in postfix form
b. implement recursion
c. convert infix form to postfix form of an expression
d. allocate resources by operating system

4. Queue

a. can be created by setting up an ordinary contiguous array to hold the items
b. can take care of delete operation automatically
c. need a one pointer to handle addition and deletion of an item.
d. None of the above

5. Data structure-
   a. is programming language dependent.
   b. need not give relationship between data items
   c. may be helpful to develop efficient algorithms in different phases of data processing.
   d. None of the above
6. "Get a node, store new element and insert the new node at the top" refers to insert operation in non empty-
   a. stack b. queue
   c. array d. None of the above
7. "Get the value of most recently inserted node and delete the node" refers to operation-
   a. POP b. PUSH
   c. EMPTY d. None of the above
8. "FRONT = REAR = NULL" pointer refers to empty-
   a. stack b. queue
   c. array d. None of the above
9. Most appropriate data structure in C to represent linked list is
   a. array b. struct
   c. union d. None of the above
10. Link of linked list in C is of type
   a. unsigned integer b. pointer to integer
   c. pointer to struct d. None of the above

Key to Multiple Choice Questions

1.	b	2.	b	3.	d	4.	a	5.	c
6.	a	7.	a	8.	b	9.	b	10.	c

TEST PAPER

Note: Answer all questions.

1. Compare the advantages and disadvantages of implementing a stack as an array with implementing a stack as a linked list.
2. How a straight queue is different from circular queue
3. Write a program in C to implement a queue using a linear linked list
4. List different applications of stacks and queues.
5. Write down the equivalent infix expression for the following postfix expression.
   ABC - DEF + * –

CHAPTER 6

Trees

6.1 INTRODUCTION

Data structure such as stacks, queues and linked list are linear data structures, whereas TREES type of data structures are non linear.

Linked list is a better type of data structure from conservation of main memory point of view. But disadvantage with the linked list is that every node has information for the next node only. For this reason, searching in linked list is a very slow process.

We will study *tree* data structure. In this, data is organised in a hierarchical way, such that each node may point to several other nodes. This makes information retrieval and searching very fast. *Tree* structure is also used in applications such as compiler construction, database design, MS-Windows operating system programs etc. Thus, data structure *tree* is a very flexible and powerful data structure that can be used for a wide variety of applications.

6.2 WHAT IS A TREE DATA STRUCTURE ?

A *tree* data structure is a dynamic data structure which represents hierarchical relationships between individual data items/nodes.

In a tree, nodes are organised in the hierarchical way such that:

- There is a specially designated node called the *root*, at the beginning of the structure except when the tree is empty.
- Lines connecting the nodes are called *branches* and every node except the root is joined to just one node at the next higher level (its parent).
- Nodes that have no children are called *leaf* nodes or *terminal* nodes. (See the tree given in Figure 6.1(a)).

☞ *Tree data structure consist of nodes (circles) connected by edges (lines).*

Thus, data structure tree consists of a collection of nodes which are joined to other nodes with the help of branches. A node which points to other nodes is said to be the *parent* of the nodes to which it is pointing to. These pointed nodes in a tree are called children of that node. In Figure 6.1(a), the tree has 13 nodes. These are: *A, B, C, D, E, F, G, H, I, J, K, L* and *M*. The node *A* is the parent of *B, C* and *D* or *B, C* and *D* are the children of *A*.

A node at the topmost position of the tree is called *root*. There is only one root in a tree. For example, in Figure 6.1(a). *A* is the *root* node. The root is the only one node in the tree that does not possess a parent.

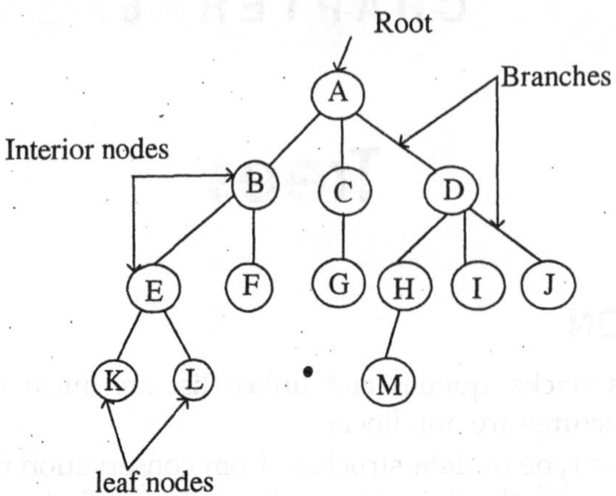

Figure 6.1(a) A tree structure for arranging data

☞ *The root is the topmost node in a tree and it has no other node as parent node.*

A node that has no children is called a *leaf node*. The leaf node is also called *terminal node*. The rest of the nodes in a tree are called *non-terminal nodes*. For example, in Figure 6.1(a) *K, L, F, G, M, I* and *J* are called leaf or terminal nodes. The nodes which possess children are known as the interior nodes.

A subtree is a subset of a tree that itself is a tree. For example *B, C, D, E,* and *H* in Figure 6.1(a) is a sub-tree. The tree in Figure 6.1(b) is a subtree of the tree in Figure 6.1(a). This subtree has the root node as B.

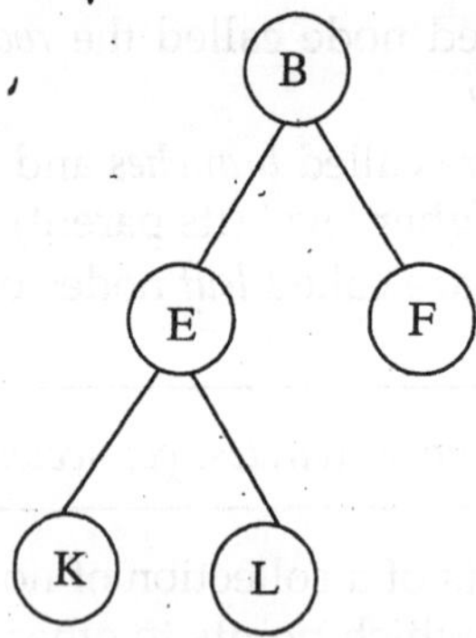

Figure 6.1(b) A subtree of the tree shown in Fig 6.1(a)

Any node can be considered to be the root of a subtree, which contains its children and its children's children and so on. If we think in terms of families, a node's subtree contains all its descendants. The descendents of a node are all the nodes along the path from node to terminal node. The ancestors of a node are all the nodes along the path from the node to the root. The ancestors of *K* are *E, B* and *A* as seen in Figure 6.1(a).

☞ *All the nodes in a tree are descendants of the root.*

The children nodes of the same parent node are called *siblings* i.e. two nodes are siblings if they are left and right children of the same node. For example, *E* and *F* are siblings as seen in Figure 6.1(b).

The number of sub-trees of a node is called the degree of the node. For example, in Figure 6.1(a) nodes *B, C, D* are sub-trees of root node *A* and the degree of node *A* is 3 since, there are three subtrees. The degree of node *I* is 0, since there is no sub-tree for node *I*.

☞ *A node with a degree zero is called leaf node.*

The level of a particular node refers to how many generations the node is from the root. If we assume the root is at level 0, its children will be at level 1, its grand children will be at level 2, and so on. For example, node *E* is at level 2 and *K* is at level 3 as seen in Figure 6.1 (a).

☞ *The nodes which are at the same level are said to be of the same generation.*

The length of the longest path from root to any node is known as *depth* or *height* of the tree. This turns out to be one more than the largest level number of the tree. For example, depth of the tree given in Figure 6.1(a) is 4.

Tree structure is ideal for representing relationships that hold among data elements. A familiar example that arises in family histories is the ancestor tree. For example, Figure 6.2 shows a typical family tree.

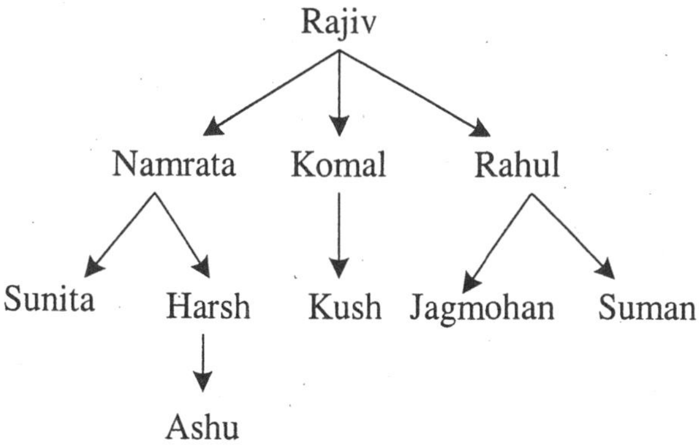

Figure 6.2 A typical family tree

Here *Rajiv* in the family tree is the root node. A node which points to other nodes is said to be the parent of the nodes to which it is pointing. The nodes in a tree that are pointed by the parent node are called children nodes. For example Rajiv is parent of Namrata, Komal and Rahul and thus, these are the children of Rajiv.

6.3 BINARY TREE

A binary tree is a special type of tree representation of data items. If every node in a tree can have at the most two children, the tree is called a *binary tree*.

A binary tree consists of a node called the root node and left and right nodes are the sub-trees. Figure 6.3(a) is an example of a binary tree. The tree shown in this figure consists of nine nodes with "+" as its root. Its left subtree is rooted at "-" and its right sub tree is rooted at "*". Note that both children of "-" are leaf nodes, whereas only the left child of "*" is a leaf node. The left subtree of the root "+" is shown in Figure 6.3(b) and the right subtree of the right subtree of "*" is shown in Figure 6.3(c).

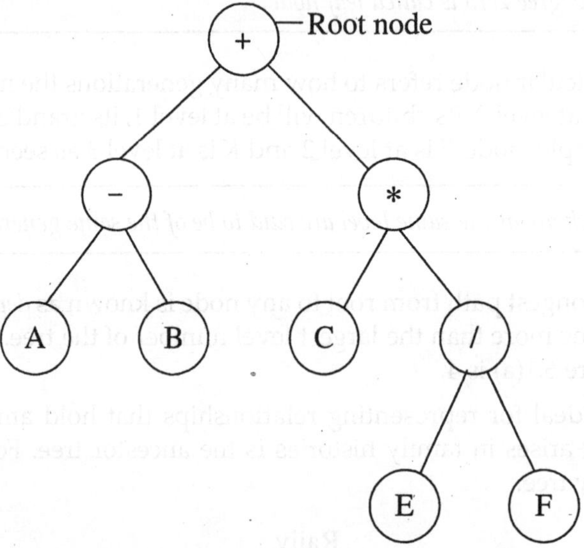

Figure 6.3(a) A binary tree where each node has no more than 2 child nodes

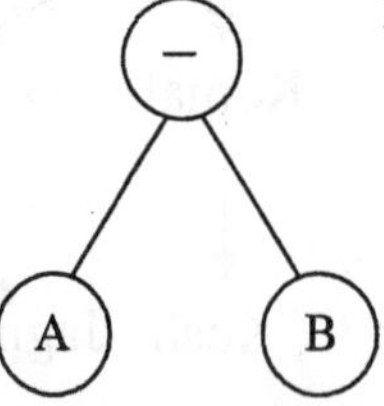

Figure 6.3(b) Left subtree of root "+" of Figure 6.3(a)

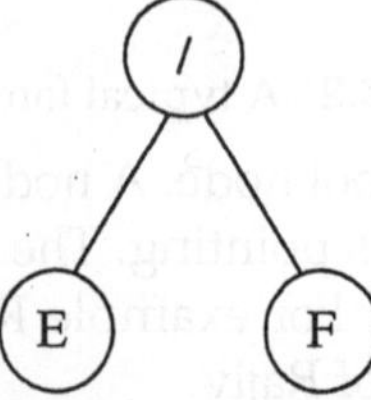

Figure 6.3(c) The right subtree of the subtree "*" in Figure 6.3(a)

The absence of a branch indicates an empty subtree. The binary trees whose roots are at A, B, C, E and F are empty subtrees.

☞ *In a binary tree, the degree of each node is less than or equal to 2.*

The two children of each node in a binary tree are called the *left child* and the *right child*. In programming language C, we can define structure of Binary tree as:

```
struct Bitree
  {
  int info;
  struct Bitree *left;
  struct Bitree *right;
  }
```

A node in a binary tree might have only one left child, and only one right child or it may have no child at all. Figure 6.4 shows different forms of the binary tree.

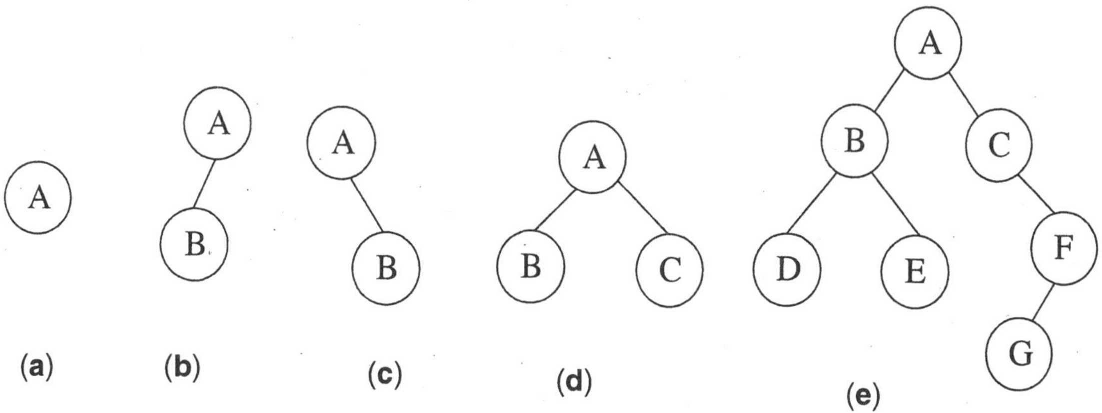

Figure 6.4 Different forms of a binary tree

In Figure 6.4(a) a binary tree is shown with a single node, i.e its left and right subtrees are empty. Figure 6.4(b) and (c) shows a binary tree with two nodes, the root node and the left child (Figure 6.4(b)) or the right child (Figure 6.4(c)). Figure 6.4(d) shows a binary tree with a left subtree and right subtree of root. In Figure 6.4(e) the binary tree has seven nodes. Root is A and its left successor is node B and right successor is node C. Similarly, left successor of node B is node D and right successor is node E.

6.3.1 Types of Binary Tree

Binary trees are of three types. These are:

- Complete binary tree
- Almost complete binary tree
- Strictly binary tree

Complete binary tree

Complete binary tree is a tree in which each leaf is at the same distance from the root. It can be defined as a binary tree whose non leaf nodes have, non empty left and right subtree. All leaves are at the same level. The tree in Figure 6.5 is an example of complete binary tree.

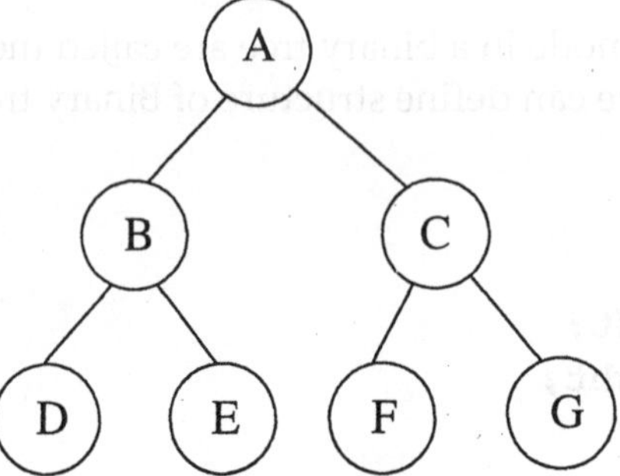

Figure 6.5 Complete binary tree

☞ *In a complete binary tree, out degree of every node is either 2 or nil.*

Almost complete binary tree

An almost complete binary tree is a binary tree in which the following conditions hold:

(a) All the leaves are at the bottom level or the bottom 2 levels.

(b) All the leaves are in the leftmost possible positions, and (except possibly for the bottom level) all levels are completely filled with nodes.

Figure 6.6(a) to (c) represent some examples of almost complete binary trees.

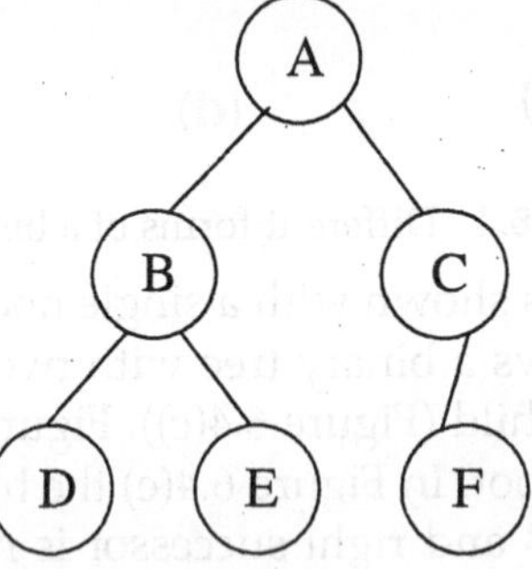

Figure 6.6(a) Almost Complete binary tree

The example shown in Figure 6.6(c) is a complete binary tree. It also fits the definition of almost complete binary tree. Since, any complete binary tree is also an almost complete binary tree.

The following data arrangement in the form of a binary tree are not almost complete binary tree representations. (See Figure 6.6(d), (e) and (f))

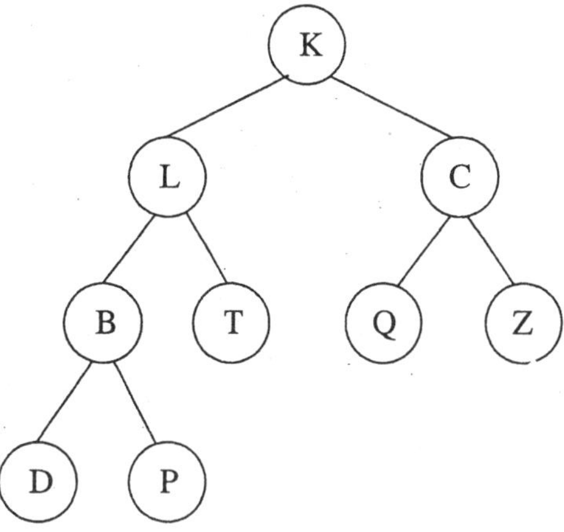

Figure 6.6(b) Almost Complete binary tree

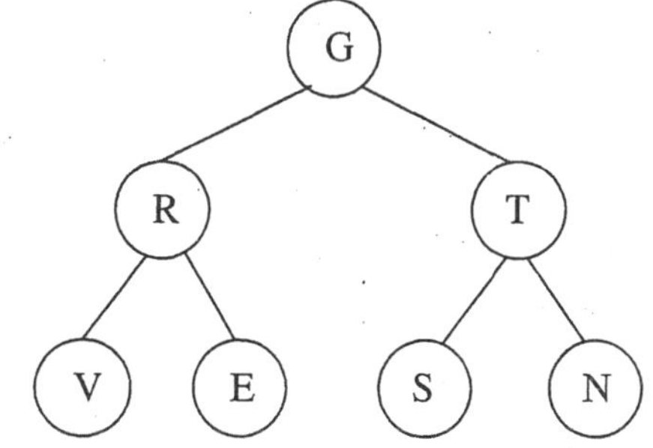

Figure 6.6(c) Almost Complete binary tree

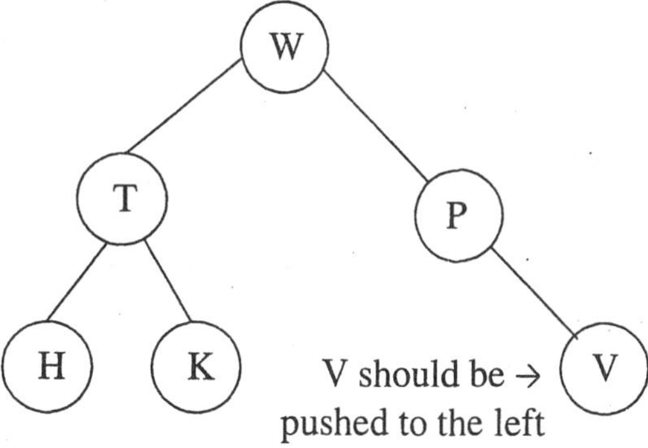

Figure 6.6(d) Not almost complete binary tree because of node V

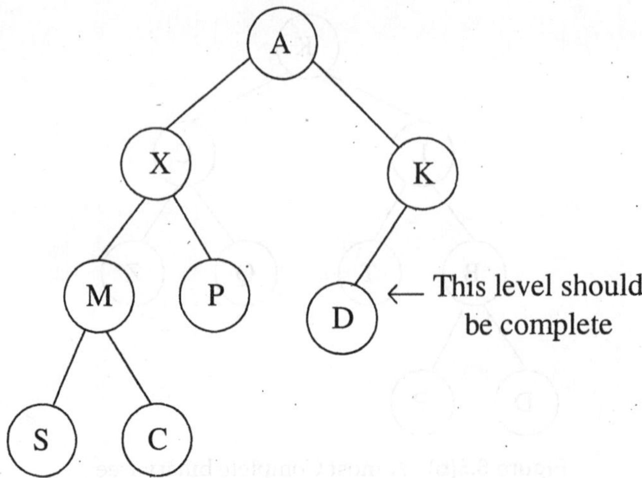

Figure 6.6(e) Not almost complete binary tree because of node D

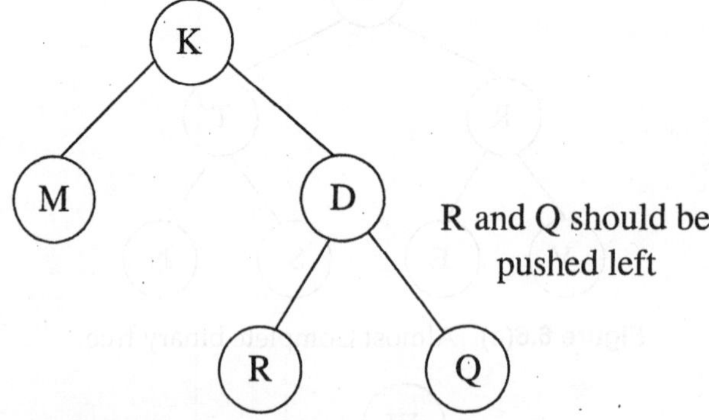

Figure 6.6(f) Not almost complete binary tree because of nodes R and Q

Strictly binary tree

A binary tree is called strictly binary tree if every non-leaf node in the tree has no empty left and right subtree. This means each node in the binary tree will either have zero or two children. (See Figure 6.7). Here every non leaf node *A, C,* and *D* has two non empty left and right children nodes, and hence it is strictly binary tree.

A strictly binary tree with *n* leaves always contain exactly (2n-1) nodes. For example in Figure 6.7, the number of leaf nodes are 4 i.e n = 4.

$$\begin{aligned}\text{Total number of nodes} &= (2 \times 4) - 1 \\ &= 8 - 1 \\ &= 7\end{aligned}$$

6.4 TRAVERSAL METHODS IN BINARY TREE

To traverse a tree means to visit all the nodes in some specified order. For example, you may visit all the nodes in the order of ascending key value.

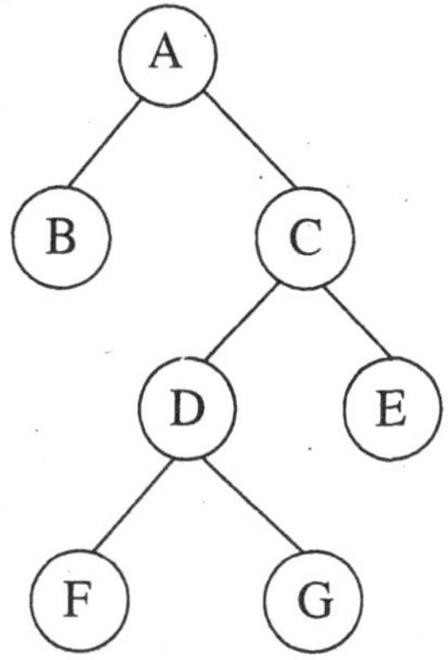

Figure 6.7 Strictly binary tree

There are three different ways to traverse a binary tree. These are:

- Inorder traversal
- Preorder traversal
- Post order traversal

☞ *Different ways of traversing a binary tree means that items can be stored in one sequence and retrieved in a different sequence.*

6.4.1 Inorder Traversal

Inorder traversal of a binary search tree will require all the nodes to be visited in the ascending order, based on their key values. Inorder traversal method is useful to create the sorted list of data.

For Inorder traversal method, the order of traversal are:

a. Traverse the left subtree

b. Visit the root

c. Traverse the right subtree.

A binary tree with 7 nodes is shown in Figure 6.8(a) and its inorder traversal is given in Figure 6.8(b).

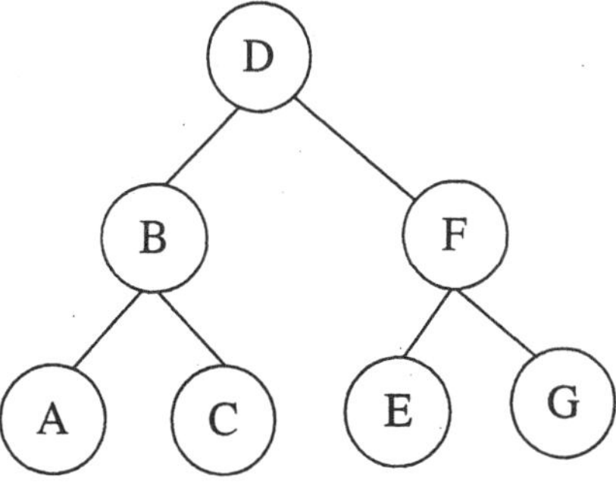

Figure 6.8(a) A binary tree with 7 nodes shown in Figure 6.8(a)

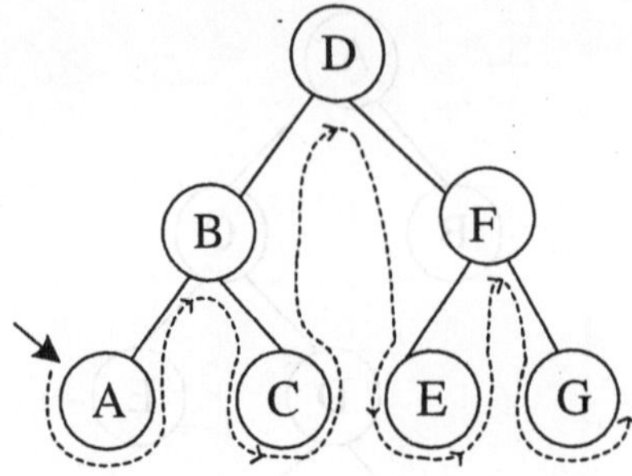

Inorder : A B C D E F G

Figure 6.8(b) Inorder traversal of binary tree shown in Figure 6.8(a)

☞ *Inorder traversal is also known as symmetric order.*

6.4.2 Preorder Traversal

The traversal order for preorder traversal are:

a. Visit the root

b. Traverse the left subtree

c. Traverse the right subtree

☞ *Preorder traversal is also known as depth first order.*

Figure 6.8(c) shows preorder traversal method of binary tree shown in Figure 6.8(a).

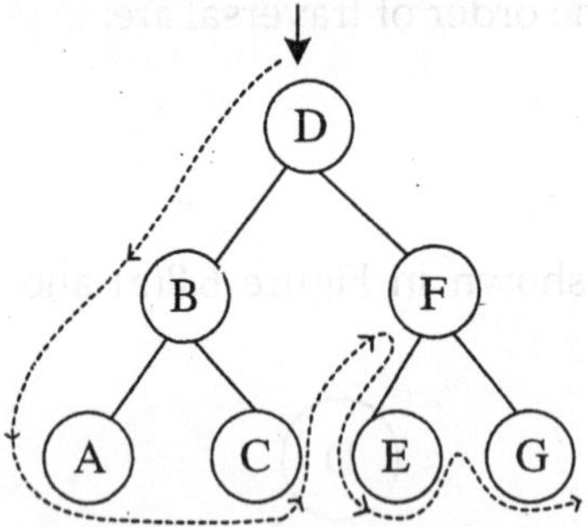

Preorder : D B A C F E G

Figure 6.8(c) Preorder traversal of binary tree

☞ *The preorder traversal of a binary tree begins with processing of the root node.*

6.4.3 Post Order Traversal

The traversal order for post order traversal are:

a. Traverse the left subtree
b. Traverse the right subtree
c. Visit the root

Figure 6.8(d) shows the post order traversal method for binary tree as seen in Figure 6.8(a).

☞ *Preorder and post order traversals are useful for parsing algebric expressions.*

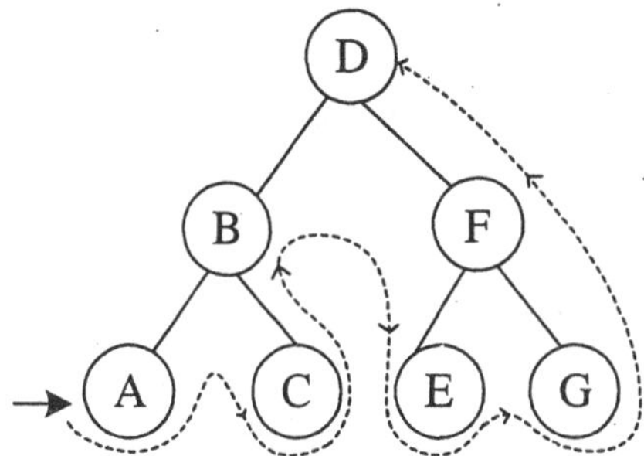

Post order : A C B E G F D

Figure 6.8(d) Post order traversal of binary tree shown in Figure 6.8(a)

☞ *The postorder traversal of a binary tree begins with the post order traversal of the left subtree.*

Example 1

Let us take a binary tree shown in Figure 6.9 and apply each of the three traversal methods, explained above.

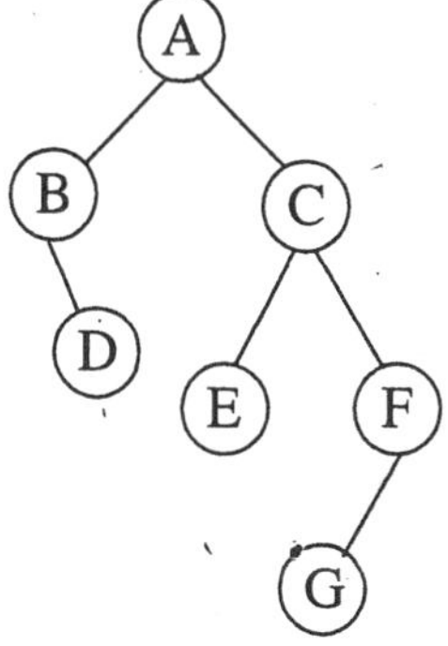

Figure 6.9 A Binary tree

Inorder traversal

The nodes are visited in inorder traversal as follows:

B D A E C G F

Preorder traversal

The nodes are visited in preorder traversal as follows:

A B D C E F G

Post order traversal

The nodes are visited in post order traversal as follows:

D B E G F C A

6.5 REPRESENTATION OF ALGEBRAIC EXPRESSION USING TREE STRUCTURE

A binary tree can be used to represent an algebraic expression, containing operands and other operators such as +, -, / and *. The root node holds an operator, and other nodes represent either a variable name (like A, B, or C) or any another operator.

☞ *The root of a strictly binary tree contains the operator and the leaf node contains operand.*

Let us perform all the traversal methods i.e inorder, preorder and post order on a binary tree shown in Figure 6.3(a). Traversing a tree means processing it in such a way that each node is visited only once.

The *inorder* traversal of binary tree for an arithmetic expression gives us the expression in the infix form *(A - B) + C * (E/F)* [See Figure 6.10(a)].

The *preorder* traversal of the corresponding tree leads us to the prefix form + - *AB * C/EF* expression, [See Figure 6.10(b)]

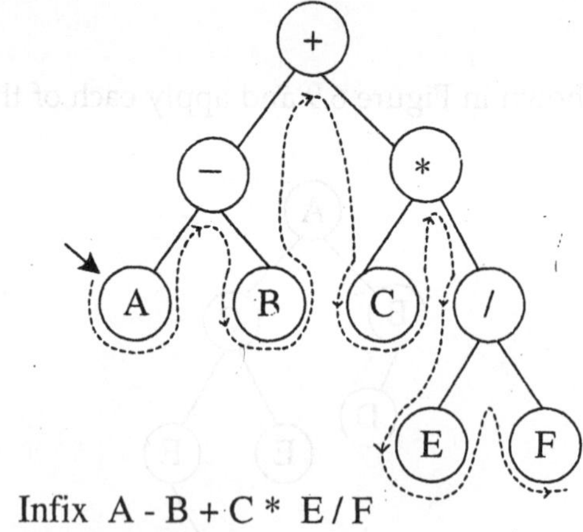

Figure 6.10(a) Inorder traversal of binary tree of Figure 6.3(a)

The *post* order traversal of the same tree yields the postfix form of expression i.e. *AB - CEF/* +* [See Figure 6.10(c)].

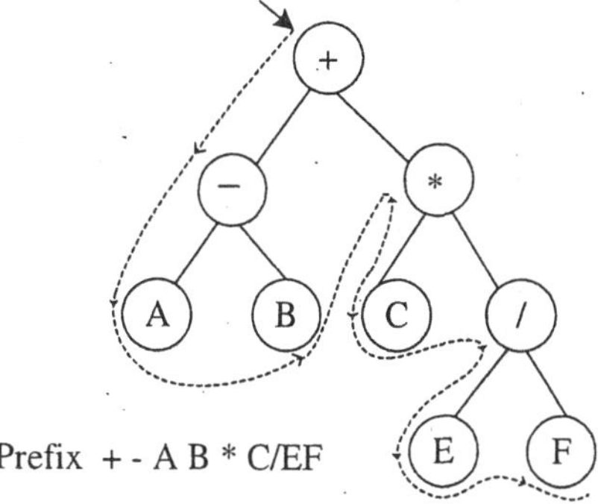

Figure 6.10(b) Preorder traversal of binary tree of Figure 6.3

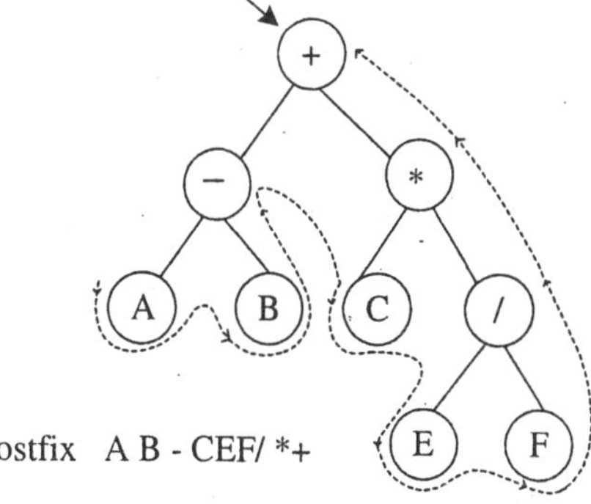

Figure 6.10(c) Post order traversal of binary tree of Figure 6.3

Example 2

Let us perform all the three traversal methods on the binary tree shown in Figure 6.11.

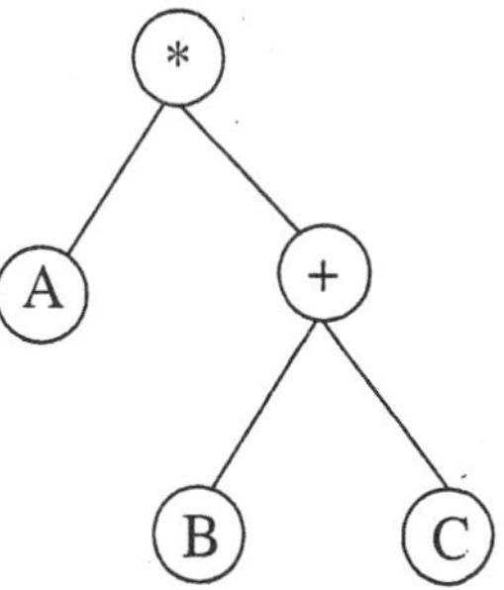

Infix : A * (B + C) [Inorder traversal]
Prefix : * A + BC [Preorder traversal]
Post fix : ABC + * [Post order traversal]

Figure 6.11 A binary tree with 5 nodes

6.6 RECURSIVE ALGORITHMS

A binary tree is recursive in which each sub-tree is also a binary tree. Thus, traversing a binary tree involves visiting the root node and traversing its left and right sub-trees. The only difference among the methods is the order in which these operations are performed. Traversing a tree using these methods can be kept quite short if we understand the recursive nature of the binary tree.

6.6.1 Inorder Traversal Algorithm

1. Begin
   Inorder (Node) /* set the current node */
2. If current node ! = Null then
   a. Call Inorder (Left_child [Node])
      /* Recursively do an inorder traversal of the left subtree of the current node */
   b. Print Info [Node]
      /* Print information at the current node */
   c. Call Inorder (Right_child [Node])
      /* Recursively do an inorder traversal of the right subtree of current node */
3. Stop

6.6.2 Preorder Traversal Algorithm

1. Begin
   Preorder (Node) /* Set the current node */
2. If current node ! = Null then
   a. Print Info [Node]
      /* Print the information at the current node */
   b. Call Preorder (Left_child [Node])
      /* Recursively do preorder traversal of left subtree of the current node */
   c. Call Preorder (Right_child [Node])
      /* Recursively do preorder traversal of right subtree of current node */
3. Stop

6.6.3 Postorder Traversal Algorithm

1. Begin
   Postorder (Node) /* Set the current node */
2. If current node ! = Null then
   a. Call Postorder (Left_child [Node])
      /* Recursively do postorder traversal of the left subtree of the current node */
   b. Call Postorder (Right_child [Node])
      /* Recursively do postorder traversal of right subtree of current node */
   c. Print Info [Node]
      /* Print information at the current node */
3. Stop

☞ *The performance of inorder, preorder and postorder traversal algorithms is directly proportional to the number of nodes in the tree.*

We can implement the traversal of binary trees in programming language 'C' by *recursive* routines. The three routines in 'C' namely *preordertrav, inordertrav* and *postordertrav* are given below.

Let tree be represented by T and NODE_PTR is the pointer of each node in a tree and each node contains a number as information.

```
void preordertrav (NODE_PTR T)
  {
    if(T != Null)
    {
      printf("%d", T → info);
                 /* print the value of root */
      preordertrav(T → left);
                 /* traverse left subtree */
      preordertrav(T → right);
                 /* traverse right subtree */
    }
  }
void inordertrav(NODE_PTR T)
   {  if (T !=Null)
      {
        inordertrav(T → left);
               /* traverses left subtree */
        printf("%d\n", T → info);
               /* print the value of root */
        inordertrav(T → right);
               /* traverse right subtree */
      }
   }
void postordertrav(NODE_PTR T)
   {  if (T !=Null)
      {
        postordertrav(T → left);
            /* traverse left subtree */
        postordertrav(T → right);
            /* traverse the right subtree */
        printf("%d", T → info);
```

```
            /* print the value of root */
        }
    }
```

6.7 NON-RECURSIVE TRAVERSAL OF A BINARY TREE

Till now we have discussed tree traversal as recursive traversal. Now we will do inorder traversal without using recursion. In all non-recursive algorithms, described in this section, a stack is used. In inorder traversal, we need to print root's left subtree, then we print the root, and finally traverse the right subtree.

Let us initialize a traversal pointer P to the root of the tree, which contains the location of the node (NODE) currently being scanned. Let us denote Left(NODE) as left child of NODE and Right(NODE) as right child of NODE. As we move pointer P to left to traverse the left subtree, we loose track of the root which is to be visited next. So we use a data structure *stack* to store these pointers as we move down so that we can retrieve them later. After reaching the left most node, we print it and pop a pointer from the stack, print the value of the node and move to the right side of the node repeating the whole process. We will keep repeating this until pointer *P* becomes *null* or we have nothing left in the stack.

6.7.1 Non Recursive Algorithm for Inorder Traversal of a Binary Tree

1. Begin
2. Initially push NULL onto STACK and then set pointer P := Root. Then, repeat the following steps until NULL is popped from stack.
3. Proceed down the left most path rooted at pointer P, pushing each NODE on to stack and stopping when a NODE with no left child is pushed onto stack.
4. While doing backtracking, pop and process the nodes on stack. If NULL is popped, then Exit. If NODE with RIGHT(NODE) is processed, set P = RIGHT(NODE) (by assigning P: = RIGHT[P]) and return to step 3.
5. Stop.

Example 3

Consider the binary tree shown in Figure 6.12 with 10 nodes. Let us use stack to print the contents using inorder traversal method. (See Figure 6.12)

Solution

a. Initially push NULL onto stack,

   Stack : NULL

   Set pointer P: = 1, the root of tree

b. Proceed down the left most path rooted at pointer P = 1 and pushing nodes 1, 2, 4, 6 and 8 onto stack. Now stack contains:

   Stack : NULL, 1, 2, 4, 6, and 8

☞ *No other node is pushed onto stack, since 8 has no left child.*

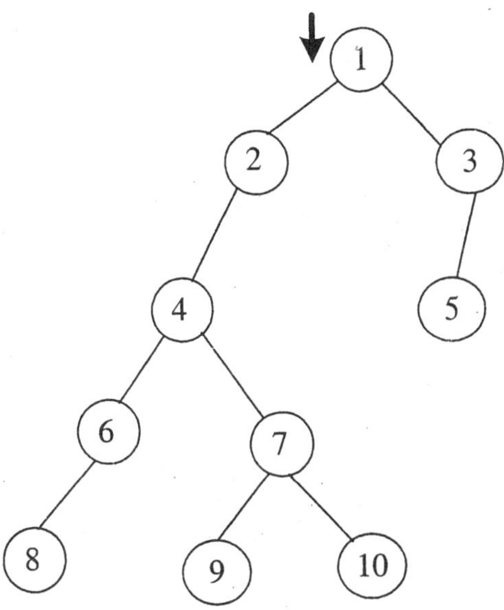

Figure 6.12 A binary tree with 10 nodes

c. While doing back tracking the nodes, the nodes 8, 6 and 4 are popped and processed. Now stack contains

Stack : NULL, 1, 2

We stop processing the node 4, since 4 has a right child). Then set pointer P: = 7, the right child of 4.

d. Proceed down the left most path rooted at pointer P = 7, pushing the node 7 and 9 onto stack. So, stack contains

Stack : NULL, 1, 2, 7 and 9

☞ *No other node is pushed onto stack, since 9 has no left child.*

---

e. While doing backtracking, the nodes 9 and 7 are popped and processed, leaving following nodes in the stack

Stack : NULL, 1 and 2

☞ *We stop the processing at 7, since 7 has right child.*

---

set pointer P : = 10, the right child of 7.

f. Proceed down the left most path rooted at pointer P=10, pushing node 10, onto stack. Now stack contains

Stack : NULL, 1, 2, and 10

☞ *Since node 10 has no left child so no other node is pushed onto stack.*

---

g. Doing backtracking, the nodes 10, 2 and 1 are popped and processed, leaving null in the stack

 Stack : NULL

☞ *No other element of stack is popped since 1 does not have a right child.*

 Set PTR : = 3, the right child of 1.

h. Proceed down the left most path rooted at pointer P = 3, pushing the nodes 3 and 5 on to the stack. Now stack contains:

 Stack : NULL, 3 and 5

i. Doing the backtracking node 5 is popped and processed. Since 5 has no right child, node 3 is popped and processed. Since 3 has no right child, the next element NULL is popped from stack.

 For *Inorder* traversal, nodes are processed in the order 8, 6, 4, 9, 7, 10, 2, 1, 5 and 3.

A formal presentation of inorder traversal algorithm is as given in Figure 6.13.

```
Inorder (Info, Left, Right, Root)
A binary tree is in memory and data structure stack is used to
temporarily hold the addresses of nodes.
1. [Push Null onto stack and initialize pointer P]
   Set Top: = 1, Stack[1]: = Null, P: = Root.
2. Repeat while P != Null : [Pushes left most path onto stack]
   a)   set Top: = Top + 1 and stack[Top]: = P [saves node]
   b)   set pointer P: = Left[P] [updates pointer P]
   [End of loop]
3. Set pointer P: = Stack[Top] and Top: = Top - 1 [Pops node
   from stack]
4. Repeat steps 5 to 7 while P != Null : [Backtracking]
5.      Apply process to Info[P]
6.      [Right child?] If Right[P] != Null then:
        a) Set P: = Right[P]
        b) Go to step 3
   [End of If loop]
7. Set P: = Stack[Top] and Top: = Top - 1 [Pops node]
   [End of Step 4 loop]
8. Exit
```

Figure 6.13 Non recursive inorder traversal algorithm

6.7.2 Non Recursive Algorithm for Preorder Traversal of a Binary Tree

1. Begin
2. Initially push NULL onto stack and set P: = Root. Then repeat the following steps until P = Null or equivalently P!=NULL

3. Proceed down the left most path rooted at P, process each node on the path and pushing each right child Right(NODE), if any onto stack. The traversing ends after a NODE with no left child LEFT(NODE) is processed, thus P is updated using assignment P: = LEFT [P], and traversing stops when LEFT[P] = NULL
4. While doing backtracking pop and assign to P the top element on stack. If P !=NULL, then return to step 3, otherwise Exit.
5. Stop.

Example 4

Consider the binary tree in Figure 6.14 with 9 nodes. Print the contents using preorder traversal method.

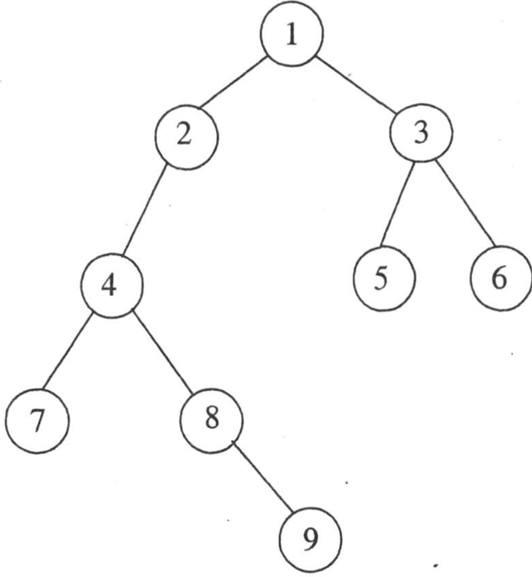

Figure 6.14 A binary tree with 9 nodes

Solution

a. Initially push Null onto stack.

   Stack : NULL

   Set pointer P : = 1, the root of tree

b. Proceed down the left most path rooted at pointer P = 1 as follows:

   (i) Process 1 and push its right child 3 onto stack

   Stack : NULL, 3

   (ii) Process 2 [Note there is no right child]

   (iii) Process 4 and push its right child 8 onto stack

   Stack : NULL, 3, 8

   (iv) Process 7 [Note there is no right child]

☞ *No other node is processed, since 7 has no left child.*

c. While doing backtracking, pop the top element 8 from stack, and set pointer P : = 8. Now stack contains

Stack : NULL, 3

d. Proceed down the left most path rooted at pointer P = 8

(v) Process 8 and push its right child 9 on to stack. So stack contains

Stack : NULL, 3, 9

since 8 has no left child, so no other node is processed.

e. While doing back tracking pop 9 from stack and set pointer P : = 9. Now stack contains

Stack : NULL, 3

f. Proceed down the left most path rooted at pointer P = 9, as follows

(vi) Process 9 [Note there is no right child]

☞ *No other node is processed, since 9 has no left child.*

---

g. While doing back tracking pop 3 from stack and set pointer P : = 3. Now stack contains

Stack : NULL

h. Proceed down the left most path rooted at pointer P = 3 as follows:

(vii) Process 3 and push its right child 6 onto stack.

Stack : NULL, 6

(viii) Process 5 [Note there is no right child]

i. While doing back tracking pop 6 from stack and set pointer P: = 6. Now stack contains only NULL.

Stack : NULL

j. Proceed down the left most path rooted at pointer P = 6, as follows

(ix) Process 6 [Note there is no right child]

k. While doing back tracking pop the top element NULL from stack and set P: = NULL. Since pointer P = NULL the algorithm is complete.

So the required preorder traversal is

1 2 4 7 8 9 3 5 6

A formal presentation of preorder traversal algorithm is seen in Figure 6.15.

```
Preorder (Info, Left, Right, Root)
A binary tree T is in memory. The data structure is used to
temporarily hold the addresses of nodes.
1. [Initially push Null onto stack, and initialize pointer P]
   Set Top: = 1, Stack[1]: = Null, P: = Root
```

(Contd...)

```
2. Repeat step 3 to 5 while pointer P != Null
3.      Apply process to Info[P].
4.      [Right child ?]
        If Right [P] != Null, then : [Push on stack]
            set Top: = Top + 1, and stack [top]: Right[P]
        [End of If structure]
5.      [Left child ?]
        If Left[P] != Null, then:
            set P: = Left [P]
        Else : [Pop from stack]
            set P: = Stack [Top] and Top: = Top - 1
            [End of If structure]
   [End of step 2 loop]
6. Exit
```

Figure 6.15 Non recursive Preorder traversal algorithm

Non recursive routines to traverse a binary tree in post order is left as an exercise for the students.

6.8 BINARY TREE REPRESENTATION

The structure of each node of a binary tree contains the *data item field,* and the *pointers* to the same structure, since binary tree is recursive in nature. Each node contains two links to the same structure, one for left child and another for right child, as shown in Figure 6.16.

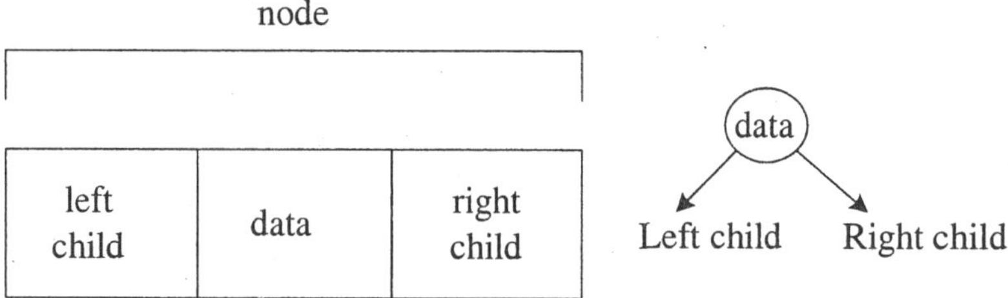

Figure 6.16 Representation of a node in a binary tree

In programming language 'C', the structure of a node can be defined as:

```
struct bt_node
    {  struct bt_node *left;
       int data;
       struct bt_node *right;
    };
```

Tree nodes may be implemented as array elements or as dynamically allocated variables. Each node of a tree contains data, left and right fields. The left field points to the node's left child and the right field points to the node's right child. Two ways to represent a binary tree are:

- Linked representation
- Sequential representation

6.8.1 Linked Representation

In linked list representation, each node has 3 fields, leftchild, data and right child. A sample binary tree is shown in Figure 6.17.

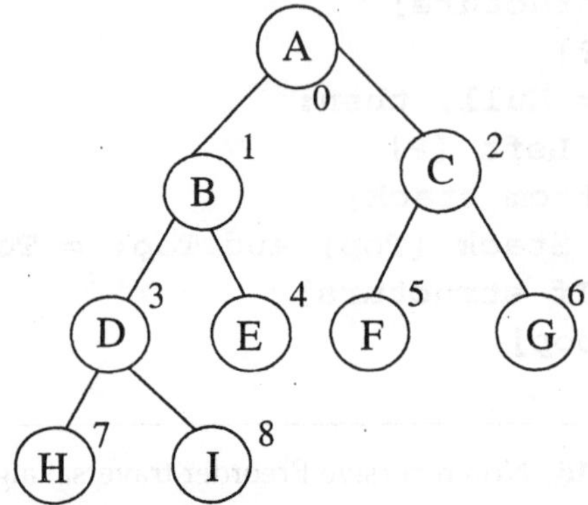

Figure 6.17 Representation of a nodes in a binary tree

The linked representation of binary tree is given in Figure 6.18.

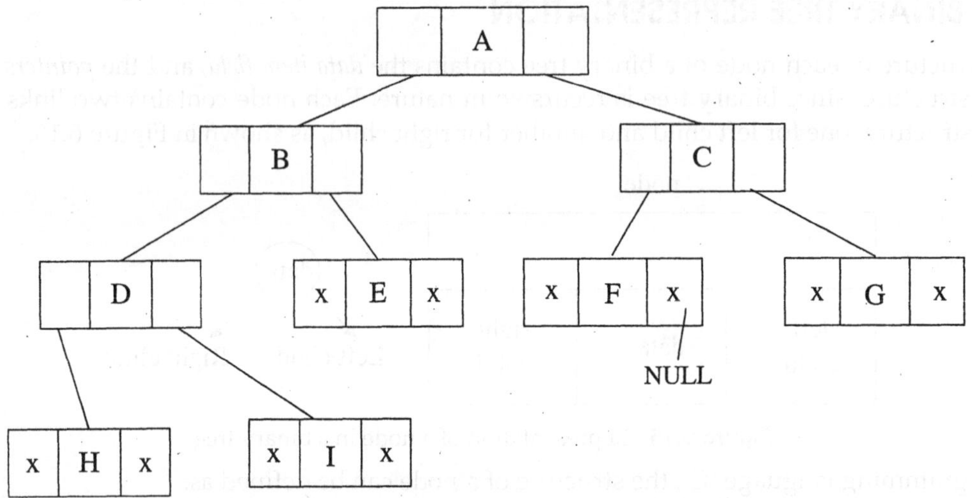

Figure 6.18 Linked list representation of a binary tree

Note that all the leaf nodes contain a NULL value represented by x in Figure 6.18. Null value (x) tells that there is no child left or right to the leaf node. In Figure 6.18 the link fields of node C contains the address of the nodes F and G. The right link field of node B contains the address of the node E.

Similarly the left node of B contains the address of D. The leaf nodes E, F, G, H and I contain a NULL (x) value in both their link fields.

6.8.2 Sequential Representation

Sequential representation of a binary tree requires numbering of nodes, starting with root node. The nodes are numbered from left to right. To represent binary tree in the form of array, three separate arrays are required. Consider the binary tree of Figure 6.18. Let the "data" field of the nodes of this tree are stored in array, "data", and two more arrays of integers say "leftchild" and "rightchild" used to represent links of the nodes as seen in Figure 6.19.

data	A	B	C	D	E	F	G	H	I
leftchild	1	3	5	7	-1	-1	-1	-1	-1
rightchild	2	4	6	8	-1	-1	-1	-1	-1

Figure 6.19 Array representation of binary tree

☞ *If the node does not have any leftchild or rightchild then the element of the array leftchild and rightchild contains a value -1.*

6.9 APPLICATIONS OF BINARY TREE

Binary tree is a useful data structure. It has the following applications:

- A binary tree is useful when two way decisions must be made at each point in a process. For example, suppose you want to find all duplicates in a list of numbers. One way of doing this is to compare each number with all those that precede it. However, this involves a large number of comparisons. The number of comparisons can be reduced by using a binary tree. The first number in the list is placed in a node that is established as the root of a binary tree with empty left and right subtrees. Each successive number in the list is then compared with the root. If it matches we have a duplicate. If it is smaller, we examine the left subtree. If it is larger, we examine the right subtree. If any or all the subtree are empty, then number is not a duplicate and is placed into a new node at that position in the tree. If the subtree is non empty, we compare the number to the contents of the root of the subtree and entire process is repeated with the values in the subtree.
- Another common operation is the traversing a binary tree, traversing each of its nodes once. We may simply wish to print the contents of each node as we enumerate it or we may wish to process it in some other order, may be *inorder, preorder* or *post order* which we have already discussed earlier. Suppose, a binary search tree is traversed in inorder (left, root, right) and the contents of each node are printed as the node is visited, the numbers are printed in ascending order.
- Another application of binary tree is the method of representing an expression containing operands and binary operators by a strictly binary tree. The root of strictly binary tree contains the operator and the leaf contains operand. For example, expression (a+b) * c - (d * e) can be represented as in Figure 6.20 as a binary tree.

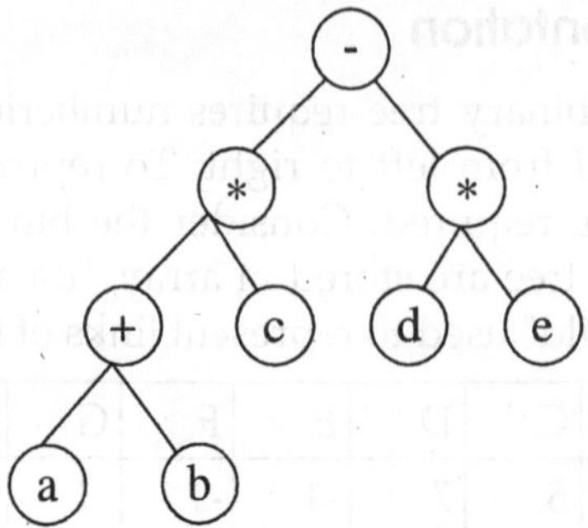

Figure 6.20 Representation of an algebraic expression in Binary Tree form

- One application of binary tree is to obtain an optimal set of codes, for messages M_1, M_2, M_3....M_n. Each code is a binary string, which will be used for transmission of the corresponding message. At receiving end, code will be decoded using a decode tree. A decode tree is a binary tree in which leaf nodes represent the messages. The binary bits in the code word for message determine the branching needed at each level of the decode tree to reach the correct leaf node.

6.10 CONVERSION OF FOREST INTO TREE

Forest is a set of several trees that are not linked to each other in any way. We can obtain a forest by removing the root from a rooted tree. For example, in Figure 6.21(a), if we remove A_1, we get a forest of three trees. (See Figure 6.21(b)). We can also build a rooted tree by starting with a forest, attaching a new vertex at the top and adding branches from the new vertex to the roots of all trees in the forest.

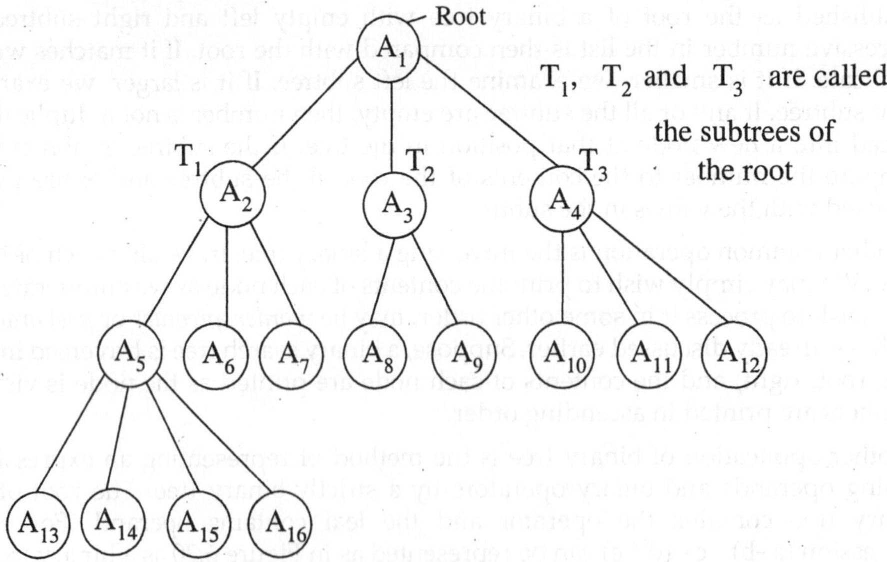

Figure 6.21(a) A Tree T with 16 nodes

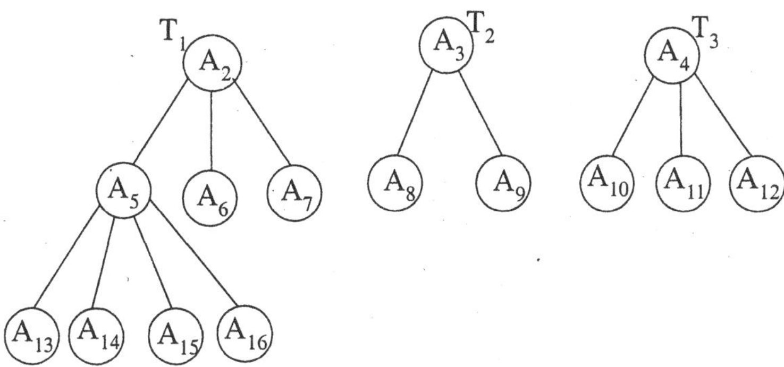

Figure 6.21(b) Forest of trees

Huffman Tree

For a given set of items and weights, a tree with minimum weighted external path length is called *Huffman tree.* Huffman algorithm constructs tree from the bottom up rather than from the top down. Huffman gave the simple algorithm shown in Figure 6.22 to construct a tree. The forest setup step builds the pieces out of which the Huffman tree will be constructed by tree building step. The tree building step requires that we are able to find and remove the smallest tree in the forest, and to add a tree in the forest.

A forest (set of trees) F, which is initially composed entirely of external nodes, one for each given weight. Each tree T in F has a weight associated with it, which is just the sum of the weights of the external nodes of T. The weight is conventionally written in the root of T. The algorithm selects two trees of minimum weight from F and combines them into one. This step is repeated until only one tree is left. For example, given the weights {3, 1, 1, 5}, at the start of each iteration of the loop, and the algorithm has produced one of the Huffman trees. (See Figure 6.21(c))

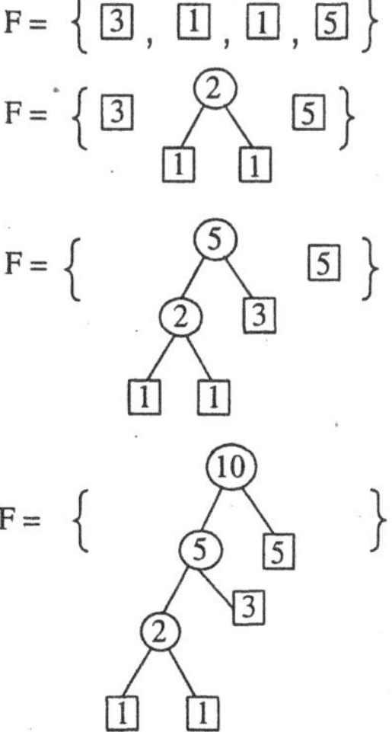

Figure 6.21(c) Huffman tree

Forest Setup Step: (a) Construct a forest of one-node trees (b) Each tree contains a single item (c) The weight of each tree is the weight of the item it contains. **Tree-Building Step:** Until the forest contains only one tree, (a) Remove two trees of smallest weights from the forest, (b) Make them children of a new node whose weight is the sum of their weights, and add the new tree to the forest.

Figure 6.22 Huffman's algorithm to construct the tree of minimum weighted external path length on a set of weighted items

☞ *Implementation of Huffman tree is very useful in coding when we want to send a message.*

6.10.1 Threaded Binary Tree

When a binary tree is represented using pointers, then pointers to empty sub-trees are set to null. That is, the 'left' pointer of a node whose left child is an empty subtree is normally set to NULL. Similarly, the 'right' pointer of a node whose right child is an empty subtree is also set to NULL. Thus, a large number of pointers are set to NULL. It will be useful to use these pointer fields to keep some other information for operations in binary tree. Traversing is the most common operation in binary tree. We can use these pointer fields to contain the address pointer which points to the nodes higher in the tree. Such a pointer which keeps the address of the nodes higher in the tree is called *thread*. A binary tree which implements these pointers is called *threaded binary tree*.

There are two types of threads. A right thread links a node to its successor node in the traversal order and a left thread links a node to its predecessor node in the traversal ordering.

The threads are drawn with dotted lines to differentiate them from tree pointers. In computer memory, an extra 1-bit tag field may be used to distinguish threads from ordinary pointers or alternatively thread may be denoted by a negative integer when ordinary pointer is denoted by positive integer.

Figure 6.23(a) shows a binary tree in which NULL pointers in nodes with empty right subtrees are replaced with threads.

In this figure, the threads are drawn with dotted lines. Observe that every null right pointer has been replaced by a thread except for the node which is the last node in the inorder traversal of tree.

☞ *There is a thread from E to A as A is accessed after E for the inorder traversal of tree.*

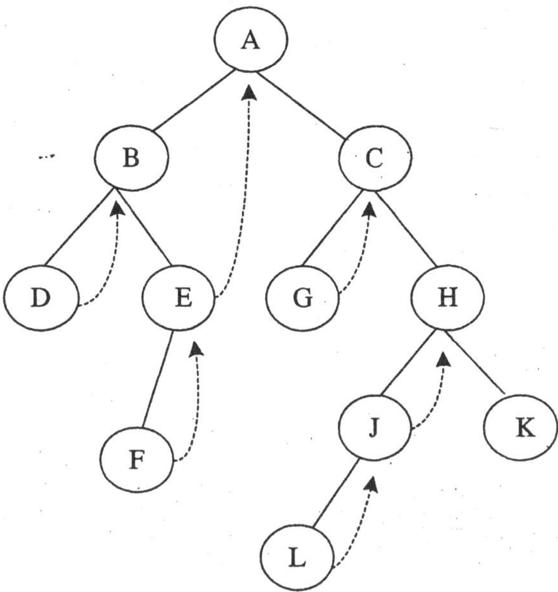

Figure 6.23(a) A binary tree with inorder threading

Advantages

There would be no need for the stack since the node directly points to its inorder successor. By changing the null links in the binary tree to special links called threads, it is possible to perform traversal, insertion and deletion without using either a stack or recursion.

☞ *Thread machnism is used to avoid recursive function call and also it saves stacks and memory.*

Time is saved, though in the structure namely, *struct*, two more bytes will be needed.

```
struct node
{
  int info;
  int rthread;
  struct node *lptr, *rptr;
};
```

There are many ways to thread a binary tree, but each threading will correspond to a particular traversal of the tree. One can choose a one-way threading or a two-way threading. In the one-way threading of tree, a thread will appear in the right field of a node and will point to next node in the inorder traversal of T. In the two way threading of T, a thread will also appear in the left field of a node and will point to the preceding node in the inorder traversal of tree. Figure 6.23(b) shows two-way inorder threading.

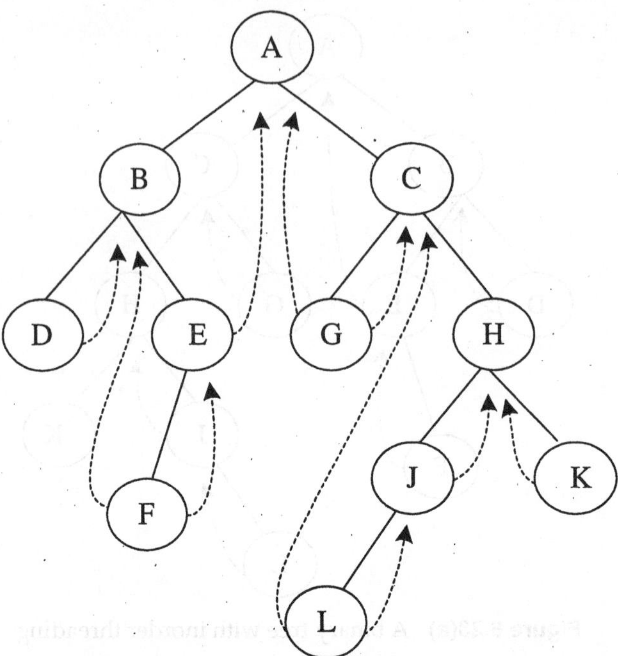

Figure 6.23(b) Two way inorder threading

☞ *Two-way inorder threading is applicable to all the three traversals but you should use it for preorder and post order only. For inorder, use one-way threaded binary tree concept.*

In two–way threading there is no recursive fuction call.

6.11 DECISION TREE AND GAME TREE

One of the very useful application of trees type of data structure is in decision making. Decision tree can describe decision processes. The decision tree of an algorithm is obtained by tracing through the action of the algorithm, representing each comparison of keys by a vertex (circle) of the tree. Inside the circle we put the Index of the key against which we are comparing the target key. Branches (lines) drawn down from the circle represent the possible outcomes of the comparison and are labeled accordingly. When the algorithm terminates, we put either F (for failure) or the location where the target is found at the end of the appropriate branch, which we call a leaf, and draw a square. Leaves are also called end vertices or external vertices of the tree. The remaining vertices are called the internal vertices of the tree.

A game tree (also called the extensive form) is a graphical representation of a sequential game. It provides information about the players, payoffs, strategies, and the order of moves. The game tree consists of nodes, which are points at which players can take actions, connected by vertices, which represent the actions that may be taken at that node. An initial (or root) node represents the first decision to be made. Every set of vertices from the first node through the tree eventually arrives at a terminal node, representing an end to the game. Each terminal node is labeled with the pay offs earned by each player if the game ends at that node.

6.12 BINARY SEARCH TREES

A binary search tree is a binary tree that is either empty or in which each node possesses a key that satisfies the following conditions:

1. Every element has a key and no two elements have the same key.
2. The key (if any) in the left subtree are smaller than the key in the root.
3. The keys (if any) in the right subtree are equal to or larger than the key in the root.
4. The left and right subtrees are also the binary search trees.

☞ *In a binary search tree each node points to two subtrees, one containing key whose value is less than the key in the given node and the other containing keys whose value is greater than or equal to the key in the given node.*

Some examples of binary search trees are shown in Figure 6.24.

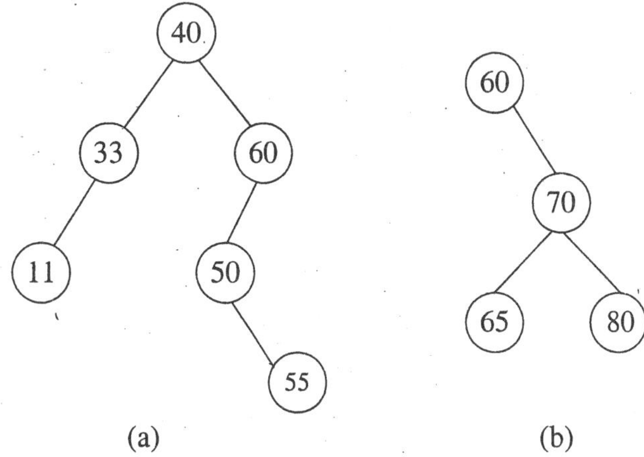

Figure 6.24 Examples of binary search trees

6.12.1 Operations Performed on a Binary Search Tree

There are several operations that can be easily performed on binary search tree. Insertion and deletion of a node are basic operations that are required to create and maintain a tree.

6.12.2 Searching a Binary Search Tree

To search any node in a binary search tree, initially the data item that is to be searched is compared with the data of the root node. If the data is equal to the data of the root node then the search is successful.

If the data is found to be greater than the data of the root node, then the searching process proceeds in the right sub-tree, otherwise searching process proceeds in the left sub-tree.

Same procedure is repeated for the left or right sub-tree until the data item is found. While searching the data item if the leaf node of the sub tree is reached and the data is not found then it is concluded that the data item is not present in the binary tree. For example consider the binary search tree shown in Figure 6.25.

Suppose the data item to be searched is 7. First compare 7 with the data of root node i.e. 19. Since 7 is less than 19, the searching would proceed in the left subtree. Now 7 is compared to 16 and since 7 is less than 16 the searching would proceed in the left subtree of the node which holds a value 16. Next 7 is compared with 5 and since 7 is greater than 5, the search proceeds in the right sub-tree of the node which holds a value 5. Now 7 is compared with the node in the right sub tree and it holds a value 7 and since 7 is found, the searching process ends here.

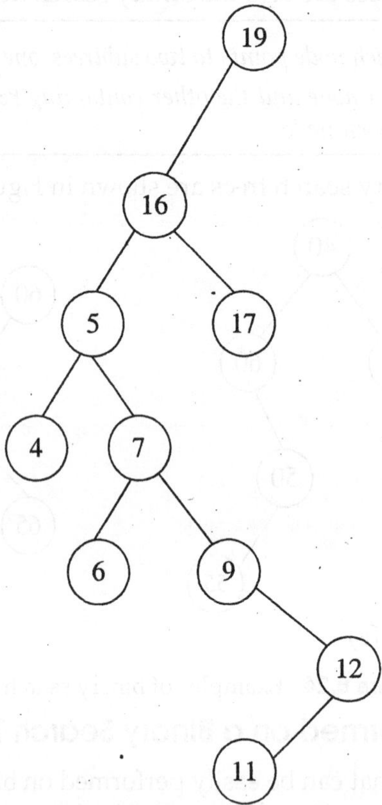

Figure 6.25 Searching data value 7 in the binary search tree

6.12.3 Insertion into a Binary Search Tree

To insert a node into a binary search tree, initially data item that is to be inserted is compared with the data of the root node. If data item is found to be greater than or equal to the data item of the root node then the new node is inserted in the right sub-tree of the root node, otherwise, the new node is inserted in the left sub tree of the root node.

Now the root node of the right or left sub-tree is taken and its data is compared with the data that is to be inserted and the same procedure is repeated. This is done till the left or the right sub-tree where the new node to be inserted is found to be empty. Finally, the new node is made the appropriate child of this current node. For example, to insert a node with value 20 into the tree of Figure 6.26, we first search for 20. Since it is not found, 20 is inserted as the right child of the node with value 18. The resulting search tree is shown in Figure 6.27.

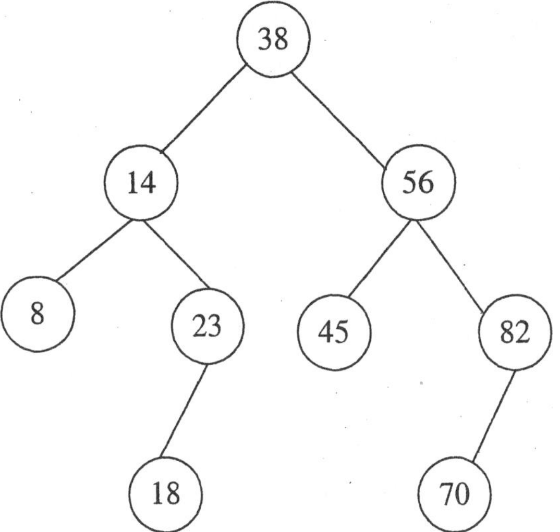

Figure 6.26 Binary search tree before insertion of node with value 20

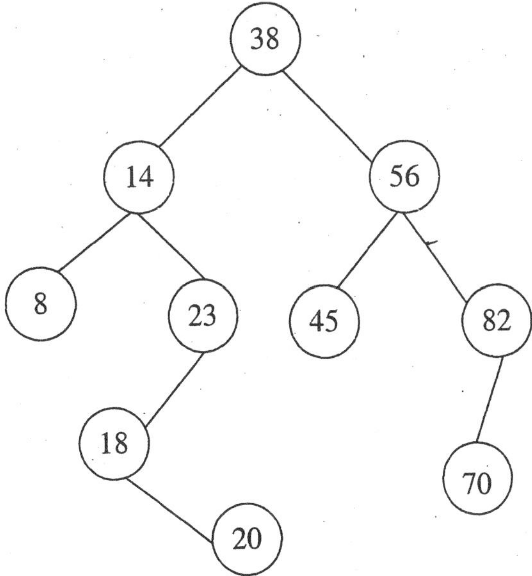

Figure 6.27 Binary search tree after insertion of node with value 20

6.12.4 Deletion from a Binary Search Tree

The deletion from a binary search tree is an easy task if the node to be deleted has only one sub-tree. In this case, we simply link the parent of the deleted node to its sub-tree. When the element to be deleted has both left and right non- empty sub-trees, the problem becomes more complicated. There are four possible cases that we need to consider:

Case 1 No node in the tree contains the specified data item.
Case 2 The node containing the data item has no children
Case 3 The node containing the data item has exactly one child.
Case 4 The node containing the data item has two children.

Let us take a binary search tree and apply delete operation. (See Figure 6.28)

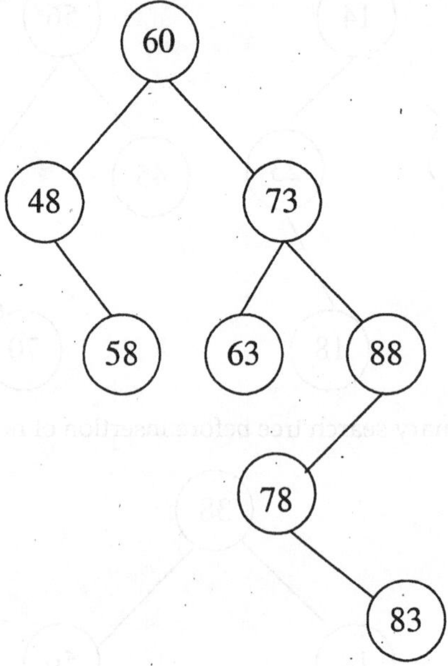

Figure 6.28 Binary search tree for delete operation

In Case 1, we need to print the message that the data item is not present in the tree. First we check the condition whether tree is empty.

The conditions is:

```
if (root == NULL)
  {
    printf("Tree is empty");
    return;
  }
```

In case 2, where node to be deleted is leaf node i.e. it has no children then its left and right pointer will contain NULL. This will be checked as follows:

```
if(location → lchild == NULL && location → rchild == NULL)
```

For example, to delete the node with value 83 in Figure 6.28, which has no children, we can delete it simply by giving NULL value to its parent's right pointer. Here 78 is the parent of 83 and 83 is the right child of 78, so after deleting 83, right pointer of 78 will have NULL value. Now the binary search tree after deleting item 83 will be as shown in Figure 6.29.

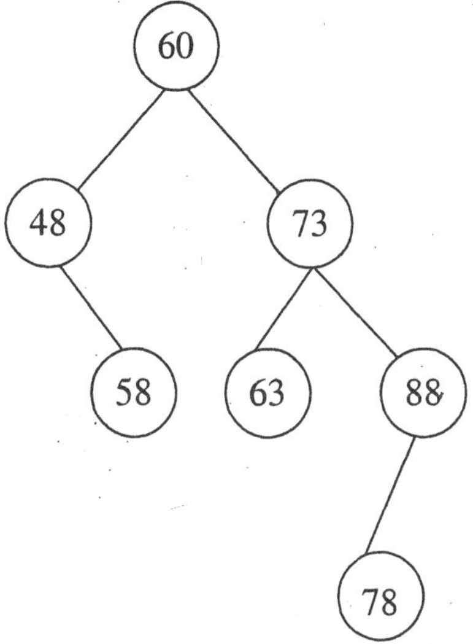

Figure 6.29 Binary Search tree after deleting node with a value 83

In Case 3, where the node to be deleted has only one child (i.e. either left child or right child), we have to adjust the pointer of the parent of the node to be deleted such that after deletion, it points to the child of the node being deleted. We need to check for both conditions namely:

```
if (location → lchild != NULL && location → right == NULL)
if (location → child == NULL && location → rchild != NULL)
```

Now we want to delete node with value 48, which has only one child, so we can delete it simply by giving the address of right child to its parent left pointer. Here 60 is the parent of 48 and 58 is the right child of 48. Binary search tree after deleting node with value 48 will be as shown in Figure 6.30.

In Case 4, the node to be deleted has two children. Now we need to consider the condition when the node has both left and right child. This can be checked as

```
if (location → lchild != NULL && location → rchild != NULL)
```

To delete the item 73, which has left and right children, we first delete the item which is inorder successor of 73. Here 78 is the inorder successor of 73. We delete 78 by simply giving the NULL value to its parents left pointer. Here 88 is the parent and 78 is the left child of 88. (See Figure 6.30)

After that, we replace the item 73 with item 78. We give the address of the left and right pointer of 73 to left and right pointer of 78 and address of 78 to the right pointer of parent 73 which is 60. Binary search tree after deleting item 73, will be as shown in Figure 6.31.

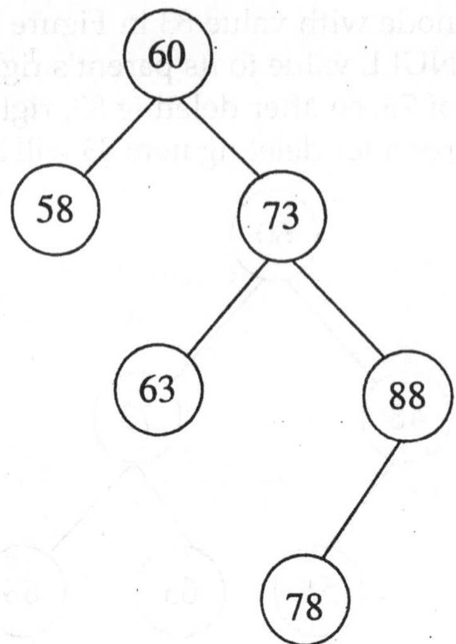

Figure 6.30 Binary search tree after deleting node with value 48

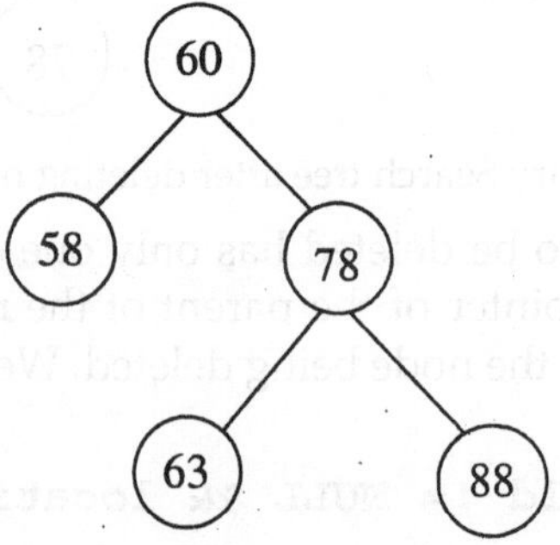

Figure 6.31 Binary search tree after deleting item 73

6.12.5 Height Balanced Tree(AVL)

Height balanced tree is a binary tree in which the difference in heights between the left and the right subtree is not more than one for every node. The height of a tree is the number of nodes in the longest path from the root to any leaf. Figure 6.32 shows some examples of the heights of trees. This property was first described in 1962 by two Russian mathematicians, G.M. Adel'son – Vel'skii and E.M. Landis. Therefore, the resulting binary trees are also called *AVL* trees in their honour.

☞ *A binary search tree in which the difference of heights of the right and left sub-trees of any node is less than or equal to one is known as an AVL tree.*

Figure 6.33 shows some examples of AVL trees. Examples of tree that are not AVL trees are given in Figure 6.34.

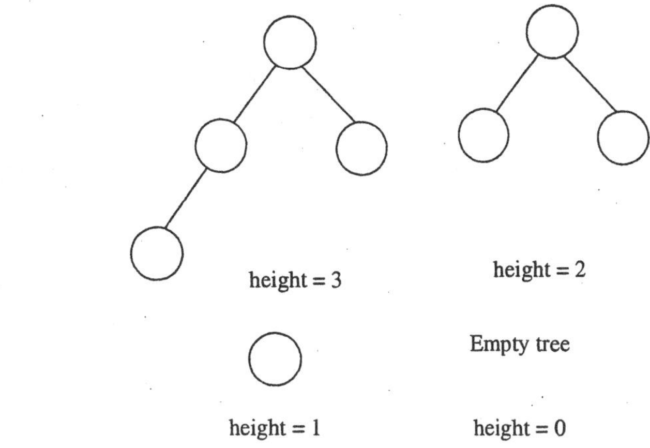

Figure 6.32 Various heights of trees

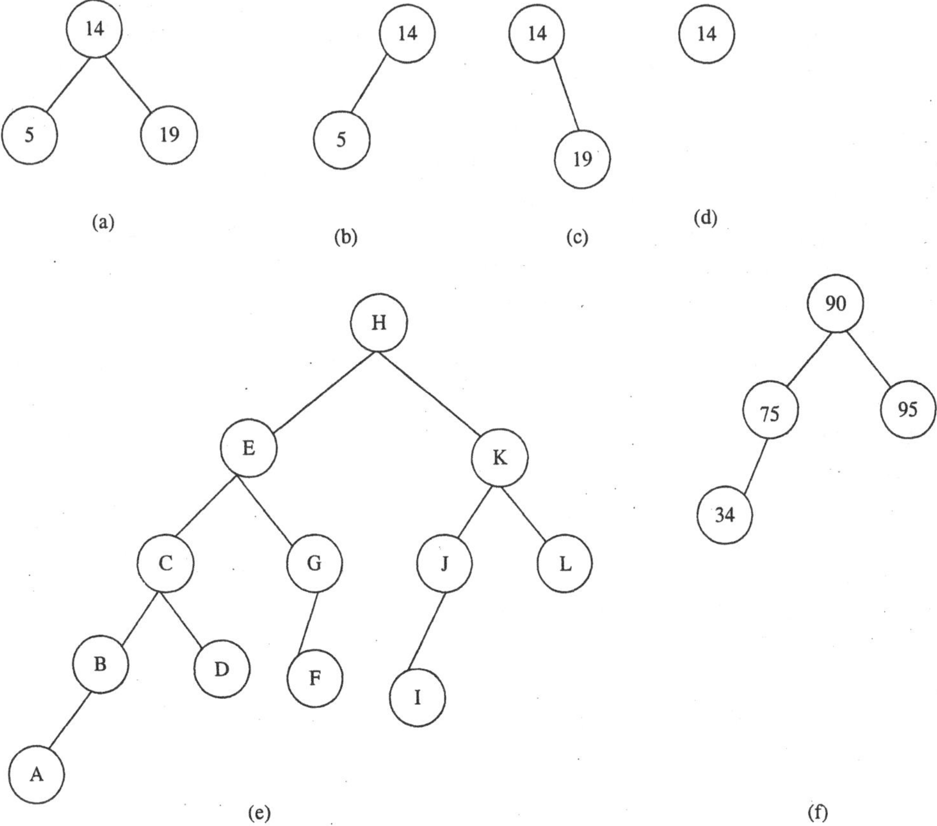

Figure 6.33 Examples of AVL trees

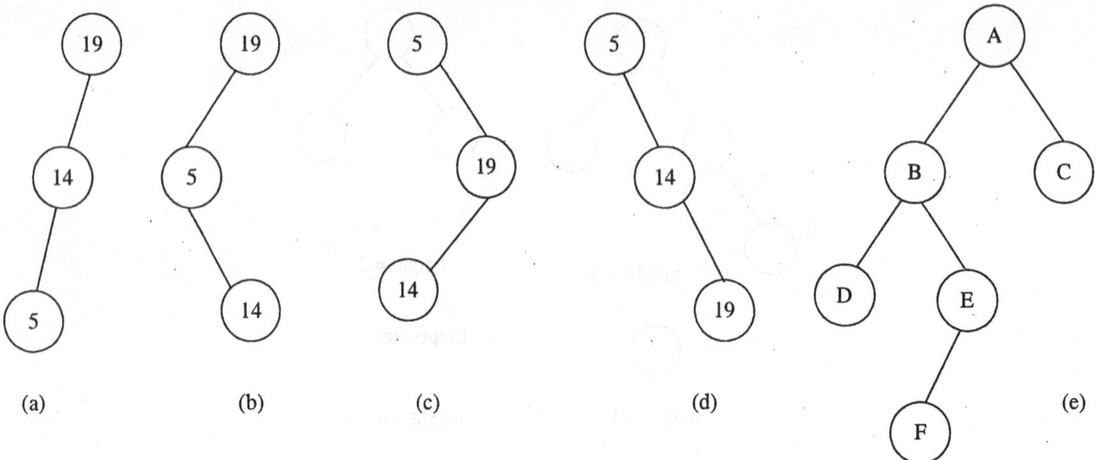

Figure 6.34 Examples of non-AVL trees

In order to represent a node in an AVL tree, a new field must be introduced. This additional field stores the "balance factor" of a node which denotes the difference of height between the left and the right sub-trees of the tree rooted at that node. Each node in a balanced binary tree has a balance of 1, -1 or 0 depending on whether the height of its leaf subtree is greater than, less than or equal to the height of its right subtree. A value of 1 indicates that the left child is 'heavier' and there is a path from root to leaf in the left child subtree of length n, whereas the longest path in the right child subtree is length n-1. A balance factor will indicate that the longest paths in the two child-subtrees are equal while a value of -1 indicates that the right child possesses the longest path.

☞ *The balance factor value can also be represented by symbols \, –, / instead of -1, 0, 1.*

The structure of a node for an AVL tree in programming language 'C' is given below:

```
struct AVL
    {
        struct AVL *left;
        int data;
        struct AVL *right;
        int bal fact;
    };
```

Figure 6.65 shows trees with values of balance factor of each node.

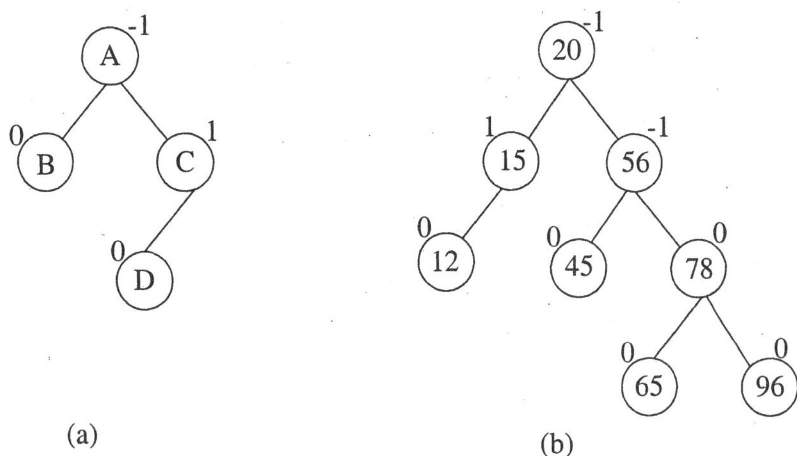

Figure 6.35 Balancing factor of trees

6.12.6 Insertion of a Node in an AVL Tree

Searching for a key in an AVL tree is quite the same as searching for a key in any ordinary binary search tree. We can insert a new node into an AVL tree by first using the binary tree insertion technique, comparing the key of the new node with that in the root and inserting the new node into the left or right subtrees accurately. But AVL tree has a property that the height of left and right subtrees will be with maximum difference of 1. Suppose after inserting new node, this difference becomes more than 1, i.e. the value of balance factor has some value other than -1, 0, 1. So our work is to restore the property of AVL tree again.

There are now two cases to consider as illustrated by Figure 6.36(a), (b) and (c). In Figure 6.36(a), the newly created node is inserted into the left subtree of B, changing the balance of B to 1 and the balance of A to Z. In Figure 6.36(b) the newly created node is inserted into the right subtree of B, changing the balance of B to -1 and the balance of A to Z. To maintain a balanced tree, it is necessary to perform a transformation on the tree so that we satisfy the following:

a. Inorder traversal of the transformed tree is the same as for the original tree, i.e the transformed tree remains a binary search tree.

b. The transformed tree is balanced.

Consider the trees shown in Figure 6.36. The tree of Figure 6.36(b) is said to be a right rotation of the tree rooted at A of Figure 6.36(a). Similarly, the tree of Figure 6.36(c) is said to be a left rotation of the tree rooted at A of Figure 6.36(a).

We illustrate insertion in AVL tree by inserting the five letters A, B, E, C and D in the same order, into an initially empty AVL tree. Without care to maintain the AVL property, this insertion order produces the binary search tree as seen in Figure 6.37.

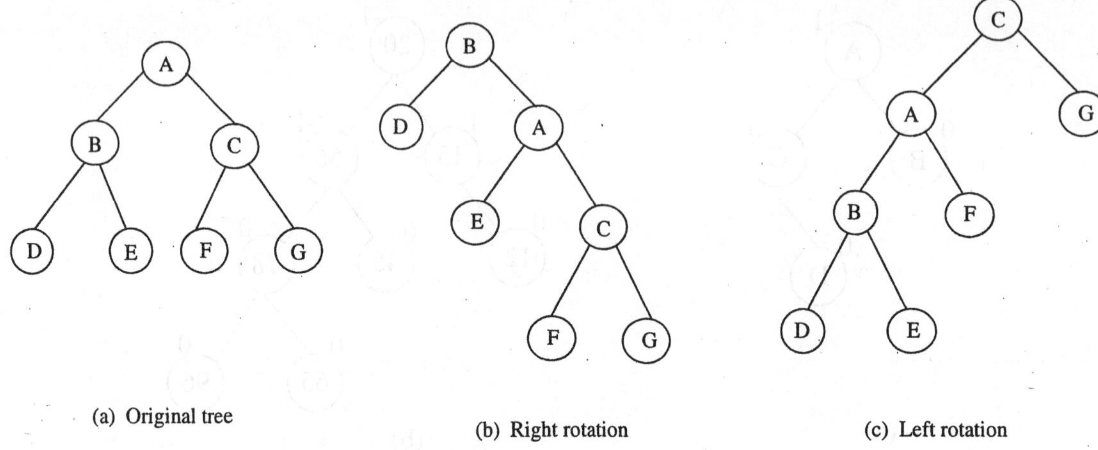

Figure 6.36 Simple rotation left or right on a tree

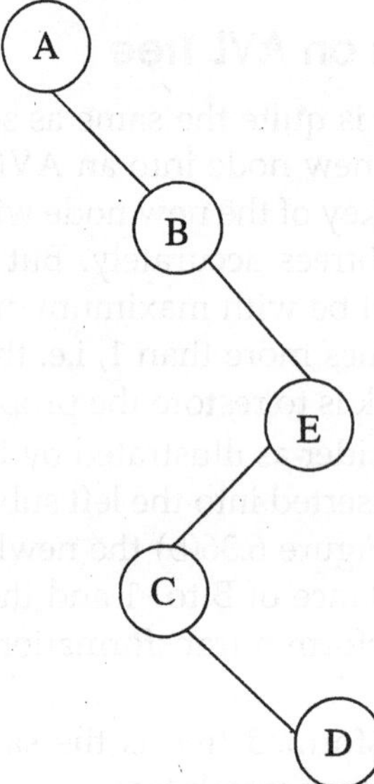

Figure 6.37 A binary search tree A, B, E, C and D after inserting nodes with values

The first two insertions of A and B require no special treatment, and they yield the AVL tree as shown in Figure 6.38.

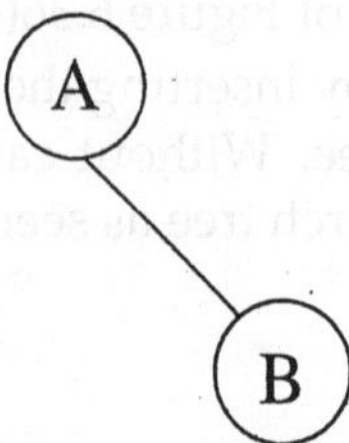

Figure 6.38 The AVL tree after insertion of nodes with values A and B

Figure 6.39(a) shows the tree that results immediately after inserting E. It does not obey the AVL rule, because the left subtree of the root is empty, while the right subtree has height two. To repair this violation, we rearrange the tree so that B is at the root and the symmetric ordering of nodes is preserved, as seen in Figure 6.39(b). This is an example of a single rotation.

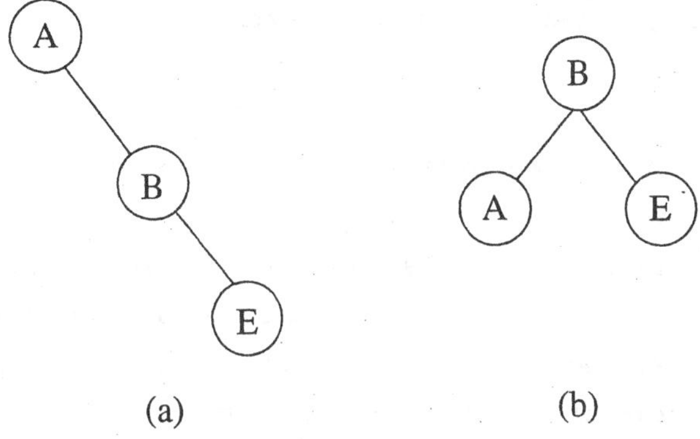

Figure 6.39 Inserting E into the AVL tree

When C is inserted into the tree, the result is still an AVL tree. After D is inserted, however, the resulting tree no longer obeys the AVL rule, (See Figure 6.40(a)). To repair the viloation, we rearrange the right subtree of the root as seen in Figure 6.40(b), restoring the AVL property and preserving the symmetric order of the nodes. This is an example of *double rotation.*

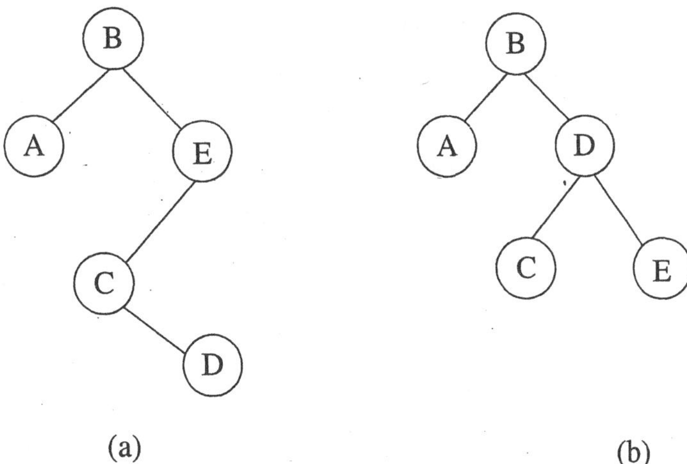

Figure 6.40 Inserting nodes with values C and D in AVL tree

Example 5

Insertion algorithm for AVL tree is given in Figure 6.41.

Step 1 :	**If this is the first insertion then allocate a node, set its fields and return.**
Step 2 :	**If the information we want to insert is not already present in the tree then link the new node to the existing tree else discard the new information and return.**
Step 3 :	**Search for an unbalanced node.**
Step 4 :	**Adjust the balance factors if there is no critical node return.**
Step 5 :	**If the node was balanced and then becomes heavy or the node was heavy and now becomes balanced then adjust the balanced factors and return.**
Step 6 :	**Rebalance the tree and return.**

Figure 6.41 Algorithm for AVL tree

Example 6

Create AVL Tree from the following A, Z, B, Y, C, X. (See steps 1 to 6 in Figure 6.42)

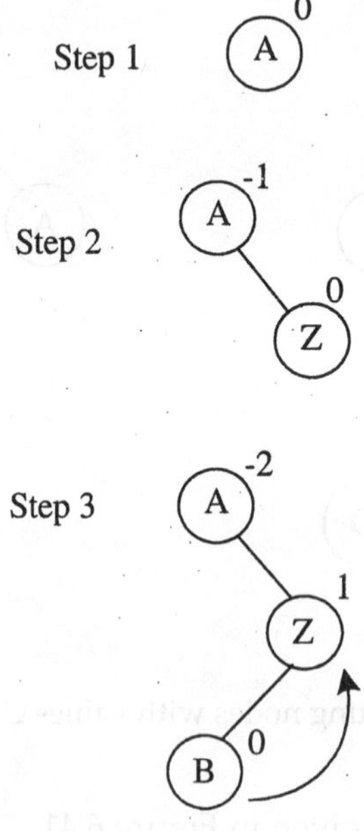

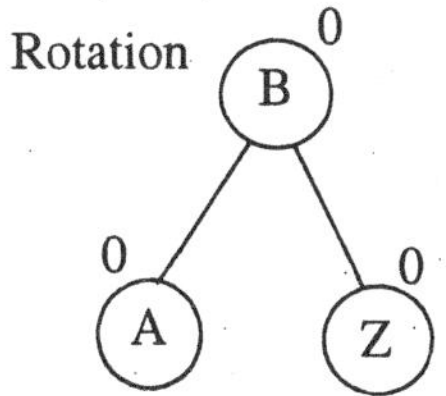
Rotation
0
B
0
A
0
Z

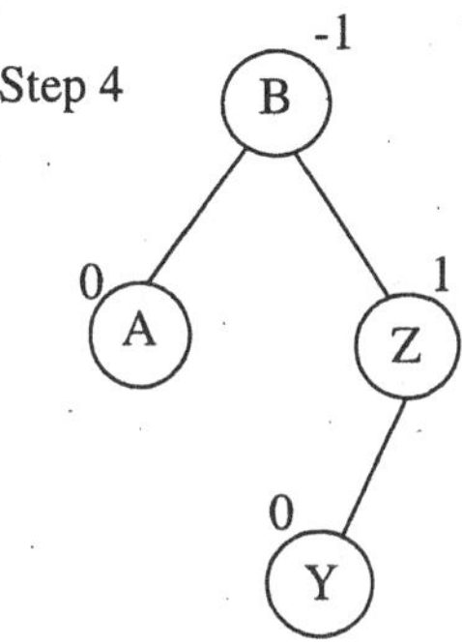
Step 4
-1
B
0
A
1
Z
0
Y

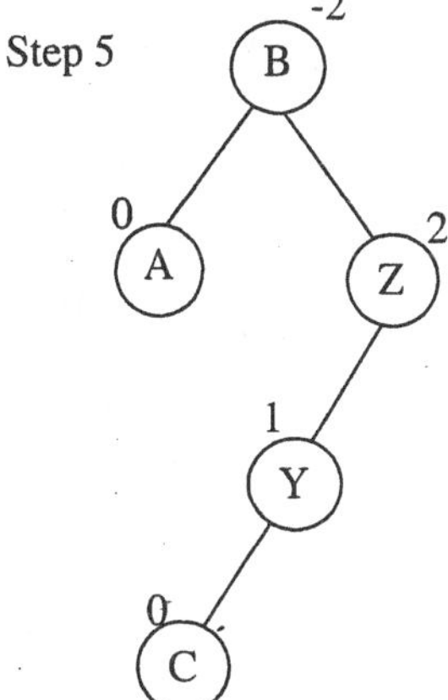
Step 5
-2
B
0
A
2
Z
1
Y
0
C

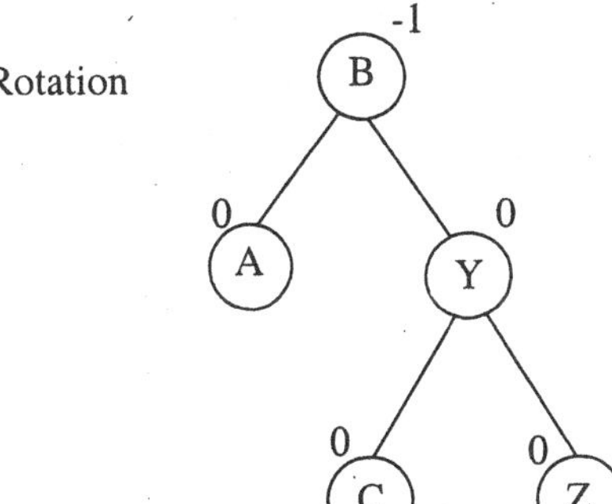
Rotation
-1
B
0
A
0
Y
0
C
0
Z

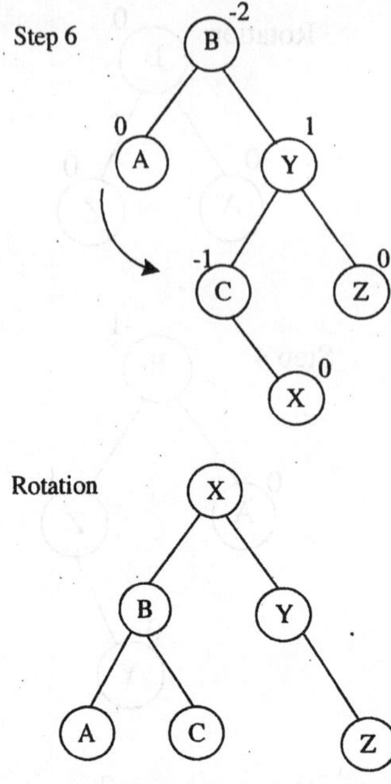

Figure 6.42 Creating AVL tree for A, Z, B, Y, C, X

Example 7

Create an AVL tree from the following: A, B, C, D, E, F (See Figure 6.43)

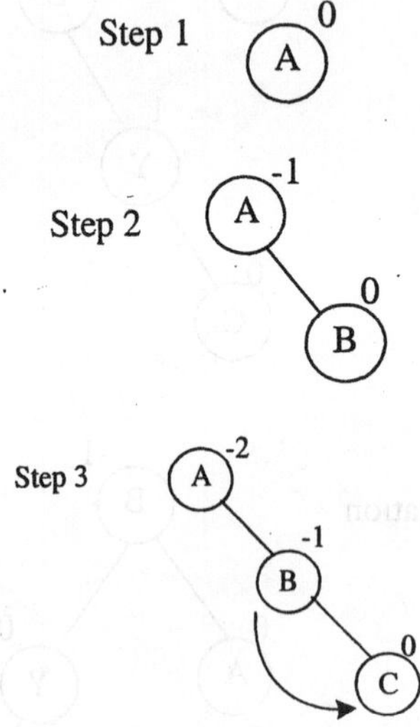

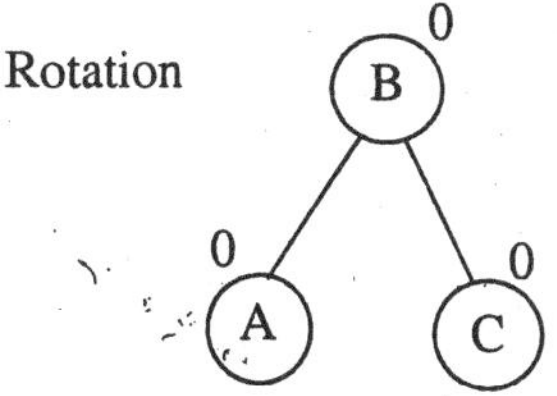
Rotation
B
0
A
0
C
0

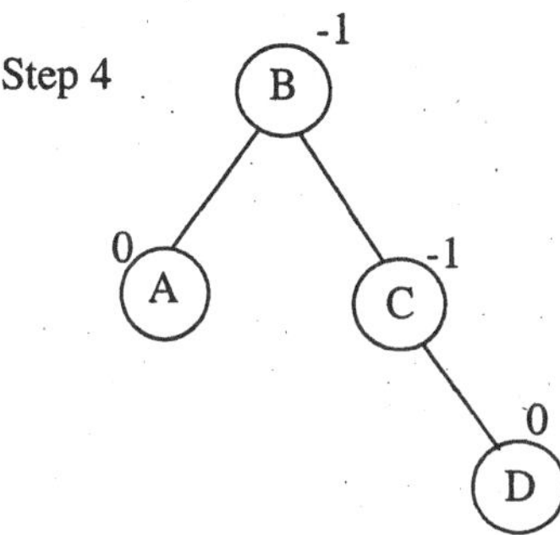
Step 4
B
-1
A
0
C
-1
D
0

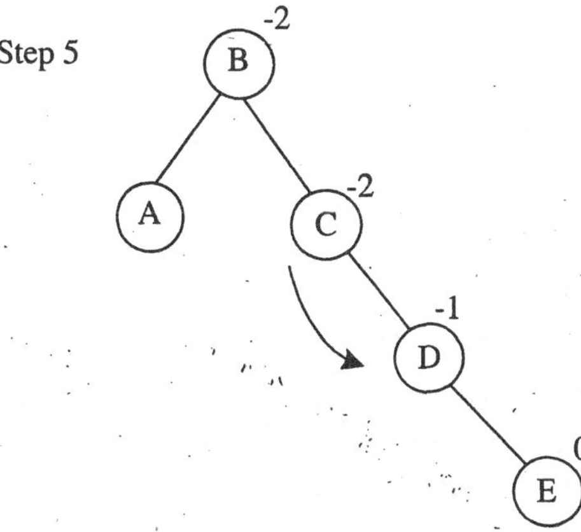
Step 5
B
-2
A
C
-2
D
-1
E
0

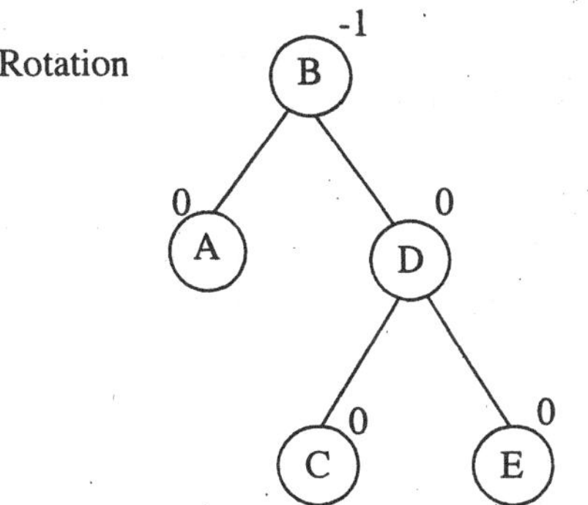
Rotation
B
-1
A
0
D
0
C
0
E
0

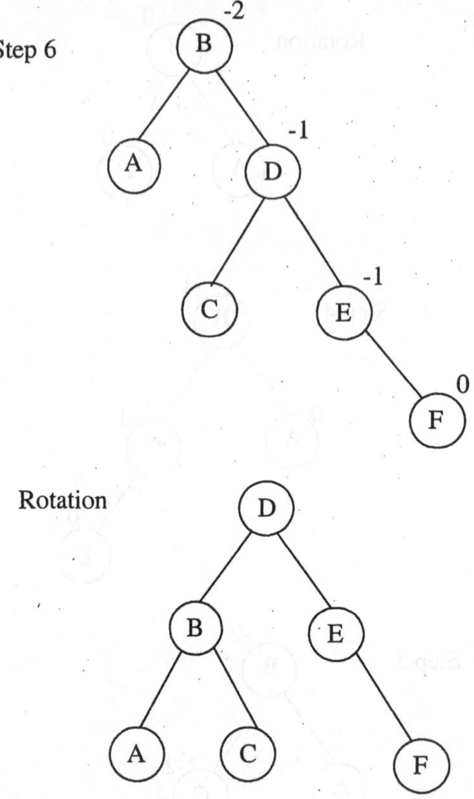

Figure 6.43 Creating AVL tree for A, B, C, D, E, F

6.12.7 Deletion from an AVL Tree

As in the case of insertion, the first step in deleting an item from AVL tree is the same as for any binary search tree. Search the item and remove it. Then rearrangement can cause the tree to lose the AVL property, so we must walk back up towards the root from the deepest node affected by the deletion to detect and repair any violations of the AVL property. This walk proceeds much as in the case of insertion, with one important difference i.e to check the balance factor of each node of the tree after the deletion of the node. The process to rebalance the tree is exactly the same as in case of inserting a node in an AVL tree described in 6.12.6.

6.13 B–Tree

B-tree is a balanced multi-way tree[1]. It is also known as balanced sort tree. It is not a binary tree. All the leaves of the B-tree must be at same level and height of the B-tree must be kept minimum.

[1] A multiway tree of order n is a tree in which any node may contain maximum (n-1) values and can have maximum of n children.

B–tree of order n can be defined as:

a. All the non-leaf nodes (except the root node) have at least (n/2) children and at the most (n) children.
b. All leaf nodes will be at the same level.
c. All leaf nodes can contain maximum (n-1) keys.
d. All non leaf nodes can contain (m-1) keys where m is the number of children for that node.
e. All the values that appear on the left most child of a node are smaller than the first value of that node. All the values that appear on the right most child of a node are greater than the last value of that node.

Figure 6.44 shows a B-tree of order 3, where all the restrictions stated above are fulfilled.

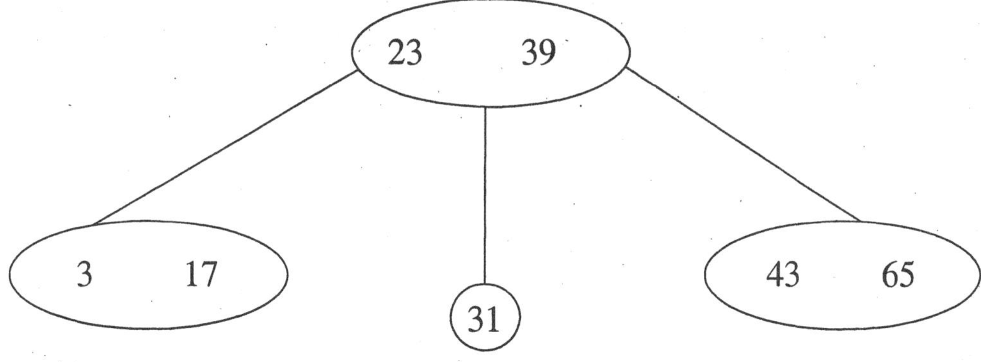

Figure 6.44 B-tree of order 3

☞ *Note that all leaf nodes are at the same level. All non leaf nodes have no empty subtree and they have keys 1 less than number of their children.*

6.13.1 Insertion in B-tree

The insertion procedure for B-tree is as follows.

First, a traversal is made to see whether the new element is in the tree or not. This search will terminate where it will return false. i.e. suppose key does not exist in tree then, it will reach leaf node through traversal. The new element is then added to the leaf node. If the node is empty then the insertion is finished.

When an element is added to non-empty node, then the node splits into two nodes on the same level, except that the median element is not put either of the two new nodes, but instead it is sent up the tree to be inserted into the parent node. When a search is later made through the tree, therefore, a comparison with median element will serve to direct the search into the proper sub-tree.

If an element is added to non-empty root, then the root splits into two and the median element sent upward become a new root.

As an example, consider B-tree of degree 4, that is a balanced four way tree where each node can hold three data values and four branches. Suppose it needs to contain the following values:

1 5 6 2 8 11 13 20 7 9 18

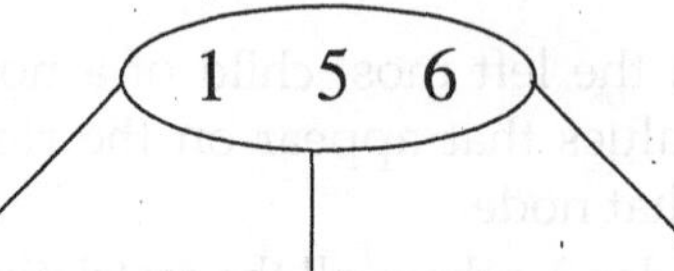

The first three elements will be inserted into one node, as illustrated above. They are sorted and put in the proper order as they are inserted. However, as there is no room for the 4th element 2, so its insertion causes the node to split into two and the median element is 5, moves up to enter a new node, which now becomes new root.

when 2 is added

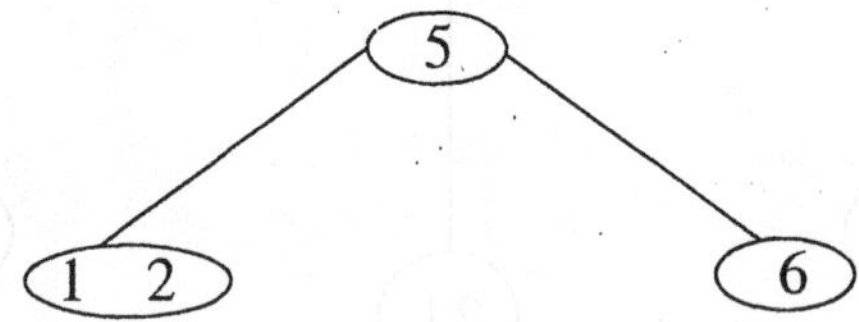

when 8 and 11 are added

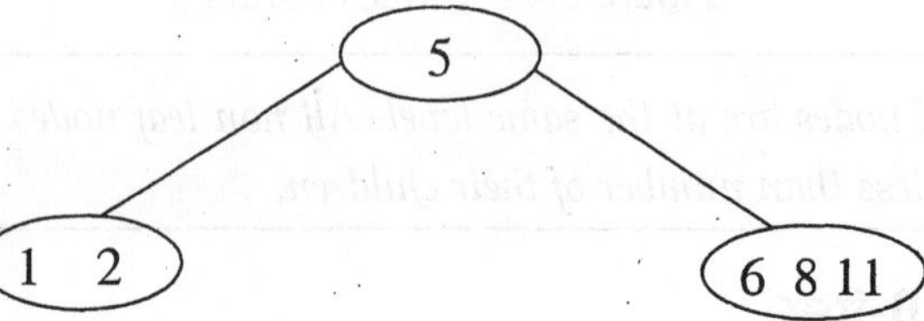

13 is to be added

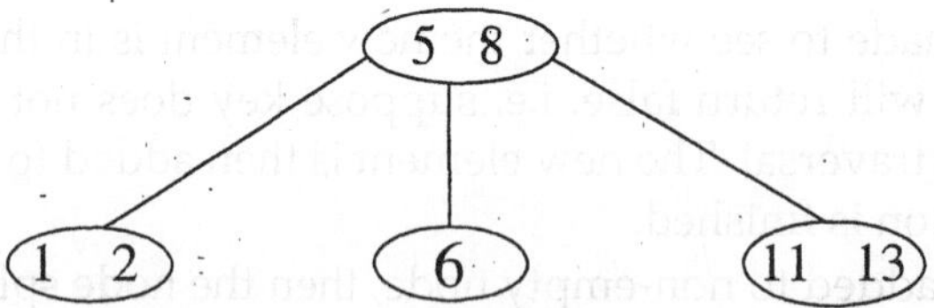

The remaining items can be added using above procedure and the final representation of a B-Tree is as seen in Figure below.

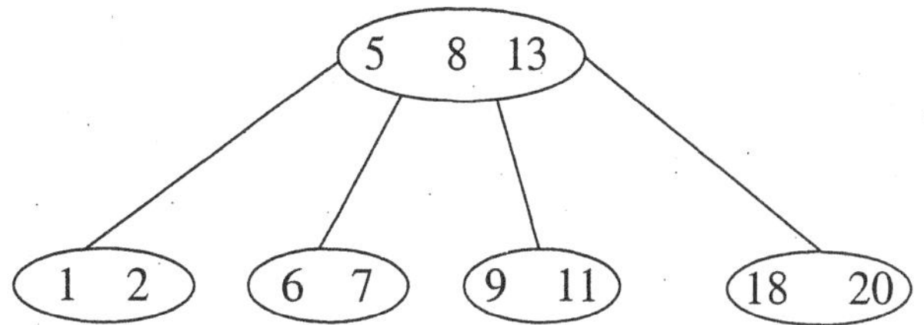

Figure 6.45 Final representation of B-tree for Example 7

☞ *Tree appears to grow at its root rather than at the leaves*

Example 8

Take a list of keys and create a B-tree of order 5. The values are: 10, 70, 60, 20, 110, 40, 80, 130, 100

Step 1 : Insert 10, 70, 60, 20

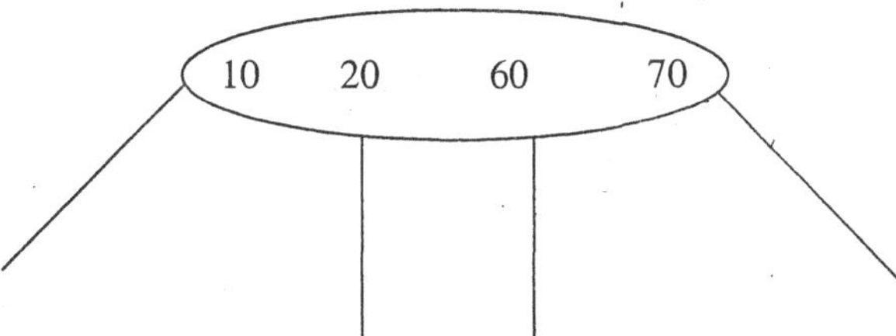

Step 2 : Insert 110

since the node is already full because it is a B-tree of order 5, where each node can hold four data values and five branches. So, after insertion of 110, it will be splitted into two nodes, 60 will be the median key so it will go in parent node but root node is splitted so it will become root.

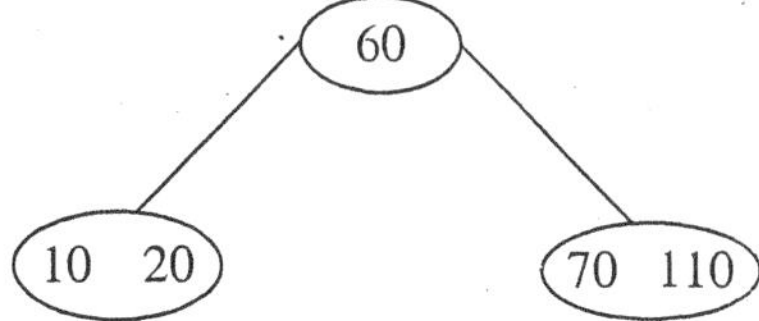

Step 3 : Insert 40

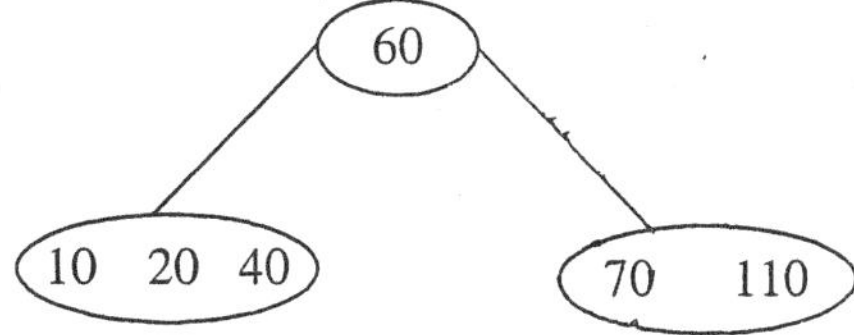

Step 4 : Insert 80

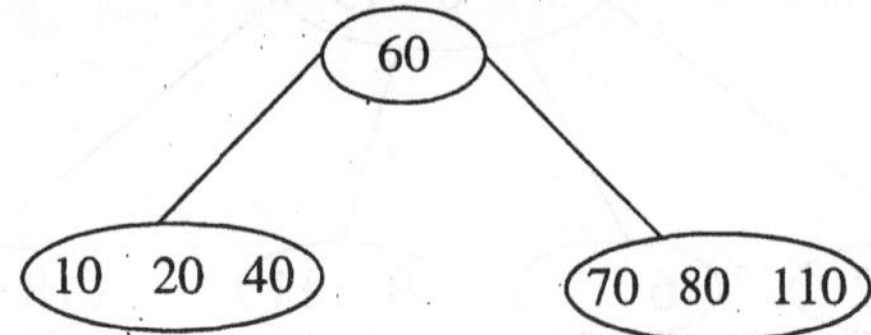

Step 5 : Insert 130

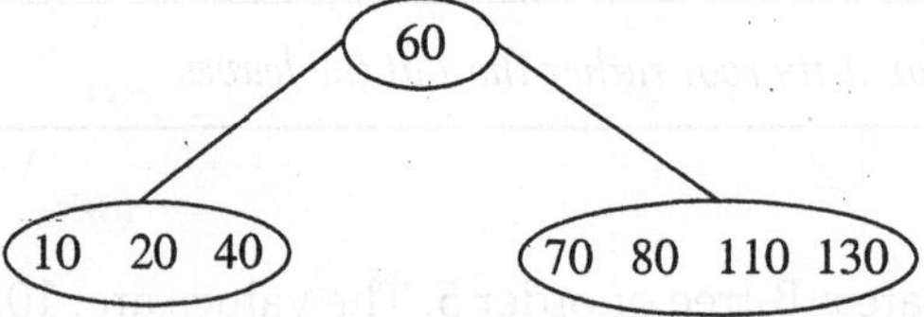

Step 6 : Insert 100
since node is already full, so after insertion of 100 it will be splitted into two nodes, 100 will be the median key, so it will go to the parent node.

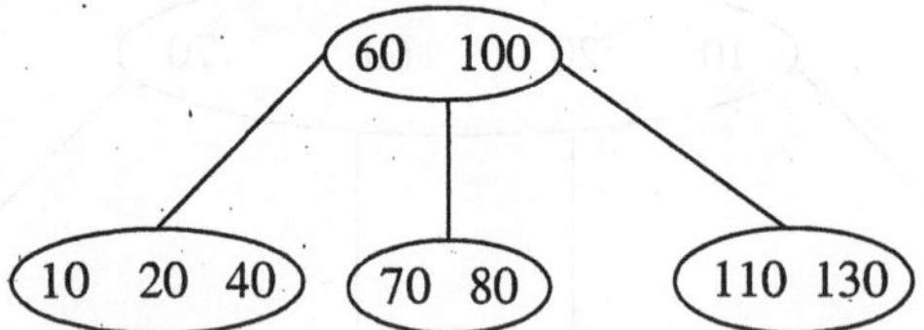

Figure 6.46 Final B-tree for Example 8

6.13.2 Deletion from B-trees

For deleting a value from the B-tree, we need to find the node from which the value is to be deleted. After the deletion of the value, we need to check, whether the balance of the tree still maintains the property of B-tree or not.

Example 9

For example consider the following B-tree of degree 5.

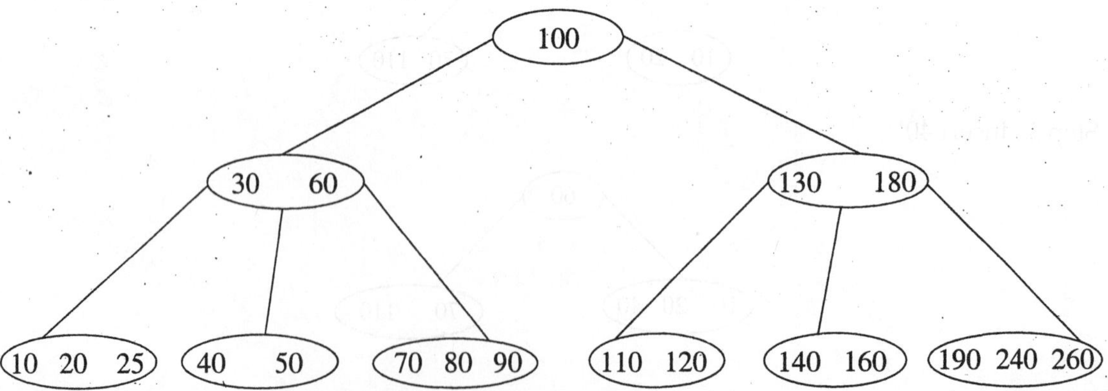

Delete 190

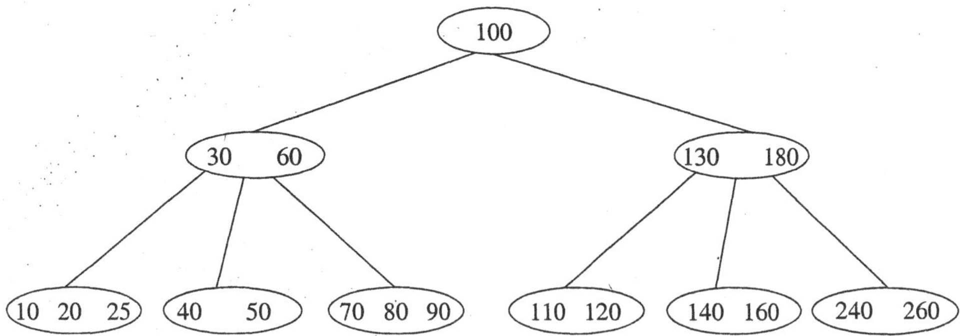

On deleting value 190, the number of values that are left in the node are 2, which satisfy the condition of a B-tree i.e. the number of values is greater than or equal to the minimum number of values required (i.e 2) for a B-tree of order 5.

Delete 60

Here 60 is in non leaf node. So first it will be deleted from the node and then the element of right side child will come in the node.

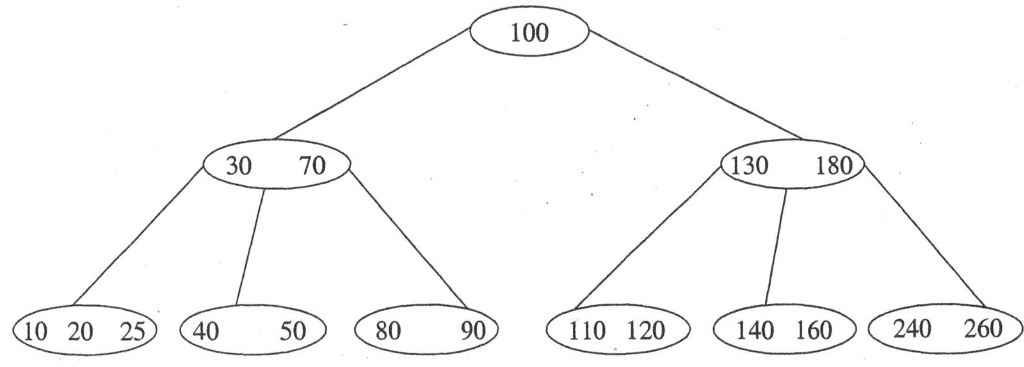

Delete 40

Here, 40 will be deleted from leaf node then left side element in the parent node will come in leaf node and then last element of the left side node of the parent node will come in parent node.

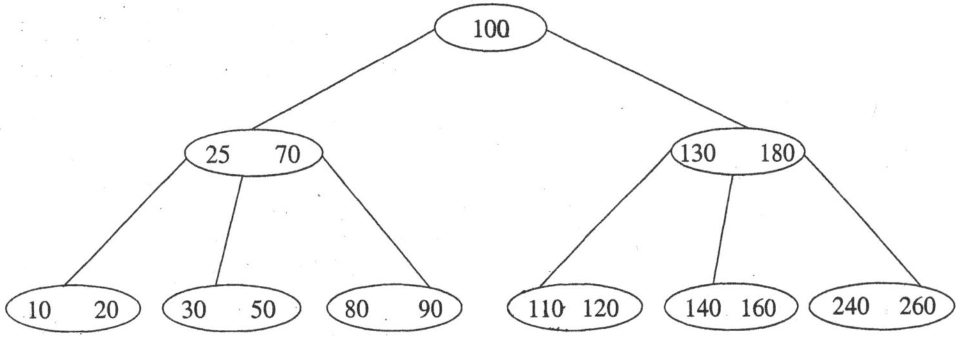

Delete 140

After deletion of the value 140, the node contains only one value 160. So, value 130 is copied from its parent and it is merge with its left sibling that contains value 110 and 120. As a result the node now contains four values 110, 120, 130 and 160.

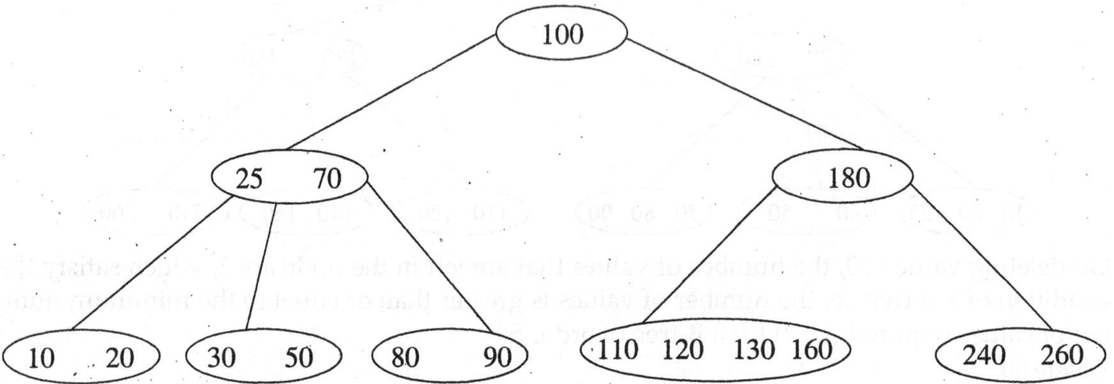

Now the parent node contains only one value 180. So the value 100 is copied from its parent and is merged with its left sibling that contains value 25 and 70. As a result, the node now contains four values 25, 70, 100 and 180.

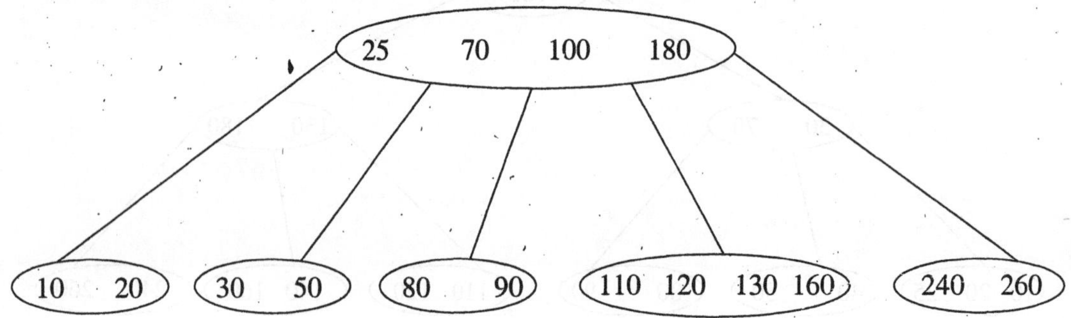

Figure 6.47 Final B-tree for Example 9

Example 10

Consider the following B-tree of order 5

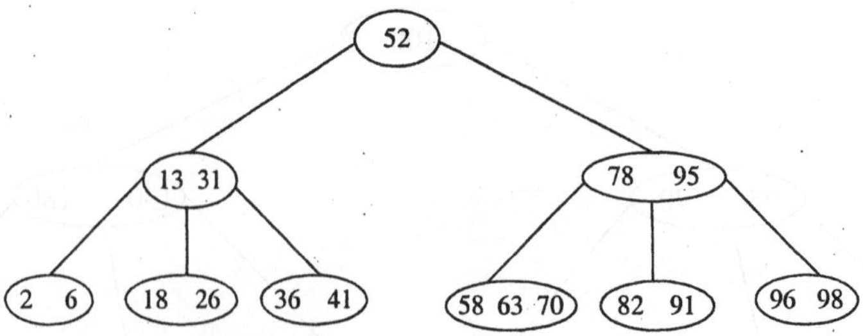

Delete 63, 91, 41

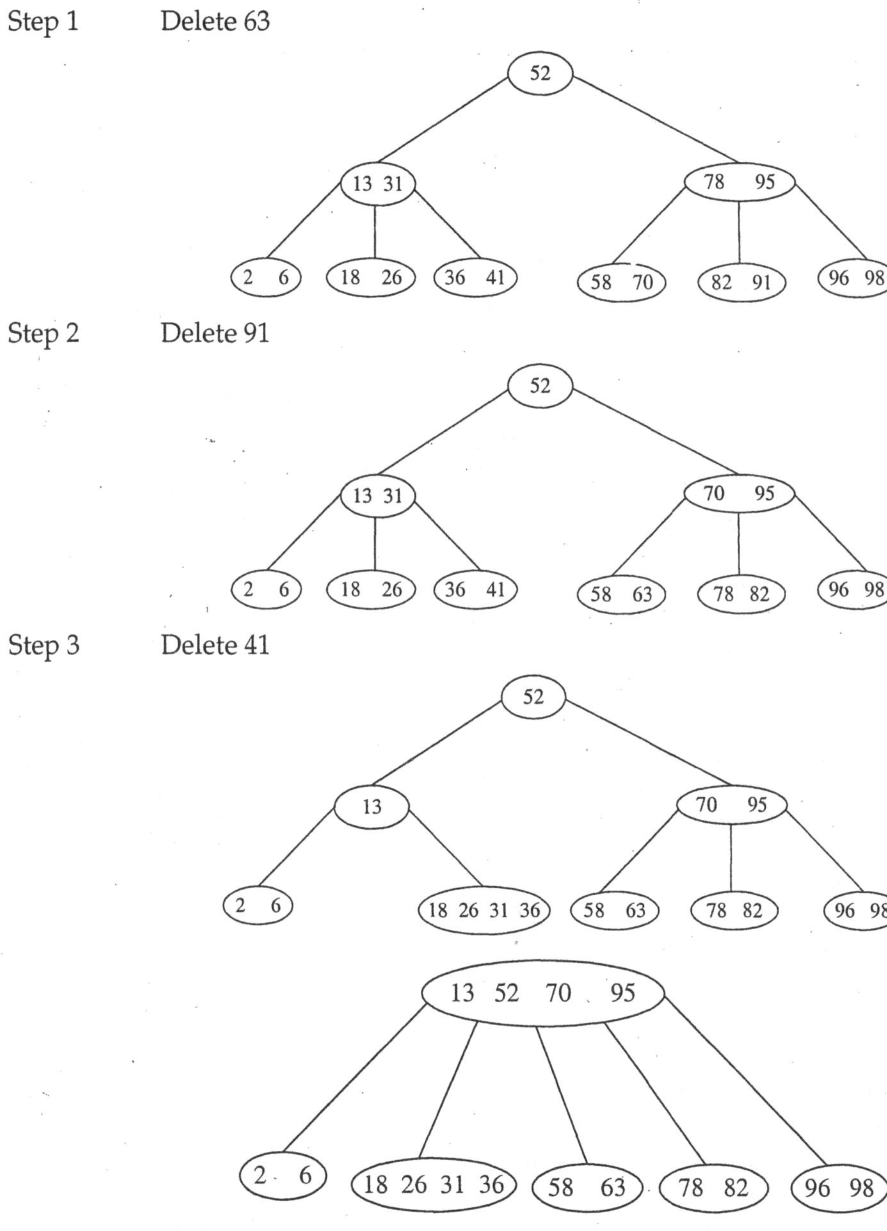

Figure 6.48 Final B-tree for Example 10

6.14 B+ Tree

One of the disadvantage of the B-tree is that we cannot traverse the record sequentially in this type of tree. Once we found particular record we cannot get the previous or next record because it does not provide sequential traversal. B+ tree has both the properties, random access as well as sequential traversal. Let us take an example of a B+ tree of order 5. In this B+ tree all the keys which are in non-leaf node will be in leaf node also and each leaf node will point to the next leaft node, so we can traverse sequentially also. (See Figure 6.49)

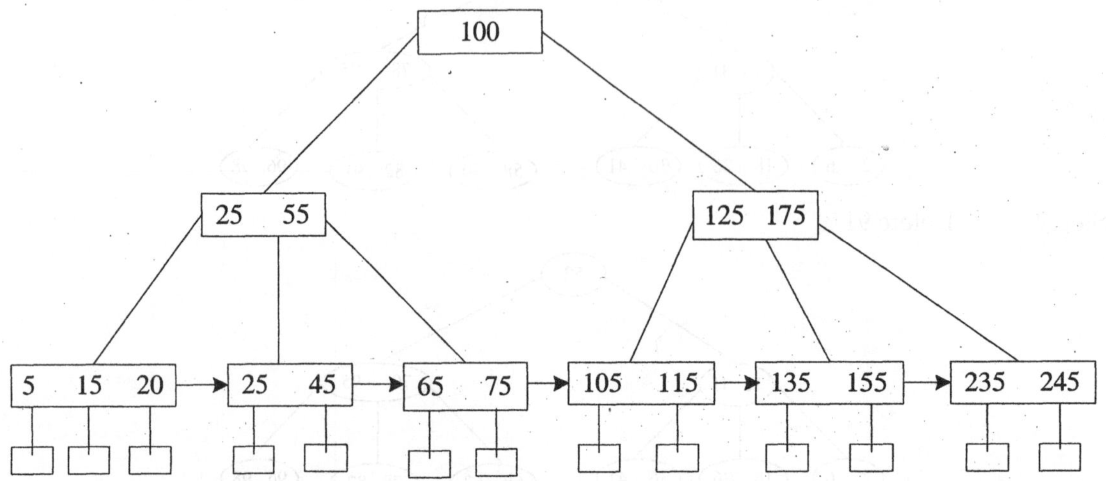

Figure 6.49 B+ tree of order 5

6.14.1 Insertion and Deletion in B+ tree

Insertion of B+ tree in similar to that in B-tree, except that when a node is split, the middle key is retained in the left half node as well as in parent node. One pointer is also needed for pointing left node to right node. When the key deleted is non-leaf node, then we should delete that key from leaf node only becuase it is a partitioning key and key in non leaf node does not point to the record.

☞ *The B+ tree retains the search and insertion efficiencies of th B-tree but increases the efficiency of finding the next record in the tree form O(log n) to O(1).*

6.15 HEAP TREE

Heap tree is a special case of *Tree* data structure, that is formed of nodes. The node which has no *parent* but can itself be the parent of zero or more *child* nodes is called the *root* node. A node that does not have any child nodes is called a *leaf* node. The nodes which are neither leaf nodes nor the root, form the internal nodes. Figure 6.50 shows a Heap tree structure. Here A is the root node. E, J, C, G, H and K are the leaf nodes. B, F, D and I are the internal nodes. B, C and D are the child nodes of A.

☞ *Heap tree is a binary tree such that the value at a node N is greater than or equal to the value at each of the children of node N.*

Figure 6.51(a) shows a heap tree H. The largest element in H appears at the top or root of the heap tree. This means that the largest element forms the root of the binary tree. Figure 6.51(b) also shows the array built from this tree. Note that the nodes of heap tree H that are on the same level, appear one after the other in the array.

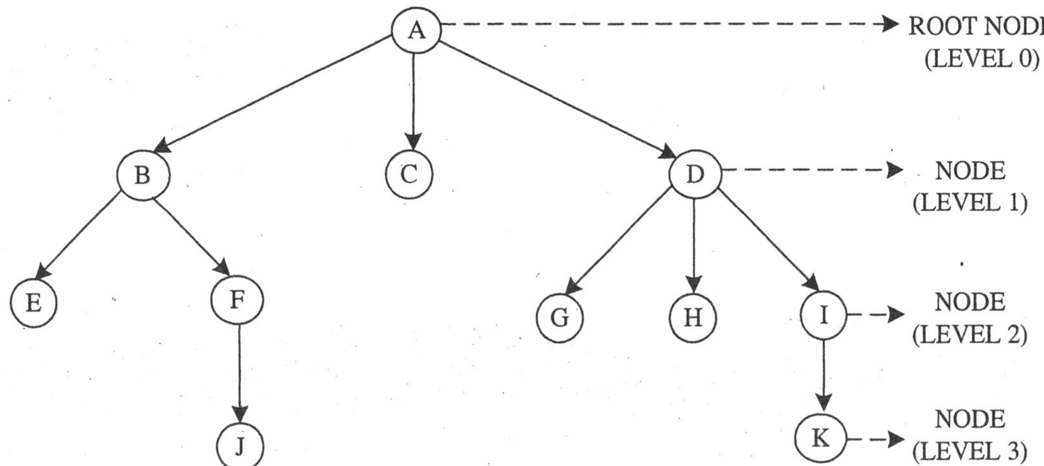

Figure 6.50 A Heap tree structure

(a)

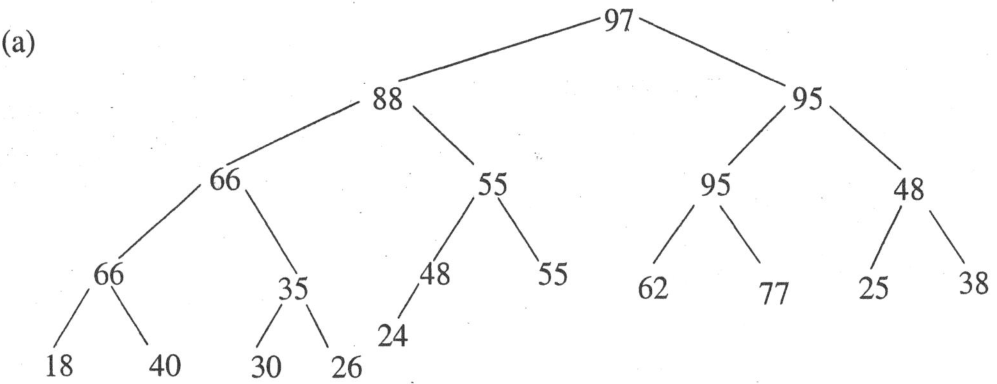

(b)

97	88	95	66	55	95	48	66	35	48	55	62	77	25	38	18	40	30	26	24

Figure 6.51 (a) A heap tree (b) Array representation of the heap tree

6.15.1 Inserting into Heap Tree

If H is a heap tree with *n* elements. To insert an element E into H, do the following:

(a) Insert E at the end of H so that H is still a complete tree but not a heap tree.

(b) Then let E to rise to its appropriate place in H so that H is finally a heap tree.

For example, suppose we want to insert 70 into the heap tree of Figure 6.51. First we will store 70 at the end of H i.e to the right of the node having value 48 (See Figure 6.52).

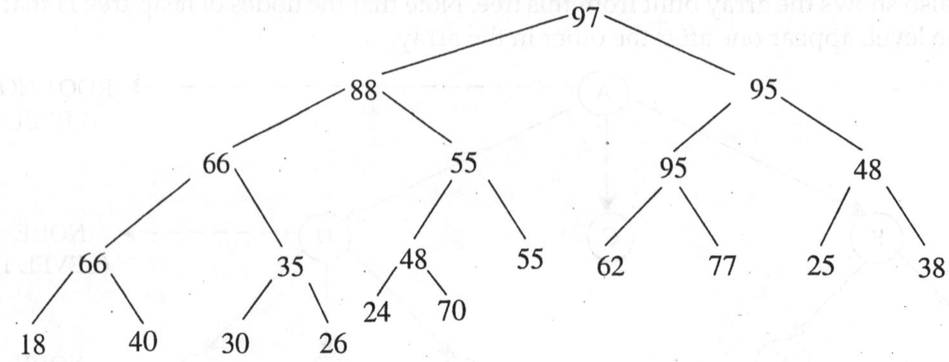

Figure 6.52 Inserting a new block 70 in a Heap tree

When compared with 48, 70 is larger than 48. Since 70 is greater then 48, interchange 70 and 48 (See Figure 6.53). Now 70 is compared with its new parent i.e 55. Since 70 > 55, interchange 70 and 55. The path will now look like the one seen in Figure 6.54.

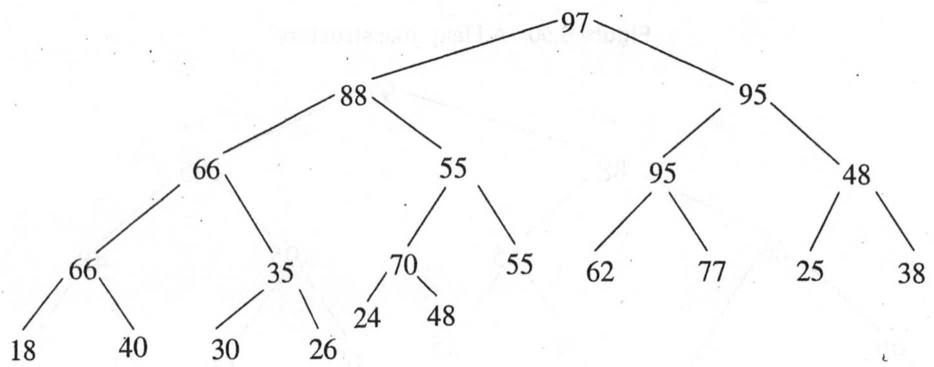

Figure 6.53 Placing 70 as it is larger than 48 in the Heap tree

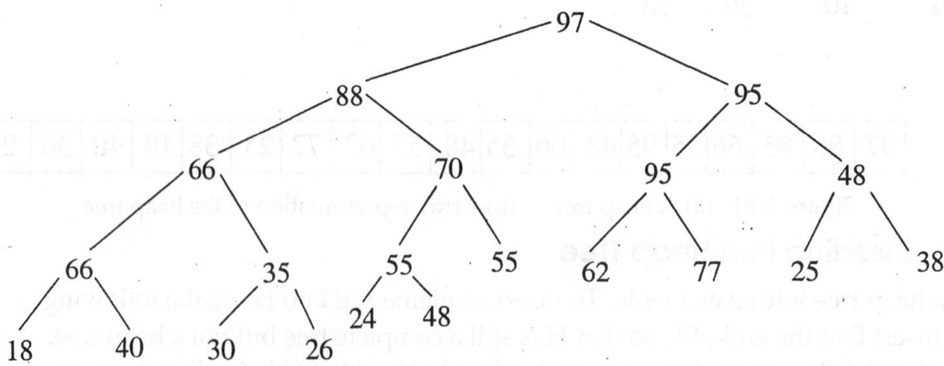

Figure 6.54 Placing 70 as it is larger than 55 in the Heap tree

Now compare 70 with its new parent i.e. 88. Sine 70 < 88, 70 has reached in its appropriate place.

6.15.2 Building a Heap Tree

Suppose we want to build a heap tree H using the following list of numbers:

44 30 50 22 60 55 77 55

The heap tree H can be constructed by inserting the above mentioned numbers one after the other into an empty heap using the methods as seen in Figure 6.55. The figure shows the different steps in building H.

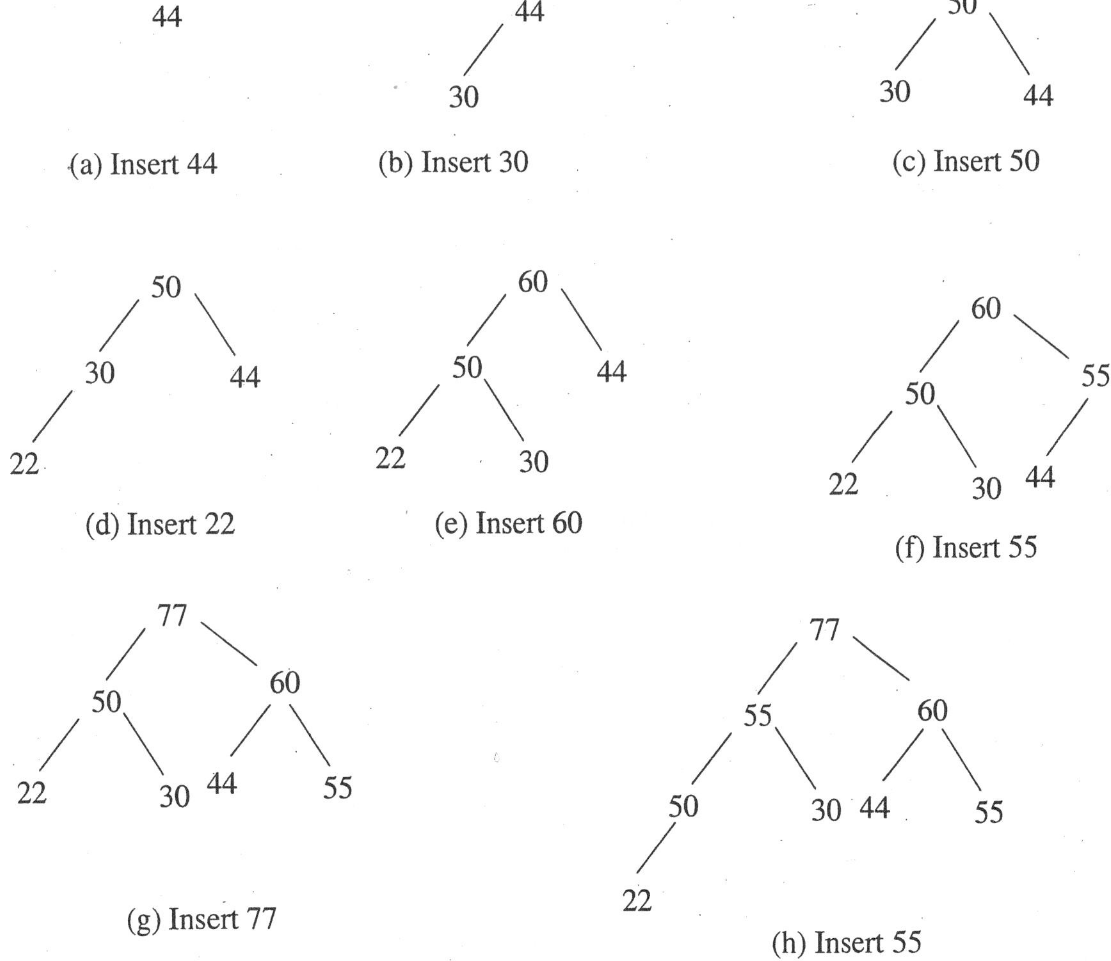

(a) Insert 44 (b) Insert 30 (c) Insert 50

(d) Insert 22 (e) Insert 60 (f) Insert 55

(g) Insert 77 (h) Insert 55

Figure 6.55 Building a Heap tree

6.15.3 Deleting from Heap Tree

To delete an element E from a heap H, do the following

(a) Assign the element E to some variable say TEMP.

(b) Replace the deleted element E by the last node L of H so that H is still a completed tree but not necessarily a heap tree.

(c) Let L sink to its appropriate position in the heap so that H is finally a heap.

For example, suppose from the heap tree shown in Figure 6.54, we want to delete element 88. For this, we will do the following:

(a) In the heap tree of Figure 6.54, 48 is the last node (L). The element E to be deleted is 88. First of all E is deleted from the tree and stored in TEMP. Thereafter, E is replaced with L as seen in Figure 6.56.

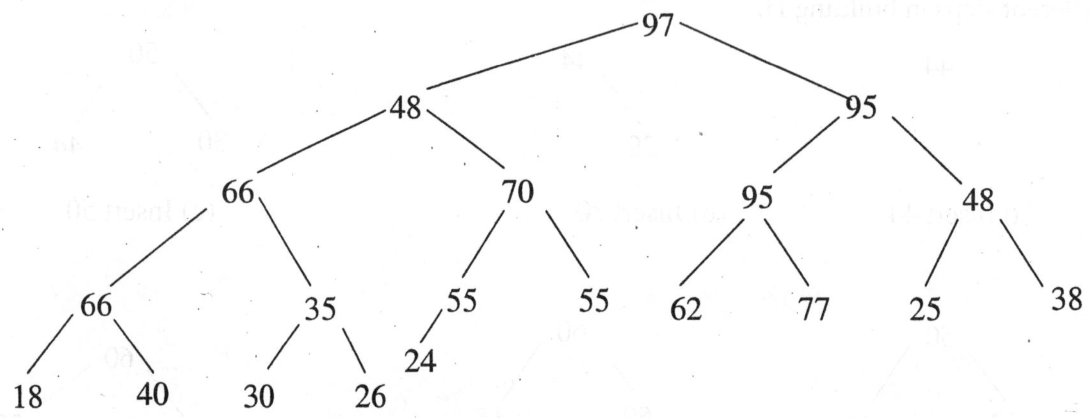

Figure 6.56 48 replaces the number 88 which is to be removed from Heap tree

(b) The tree shown in Figure 6.56 is a complete binary tree but it is not a heap tree.

(c) Compare 48 with its new children which are 66 and 70. Since 48 is less than the larger child that is 70, interchange 48 and 70. The tree will now look like as seen in Figure 6.57.

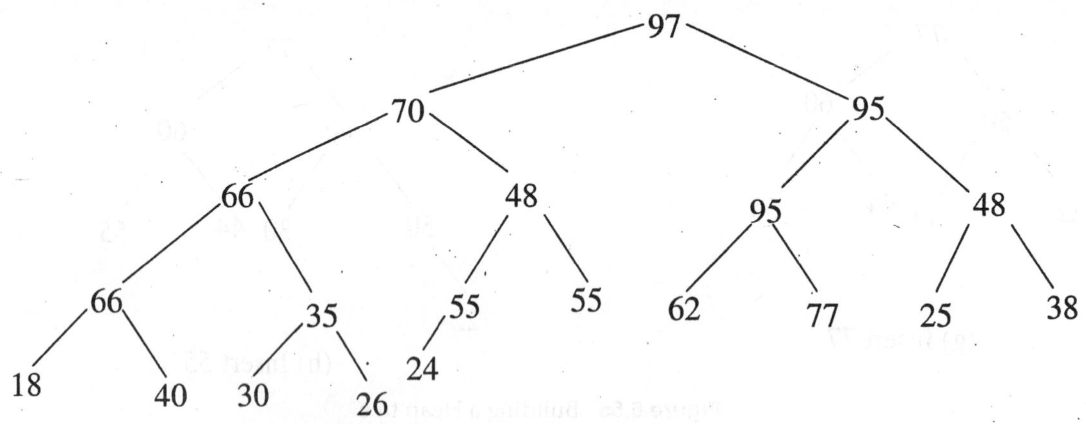

Figure 6.57 70 being larger than 48, replace 48 by 70

(d) Now compare 48 with its new children which are 55 and 55. Since 48 is less than both, interchange 48 and 55. Since there are no more children of 48, 48 has reached it correct position (See Figure 6.58).

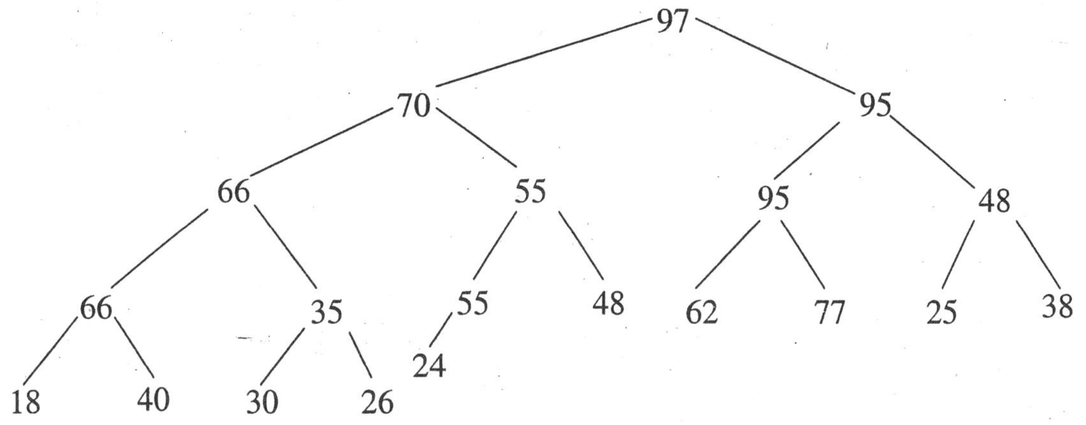

Figure 6.58 Heap tree after deleting 88

DESCRIPTIVE QUESTIONS

Q. No. 1 Find the preorder, inorder and postorder traversals of the tree shown below:

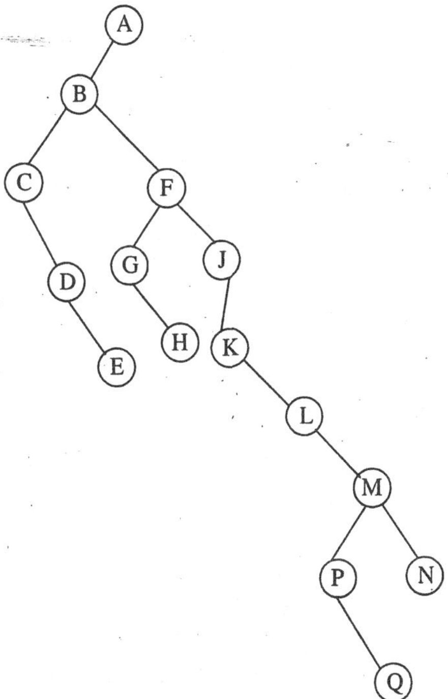

Figure 6.59 Tree structure for Q.No.1

Ans to Q. 1 Preorder: A, B, C, D, E, F, G, H, J, K, L, M, P, Q, N

Inorder: C, D, E, B, G, H, F, K, L, P, Q, M, N, J, A

Postorder: E, D, C, H, G, Q, P, N, M, L, K, J, F, B, A

Q. No. 2 What is the meaning of traversing a tree? What are different ways to traverse a tree.

Ans to Q. 2 Traversing a tree means visting each node in a specified order. There are three simple ways to traverse a tree. These are preorder, inorder and post-order.

Preorder Traversal

1. Process the root R
2. Traverse the left subtree of R
3. Traverse the right subtree of R

Inorder Traversal

1. Traverse the left subtree of R
2. Process the root R
3. Traverse the right subtree of R

Postorder Traversal

1. Traverse the left subtree of R
2. Traverse the right subtree of R
3. Process the root R

Q. No. 3 Write recursive algorithm for binary tree creation.

Ans to Q. 3 Create_Tree(Info, Node)

where Info -> Information for which we have to create node.

Node -> Structure type variable to print both left and right child

Step 1: [Check whether the tree is empty]

If node = NULL
Node = Create a Node
Left_Child [Node] = Null
Right_Child [Node] = Null

Step 2: [Test for the left child]

If Info [Node] ≥ Info
Left_Child [Node] = Call Create_Tree
(Info, Left_Child [Node])
Else
Right_Child [Node] = Call Create_Tree
(Info, Right_Child [Node])

Step 3: Return (Node)

Q. No. 4 Build a heap H from the following list of numbers:

44 30 50 22 60 55 77 55

Ans to Q. 4

44, 30, 50, 22, 60, 55, 77, 55

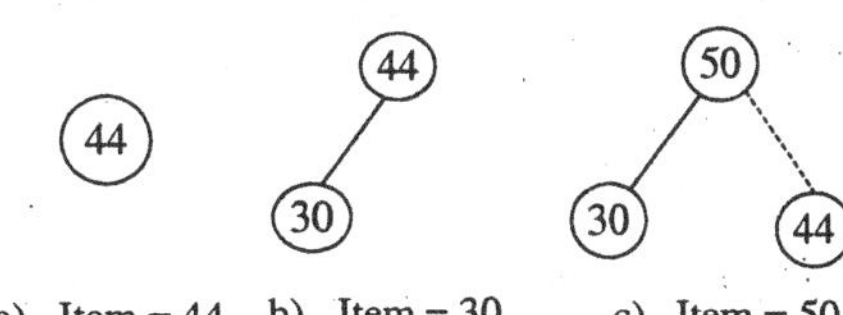

a) Item = 44 b) Item = 30 c) Item = 50

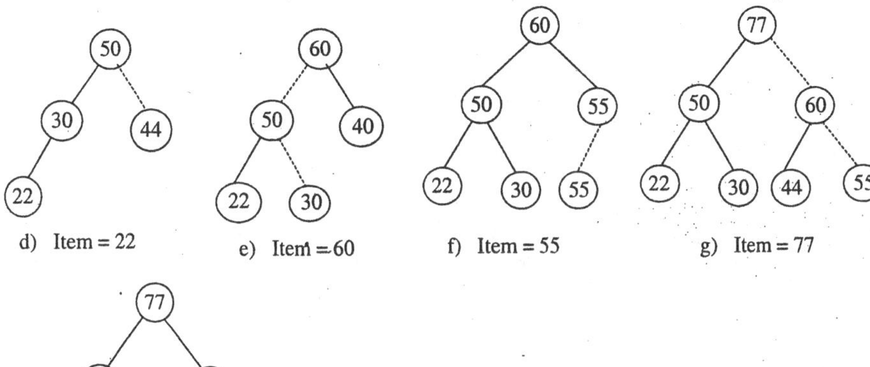

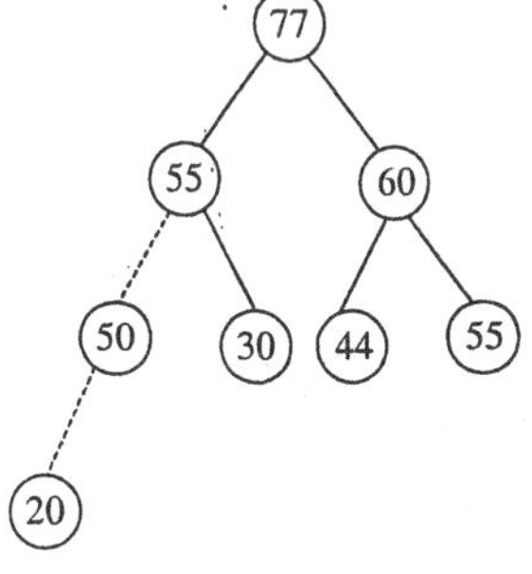

h) Item = 55

Figure 6.60 Heap tree for Q.No.4

Q. No. 5 Write recursive and non recursive functions for the following:

(a) Inorder traversing
(b) Postorder traversing

Ans to Q. 5 (a) *Recursive Function*

```
inorder (tree)
NODEPTR tree;
{
  if (tree != Null)
  {
     inorder(tree -> left);
     printf("%c", tree -> info);
     inorder(tree -> right);
  }
}
```

Non Recursive Function

```
void non_rec_inorder (root)
NODEPTR root;
{
  NODEPTR p;
  int top = -1; /* initialize stack */
  NODEPTR stack[MAX_STACK_SIZE];
  p = root;
  for (; ;)
  {
  for (; p ; p = p -> left) push(stack, p);
  /* add to the stack */
  p = pop(stack);
  if (!p) break;
  /* empty break; */
  printf("%d", p -> info);
  p = p -> right;
  }
}
```

(b) *Recursive Function*

```
postorder(tree)
NODEPTR tree;
{
  if(tree != NULL)
  {
    postorder(tree -> left);
    postorder(tree -> right);
    printf("%c", tree -> info);
  }
}
```

Non Recursive Function

The non recursive stack less function of the post order traversal in pseudocode is

```
p <- root
repeat
  while(left [p] != right[p])
  while(left [p] != null)
  p <- left[p]
  visit(p)
  if(right [p] != null)
  p <- right[p]
  visit (p)
```

```
while ((p != root) AND ((right(parent[p])=p) or
    (right (parent[p]) = null))
    p <- parent [p]
    if(p != root)
p <- right[parent[p]]
    visit(p)
    else exit;
```

EXERCISE

Multiple Choice

1. Which of the following process is faster for threaded trees compared with their unthreaded counterparts?
   (a) Insertion (b) Deletion
   (c) Traversal (d) None of these
2. Which of the following statements is TRUE in view of a threaded binary tree? It can have:
   (a) NULL links but no structural links
   (b) only structural links but no NULL links
   (c) structural links and NULL links
   (d) None of the above
3. Which of the following steps is performed first for inorder traversal of a binary tree?
   (a) Traversal of the left subtree in postorder.
   (b) Processing of the root node
   (c) Traversal of the left subtree in inorder
   (d) None of the above.
4. A B-tree of order n is also called:
   (a) (n-n)-1 tree (b) n-(n-2) tree
   (c) (n-1)-n tree (d) None of these.
5. The preorder traversal of a binary tree begins with:
   (a) Processing of the root node
   (b) Traversal of the right subtree in preorder
   (c) Traversal of the left subtree in preorder
   (d) None of the above
6. If a binary search techniques is used for accessing and implementing a symbol table, which of the following statements is TRUE? The ratio of:
   (a) insertion time to access time for its entries is quite high
   (b) access time to insertion time is quite high
   (c) search time to insertion time is very high
   (d) None of the above

7. The postorder traversal of a binary tree begins with:
   (a) the postorder traversal of the left subtree
   (b) processing of the root node
   (c) the postorder traversal of the right subtree
   (d) None of the above
8. Which of the following figures is not possible as a balance of any node of an AVL tree?
   (a) 1 (b) -1
   (c) 0 (d) None of these
9. The inorder traversal of some binary tree produced the sequence DBEAFC, and the postorder traversal of the same tree produced the sequence DEBFCA. Which of the following is a correct preorder traversal sequence?
   (a) DBAFCF (b) ABEDFC
   (c) ABDECF (d) None of these
10. The inorder traversal of some binary tree produced the sequence DBEAFC, and the postorder traversal of the same tree produced the sequence DEBFCA. What will be the total number of nodes in the left subtree of the given tree?
   (a) 1 (b) 4
   (c) 5 (d) None of these

Key to Multiple Choice Questions

1.	c	2.	d	3.	c	4.	c	5.	a
6.	a	7.	a	8.	d	9.	c	10.	d

TEST PAPER

Note: Answer all questions.

1. Define a B-tree. Taking an example to show how insertion is handled here.
2. Write a general, non-recursive C program, for postorder traversal of a binary tree. Explain it giving an example.
3. Discuss an algorithm for deletion of a node from B-tree.
4. Write C functions required for deletion of a node from an AVL tree.
5. Define the term *binary tree* and *binary search tree*.
6. What is the difference between a *binary tree* and an *ordinary tree* in which each vertex has at most two branches?
7. Define hashing. Explain different hashing techniques.
8. What is the use of AVL trees? What isolates an AVL tree from all binary search trees?
9. Draw a picture showing how balance is restored when an insertion into an AVL tree puts a node out of balance.

CHAPTER 7

Searching and Sorting

7.1 WHAT IS SEARCHING ?

Locating a particular data item in a database is known as *Searching*. The application of search process occurs in computer when a particular data item is required from a set of stored data items. The search is said to be *successful* if the desired data item is located otherwise the search is considered to be *unsuccessful*.

Consider an example of telephone directory, where information of subscribers, such as name, address, telephone number etc are stored. It is required to find the address when the telephone number is given. Take another example of employee table, where we may want to find the name and address of the employee if emp_code is given.

In the above examples, we are given one piece of information, called *key* and we are asked to find a record that contains other set of information associated with the key. Thus, the key is used to differentiate the specific record from other records.

For every database, there is atleast one key which is unique i.e no two records have the same key field value. Such a key is called the *primary* key.

☞ *Computer systems are used to store large amounts of data from which individual records may be retrieved according to some search criterion. Thus the efficient storage of data to facilitate fast searching is very important.*

Searching in computer systems is of two types:

a. *Internal* search

b. *External* search

In case of Internal search, the data items are stored entirely within the computer's main memory. In case of External search, tables, records etc are stored in files kept on disk or tape which are external to computer's main memory.

7.2 SEQUENTIAL AND BINARY SEARCH

There are two simple techniques for carrying out search. These are:

a. Linear or Sequential Search

b. Binary Search

7.2.1 Linear or Sequential Search

Sequential search is to find the specific data item in a linear i.e. one after the other. It needs traversing each and every element of data items and checking if it is the one required.

The sequential search technique is the simplest method but suitable for data items stored as a table that are organised either as an array or as a linked list. This method can be applied on sorted or unsorted list of data items.

In sequential search, each element of an array is compared one by one with the required ITEM to be searched, until either the desired element is found or the end of the list is reached.

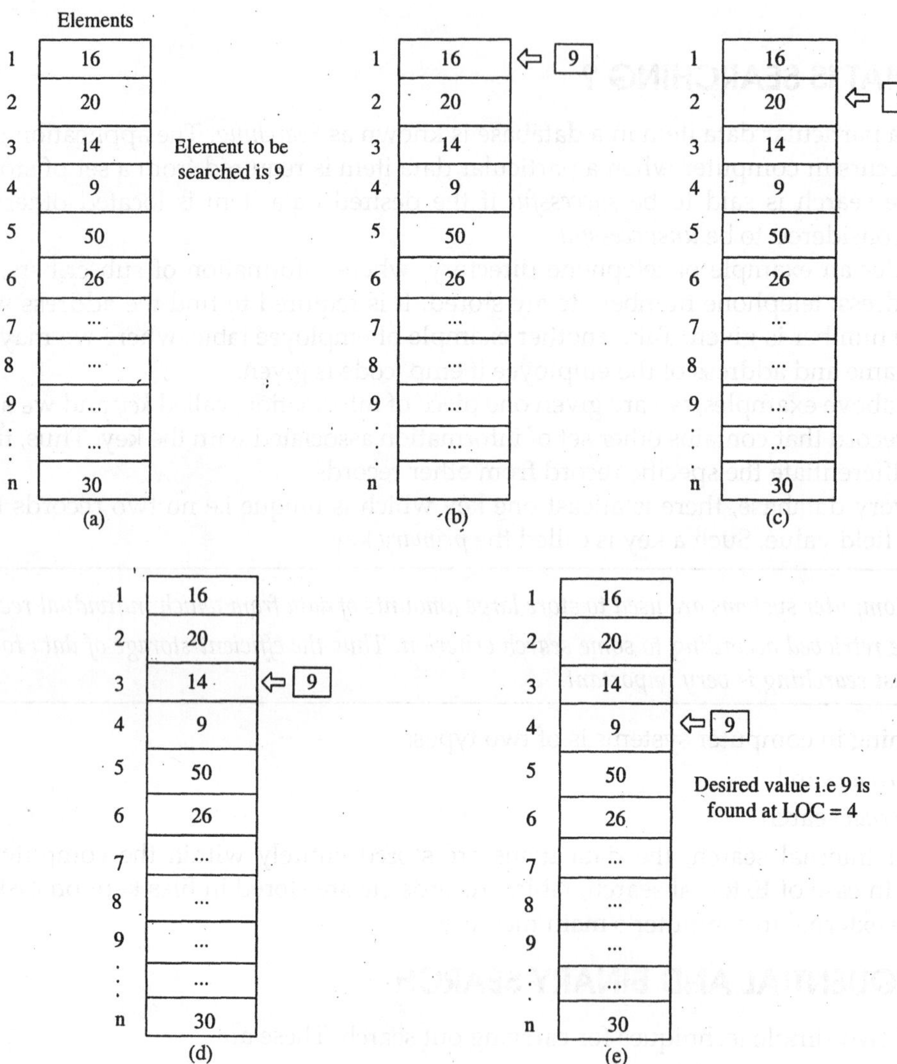

Figure 7.1 Illustration of Linear search

☞ *A method in which we traverse every item of the array sequentially to locate the given ITEM is called sequential or linear search.*

Let us take an example to understand linear search in a better way. Consider the unsorted list shown in Figure 7.1(a). This list contains n elements. Suppose the element that is to be searched is 9. The concept of sequential search states that the element 9 is compared with each element of array. If it matches, then the search is completed. Otherwise, next element from the list is fetched and compared. This process is continued until either the desired element is found or list is exhausted. (See Figure 7.1)

The algorithm in Figure 7.2 gives a method to search an Item using linear search in an array, using *Repeat until* loop.

```
(Sequential Search) Sequential (DATA, N, ITEM, LOC)
Here DATA is a linear array with N elements, and ITEM is a given item
of information to be searched. The algorithm finds the location LOC of
ITEM in DATA or sets LOC: = 0 if the search is unsuccessful
Step 1    Insert ITEM at the end of DATA [Initialize Counter]
          set DATA[N + 1] : = ITEM
Step 2    [Initialize Counter] set LOC : = 1
Step 3    [Search for ITEM]
          Repeat while DATA[LOC] ≠ ITEM
          set LOC : = LOC + 1
          [End of loop]
          [End of loop in Step 2]
Step 4    [Successful?] If LOC = N + 1, then set LOC : = 0
Step 5    Exit
```

Figure 7.2 Algorithm for sequential search in an array using Repeat loop

The efficiency of the sequential search is very poor. On the average, it will require NUMBERREC/2 accesses to the list to find a key. In the worst case, the target being sought is not in the list of keys and each record must be accessed. This worst case efficiency can be improved somewhat if the list is in a sorted order. The efficiency of the sequential search is basically proportional to the number of records in the list. Hence, users searching an external file of 50,000 records for which the average retrieval time per record is 5 milliseconds will have to wait over 2 minutes for responses to their requests. Obviously, that sort of performance is not good, something better method is needed.

☞ *Sequential search is a simple and easy method, but it is efficient only for small sized array list and highly inefficient for large sized list. If the array list is big, then the number of comparisons are very large. In the worst case, we will have to make N comparisons, to search for the record in the end of the list. Where N is the maximum number of elements in the array.*

Example 1

A program and the output for sequential search in the array is shown in Figure 7.3.

```
#include <stdio.h>
main()
{
  int arr[15], n, i, item;
  printf("Enter Total Number of elements you want to store in the
          array:");
  scanf("%d", &n);
  for(i=0; i<n; i++)
     {
       printf("Enter element %d:", i+1);
       scanf("%d", &arr[i]);
     }
  printf("Enter the element to be searched:");
  scanf("%d", &item);
  for(i=0; i<n; i++)
     {
       if(item == arr[i])
     {
       printf("%d found at position %d\n", item, i+1);
       break;
     }
  } /* End of for loop */
    if(i==n)
       printf("Item %d not found in array\n", item);
 }
```

RUN

```
Enter Total Number of elements you want to store in the array : 5

Enter element 1 : 45
Enter element 2 : 87
Enter element 3 : 23
Enter element 4 : 65
Enter element 5 : 72
Enter the element to be searched : 65
65 found at position 4
```

Figure 7.3 Program and the output for linear search in an array

7.2.2 Binary Search

When you want to locate an item in an *ordered* or *sorted* list (array) then, you can do so more efficiently by using a *binary* search. This is a technique in which each comparison either locates the item or divides the remaining list (array) in to half. Because the array (list) is in the order (ascending or descending order), it will only be necessary to repeat this process again on one of the two segments. In this way, we are reducing the remaining search operations very rapidly. Thus, in binary search, we first compare the value of the desired item with the element in the middle position of the array. If there's a match, we found the match immediately. If the value is less than the middle element value, then the item sought must lie in the lower half of the array. If it is greater than the item sought, then it must lie in the upper half of the array. So we repeat the procedure on the lower (or upper) half of the array depending upon the value of the middle element of the array.

☞ *The binary search method requires the elements of the array in the sorted order descending or ascending.*

Example 2

Suppose, we are required to locate 29 in the sorted array shown in Figure 7.4 using binary search technique. Then, we do the following:

Step 1 Split the ten element list into half (10/2 = 5), and check the fifth element. The result is 23. Since 29 > 23 we will proceed with the lower half of the array.

Step 2 Split the five elements in the second half of the list into half, i.e. ((10 – 5)/2 + 5) = 7.5 (rounded to 8). Check the 8th element. The result is 52 but 29 < 52. Thus search is upper half in the list.

Step 3 Split the distance between the fifth and the eighth into half (8 – 5)/2 + 5 = 6.5 (rounded to 7). So check the seventh element. The result is 35 and 29 < 35. So continue with upper half in the list.

Step 4 Split the distance between the fifth and the seventh element into half ((7 – 5)/2 + 5). So check the sixth element which is 29. That is the match.

	N	
1	1	
2	5	
3	11	
4	17	
5	23	**Comp 1 (29 > 23)**
6	29	**Match comp 4**
7	35	**Comp 3 (29 < 35)**
8	52	**Comp 2 (29 < 52)**
9	71	
10	93	

Figure 7.4 Locating an array element containing 29

☞ *At each stage, the number of elements in the remaining set is decreased by about one half. Therefore the binary search is faster than the sequential search.*

Example 3

Locate MERCURY in the list given in Figure 7.5 using binary search technique.

Step 1 Check the item number (13 + 1)/2 or the seventh item.

Step 2 Since MERCURY comes after MERCEDES which is the 7th item in the list, so the second comparison is for 7 + (13 – 7)/2 = 7 + 3 = 10. i.e. lower half. The 10th item is PLYMOUTH. But alphabetically, MERCURY comes before PLYMOUTH.

Step 3 The third comparison will be for 7 + (10 – 7)/2 = 7 + 1.5 ≅ 9. But MERCURY comes before OLDS in the alphabetic list.

Step 4 The fourth comparison is for 7 + (9 – 7)/2 = 8th item. It is MERCURY. Hence the match is obtained.

	M$	
1	AMC	
2	CADILLAC	
3	CHEVY	
4	CHRYSLER	
5	DATSUN	
6	FORD	
7	MERCEDES	Comparison 1 (MERCURY > MERCEDES)
8	MERCURY	Comparison 4 (MATCH)
9	OLDS	Comparison 3 (MERCURY < OLDS)
10	PLYMOUTH	Comparison 2 (MERCURY < PLYMOUTH)
11	PONTIAC	
12	TOYOTA	
13	VW	

Figure 7.5 Locating array element containing PLYMOUTH

Procedure to write the algorithm for binary search

Suppose DATA is an array which is already sorted in ascending order, of numeric or alphabetic values. Then binary search algorithm can be used to find the location LOC of a given ITEM of information in DATA.

The algorithm works as follows:

After every state of search for ITEM, the segment of DATA elements reduces by half. Suppose DATA [BEG], DATA [BEG + 1] . . . . . . DATA [END] is the array DATA with its subscripts BEG meaning the *beginning*, and END meaning the last location of the segment under consideration. The algorithm compares the ITEM with the *middle* element DATA (MID) of the segment, where:

MID = INT((BEG + END)/2)

We use INT(A) for the integer value of A.

If

DATA[MID] = ITEM,

then the search is successful and we set

LOC: = MID,

otherwise a new segment of DATA is obtained as follows:

a. If ITEM < DATA[MID] then ITEM can appear in the first half of the segment. It means that the item is in the segment:

```
DATA [BEG], DATA [BEG + 1], . ,
DATA [MID-1]
```

So we reset END := MID – 1 and begin searching again.

b. IF ITEM > DATA[MID] then ITEM can appear only in the second half of the segment. It means that the item is in that segment which is:

```
DATA[MID + 1], DATA[MID + 2], . .  DATA [END]
```

So we reset BEG : = MID + 1 and begin searching again.

Initially, we begin with the entire array DATA, i.e. we begin with BEG = 1 and END = *n* or more generally with BEG = LB and END = UB.

Here LB means *lower bound* and UB means *upper bound* of the array DATA.

If ITEM is not in DATA, then eventually, we obtain

END < BEG.

This condition signals that the search is *unsuccessful* and in such a case, we assign:

LOC := NULL

Here NULL is a value that is outside the set of elements or indices of array DATA. The binary search algorithm is as shown in Figure 7.6.

```
BINARY SEARCH (DATA, LB, UB, ITEM, LOC).
(Here DATA[] is a sorted array with lower bound LB, and upper bound UB
and ITEM is a given item of information to be searched. The variables
BEG, END and MID denote respectively the beginning, ending and middle
location of segment of the elements of array DATA[]. This algorithm
finds the LOC of ITEM in DATA[] or sets LOC = NULL) if search is
unsuccessful.
Step 1. (Initialize the segment variables)
        Set BEG: = LB,  END: = UB and
        MID = INT((BEG + END)/2)
```

(Contd...)

```
Step 2. Repeat Steps 3 and 4 while BEG < END
            and DATA(MID) ≠ ITEM
Step 3. IF ITEM < DATA(MID) Then
            SET END := MID - 1
        ELSE
            SET   BEG := MID + 1
        END IF
Step 4. Set MID:= INT [(BEG + END)/2]
            (End of step 2 loop)
Step 5. IF DATA[MID] = ITEM then
            Set LOC:= MID and print search successful
        ELSE
            Set LOC:= NULL and print search unsuccessful
        END IF
Step 6. EXIT
```

Figure 7.6 Algorithm for binary search of a linear array DATA[ ]

Example 4

The program shown in Figure 7.7 implements binary search technique in an array which is already sorted.

```
/* Binary Search */
#include<stdio.h>
main()
{
    int a[50],i,n,low,high,mid,term,flag = 1;
    printf("Enter no. of elements in an array ? ");
    scanf("%d",&n);
    printf("\n\nEnter elements in ascending order:\n");
        for(i=0;i<n;i++)
    scanf("%d",&a[i]);
        for(i=0;i<n;i++)
    printf("%5d",a[i]);
    printf("\n");
    printf("\nEnter element to be searched? ");
    scanf("%d",&term);
    low = 0;
    high = n-1;
    while(low <= high)
    {
        mid = (low+high)/2;
    if(term < a[mid])
```

(*Contd...*)

```
        /*Term in lower half */
    high = mid - 1;
    else
    if(term > a[mid])
        /* Term in upper half */
    low = mid + 1;
    else
    {
        printf("\nSearch successful.\n");
        printf("%d found at location %d \n",term,mid+1);
        flag = 0;
        break;
    }
    }
    if(flag) /* same as flag == 1 */
    printf("\nSearch Unsuccessful.\n");
    return 0;
}

RUN

Enter no. of elements in an array? 5

Enter elements in ascending order:
2
4
9
16
19
    2  4  9  16     19
Element to be searched? 9

    Search successful
9 found at location 3
```

Figure 7.7 Program and its output to carry out binary search in a sorted array

7.3 INDEXED SEARCH

You can improve search efficiency for sorted file by indexed sequential search method. An indexed sequential file is basically a sequential file organised on search a key field. In addition, an index is maintained which speeds up the access of isolated records. Just as you may use indexes to locate information in a book, an index can be provided for a file. The file is divided into a number of blocks and the highest key in each block is indexed as shown in Table 7.1.

Table 7.1 Keys and starting address of each block

Key	Starting address of block
125	12
860	19
1420	24
1600	42
1829	49

All the records with index value upto 125 are in the first block on the storage medium which starts at the address 12 on the disk. If a record with key 1236 is required, it will be in the third block starting at address 24, within this block the record is searched sequentially.

This method of locating an item is much faster than searching the entire file i.e. sequential search. It is also possible to have more than one level of indexing to make the search much faster. Hence, the general strategy of an indexed search is to use the key to search the index, find the relative record position of the associated data, and from there make only one access into the data. Because the parallel lists of keys and relative record positions require much less storage than do the data, frequently the entire index can be loaded and held in the main memory. For large sized indexes, large blocks of keys and associated pointer can be manipulated in the main memory. This will enhance search as well as the efficiency of search.

7.4 HASHING SCHEMES

Hashing algorithm is a method that provides very fast access to specific records depending on certain search criteria. This type of data organization is stored in file called *hash file*.

Suppose a manufacturing company has an inventory file containing data of 1000 parts, each *part* having a unique three-digit number. Then, the obvious way to store this file is to use an array of size 1000. Let the array be represented as part[1000], where part[i] represents the ith record with a part number. (value of *i* ranges from *000* to *999*). In this case, part numbers are keys, which are used as *indices* to the array.

There is an obvious drawback in the array system of storing data. If the company stores less than 1000 parts, the same array structure can be used. But, if the company wishes to stock more than 1000 parts, then this structure will have to be modified as the part number will now contain four digit numbers in place of three digits earlier.

Suppose the key to each record is a five digit part number. To employ direct indexing using the entire five digit number, an array of 1 lakh elements would be required. This will clearly wastes main memory space of a computer because a company may not stock more than a few thousand parts.

Such a problem can be solved easily if we use some method of converting the *key* values into integers of a limited range. This process of manipulating the key values to generate integer numbers of limited range is known as *hashing* technique. The function used for key manipulation is called *hash function*.

A good hash function must have the following properties:

(a) The hash function must uniformly distribute the keys into the available range of integers.

(b) No two keys should be converted into the same integer value.

Suppose we know in advance that a manufacturing company will not be having more than 2000 parts in its inventory at any point of time. Then we can create an array of size 2000. The company uses a seven-digit part number. The last three digits of the part number can then form the index for the array. Choosing the last three digits for forming the array index has an advantage. The advantage is that two keys which are relatively close to each other numerically, such as 4618396 and 4618996 will be farther from each other in the array. And the keys that are widely separated numerically, such as 000991 and 9846995 will be closer to each other in the array, as we are looking for the last three numerical digits only.

☞ ***Hashing** refers to the process of deriving a storage address from a record key. A function that transforms a key into a table index is called **hash function**.*

☞ *Hashing avoids unnecessary comparisons or searches and each key can be retrieved in a single access.*

7.5 HASHING FUNCTIONS

Conversion of the key to an address is done by a relation (formula) which is known as '*hashing*' function. A *hashing* function is actually just a relation which operates on a key to give its hash value (a number). It converts key to yield a location (position) at which the record should be found. The hash function is used to generate the location at which a record will be inserted. During retrieval, the same hash value is used to find the location at which the record is stored. Alphanumeric keys are usually converted into numeric keys before the hashing function can operate on it.

There are three different hashing functions. These are:

(a) Division/Remainder

(b) Mid square

(c) Folding

  (i) Shift folding

  (ii) Folding at boundaries

7.5.1 Division/Remainder Methods

In this method, primary key value is divided by an appropriate integer and the remainder is used as the relating address for the record. If *D* is the divisor, then remainder always falls between 0 and D (both inclusive). It is a common practice to *add* 1 to the remainder. Then the maximum number of addresses it can produce is D. Let us consider a file with 20 records and with the key values of records ranging between 100 to 2000. Let the divisor be 100. Now let the key values are given as 400, 780, 902, the remainders after dividing by 100 will be 0, 80, 2.

Adding 1 to the remainder will give us the addresses as 1, 81 and 3 respectively. Take another case, we have the key values of the addresses as 450, 650, 750. They will give the remainders as 50, 50, 50 respectively. Now adding 1 to the remainder will also give the addresses as 51, 51, 51. Such a key address value gives the same address for all the three records. Such a situation is called *hash collision*. There is a collision in addresses and they are to be resolved. Hence, we need to select a divisor such that the possibility of collision is minimized.

☞ *Two records cannot occupy the same position. Such a situation is called a* ***hash collision****.*

Therefore, we select the divisor such that possibility of number of collision is quite low. So if we select a number which is a prime number closer to the number of records, i.e. say 19, then the remainders for 450, 650 and 750 would be 13, 4 and 9 respectively. Adding 1 to the remainders will give the physical addresses in the memory as 14, 5 and 10 respectively. These are all different addresses. Hence we can resolve the collision problem of the same physical address locations by taking a different divisor values.

7.5.2 Mid Square Method

In Mid square hashing function method, the key is multiplied by itself (squared) and the middle few digits of square are used as address. In order to calculate the address of the main memory where the record will be stored, we use the following algorithm:

Step1 : Square the key value of the record

Step2 : Extract the number of digits from the middle of the squared value to get the address of the memory.

For example, if we have a file with 100 records then we shall need 2 digits address to reach all the records. Thus 0 to 99 will give us 100 records. Now if the key value of a record is 784, then square of 784 = 614656. Hence if we drop the first two and last two digits of this (614656), number we shall get 46. Thus we shall take the physical address of the location of the record to be 46 which is the middle digits of the square of the address value.

Advantages and disadvantages of mid squared method

The mid square method has the advantage that it is a flexible method and it can be suitably modified if needed. The disadvantage of this method is that it does not yield uniform hash values.

7.5.3 Folding Method

In the folding method, a key is partitioned into a number of parts. Each part has the same length as that of the required address except the last part. The parts are then added together, ignoring the last carry. For example, an eight digit integer (92965274) can be divided into two parts consisting of three digits and one part consisting of two digits i.e. 929 + 652 + 74, are added together, ignoring the last carry. So the total of 929 + 652 + 74 = 1655. So, after ignoring the last carry i.e 1, the address will be 655.

☞ *The folding method breaks up a key into several segments that are added or exclusively order together to form a hash value.*

This method is also flexible like the 'mid square' method and can be modified as desired. In case the key is string of characters, this can be converted into a number consisting of string of ASCII value of the characters.

Following are two ways of carrying out this addition.

a. *Shift folding*: In shift folding method, all but the last partition are shifted so that the least significant bit of each lines up with the corresponding bit of last partition. For example, let x = 12320324111220. We will partition this digit into five parts, four are three digits long and one is two digit long.

$x =$	123	203	241	112	20
	P_1	P_2	P_3	P_4	P_5

$$h(x) = 123 + 203 + 241 + 112 + 20 = 699$$

↑ right shifted

b. *Folding at boundaries*: In folding at boundaries method, the identifier is folded at the partition boundaries and digits falling into the same position are added together.

For example, x = 12320324111220, before folding at boundaries is used, we first reverse P_2 and P_4 to obtain 302 and 211 respectively.

$x =$	123	← 203	241	← 112	20
	P_1	P_2	P_3	P_4	P_5

$$h(x) = 123 + 302 + 241 + 211 + 20 = 897$$

Regardless of whether shift or boundary folding is used, one of the great advantages of folding method is its ability to transform non integer keys into integer values that are suitable for further hashing action.

7.6 WHAT IS HASH COLLISION?

Two records cannot occupy the same position in main memory of a computer. If such a situation occurs, then it is called *hash collision*. There are three basic methods of dealing with hash collision.

a. Linear probing
b. Chaining
c. Bucketing

7.6.1 Linear Probing

A simple approach to resolving collisions is to store the colliding record (element) into the next available space. This technique is known as linear probing.

This hashing technique finds the hash key value through hash function and maps the key on particular position in the hash table. In case, if key has same hash address then it will find the next empty position in the hash table. We take the hash table as circular array. So, if table size is N then after $(N-1)^{th}$ position it will search from 0th position in the array.

In linear probing we search sequentially for vacant cells when collision occurs. A sequence of filled cells in a hash table is called filled sequence. When we add more and more items, the filled sequences becomes longer. This is called *clustering* as seen in Figure 7.8.

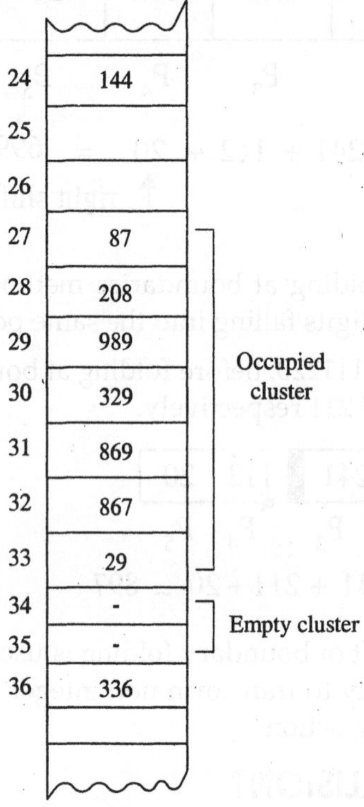

Figure 7.8 Clustering

Most items will go into the first cell but some will suffer collisions and need to step along to find empty cell. The number of steps they take is called *probe length*. Most probe length are only a few cells long. Sometimes, however, you might see probe lengths of four or five cells or even longer as array becomes excessively full. Clustering can result in very long probe lengths. This means that it is very slow to access cells at the end of sequence. More full is the array, the worse clustering becomes.

7.6.2 Chaining

The second technique, called chaining, builds a linked list of all items whose keys hash to the same values. During search, the short linked list is traversed sequentially for the desired key. This technique involves adding an extra link field to each table position. (See Figure 7.9)

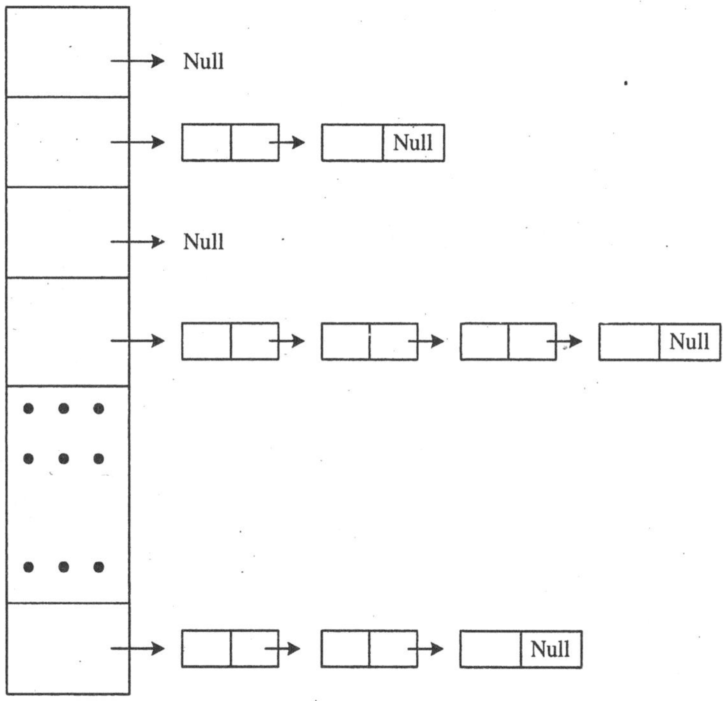

Figure 7.9 Hash table contains pointer

Here, we can maintain the linked list in sorted order and the elements which have the same hash address will be in this linked list. Each element of linked list will contain the whole record with key.

☞ *The main advantage of chaining is saving of memory space and perfect collision resolution.*

7.6.3 Bucketing

Another approach similar to chaining is to use an array at each location in the hash table, instead of a linked list. Such arrays are called *buckets* (See Figure 7.10). This approach is not as efficient as the linked list approach. However, because of the problem of choosing the size of buckets. If they are too small they might overflow and they waste memory.

☞ *Linked lists which allocates memory dynamically do not have this problem.*

0	empty	empty	empty
1	01	21	empty
2	empty	empty	empty
3	03	empty	empty
4	04	24	14
5	empty	empty	empty
6	16	empty	empty
7	17	27	07
8	empty	empty	empty
9	99	89	empty

Figure 7.10 Bucketing

7.7 SORTING

Sorting is the process of arranging data items in a particular order (ascending or descending).

Sort algorithms are designed with the following objectives:

1. Minimize exchanges or wholesole movement of data items. When the number of data items is very large, swapping of data items may take an inordinate amount of processing time.
2. Move data from secondary storage to main memory in large blocks, because the larger the data block to be moved, the more efficient is the corresponding algorithm. This is a key part of external sorting.
3. If possible, retain all the data in main memory. In this case, random access into an array can be effectively used. This is a key part of internal sorting.

The two basic categories of sorting methods are:

- Internal sorting
- External sorting

In the internal sorting method, all data items to be sorted are accomodated in main memory at one time. The time required to read or write is not considered to be significant in evaluating the performance of internal sorting methods. External sorting methods are applied to larger collection of data which reside on secondary devices. The read and write access time are major concern in determining performance of external sorting methods.

There are basically three main considerations that should effect a programmer's decision to choose from a variety of sorting methods:

- Programming time
- Execution time of the program
- Memory or auxiliary space needed for the program environment.

Arrays are convenient for storing many forms of data, because they allow the access of the entry using its index. Here, we shall look at several methods of sorting data held in one-dimensional arrays. Although the data items can be of one type which are not in the desired order—that is, type of data items for which relations such as "greater than" and "less than" would make sense. Hence, we will assume that we are sorting numerical or alpha numeric data.

The first group of sorting methods we will look into consist of sequential methods. These methods keep scanning through the data elements from one end to the other, passing entries that are out of order into correct ordered position. These methods are conceptually simpler to program, and for small amount of data items they are very effective.

However, these methods become slow for large amount of data items. We will therefore also examine a type of *binary sort* techniques that provide a greater degree of speed over the sequential sort technique, specially when number of elements to be sorted are very large.

7.8 SELECTION SORT

The first linear sorting method we will examine is called the selection sort. We perform a search through the table, starting from the first record, to locate the element with the smallest key. When this record is found, we interchange it with the first record in the table. As a result of this interchange, the smallest key is placed in the first position of the table. Second time, we locate second smallest key examining the keys of the records starting from the second record onwards. We then interchange this record with the second record in the table. We continue this process of searching for the record with the smallest key in the remaining unsorted portion of the table and placing it in its proper place until we have placed all the records in the proper order.

Suppose we want to sort an N-entry array as in Figure 7.11 into an ascending order. We first find the smallest entry and move it into the first position, by switching it with the element originally in that position. Then we know that the first element is correct, and we can proceed in the same way to sort the remaining N – 1 elements in positions 2 through N of the array. This process is shown in Figure 7.11, for N = 5.

Each successive pass moves one more element into its correct position. After N – 1 passes, the array will be in the sorted order. The overall form of the algorithm is shown in Figure 7.12. Each pass through the outer loop moves the smallest element of the array ID[I], for I from K to N, into position ID[K]. We can further "refine" the two steps of finding the smallest value in the sub-array and then switching the elements. Those sections of pseudocode are shown in the refined version as seen in Figure 7.13(a).

The sorting algorithm given in Figure 7.12 requires a longer time to execute. In the first pass through the outer loop, the inner loop is executed for I from 2 to N; on the second pass, from 3 to N; and so on. A refined algorithm is shown in Figure 7.13(a) which needs lesser time.

The total number of passes needed through the inner loop is (N – 1) + (N – 2) + (N – 3) + . . . + 3 + 2 + 1, which comes to N × (N – 1)/2. If N is 100, this means that the inner loop must be executed 4950 times, regardless of the original order of the data— even if it is already in order and needs no sorting.

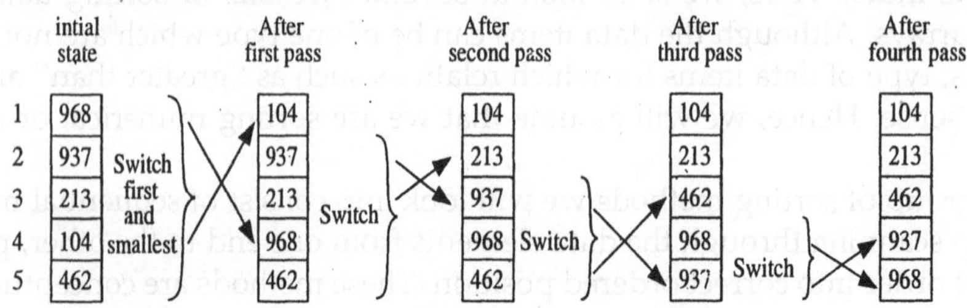

Figure 7.11 Representation of selection sort

```
BEGIN
integer K, N, ID(N)
do for K ←1 to N - 1
  First K - 1 elements are now in order. Find the
    smallest remaining element and move it to position K.
  Set I to index of the smallest element between ID(K) and ID(N)
  switch ID(I) and ID(K)
end do
END
```

Figure 7.12 Algorithm for selection sort

```
BEGIN
integer  I, J, K, N, ID(N), SMALL
do for K ← 1 to N - 1
        First K - 1 elements are now in order. Find the
        smallest remaining element and move it to
        position K.
        I ← K
        SMALL ← ID(K)
    do
        for J ← K + 1 to N
        SMALL contains the smallest element between ID(K)
        and ID(J - 1). I is its index.
        if ID(J) < SMALL
           then I ← J
                SMALL ← ID(J)
        end if
    end do
ID(I) ← ID(K)
ID(K) ← SMALL
end do
END
```

Figure 7.13(a) Refined algorithm for selection sort

The observation that the sorting method just described can take a longer time even if the elements are already in order. Thus, it prompts us to look for methods that are faster when data is already sorted order or nearly so.

Example 5

Program in 'C'and the output for sorting an array using selection sort, is given in Figure 7.13(b).

```
/* Selection Sort */
#include<stdio.h>
void main()
{
  int a[50],i,j,k,n,pass,min;
  printf("Enter no. of elements in an array ? ");
  scanf("%d",&n);
  printf("\nEnter array elements :\n");
  for(i=0;i<n;i++)
       scanf("%d",&a[i]);
  printf("Unsorted array:\n");
  for(i=0;i<n;i++)
       printf("%5d",a[i]);
  printf("\n");
/* Selection Sort */
  for(pass = 0;pass < n-1;pass++)
  {
/* Assume that pass is the minimum index */
    min = pass;
    for(j = pass+1;j <n ;j++)
    {
       if(a[min] > a[j])
/* Update min */
       min = j;
    }
    if(min != pass)
    {
/* Swap elements */
       k = a[pass];
       a[pass] = a[min];
       a[min] = k;
    }
  }
  printf("\nSorted array:\n");
  for(i = 0; i < n;i++)
    printf("%5d",a[i]);
  printf("\n");
}
```

(Contd..)

```
RUN
Enter no. of elements in an array ? 4
Enter array elements :
0
67
-5
23
Unsorted array :
0
67
-5
23
Sorted array:
-5
0
23
67
```

Figure 7.13(b) Program and output for sorting an array using selection sort

7.9 BUBBLE SORT

The basic idea underlying the bubble sort method is to pass through the table sequentially several times. Each pass puts the largest unsorted element in its correct place by comparing each element in the table with its successor and interchanging the two elements if they are not in proper order. The first pass puts the largest element of the array in the last (n th) place, the second pass puts the second largest element in the second last $(n-1)^{th}$ place. In general, the ith iteration puts the $(n-i)^{th}$ element in its correct place. This way, each element slowly "bubbles" upto its proper place. This is why the method is called *bubble sort*. The process is illustrated in Figure 7.14 which shows the following steps:

1. Compare the first pair 621 and 104. They are out of order, so switch them.
2. Compare the second pair, 621 and 836. They are already in order, so leave them.
3. Compare the third pair, 836 and 424. They are out of order, so switch them.

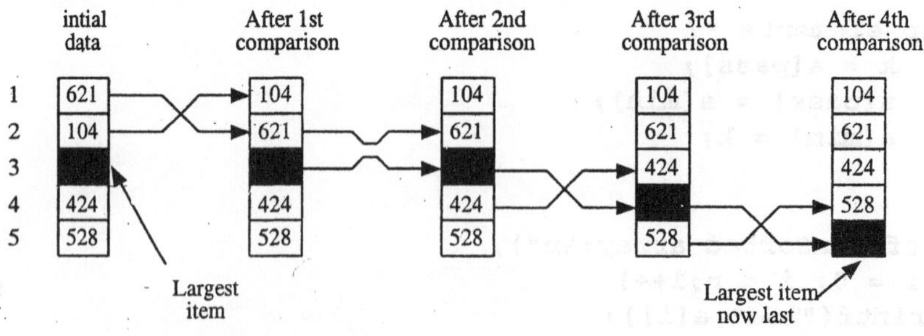

Figure 7.14 Representation of bubble sort

4. Compare the fourth pair, 836 and 528. They are out of order, so switch them.

This is the first pass of a bubble sort.

As a result of these operations, at the end of the first pass, the largest element in the list, 836 has "bubbled" to the last position. The next pass will work with the first *N* – *1* elements, and will move the next largest to the next-to-last position, and so on. Notice that if an *N*-element list is already sorted to begin with, we will find this out on the first pass, after only *N* – *1* comparisons—the minimum possible to determine that *N* elements are already sorted. The bubble-sort algorithm is given in Figure 7.15(a).

```
BEGIN
integer I, J, K, N, ID(N), TEMP
I ← N
K ← 1
The flag K is non zero on the first pass of the outer loop and when-
ever switches are made on the previous pass.
do while I > 2 and K = 1
    The largest N - I elements of ID are now in order in position ID(I
+ 1) to
    ID(N). Float the largest of the first I elements to position
ID(I).
    K ← 0
    do for J ← 1 to I - 1
        The largest of the first J elements is now in position ID(J).
        if ID(J) > ID(J + 1)
        then
            Switch entries ID(J) and ID(J + 1).
            TEMP ← ID(J)
            ID(J) ← ID(J + 1).
            ID(J + 1) ← TEMP
            K ← 1
    endif
    enddo
I ← I - 1
enddo
END
```

Figure 7.15(a) Algorithm to sort an array into an ascending order using bubble sort.

I is the loop counter, and decrements from *N* to *2* on successive passes through the outer loop. On each pass, the counter for the inner loop, *J*, need run only from 1 to *I* – 1, since the last *N* – *I* positions already contain the *N* – *1* largest elements.

At most, *N* – *1* passes through the outer loop are needed to sort the array or list into an ascending order, but it may take lesser number of passes. If no switches are made on any given pass, then we have finished the job. Accordingly, a variable *K* is used to remember whether any switches have yet been made. On the current pass, it is set to zero at the beginning of the pass, and changed to non zero whenever a switch is made. If *K* is still zero at the beginning of the next pass, the outer loop terminates. Otherwise, it terminates when *I* becomes less than *2*.

In the best case, when the data is already in sorted order, the bubble sort takes only one scan through the list, and no sorting method can do better. However, in the worst case, the bubble sort takes maximum of $N \times (N-1)/2$ comparisons, as does any sequential method. The worst case occurs when the data is in reverse order. For example, a bubble sort of 5, 4, 3, 2, 1 into ascending order requires 10 switches. After the first pass through the outer loop, four switches have been made and the list is 4, 3, 2, 1, 5. Furthermore, in the worst case, each of the comparisons will cause a switch of two data items (which requires three assignment statements).

☞ *Bubble sort is a reasonable sort method for sorting a small number of items and is easy to implement.*

Example 6

A program and the output to sort numbers in an array using Bubble sort technique is given in Figure 7.15(b).

```
/* Program to arrange a set of numbers in ascending order using bubble
sort */
#include<stdio.h>
main()
{
  int n,i,j,num[50],temp, flag;
  printf("Enter numbers to be sorted : ");
  scanf("%d",&n);/* Gets the size of the array*/
  for (i=0; i<n; i++)
  {
     printf("Enter number %d\n",i+1);
     scanf("%d",&num[i]);/* Array elements are accepted*/
  }
/* Bubble sorting begins */
  for (i=0;i<n-1;i++)
  {
     flag = 1;
     for (j=0; j<n-1-i; j++)
     {
        if (num[j]>num[j+1]) {
        temp = num[j];
        num[j] = num[j+1];
        num[j+1] = temp;
        flag = 0;
     }
     if (flag)
     break;
  }
```

(Contd...)

```
  printf("\nThe numbers after sort\n");
  for(i = 0;i<n;i++)
  printf("%d  ",num[i]);
  return 0;
}
RUN
Enter numbers to be sorted? : 4

Enter number  1
0

Enter number  2
45

Enter number  3
67

Enter number  4
-5

The numbers after sort
   -5  0  45  67
```

Figure 7.15(b) Program and output to arrange a set of numbers in ascending order using bubble sort

7.10 INSERTION SORT

The third sequential sorting method we will consider is the insertion sort. In this method, the list is scanned until an out-of-order element is found. The scan is then temporarily halted while a backward scan is made to find the point at which to insert the out-of-order element. Elements biased during this backward scan are moved up one position to make room for the element being inserted. Thus, in Figure 7.16, if the first K elements are in order but the $(K + 1)^{st}$ is not—that is, if $ID(1) < ID(2) < ID(3) < .... < ID(K)$ but $ID(K) > ID(K + 1)$—then $ID(K + 1)$ is out of order and must be moved to an earlier position. It is removed from the array, that is, a copy of its value is saved somewhere, say at *TEMP*, and the elements $ID(K), ID(K - 1), \ldots$ are examined until an $ID(J)$ is found such that $ID(J) <$ *old* $ID(K + 1)$. In the process, the old elements $ID(J + 1)$ through $ID(K)$ will be moved to positions $ID(J + 2)$ through $ID(K + 1)$, clearing the $(J + 1)^{st}$ position for the value saved at *TEMP*.

The algorithm shown in Figure 7.16 is based on this method. The inner loop is in the *then* clause of an *if* statement, and is executed only when an out-of-order element is found. Like the bubble sort, it requires only $N - 1$ comparisons in the best case (when the data is already sorted initially). Again like the bubble sort, it requires $N \times (N - 1)/2$ comparisons and moves in the worst case—but unlike the bubble sort, it completes each move in only one assignment statement instead of three.

```
BEGIN
integer J, K, N, ID(N), TEMP
    do for K ← 1 to N - 1
    ID(1) to ID(K) are now in an ascending order.
    Extend to ID(K + 1).
    if ID(K) > ID(K + 1)
      then
        Move, ID(K + 1) back to its place in the array.
        First save its value in TEMP, then move the earlier
        elements up one place until the right positionis found
        TEMP ← ID(K + 1)
        J ← K
    do while J > 1 and ID(J) > TEMP
        ID(J + 1) ← ID(J)
        J ← J - 1
    end do
      ID(J + 1) ← TEMP
    end if
end do
END
```

Figure 7.16 Algorithm to sort an array containing integers into an ascending order using insertion sort

Although the insertion sort is almost always better than the bubble sort, the time element in both methods is approximately the same – that is, it is proportional to n^2, where n is the number of the data items in the array. The number of interchanges needed in both the methods is on the average $(n^2)/4$, and in worst cases it is about $(n^2)/2$. Where the data items are already partially ordered, the insertion sort will normally take less time than the bubble sort. The insertion sort is highly efficient if the array is already in almost sorted order.

☞ *Inspite of the superiority of the selection sort over the bubble sort and insertion sort, there is no significant gain in run time, its efficiency is also of the order of n^2 ($O(n^2)$) for n data items.*

Example 7

A program in 'C' language along with the output for insertion sort is given in Figure 7.17

```
/* Insertion Sort */
#include <stdio.h>
void main()
{
  int i,j,k,x, a[50];
  printf ("Enter element to be inserted or type -99 to terminate : ");
  scanf ("%d", &x);
  printf("\n");
  i = 0;
```

(Contd...)

```
   while (x != -99)
   {
      k = i - 1;
      while ((x < a[k] ) && (k >= 0))
      {
         a[k+1] = a[k]; --k;
      }
      a[k+1] = x;
      printf ("Array after inserting element %d :\n", x);
      for (j = 0; j <=i; j++)
         printf ("%5d", a[j]);
      printf ("\n\n Enter element to be inserted or type -99
                    to terminate  :");
      scanf ("%d", &x);
      printf ("\n");
      ++i;
   }
      printf ("The final sorted array using insertion sort : \n");
      for (j = 0; j < i; j++)
         printf("%5d", a[j]);
      printf ("\n");
   }

RUN

Enter element to be inserted or type -99 to terminate : 66

Array after inserting element 66:
   66

Enter element to be inserted or type -99 to terminate : 22

Array after inserting element 22:
   22   66

Enter element to be inserted or type -99 to terminate : 77

Array after inserting element 77:
   22   66   77

Enter element to be inserted or type -99 to terminate : 33

Array after inserting element 33:
   22   33   66   77
```

(Contd...)

```
Enter element to be inserted or type -99 to terminate : 11

Array after inserting element 11:
   11   22   33   66   77

Enter element to be inserted or type -99 to terminate: -99

The final sorted array using insertion sort:
   11   22   33   66   77
```

Figure 7.17 Program and the output of Example 7 using insertion sort

7.11 QUICK SORT

Quick sort names a family of related algorithms that sort data items using a divide-and-conquer strategy. Quick sort method is also called *partition exchange sort.* To partition the list, we first choose some key from the list for which about half the items will come before and half after. This selected key is called *pivot.* In the quicksort method, list is partitioned into lower and upper sublists for which all keys are, respectively, less than some pivot key or greater than the pivot key. The sort then recursively invoke itself with both lists. Each time when the sort is invoked, it further divides the elements into smaller sub-lists. The algorithm shown in Figure 7.18(a) outlines the quick sort algorithm.

```
/* Elements to be sorted are in x[low : high] */
Split selection step:
    choose an element s in x[low : high]
Partition step:
    partition x[low : high] using variable a so that for some i,
    x[i]=a, x[low:i-1] are all <=a, and x[i+1: high] are all >=a
Recursive step:
    call quicksort recursively on x[low:i-1] and x[i+1:high]
```

Figure 7.18(a) Algorithm for quick sort

Quick sort was introduced by Hoare in 1962 and it is a faster method for sorting. Quick sort treats an array as a list of elements and we divide the original list into two sublists. To partition the list, we first choose some key from the list for which about half the keys will come before and half after. This selected key is called *pivot.* We next partition the entries so that all the keys which are less than the pivot come in one sublist and all the keys which are greater than the pivot come in another sublist. We will repeat the same process until all elements of list are at proper position in the list.

The Algorithm shown in Figure 7.18(a) gives the outline of quick sort and Figure 7.18(b) gives schematically the progress of one recursive call.

Let us consider the following unsorted array and try to sort it using quick sort method.

20 55 46 37 9 89 82 32

From the above list we will choose first number as the pivot i.e 20, and the list is partitioned into two sublists.

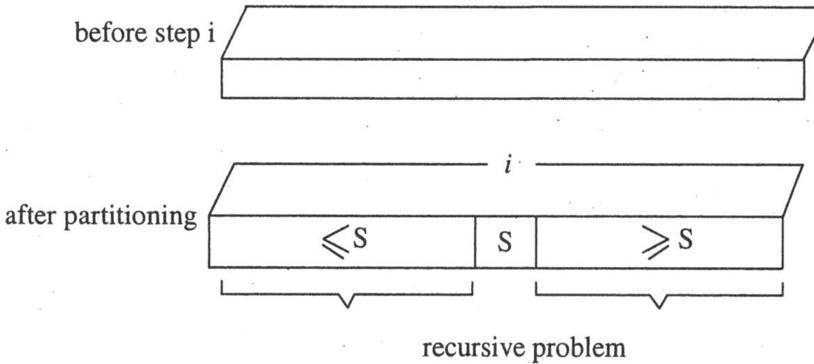

Figure 7.18(b) Quicksort after partitioning on the elements

(9) and (55 46 37 89 82 32)

At this point 20 is in its proper position in the array x[1], each element below that position (9) is less than or equal to 20, and each element above that position (55 46 37 89 82 32) is greater than or equal to 20.

Our problem is broken into two sub problems that is to sort the two subarrays. Since the first sub array contains only a single element, so it is already sorted. To sort the second sub-array we choose its first element 55 as the pivot and again get two subarrays:

(46 37 32) and (89 82)

The entire array can be represented as

9 20 (46 37 32) 55 (89 82)

☞ *Sublist to be sorted are kept in parenthesis.*

Repeating the process on subarrays yields the following result.

9	20	(37	32)	46	55	(89	82)
9	20	(32)	37	46	55	(89	82)
9	20	32	37	46	55	(89	82)
9	20	32	37	46	55	(82)	89
9	20	32	37	46	55	82	89

Note that final array is in sorted order.

The average run time efficiency of the quick sort is $O(n(\log_2 n)$, which is the best that has been achieved for a large array of size n. In the worst case situation, when the array is already sorted, the efficiency of quick sort may drop down to $O(n^2)$ due to the continuous right to left scan all the way to the last left boundary.

☞ *Quick sort is very fast on the average case, but it is very slow in the worst case and could cause a stack overflow.*

Example 8

A program and output for quick sort is given in Figure 7.19.

```
/* Quick sort*/
#include <stdio.h>
#include <conio.h>
int n;
main()
{
   int a[50], x,l,r;
   void quick_sort();
   clrscr();
   printf ("\nEnter number of elements in array: ");
   scanf ("%d", &n);
   printf ("Enter elements of array : ");
   for (x=0; x<n; x++)
      scanf ("%d", &a[x]);
 /* Invoke Quick sort function */
l = 0;
r = n - 1;
quick_sort (a,l,r);
printf ("\nQuick Sorted array is : ");
for (x=0; x<n; x++)
   printf ("%5d", a[x]);
} /* end of main() */
/* Quick Sort Function */
void quick_sort (b, left, right)
int b[50], left, right;
{
   int x,y,p,tmp, over, k;
   if (right > left)
   {
      x = left;
      y = right;
      p = b[left];
      printf ("P, the partitioning element is : %d .", p);
      over = 0;
      while (!over)
      {
         do {
            ++x;
         } while ((b[x] <= p) && (x <= right));
         while ((b[y] >=p) && (y > left))
         {
            --y;
         }
      if (y < x)
```

(Contd...)

```
        over = 1;
      else {
        printf (" Swapping %d & %d. \n", b[x], b[y]);
        tmp = b[x];
        b[x] = b[y];
        b[y] = tmp;
        for (k = 0; k < n; k++)
          printf ("%5d", b[k]);
          }
      } /* while */
      printf ("\nI is greater than J, so b[left] and b[y] are
            swapped.Swapping %d & %d.\n", b[left], b[y]);
      tmp = b[left];
      b[left] = b[y];
      b[y] = tmp;
      for (k = 0; k < n; k++)
        printf ("%5d", b[k]);
      printf("\n");
      printf("\nSubfile one is: elements %d to %d.\n",left,y-1);
      quick_sort(b,left,y-1);
      printf("\nSubfile two is : elements %d to %d .\n",x,right);
      quick_sort (b, x, right);
    } /* IF */
    else {
      if (right != left)
        printf ("Right (%d) is less than left (%d). \n", right, left);
      else {
        printf ("Right (%d) is equal to Left (%d). \n", right, left);
        printf ("Subfile has only one element. \n");
        }
      }
      return;
    }
RUN

Enter number of elements in an array : 4
Enter elements of array: 23 79 54 13

P, the partitioning element is: 23. Swapping 79 & 13
   23   13   54   79
I is greater than J, so b[left] and b[y] are swapped. swapping 23 & 13.
   13   23   54   79

Subfile one is: element 0 to 0
Right(0) is equal to left (0)
```

(Contd...)

```
Subfile has only one element
Subfile two is: elements 2 to 3
P, the partitioning element is : 54
I is greater than J, so b[left] and b[y] are swapped. swapping 54 & 54.
   13    23    54    79

Subfile one is: elements 2 to 1
Right(1) is less than left (2)

Subfile two is: elements 3 to 3
Right(3) is equal to left(3)
Subfile has only one element.

Quick sorted array is : 13    23    54    79
```

Figure 7.19 Program and the output of Example 8 using quick sort

7.12 MERGE SORT

A common algorithm used in external sorting is the merge sort. A file (or subfile) is divided into 2 files, O_1 and O_2. These 2 files are then compared, 1 pair of records at a time, and merged. This is done by writing them on 2 separate new file M_1 and M_2. The elements that do not pair off are simply rewritten into the new files. The records in M_1 and M_2 are now blocked with 2 records in each segment. The 2 blocks (that is, 4 records), 1 from M_1 and 1 from M_2, are merged and written onto the original files O_1 and O_2. The length of the segments in each O_1 and O_2 is now increased to 4, the merge process applied again, and new files are written to M_1 and M_2. The process is continued until 1 of the 2 files O_1 or O_2 is empty.

In order to clarify these concepts, suppose we have an external file containing the data:

(2, 6, 3, 1, 4, 31, 23, 8, 11, 19, 21, 37, 14, 57, 28, 45, 30, 9, 35, 12, 13, 18, 5, 89, 77)

We divide it into two original file as:

O_1 : (2, 6, 3, 1, 4, 31, 23, 8, 11, 19, 21, 37)

O_2 : (14, 57, 28, 45, 30, 9, 35, 12, 13, 18, 5, 89, 77)

After 1st pass of segments the length 1, we have

M_1 : ((2,14), (3,28), (4,30), (23,35), (11,13), (5,21))

M_2 : ((6,57), (1,45), (9,31), (8,12), (18,19), (37,89), 77))

After the 2nd pass of segments of length 2:

O_1 : ((2,6,14,57), (4,9,30,31), (11,13,18,19))

O_2 : ((1,3,28,45), (8,12,23,35), (5,21,37,89), 77))

After the 3rd pass of segments of length 4:

M_1 : ((1,2,3,6,14,28,45,57), (5,11,13,18,19,21,37,89))

M_2 : ((4,8,9,12,23,30,31,35),77))

After the 4th pass of segments of length 8:

O_1 : ((1,2,3,4,6,8,9,12,14,23,28,30,31,35,45,57)

O_2 : (5,11,13,18,19,21,37,77,89)

After the 5th pass of blocks of length 16:

M_1 : (1,2,3,4,5,6,8,9,11,12,13,14,18,19,21,23,28,30,31,35,37,45,57,77,89)
M_2 : is empty

In merge sort, we take elements in pairs and merge with another pair after sorting. So, merge sort requires maximum log_2n passes. In each pass, total number of comparisons can be maximum n. Hence we can say merge sort requires maximum $n * log_2n$ comparisons which is of $O(nlog_2n)$. The main disadvantage of merge sort is space requirement. It requires extra space of $O(n)$.

☞ *Merge sort is simple to understand but requires as much memory as the original array.*

Example 9

A program and the output of merge sort is given in Figure 7.20.

```
/* Mergesort*/
#include <stdio.h>
main()
{
   float arr[50];
   int x,y;
   void merge_sort();
   void merge_pass();
   printf ("Please enter the size of the list:  ");
   scanf ("%d", &y);
   printf ("\n Enter elements of the list \n");
   for (x = 0; x < y; x++)
      scanf ("%f", &arr[x]);
   for (x = 0; x < y; x++)
      printf ("%8.1f", arr[x]);
   printf ("\n");
   x = 0;
   merge_pass (arr, x, y-1);
   printf ("\n\nThe merge sorted list is : \n");
   for (x = 0; x < y; x++)
      printf ("%8.1f", arr[x]);
   printf ("\n");
}
void merge_sort(list,top,size,bot)
float list[50];
int top, size, bot;
{
   int u, f1, s1, t1;
   float tmp[50];
```

(Contd...)

```
   f1 = top;
   s1 = size + 1;
   t1 = top;
   while ((f1 <= size) && (s1 <= bot))
   {
      if (list[f1] <= list[s1])
      {
         tmp[t1] = list[f1];
         f1 = f1 + 1;
      }
      else
      {
         tmp[t1] = list[s1];
         s1 = s1 + 1;
      }
      t1= t1+1;
   }
      if (f1 <= size)
      {
         for (f1 = f1; f1 <= size; f1++)
         {
            tmp[t1] = list[f1];
            t1 = t1 + 1;
         }
      }
         else {
            for (s1 = s1; s1 <= bot; s1++)
            {
               tmp[t1] = list[s1];
               t1 = t1 + 1;
            }
      }
      for (u = top; u <= bot; u++)
         list[u] = tmp[u];
      return;
   }
void merge_pass (a,m,y)
float a[50];
int m,y;
   {
      int h;
      if (m != y)
      {
         h = (m + y)/2;
         merge_pass (a,m,h);
```

(Contd...)

```
        merge_pass (a,h+1,y);
        merge_sort (a,m,h,y);
      }
      return;
  }

RUN

Please enter the size of the list: 5
Enter elements of the list : 5

23.9
65.2
-33.4
45.0
-35.7

23.9   65.2   -33.4   45.0   -35.7

The merge sorted list is:
-35.7   -33.4   23.9   45.0   65.2
```

Figure 7.20 Program and the output of Example 9 using merge sort

7.13 RADIX SORT

Radix sort is based on the positional value of the actual digits of the numbers being sorted. This method was earlier performed on a mechanical card sorter. For example, the number 245 in decimal notation is written with a 2 in the hundreds position, 4 in the tens position, and 5 in the units position. This three digit number (i.e 245) will be sorted in maximum 3 passes. In the first pass, the unit digit will be sorted, in the second pass, the tens digit will be sorted and in the third and final pass, the hundreds digit will be sorted.

Radix sort technique is also used when large lists of names are to be sorted alphabetically. To sort the large list we start with alphabet 'A' and then we take the names which start from alphabet 'B' and so on. Using the radix sorting technique one can classify the list of names into 26 groups (all alphabets). We can take all the names in different parts. In second pass, we take the names in parts on the basis of second alphabets of names. Similar process we can do for other passes also.

If we have a list of ten numbers, then there will be 10 parts from 0 to 9 because radix is 10. In first pass we take the numbers in parts on basis of unit digit (least significant digit). In second pass the base will be tens digit and similarly for other passes.

Let us take numbers in unsorted order and sort them by applying radix sort:

42 20 64 51 34 70 31 16 15 12 19 33
↑
unit digit position

In the first pass, the unit digits (first from last) are sorted.

Pass 1

Numbers	0	1	2	3	4	5	6	7	8	9
42			42							
20	20									
64					64					
51		51								
34					34					
70	70									
31		31								
16							16			
15						15				
12			12							
19										19
33				33						

After pass 1, numbers are as follows:

20 70 51 31 42 12 33 64 34 15 16 19
↑

In the second pass, the tens digit are sorted according to tens digit position

Pass 2

Numbers	0	1	2	3	4	5	6	7	8	9	10	11	12
20			20										
70								70					
51						51							
31				31									
42					42								
12		12											
33				33									
64							64						
34				34									
15		15											
16		16											
19		19											

After second pass sorted list will be as follows

12 15 16 19 20 31 33 34 42 51 64 70

☞ *The disadvantage of radix sort is extra space requirement.*

Example 10

A program and output of radix sort is given in Figure 7.21.

```
/* Radix Sort */
#include <stdio.h>
#include<conio.h>
#define NULL 0
struct element_list
{
   int info;
   struct element_list *next;
};
typedef struct element_list node;
node *initial;
node *bot[10], *top[10];
main()
{
   node *start, *ptr;
   void create();
   void display();
   node *radix();
   clrscr();
   printf("Enter the elements of the array.\n ");
   start = (node *) malloc(sizeof(node));
   create(start);
   printf("\nGiven list is : ");
   display(start);
   printf("\n");
   initial = start;
   start = radix(start);
   printf("\nSorted list is : ");
   display(start);
   printf("\n");
}
void create(record)
node *record;
{
   int num;
   printf("Enter -99 to stop\n");
   scanf("%d", &record -> info);
   if (record -> info == -99)
   {
      record -> next = NULL;
      return;
   }
   else
   {
      record -> next = (node *) malloc(sizeof(node));
```

(Contd...)

```
      create(record -> next);
   }
   return;
}
void display(record)
node *record;
{
   if (record != NULL)
   {
      if (record -> info != -99)
      {
         printf("%4d", record -> info);
         display(record -> next);
      }
   }
   return;
}
node *radix(record)
node *record;
{
   int lar, m,i,j,k, dig, poc;
   node *nex, *r, *prev;
   int large();
   int numdig();
   int digit();
   void update();
   node *link();
   lar = large(record);
   m = numdig(lar);
   for (k=0; k<10; k++)
   {
      top[k] = (node *) malloc(9 * sizeof(node));
      bot[k] = (node *) malloc(9 * sizeof(node));
   }
   for (j=1; j<=m; j++)
   {
      for (i=0; i<10; i++)
      {
         top[i] = NULL;
         bot[i] = NULL;
      }
   r = record;
   while (r -> next != NULL)
   {
```

(Contd...)

```
      dig = digit(r -> info, j);
      nex = r -> next;
      update(dig, r);
      r = nex;
   } /* end of while */
   if (r -> info != -99)
   {
      dig = digit(r ->info, j);
      update(dig, r);
   }
   poc = 0;
   while (bot[poc] == NULL)
      poc++;
   record = link(poc, record);
   printf("\n Newly ordered list is :  ");
   display(record);
   printf("\n");
   }
   return(record);
}
int large(record)
node *record;
{
   node *save;
   int p;
   p = 0;
   save = record;
   while (save -> next != NULL)
   {
      if (save -> info > p)
      {
         p = save -> info;
      }
      save = save -> next;
   }
   printf("Largest element in list is %d\n", p);
   return(p);
}
int numdig(large) /* Digits of the largest number */
int large;
{
   int temp, num;
   temp = large;
```

(Contd...)

```
num = 0;
while (temp !=0) {
   ++num;
   temp = temp/10;
}
printf("Number of digits of the number %d is %d\n",large,num);
return(num);
     }
int digit(num,j) /* to find the next digit to be sorted */
int num, j;
{
   int i, dig, temp;
   temp = num;
   for (i=0; i<j; i++)
   {
     dig = temp % 10;
     temp = temp/10;
   }
   printf("%dth digit of no. %d is %d \n", j, num, dig);
   return(dig);
}
void update(dig, r)
node *r;
int dig;
{
   int i;
   if (top[dig] == NULL)
   {
   top[dig] = r;
   bot[dig] = r;
   }
   else
   {
      top[dig] -> next = r;
      top[dig] = r;
   }
   r -> next = NULL;
   return;
}
node *link(poc, record)
node *record;
int poc;
{
   node *pr;
   int i;
```

(Contd...)

```
      record = bot[poc];
      for (i=poc+1; i<10; i++)
      {
         pr = top[i - 1];
         if (top[i] != NULL)
            pr -> next = bot[i];
         else
            top[i] = pr;
      }
      return(record);
   }
```

RUN

```
Enter the elements of the array

Enter -99 to stop
   45
Enter -99 to stop
   76
Enter -99 to stop
   23
Enter -99 to stop
   12
Enter -99 to stop
   -99

Given list is: 45   [illegible]   23   2
Largest element in lis[illegible] is 76
Number of digits of th[illegible] number 76 is 2

1th digit of no. 45 is 5
1th digit of no. 76 is 6
1th digit of no. 23 is 3
1th digit of no. 12 is 2

Newly ordered list is : 12   23   45   76

2th digit of no. 12 is 1
2th digit of no. 23 is 2
2th digit of no. 45 is 4
2th digit of no. 76 is 7

Newly sorted list is : 12   23   45   76
Sorted list is: 12   23   45   76
```

Figure 7.21 Program and the output of Example 10 using radix sort

7.14 SHELL SORT

Shell sort is a modification of insertion sort, proposed by D.L. Shell in 1959. In case of insertion sort, we can move entries only one position because it compares only adjacent keys. If we take the item at a particular distance (increments) then we can compare items which are far apart and we can sort them. Afterwards, we decrease the increment and repeat the process again. Finally we take the increment 1 to ensure that the file is completely sorted.

Assume that starting increment is 5, then the subfile is made up of elements 1, 6, 11, 16, 21.... < n ('n' is size of the array). This subfile is sorted by swapping elements. Once this subfile is sorted, the next increment is taken and the new subfile is again sorted; till the final pass, the increment will be a 'one'.

Let us take a list of elements in unsorted order and sort them by applying Shell sort:

24 56 47 36 11 91 85 32

we choose here the sequence (5, 3, 1) as increments.

☞ *Any other sequence may be chosen which might work better. But avoid choosing increments as power of 2 such as 8, 4, 2, 1, because in such a case, items compared at one pass will again be compared in the next pass.*

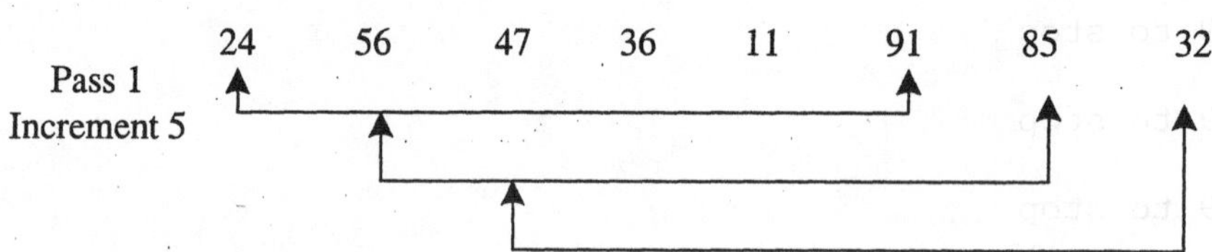

Result after first pass by swapping 47 and 32 will be:

24 56 32 36 11 91 85 47

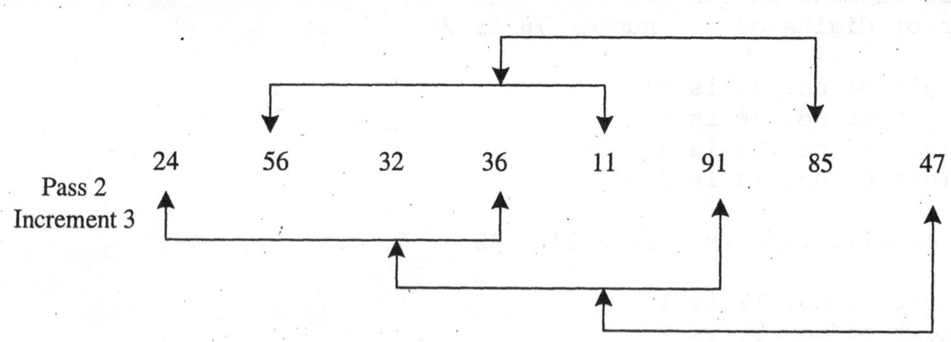

Result at a distance 3 are swapped if necessary

Swapping 56 and 11

Swapping 56 and 47

24 11 32 36 47 91 85 56

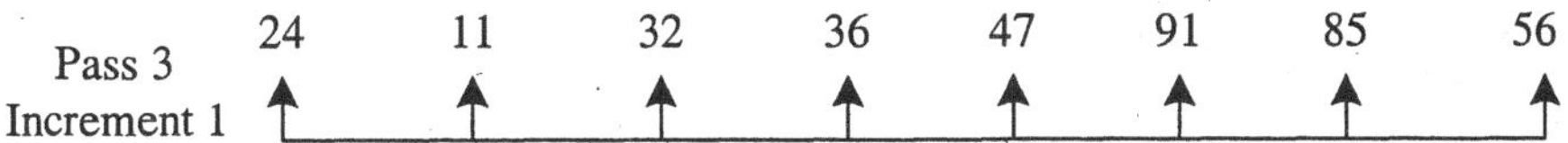

Result at a distance 1 are swapped if necessary

Swapping 24 and 11
Swapping 91 and 85
Swapping 85 and 56
Swapping 91 and 85

Finally of sorted list would be

11 24 32 36 47 56 85 91

The Shell sort is also called the *diminishing increment sort* because the value of k (the number of segments) continually decrease.

The Shell sort is very efficient when applied on arrays that are nearly in the sorted order. In fact, the first chosen value of *k* is large to ensure that the whole array is fragmented into small individual arrays, for which the insertion sort is very effective. Each subsequent sort causes the entire array to be more nearly sorted. So that the efficiency of the insertion sort as applied to larger partially sorted arrays is increased.

Example 11

A program and along with output by using Shell sort is given in Figure 7.22.

```
/*Shell Sort*/
#include <stdio.h>
main()
{
   int a[20], x, y;
   void shell_sort();
   printf ("Enter number of elements in the array : ");
   scanf ("%d", &y);
   printf ("\nEnter array elements : \n");
   for (x = 1; x <=y; x++)
      scanf ("%d", &a[x]);
   for (x = 1; x <= y; x++)
      printf ("%5d", a[x]);
   printf ("\n");
   shell_sort (a,y);
   printf ("\nShell sorted array is : \n");
   for (x = 1; x <= y; x++)
      printf ("%5d", a[x]);
   printf ("\n");
}
```

(Contd...)

```
void shell_sort (b,y)
int b[20], y;
{
   int x,j,k, inc, temp;
   inc = 1;
   /* Sequence of increments chosen */
   while (inc <= y) {
      inc = inc * 3 + 1;
   }
   do {
   inc = inc / 3;
   x = inc + 1;
   printf ("\nIncrement is %d \n", inc);
   printf ("Elements at a distance %d are swapped if
                    necessary :\n ", inc);
     while (x <= y) {
       temp = b[x];
       j =x;
     while ((b[j - inc]) > temp) {
        printf ("Swapping %d & %d \n", temp, b[j - inc]);
        b[j] = b[j - inc];
        j =j - inc;
        if (j <= inc)
        break;
     }
     b[j] = temp;
     x++;
   }
   printf ("\nArray at end pass :\n");
   for (k = 1; k <= y; k++)
     printf ("%5d", b[k]);
   printf ("\n");
   } while (inc != 1);
   return;
}
```

RUN

```
Enter number of elements in the array: 5

Enter array elements:
12   45   63   24   52
Increment is 4
Elements at a distance 4 are swapped if necessary.
```

(Contd...)

```
Array at end pass:
Increment is 1
Elements at a distance 1 are swapped if necessary.

swapping 24 & 63
swapping 24 & 45
swapping 52 & 63

Array at end pass:
12  24  45  52  63

Shell sorted array is
12  24  45  52  63
```

Figure 7.22 Program and the output of Example 11 using shell sort

7.15 HEAP SORT

Heap sort is an improvement over the binary tree sort. It does not create nodes as in the case of binary tree sort. Instead it builds a heap by adjusting the position of the elements within the array itself.

The efficiency of heap sort is nearly equivalent to that of the quick sort. The two phases involved in sorting the elements using heap sort algorithm are as follows:

(a) Construct a heap by adjusting the array elements.

(b) Replace the root with last node of heap tree.

(c) Keep the last node (new root) at the proper position. It means, do the delete operation in heap tree but here deleted node is the root.

The root element of a max-heap is always the largest element. The sorting ends when the root element of each successive heap has been moved to the end of the array (i.e when the tree is exhausted). The resulting array now contains a sorted list.

Let us consider the heap tree of Figure 7.23 and see how to process it.

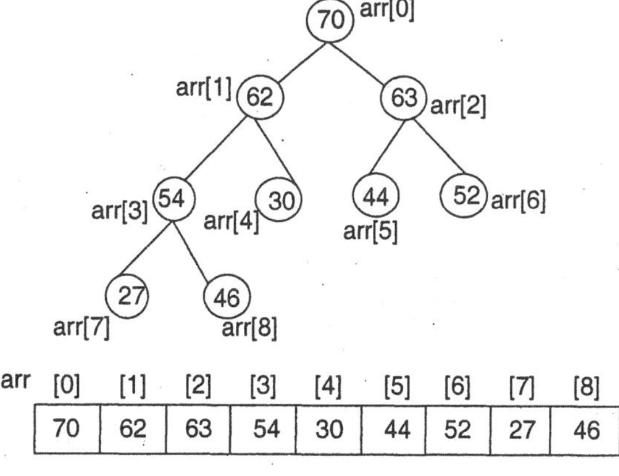

arr	[0]	[1]	[2]	[3]	[4]	[5]	[6]	[7]	[8]
	70	62	63	54	30	44	52	27	46

Figure 7.23 Array and its equivalent representation as heap tree

Step 1

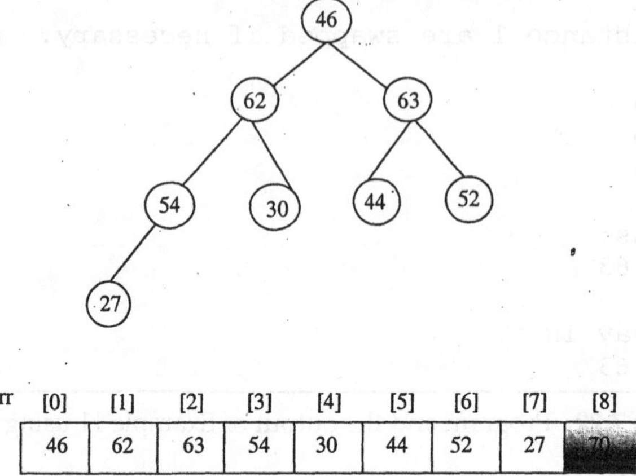

Figure 7.24 Heap after eliminating root element 70

Similarly, one by one the root element of the heap is eliminated, the following figures show the heap and array after each elimination.

In Figure 7.24 root is at the position of last node and the last node is at the position of root. Here left and right child of 46 is 62 and 63. Both are greater than 46, but right child 63 is greater than left child 62, hence replace it with right child 63.

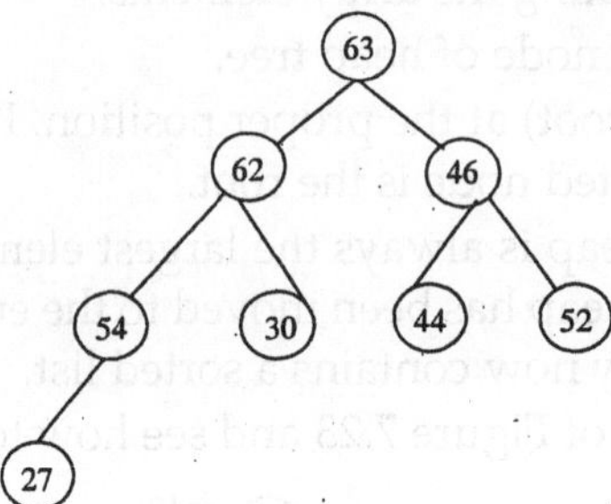

Here right child of 46 is 52, which is greater than 46, hence replace it with 52.

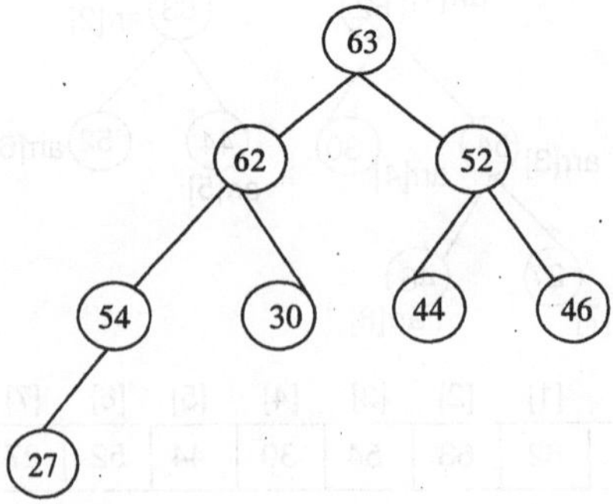

Now the elements of heap tree in array are as follows:

arr [0]	[1]	[2]	[3]	[4]	[5]	[6]	[7]	[8]
63	62	52	54	30	44	46	27	70

Now 27 is the last node. So replace it with root 63 and do the same operation.

Step 2

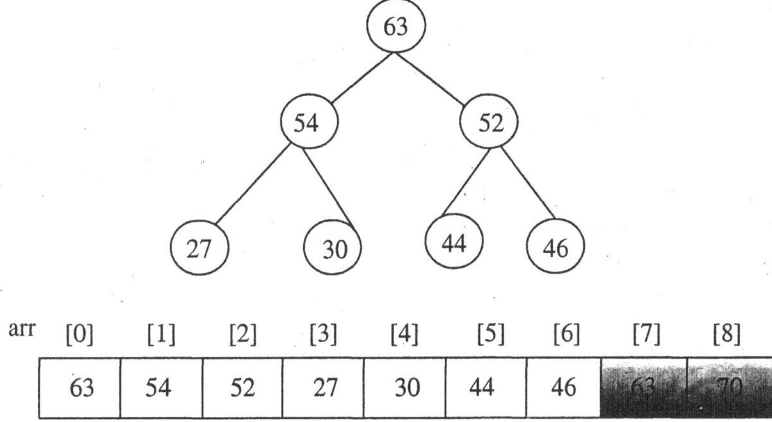

arr [0]	[1]	[2]	[3]	[4]	[5]	[6]	[7]	[8]
63	54	52	27	30	44	46	63	70

Step 3

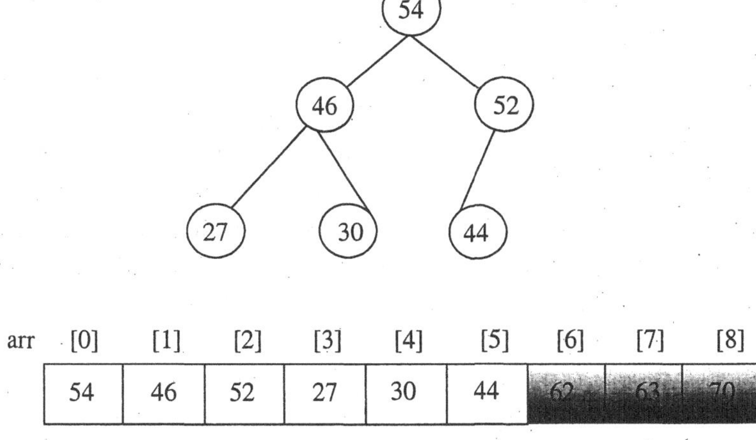

arr [0]	[1]	[2]	[3]	[4]	[5]	[6]	[7]	[8]
54	46	52	27	30	44	62	63	70

Step 4

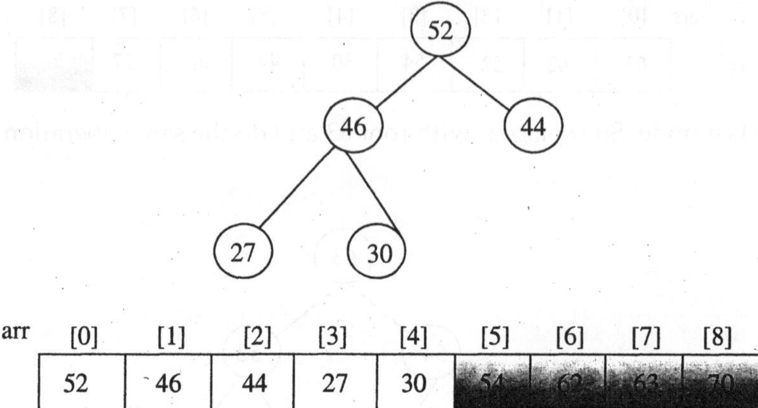

Step 5

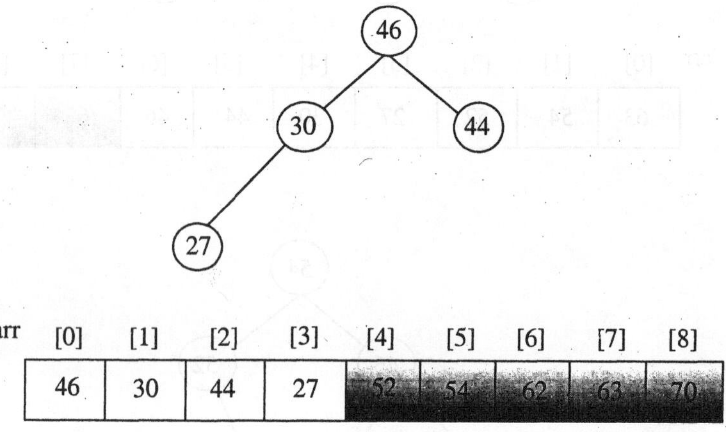

Step 6

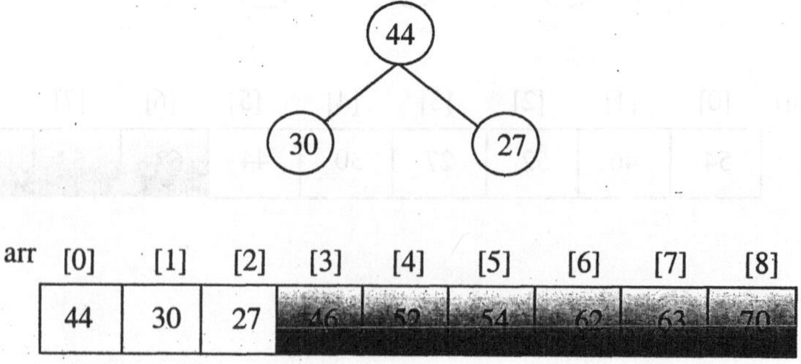

Step 7

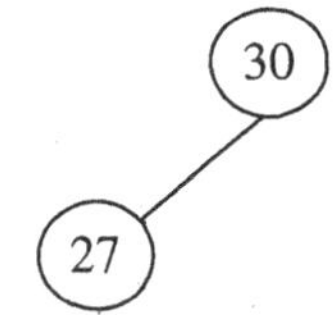

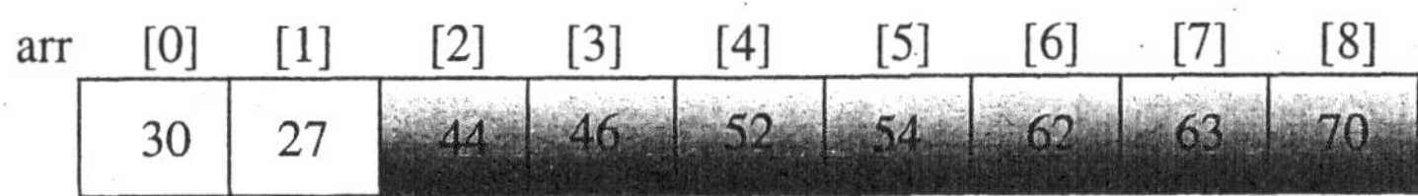

Step 8

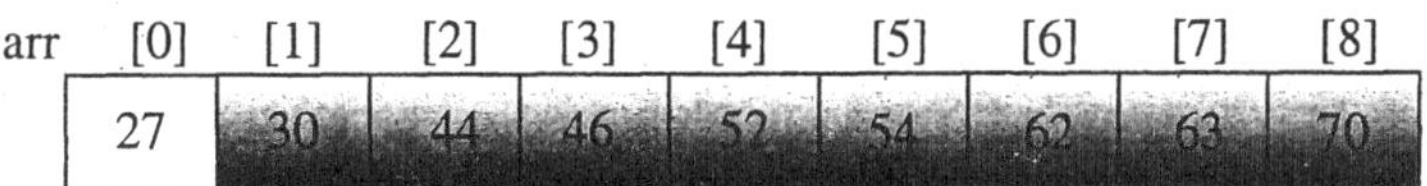

Example 12

A program and output for Heapsort is given in Figure 7.25

```
/*Heapsort */
#include <stdio.h>
#include <conio.h>
main()
{
   int a[30], x, n;
   clrscr();
   printf("Please enter the size of the array : ");
   scanf("%d", &n);
   printf("Enter elements of array : ");
   for(x=1; x <= n; ++x)
      scanf("%d", &a[x]);
   heap_sort(a,n);
   /* To print the sorted elements of the array */
      printf("The sorted array is : ");
      for(x = 1; x <= n; ++x)
         printf("%3d", a[x]);
}
```

(Contd...)

```
crheap(a,n)
int a[30], n;
{
   int i,j,key,q;
   for(q = 2 ; q <= n; ++q)

   {
      i = q;
      key = a[q];
      j = (int)(i/2);
      while ((i > 1 ) && ( key > a[j]))
      {
         a[i] = a[j];
         i = j;
         j = (int)(i/2);
         if (j < 1)
            j = 1;
      }
      a[i] = key;
   }
}
/* Function of heap sort */
heap_sort(a,n)
int a[30], n;
{
   int q, temp, i, j, key;
   crheap(a, n);
   for(q = n ; q >= 2; -- q)
   {
      temp = a[1];
      a[1] = a[q];
      a[q] = temp;
      i = 1;
      key = a[1];
      j = 2;
      if((j + 1) < q)
         if (a[j+1] > a[j]) j = j+1;
      while ((j <= (q-1) && (a[j] > key)))
      {
         a[i] = a[j];
         i = j;
         j = 2*i;
         if ((j+1) < q)
            if (a[j+1] > a[j]) j = j+1;
```

(Contd...)

```
            else if (j > n) j = n;
          a[i] = key;
       }  /*End of while loop */
    } /* End of for loop */
} /* end of function main */

RUN

Please enter the size of the array: 8

Enter elements of array: 12  67  89  43  65  3  4  99

The sorted array is: 3  4  12  43  65  67  89  99
```

Figure 7.25 Program and the output of Example 12 using heap sort

7.16 COMPARISON OF TIME COMPLEXITY

The performance of programs can be judged by criteria such as whether it satisfies the original specification of the task, whether the code is readable, whether the documentation is appropriate and so on. These factors affect the computing time and storage requirements of the program.

The *space* complexity of a program is the amount of memory it needs to run the completion.

The *time* complexity of a program is the amount of computer time it needs to run to completion. In most cases the time needed by a sort program depends on the original sequence of the data. For some sorts input data which is almost in sorted order can be completely sorted in time O(n), whereas input data that is in reverse order needs time that is $O(n^2)$. For other sorts the time required is O(n log n) regardless of original order of the data. Thus, if we have some knowledge about the original sequence of the data we can make a more intelligent decision about which sorting method to select.

As with the choice of data structure, it's worthwhile initially to try a slow but simple sort, such as the insertion sort. Insertion sort is also good for almost sorted files, operating in about O(n) time if not too many items are out of place. This is typically the case where a few new items are added to an already sorted file.

If the insertion sort proves too slow, then the shellsort is the next choice. It's very easy to implement.

Only when the shellsort proves too slow you should use one of the more complex but faster sorts: mergesort, heapsort, or quick sort. Merge sort requires extra memory, heap sort requires heap data structure, and both are somewhat slower than quicksort. So, quick sort is the usual choice when the fastest sorting time is necessary. For potentially non-random data, heapsort is better.

List of the best, average and worst case behaviour of sorting techniques in terms of O notation is as follows:

Sorting Technique	Best case	Average case	Worst case
Bubble	O(n)	$O(n^2)$	$O(n^2)$
Insertion	O(n)	$O(n^2)$	$O(n^2)$
Selection	$O(n^2)$	$O(n^2)$	$O(n^2)$
Shell	–	–	–
Quick	$O(n^2)$	O(n log n)	$O(n^2)$
Merge	O(n log n)	O(n log n)	O(n log n)
Radix	$O(n^2)$	O(n log n)	O(n log n)
Heap	O(n log n)	O(n log n)	O(n log n)

DESCRIPTIVE QUESTIONS

Q. No. 1 What is sorting? Why there is a need for sorting?

Ans to Q. 1 The process of arranging elements of a list or array in a specified order of some key for each element of the array is called sorting.

Need for sorting

Practicaly, data processing requires accessing records quickly and efficiently. Search algorithms are most efficient only when the records are sorted. If the records in a file are not in sorted order searching for a particular record would require checking every record until the match is made. This is unnecessary waste of precious computer time. If the file size is large, time wasted will be much larger.

Consider, for example, a file consisting of 1000 unsorted records. To find a record in this file we may, in worst case, need to make 1000 comparisons. If the same file is sorted on some key, then a binary search algorithm can catch the record in less than 10 comparisons.

Q. No. 2 Compare Average and worst case of different sorting algorithms.

Ans to Q. 2 *Comparison of sorting algorithms*

	Sort	Average	Worst	Comparison	Extra memory
1.	Bubble	$O(N^2)$	$O(N^2)$	Poor	No
2.	Selection	$O(N^2)$	$O(N^2)$	Fair	No
3.	Insertion	$O(N^2)$	$O(N^2)$	Good	No
4.	Shell sort	$O(N^{3/2})$	$O(N^{3/2})$	—	No
5.	Quick sort	O(N*log N)	$O(N^2)$	Good	No
6.	Merge sort	O(N*log N)	O(N*log N)	Fair	Yes
7.	Heap sort	O(N*log N)	O(N*log N)	Fair	No

Q. No. 3 Write 'C' routine for the following.

(a) Heapsort

(b) Radix sort

Ans to Q. 3 (a)

```
sort(r,lo,up)
ArrayToSort r;
int lo, up;

{int i;
/*** construct heap ***/
for (i=up/2; i>1; i--) siftup(r, i, up);
/*** repeatedly extract maximum ***/
for ( i=up; i>1; i-- )    {
   siftup(r, 1, i);
   exchange( r, 1, i );
   }
};
```

(b)

```
list sort (r)
list r;

{
list head[M], tail[M];
int i, j, h;
for (i=D; i>0; i--)   {
   for (j=0; j<M; j++)  head[j] = NULL;
   while ( r != NULL 0   {
      h = charac( i, r->k );
      if ( head[h] ==NULL ) head[h] = r;
      else tail[h] -> next = r;
      tail[h] = r;
      r = r-> next;
      };
   /*** Concatenate lists ***/
   r = NULL;
   for (j=M-1; j>=0; j--)
      if ( head[j] != NULL )   {
         tail[j] -> next = r;
         r = head[j];
         }
   };
return( r );
};
```

Q. No. 4 Write an algorithm for Shell sort.

Ans to Q. 4 Shell_sort (array, size)

```
where array -> Represents the list of elements
     size -> Represents the size of the list
Step 1: [Initialize]
        gap = size/2
Step 2: Repeat through step 6 while (gap = gap/2)
Step 3: Swap = 0
Step 4: Repeat through step 6 while (swap)
Step 5: Repeat through step 6 for I = 0, 1, 2, 3, . . . i <
(size - gap)
Step 6: If (array [i] > array [i + gap])
(i)   temp = array[i]
(ii)  array[i] = array[i + gap]
(iii) array[i + gap] = temp
(iv)  Swap = 1
[End of for loop]
[End of inner while loop]
[End of outer while loop]
Step 7: Output array elements (sorted)
Step 8: Exit
```

Q. No. 5 What is a heap? How heap sort works?

Ans to Q. 5 *[Refer to Section 7.15]*

EXERCISE

Multiple Choice

1. Name the sort for which time is not proportional to n^2
   a. Selection sort b. Bubble sort
   c. Quick sort d. None of these
2. This sort does not use divide & conquer methodology
   a. Merge sort b. Bubble sort
   c. Quick sort d. None of these
3. Name the sorting method in which array to be sorted is partitioned again and again in such a way that all elements less than or equal to partition element appear before it and those which are greater appear after it.
   a. Merge sort b. Quick sort
   c. Selection sort d. None of these

4. Worst case efficiency of this search is n.
   a. Sequential search
   b. Binary search
   c. Indexed search
   d. None of these
5. Which is not a hashing technique ?
   a. Division remainder method
   b. Folding
   c. Mid square
   d. All are hashing techniques
6. Extra space in each record is kept for which collision processing method?
   a. Linear collision processing
   b. Linked collision processing
   c. Quadratic collision processing
   d. None of these
7. Which method of collision processing requires prime area and overflow area?
   a. Linked collision processing
   b. Quadratic collision processing
   c. Linear collision processing
   d. None of these
8. In which method of collision processing some of the addresses may remain unchecked.
   a. Linear collision processing
   b. Quadratic collision processing
   c. Linked collision processing
   d. None of these
9. In which search method, keys must be ordered?
   a. Sequential search
   b. Hashing
   c. Binary search
   d. None of these
10. The searching method which requires all keys must reside in internal memory.
   a. Binary search
   b. Sequential search
   c. Hashing
   d. None of these

Key to Multiple Choice Questions

1.	c	2.	b	3.	b	4.	a	5.	d
6.	b	7.	a	8.	b	9.	c	10.	a

TEST PAPER

Note: Answer all questions.

1. What is sorting? Explain the bubble sorting method with an example.
2. Explain sequential search with an example.
3. Define hashing. Explain different hashing techniques.
4. What is Insertion sort? Give a suitable example.
5. Construct heap from following items:
   44 30 50 22 60 55 77
6. Explain merge sort with suitable example.
7. Explain how tree sort is carried out? What is the relationship between tree sort and quick sort methods.

CHAPTER 8

Graphs

8.1 INTRODUCTION

In the tree structure, the relationship between data items is hierarchical or like parent and child. A general graph, on the other hand, is a structure that represents a less restrictive relationship between data items. A common example of a graph is a collection of cities and the roads connecting them. The two cities are related if there is a road between them. Their relationship may not be hierarchical because traffic on the road routes between cities can flow in both the directions.

Graphs are data structures which have wider applications in real life namely, analysis of electrical circuits, finding shortest routes, cities and highway connections etc.

☞ *A graph is a non-linear arrangement of data items.*

8.1.1 What is a Graph ?

A graph G is an ordered pair of sets (V, E), where V is a set of *vertices* or *nodes* and E is a set of *edges* or *arcs*. A graph is thus defined as a set of objects called nodes and edges. In this context, a node is a data element of a graph, and an edge is a path between two nodes. (See Figure 8.1).

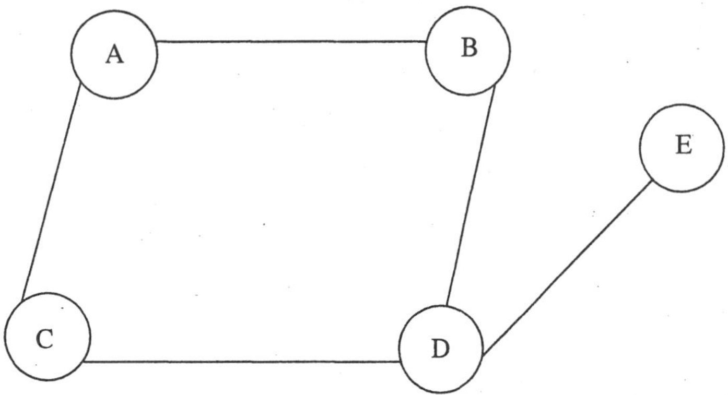

Set of vertices = {A, B, C, D, E}
Set of edges = {(A,B), (A,C), (B,D), (C, D), (D, E)}

Figure 8.1 Graphs with 5 vertices and 5 edges

Point and node are other names for vertex. Line and arc are other name for edge.

☞ *A graph **G** consists of a set **V**, whose members are called the vertices of **G**, together with a set of **E** of pairs of distinct vertices from **V**. These pairs are called the edges of **G**. If **e** = (v, w) is an edge with vertices v and w, then v and w are said to lie on **e**, and **e** is said to be incident with v and w.*

A graph can be of two types:

- Undirected graph
- Directed graph

For a graph G = (V, E), an edge that is directed from one vertex to another is called a *directed edge*, while an edge which has no specific direction is called an *undirected* edge.

☞ *A graph in which every edge is directed is called a directed graph or a digraph.*

In Figure 8.2, the directed edges are shown by means of arrows which also show the direction.

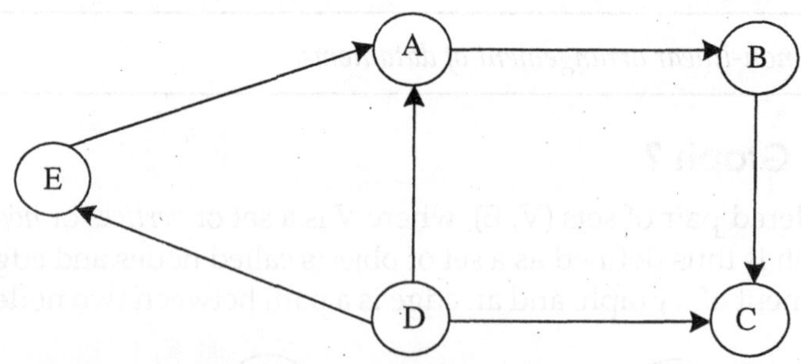

Set of vertices = {A, B, C, D, E}

Set of edges = {(A,B), (B,C), (D,C), (D,A), (D,E), (E,A)]

Figure 8.2 The directed graph with 5 vertices and 6 edges

A graph in which every edge is undirected is called *undirected graph*. Figure 8.3 shows a undirected graph with 6 vertices and 9 edges.

☞ *If the pairs v and w, of graph **G**, are unordered, then **G** is called undirected graph. If the pairs v and w are ordered then **G** is called a directed graph or digraph. The term graph usually means **undirected** graph.*

If some edges are directed and some are undirected in a graph, the graph is called *mixed graph* as seen in Figure 8.4.

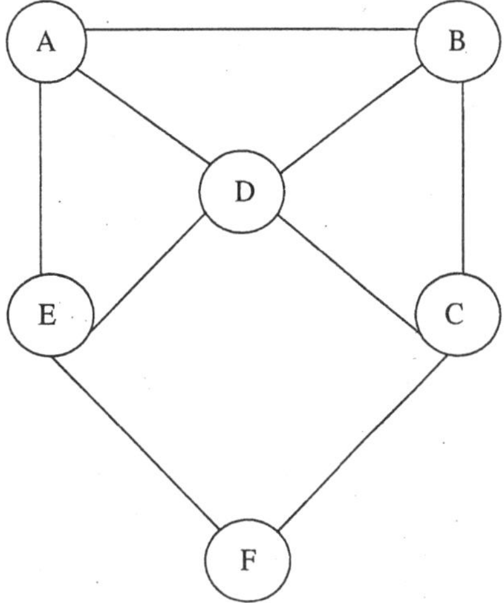

Set of vertices = {A, B, C, D, E, F}
Set of edges = {(A,B), (A,D), (A, E), (B,C), (B,D), (C,D), (C,F), (E,D) (E,F)}

Figure 8.3 The undirected graph with 6 vertices and 9 edges

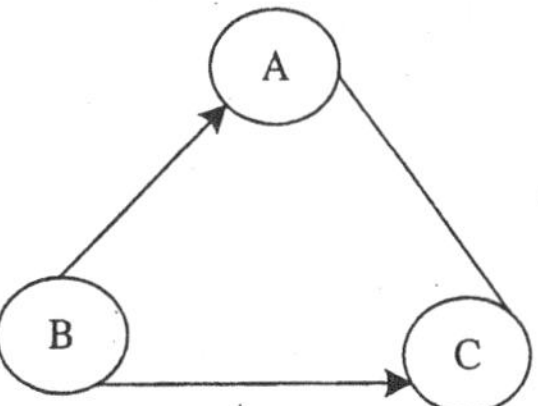

Figure 8.4 A mixed graph with 3 vertices and 3 edges

In order to use graphs effectively, we need to know which nodes are directly connected by an edge, and also which nodes are indirectly connected by a set of edges. For example in Figure 8.5, A is directly connected to B, and B is indirectly connected to E via the arcs B → C, C → D, and D → E. In a *digraph*, therefore, we may say that there is a directed path connection from node I to node J if there is a sequence of nodes $I = I_1, I_2 \ldots, I_n = J$ such that I_{i-1} is connected to I_i via an arc. In Figure 8.5, there is no path from node E to node A, although there is a path from node A to node E.

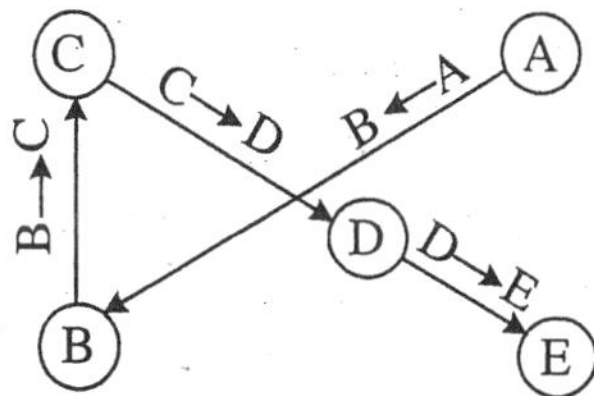

Figure 8.5 Directed graph

☞ *Any graph is considered as connected graph, provided that there exists a path between any 2 nodes.*

A digraph is said to be *strongly connected* if, for any two node I and J, there is a path from I to J and also a path from J to I. A digraph is said to be weakly connected if for any two nodes I and J, there is a directed path from I to J or J to I. The digraph in Figure 8.5 is weakly connected. It is not strongly connected because, for the nodes C and E, there is a directed path from C to E but none from E to C.

The digraph shown in Figure 8.6, is strongly connected.

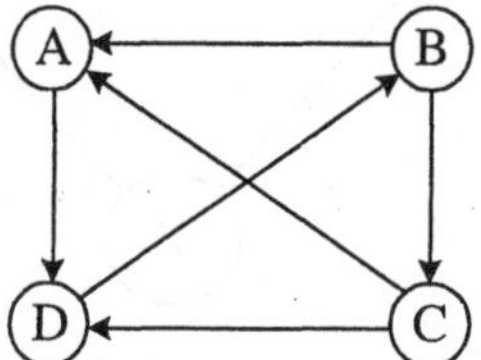

Figure 8.6 Strongly connected digraph

The *outdegree* of a node in a digraph is the number of arcs exiting from the node. The indegree of a node is the number of arcs entering the node. In Figure 8.6, the indegree of A is 2 and out degree is 1. The indegree of C and D are 1 and 2 respectively. The indegree and outdegree of a node in a digraph indicate its relative importance in data processing of that graph.

A cycle in a directed graph is a directed path of length at least 1 that originates and terminates at the same node. For example, in Figure 8.6:

A → D → B → A is a cycle of length 3.

In a graph, two vertices are said to be adjacent if there is an edge joining them. Similarly, two edges are said to be adjacent if they pass through a common vertex.

For example in the graph shown in Figure 8.7:
A and C are adjacent vertices,
A and D are adjacent vertices,
AC and AD are adjacent edges,
B and D are adjacent vertices,
BD and DA are adjacent edges,
Vertices A and B are not adjacent
Vertices B and E are not adjacent
AC and BD are not adjacent edges

If a node that has no edges connected with any other node, then its degree will be 0 and it will be called *isolated node*. In Figure 8.7, the node E is an isolated node.

It should be noted that while drawing a graph, it is immaterial whether a line is drawn straight or curved, long or short. What is important is the incidence between the edges and the vertices. For example, graph shown in Figure 8.7 can also be drawn as in Figure 8.8.

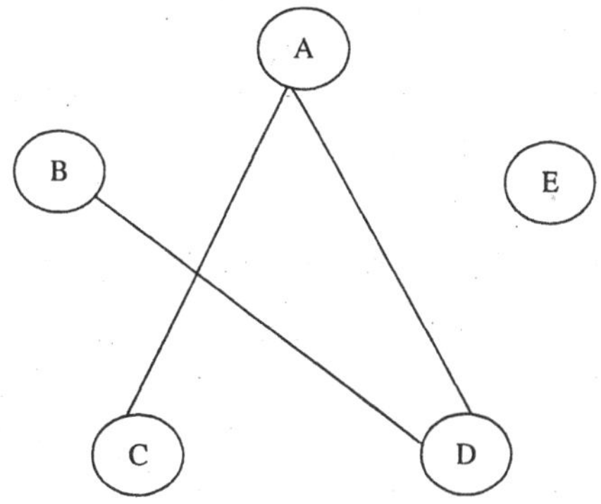

Figure 8.7 A graph with adjacent vertices

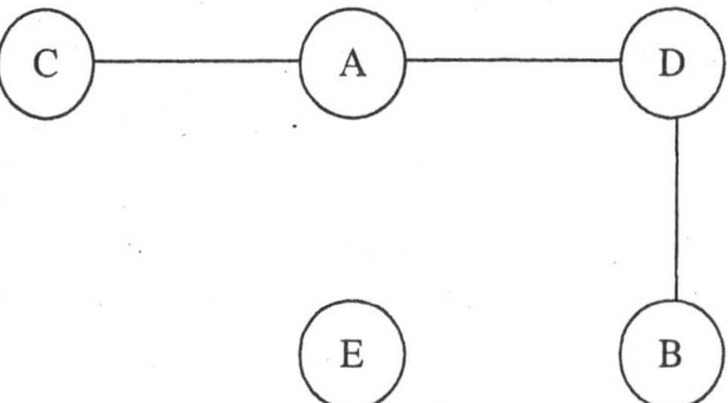

Figure 8.8 Incidence between edges and the vertices

An edge of a graph which joins a node to itself is called a *loop*. An edge will be called a *loop* or *self edge* if it starts and ends on the same node. The direction of loop has no significance. (See Figure 8.9)

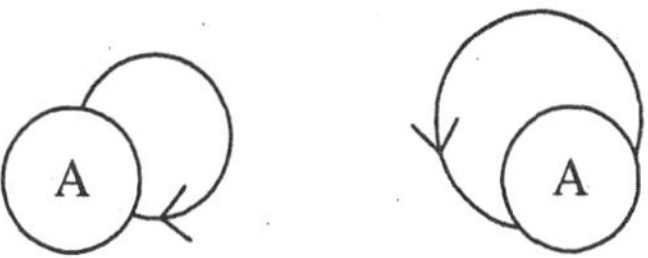

Figure 8.9 Loop

Certain pairs of nodes are joined by more than one edge. If between a pair of nodes, there are more than one edges then they are known as *parallel edges*. In the graph shown in Figure 8.10, parallel edges are shown between nodes A and C.

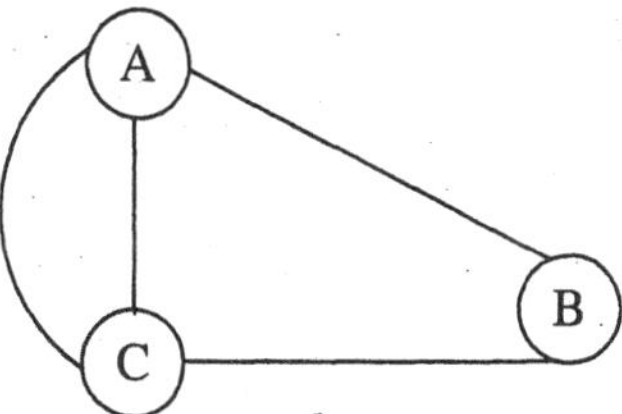

Figure 8.10 Parallel edge

8.2 GRAPH REPRESENTATION

There are three major approaches to represent graphs. These are:

- Adjacency Matrix
- Adjacency Lists
- Adjacency Multilists

8.2.1 Adjacency Matrix

The nodes that are adjacent to one another are represented as matrix. Thus, adjacency matrix is the matrix, which keeps the information of adjacent or near by nodes.

☞ *The Adjacency matrix keeps the information whether the node is adjacent to any other node or not.*

The adjacency matrix is a sequence matrix with one row and one column for each vertex. The values in the matrix are either 0 or 1. The adjacency matrix of the graph G is a 2 dimensional array of size n × n (where n is the number of vertices in the graph) with the property that a[i] [j] = 1, if the edge (V_i, V_j) is in the set of edges and a[i] [j] = 0 if there is no such edge.

For example, consider the graph G illustrated in Figure 8.11(a). Figure 8.11(b) shows the adjacency matrix for the graph in Figure 8.11(a).

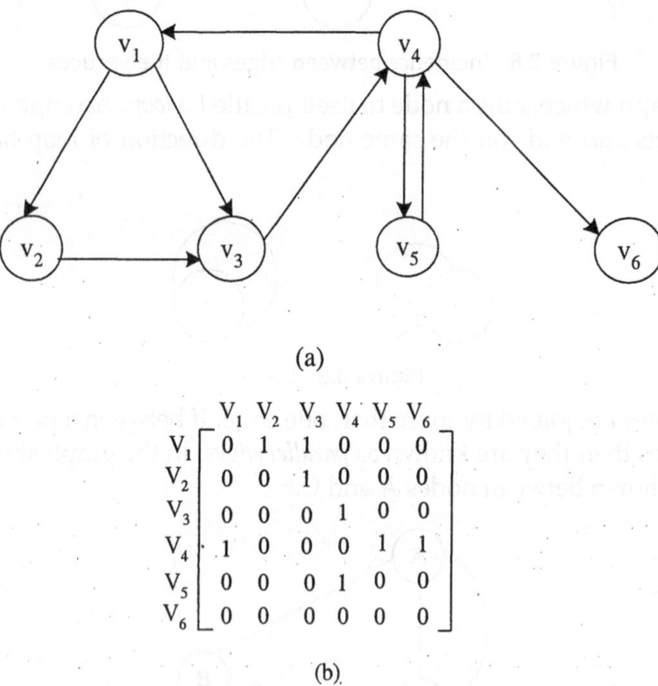

	V_1	V_2	V_3	V_4	V_5	V_6
V_1	0	1	1	0	0	0
V_2	0	0	1	0	0	0
V_3	0	0	0	1	0	0
V_4	1	0	0	0	1	1
V_5	0	0	0	1	0	0
V_6	0	0	0	0	0	0

Figure 8.11 Adjacency matrix for the graph

From the matrix in Figure 8.11(b), it is clear that the vertices are used as headings for both rows and columns. An edge between two vertices is indicated by a 1; the absence of an edge is indicated by a 0. As we can see, vertex V_1 is adjacent to V_2 and V_3, V_2 is adjacent to V_3, V_3 is adjacent to V_4 and so on. In this example, the connection of vertex to itself is indicated by 0, so the diagonal, values are all 0s.

☞ *Adjacency matrix does not depend on the ordering of the vertex of a graph, that is different ordering of the vertices may result in a different adjacency matrix. One can obtain the same matrix by interchanging rows and columns.*

Figure 8.12 shows the adjacency matrix for the digraph shown in Figure 8.5.

	A	B	C	D	E
A	0	1	0	0	0
B	0	0	1	0	0
C	0	0	0	1	0
D	0	0	0	0	1
E	0	0	0	0	0

Figure 8.12 Adjacency matrix for the digraph in Figure 8.6

8.2.2 Adjacency List

The use of adjacency matrix to represent a graph is *inadequate* because of the *static* implementation. The solution to this problem is by using a linked list structure, which represents graph using adjacency list. If the graph is not dense, that is if the graph is sparse, adjacency list representation is a better solution.

For each vertex, we keep a list of all adjacent vertices. In adjacency list representation of graph, we will maintain two lists. First list will keep track of all nodes in the graph and in second list, we will maintain a list of adjacent nodes for every node. Each list has a header node, which will be the corresponding node in the first list. The header nodes are sequential providing easy random access to the adjacency list for any particular vertex. Figure 8.13 shows the adjacency list representation for the graph in Figure 8.11(a).

The arrow (→) symbol indicates a link in a linked list. Each link in the list is a vertex. N stands for NULL in the figure.

☞ *Note that vertices may appear on the adjacency lists in an arbitrary order.*

The adjacency list can be declared in programming language 'C' as follows:

```
#define MAX_VERTICES 10
typedef struct node{int vertex;
                    struct node *link;
                 } *NEXTNODE;
NEXTNODE headnode[MAX_VERTICES];
```

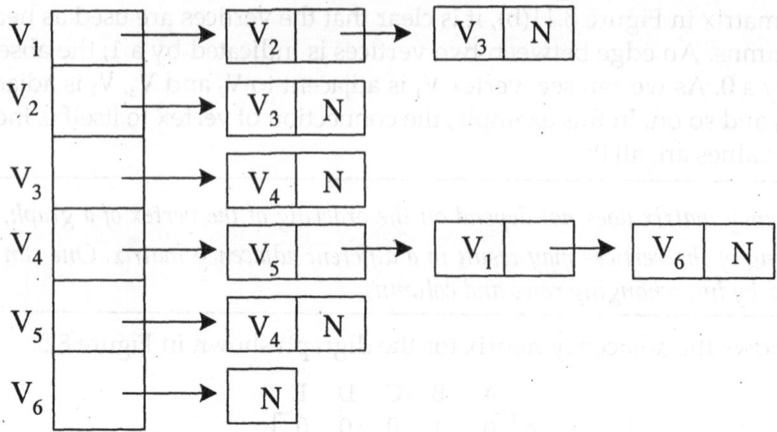

Figure 8.13 Adjacency list representation of the graph in Figure 8.11(a)

The vertex field contains the indices of vertices. The headnodes are sequential providing easy random access to the adjacency list for any particular vertex.

8.2.3 Adjacency Multicasts

When adjacency lists are maintained in a multi-list, the representation is called adjacency multi-lists or adjacency multicasts. A multi-list representation consists of two parts:

(a) directory of node information

(b) set of linked lists of edge information.

The node directory contains one entry for each node of the graph.

A multilist representation of the graph of Figure 8.14(a) is given in Figure 8.14(b). This representation is based on the set of edges {(1,2), (2,2), (2,3),(4,3),(3,5),(3,6)}.

8.3 TRAVERSAL SCHEMES

A number of graph problems involve traversal of a graph. *Traversal* of a graph means visiting each of its vertices exactly once. The solution is accomplished by visiting the vertices in a systematic way. In many practical applications of graph, there is a need to visit systematically all the nodes on a graph. One such application occurs when the organizers of a political campaign want their candidate to visit all important political constituencies. The presence or absence of direct transportation routes (edges) between such constituencies or centers will determine the possible ways in which all these centers could be visited. Two techniques of graph traversal are:

- Depth-first search
- Breadth-first search

8.3.1 Depth-first Search

This is one popular technique for systematically traversing the vertices of a graph. Depth-first traversal of an undirected graph is roughly analogous to preorder traversal of an ordered tree.

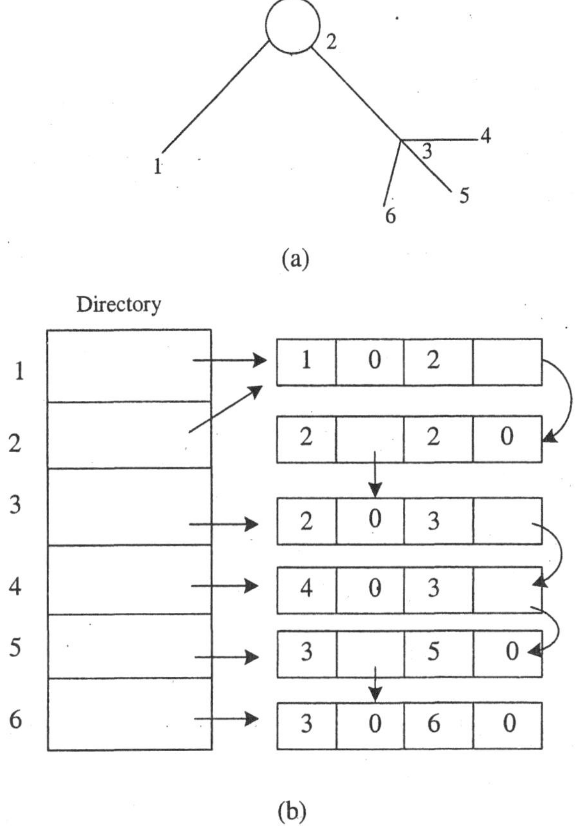

Figure 8.14 Multilist representation

In depth-first search technique, we take one node as a starting node. Then go to the path which is from starting node and visit all the nodes which are in that path. When we reach at the last node then we traverse another path starting from that node. If there is no path in the graph from the last node then it returns to the previous node in the path. It is accomplished recursively as follows:

1. Choose any node in the graph. Designate it as the *search node* and mark it *visited*.

☞ *To avoid going over the same path multiple times, we mark each vertex as "visited" when we first encounter it. We do not consider visited vertices more than once.*

---

2. Using the adjacency matrix of the graph, find a node adjacent to the search node (that is, connected by an arc from the search node) that has not been visited yet. Designate this as the new search node (but remember the previous one) and mark it as visited.
3. Repeat step 2 using the new search node. If no nodes satisfying step 2 can be found, return to the previous search node and continue from there.
4. When a return to the previous search node in step 3 is impossible, the search from the originally chosen search node is complete.

5. If the graph still contains unvisited nodes, choose any node that has not been visited and repeat steps (1) through (4).

☞ *The algorithm is called a depth – first search because the search continues progressively deeper in recursive manner.*

To illustrate depth-first search procedure more clearly, we consider the directed graph in Figure 8.15(a). Its adjacency matrix is shown in Figure 8.15(b).

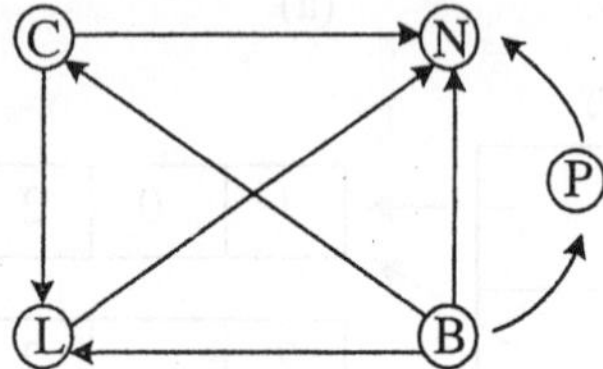

Figure 8.15(a) Directed graph illustrating a depth-first search

	C	L	N	B	P
C	0	1	1	0	0
L	0	0	1	0	0
N	0	0	0	0	0
B	1	1	1	0	1
P	0	0	1	0	0

Figure 8.15(b) Adjacency matrix of graph in Figure 8.15(a)

Suppose we have a procedure, SEARCH, that is invoked to begin a depth-first search from a given node on the graph. The steps followed by the algorithm for Figure 8.15(b) are:

1. Begin by marking C visited and invoking SEARCH(C).
2. Because both N and L are adjacent to C on the adjacency matrix of the graph, L is encountered first on a left scan of the C row, so we go to L. Invoke SEARCH(L) and mark L as visited.
3. Because N is the only node adjacent to L, we go to N, invoke SEARCH(N), and mark N as visited.
4. Because there is no node adjacent to N - that is N has exhausted the search so we go back to N's predecessor, which is node L.
5. All nodes adjacent to L also have been visited, so return to C.
6. N is the next node adjacent to C. However, N is already visited, so the search from C is now completed.
7. All nodes except P and B have been visited. Choose node B next and mark it as visited. Because P is the only unvisited node adjacent to B, proceed to P and invoke SEARCH (P). N being the only node adjacent to P, go to N – which has already been visited. Then back track to B; the total search is complete.

☞ *The depth-first search uses stack to hold the nodes for future processing.*

In tree traversal, there was no danger of repeating a path because there are no cycles in a tree. This is not true for graph traversal.

In graph traversal, two problems arise that cannot appear for tree traversal. These are:

- First, the graph may contain cycles, so our traversal algorithm may reach the same vertex second time.
- Second, the graph may not be connected, so the traversal algorithm may fail to reach all vertices from a single starting point.

8.3.2 Breadth-first Search

This is another popular way to visit the vertices of a graph systematically. This graph traversal technique uses queue for traversing all the nodes of the graph. In this, first we take any node as a starting node then we take all the nodes adjacent to that starting node. Similar approach we take for all other adjacent nodes, which are adjacent to the starting node and so on. We maintain the status of visited node in one array so that no node can be traversed again.

Although Breadth-First search can be used for directed and undirected graphs, we shall describe it in relation to undirected graphs. The breadth-first search begins at a given node and then proceed to all the nodes directly connected to that node. The following steps are involved in the algorithm.

1. Begin with any node, mark it as visited.
2. Proceed to the next node having an edge connection to the node in step (1). Mark it as visited.
3. Come back to the node in step (1), descend along an edge towards an unvisited node, and mark the new node as visited.
4. Repeat step (3) untill all nodes adjacent to the node in step (1) have been marked as visited.
5. Repeat step 1 through 4 starting from the node visited in (2), then starting from the nodes visited in step (3) in the order visited. Keep this up as long as possible before starting a new scan.

A queue is a convenient structure to keep track of nodes that are visited during a breadth-first search. As the given node is visited, it is entered into the queue of nodes waiting to have their children visited. Once all the children of a given node have been visited, the node currently at the front of the queue is removed and all its children are visited.

The undirected graph in Figure 8.16(a) shows the breadth-first searching for Figure 8.16(b), assuming that we have begun the traversal at P.

Difference between depth-first and breadth-first traversal

Depth-first traversal of graph is roughly analogous to preorder traversal of an ordered tree and breadth-first traversal of a graph is roughly analogous to level by level traversal of an ordered tree.

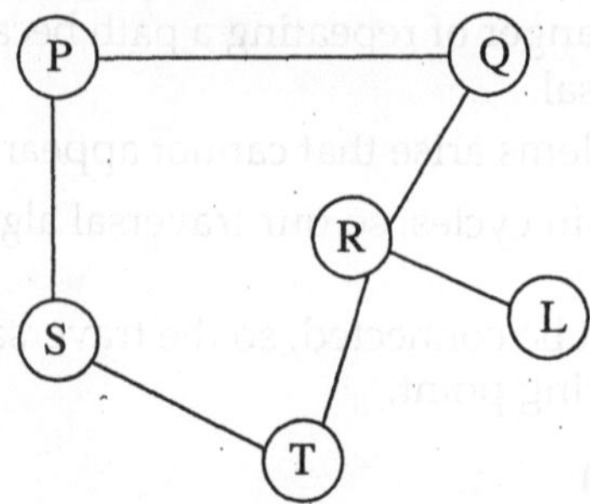

Figure 8.16(a) Undirected graph

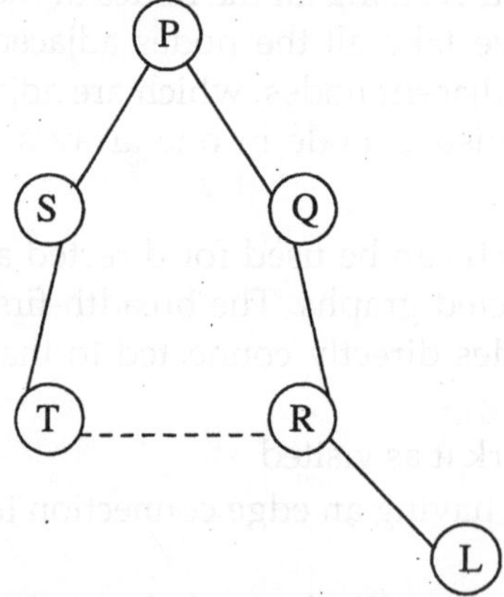

Figure 8.16(b) Breadth-first search for Figure 8.16(a)

The breadth-first traversal differs from depth-first traversal in that all unvisited vertices adjacent to V are visited after visiting the starting vertex U and marking it as visited. Next, the unvisited vertices adjacent to these vertices are visited and so on until the entire graph is traversed. The breadth-first traversal algorithm uses a queue instead of stack to store the nodes of each level of the graph as and when they are visited.

☞ *Breadth-first search of a graph is similar to level by level examination of an ordered tree.*

Figure 8.17 and 8.18 show the order of visiting the vertices of one graph under both depth-first and breadth-first traversal.

Procedure

We shall now try to understand the use of stack for depth-first search. Take an array stack which will be used to keep the unvisited neighbours of the node. Take a visited boolean array which will have *true* value if the node has been visited and will have value *false* if the node has not been visited. Initially stack is empty and top = -1. Initially visited[i] = *false* where i = 1 to *n*, *n* is the total number of nodes.

1. Initially push starting node into the stack

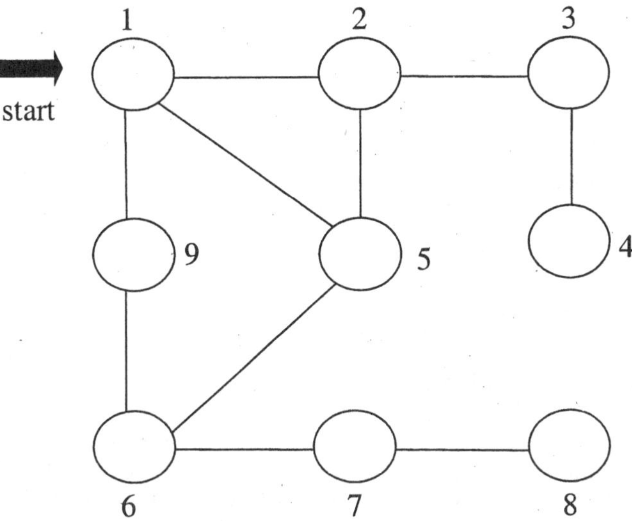

Figure 8.17 Graph traversal under depth-first search

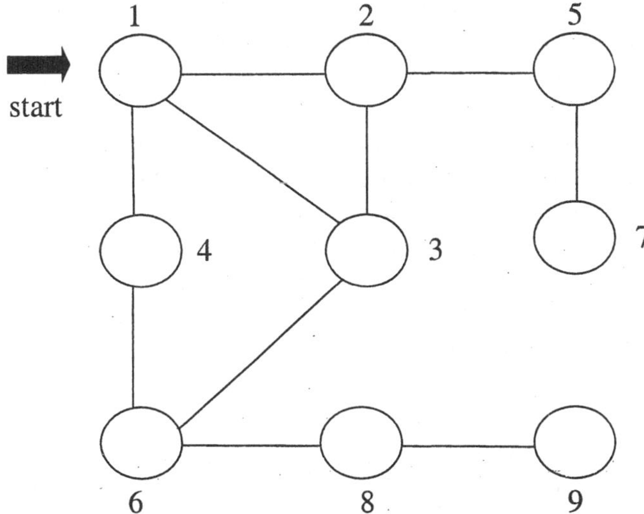

Figure 8.18 Order of visiting the vertices of graph under breadth-first search

2. Pop an element from the stack, if it has not been traversed then traverse it. If it has already been traversed then just ignore it. After traversing make the value of visited array true for this node.
3. Now push all the unvisited adjacent nodes of the popped element on stack. Push the element even if it is already on the stack.
4. Repeat steps 2 and 3 until stack is empty.

In breadth-first search, a *queue* will be used to keep the unvisited neighbours of the node. Take a boolean array visited which will have value *true* if the node has been visited and will have value *false* if the node has not been visited.

Initially, queue is empty and front = -1 and rear = -1. Initially visited[i] = *false*, where i = 1 to n, n is total number of nodes.

1. Insert starting node into the queue.
2. Delete front element from the queue and insert all its unvisited neighbours into the queue at the end, and traverse them. Also make the value of visited array *true* for these nodes.
3 Repeat step 2 until the queue is empty.

8.4 TOPOLOGICAL SORTING

Topological sorting arises as a natural subproblem in most algorithms on directed acyclic graphs (DAG). Topological sorting orders the vertices and edges of a DAG in a simple and consistent way and hence plays the same role for DAGs that depth-first search does for general graphs.

Topological sorting can be used to schedule tasks under precedence constraints. Suppose we have a set of tasks to do, but certain tasks have to be performed before other tasks. These precedence constraints form a directed acyclic graph, and any topological sort (also known as a *linear extension*) defines an order to do these tasks such that each is preformed only after all of its constraints are satisfied.

If *G* is a directed graph with no directed cycles, then a topological order for *G* is a sequential listing of all the vertices in G, such that, for all vertices $v, w \in G$1. If there is an edge from v to w, then v precedes w in the sequential listing.

For example, the courses available in a university are arranges in topological order. The courses are the vertices of a directed graph, where there is an edge from one course to another, in case, the first course is a prerequisite for the second course. A topological order is the listing of all the courses such that all prerequisites for a course appear before that course.

An example of two different topological orders of a directed graph is shown in Figure 8.19.

We shall develop functions that produce a topological ordering of the vertices of a directed graph that has no cycles. We shall develop two functions, first for depth-first traversal and then for breadth-traversal.

8.5 SHORTEST PATH ALGORITHMS

Shortest Path Algorithms are the set of steps or algorithms used to determine the shortest paths that exist in a graph. There are different types of shortest path problems. For example, we may need to find out the:

(a) shortest path between two specified vertices

---

[1]The sign ∈ means belongs to. Thus, v, w belongs to G in v, w, ∈ G.

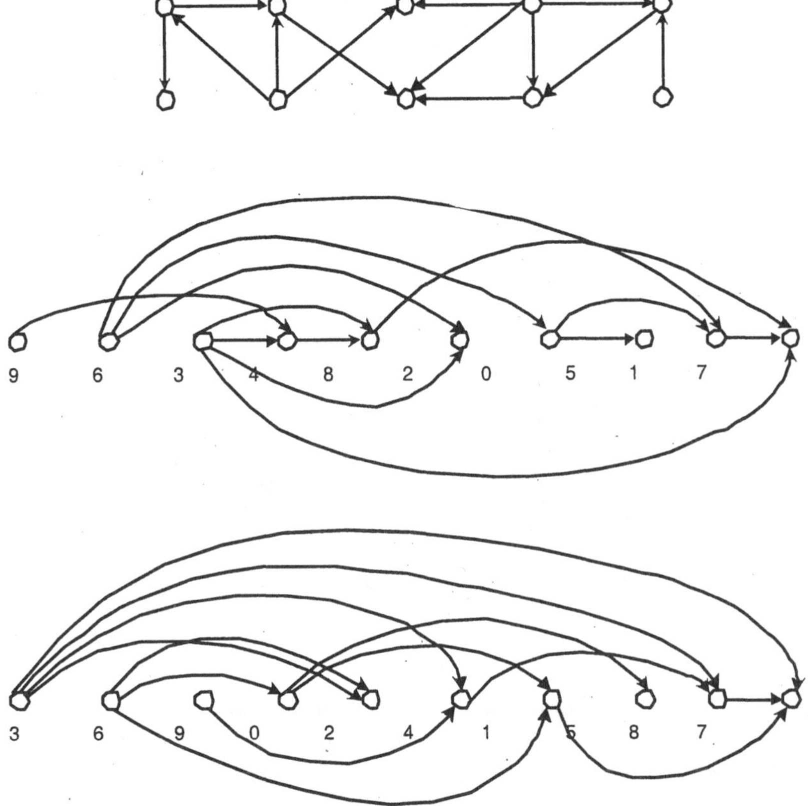

Figure 8.19 Topological ordering for a directed graph

(b) shortest path between all pairs of vertices

(c) shortest path from a specified vertex to all others

(d) shortest path between specified vertices that passes through specified vertices, etc.

Among several algorithms that have been proposed for the shortest path between a specific vertex pair, the most efficient one is the Dijkstra's Algorithm.

8.5.1 Dijkstra's Algorithm

Dijkstra's algorithm labels the vertices of a given digraph. At each stage in the algorithm some vertices have permanent labels and others temporary labels. The algorithm begins by assigning a permanent label 0 to the starting vertex s, and a temporary label ∞ to the remaining n-1 vertices. In each iteration, another vertex gets a permanent label, according to the following rules:

Rule 1 Every vertex j that is not yet permanent labeled gets a new temporary label, whose value will be $\min(j, (i + d_{ij}))$.

Here i is the most recent vertex that has been permanently labeled. And d_{ij} is the distance between the vertices i and j. If i and j are not joined, $d_{ij} = \infty$.

Rule 2 The smallest value among all the temporary labels becomes the permanent label of the corresponding vertex. In case of a tie, any one of the values is chosen for permanent labeling.

Steps (a) and (b) are repeated until the destination vertex t gets a permanent label. The first vertex to get a permanent label is s, the second vertex to get a permanent label (out of the remaining n-1 vertices) is the vertex closest to s. And so on. The permanent label of each vertex is the shortest distance of that vertex from s.

For example, let us find out a shortest path between vertex B and G, in the digraph shown in Figure 8.20, using Dijkstra's algorithm.

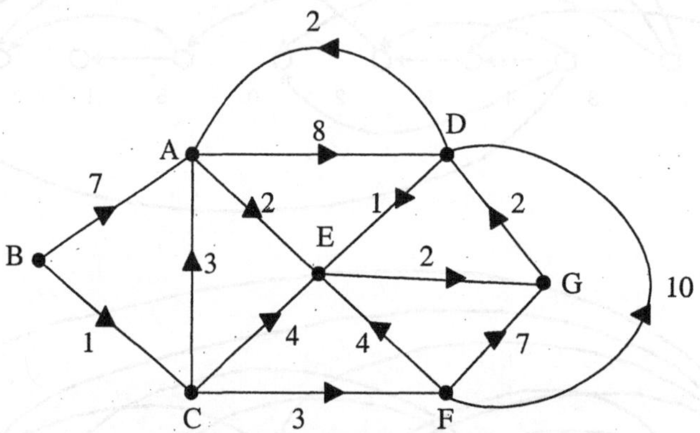

Figure 8.20 A weighted digraph

We will mark the permanent labels in squares (□), and the most recently assigned permanent label will be indicated by a cross inside a circle (⊗). The steps are as follows:

A	*B*	*C*	*D*	*E*	*F*	*G*	
∞	0⊗	∞	∞	∞	∞	∞	Starting vertex B is labeled as 0
7	0	1	∞	∞	∞	∞	All successors of B get labeled
7	0	1⊗	∞	∞	∞	∞	Smallest label becomes permanent
4	0	1	∞	5	4	∞	Successors of C gets labeled as per rule 1.
4	0	1	∞	5	4⊗	∞	One of the smallest of the temporary labels is made permanent as per rule 2
4	0	1	14	5	4	11	Successors of F gets labeled
4⊗	0	1	14	5	4	11	A gets permanently labeled
4	0	1	12	5	4	11	Successors of A gets labeled as per rule 1
4	0	1	12	5⊗	4	11	
4	0	1	12	5	4	7	
4	0	1	12	5	4	7⊗	Destination vertex gets permanently labeled

Thus, we have found out that the shortest distance between *B* and G is 7. If we had continued the labeling until every vertex got a permanent label, we would have got shortest paths from starting vertex *s* to all other vertices.

In this algorithm, as more vertices acquire permanent labels, the number of additions and comparisons needed to modify the temporary labels continue to decrease. We need n(n-1)/2 additions and 2n(n-1) comparisons. Thus, the computation time is proportional to n^2.

8.6 SPANNING TREE

A spanning tree of a graph is an undirected tree consisting of only those edges that are necessary to connect all the vertices in the original graph. A spanning tree has a property that for any pair of vertices there exists only one path between them, and the insertion of any edge to a spanning tree forms a unique cycle.

☞ *The edges traversal form a tree which includes all the visited vertices in the graph. This tree is called a spanning tree.*

A tree T is said to be a spanning tree of connected graph G, if T is a subgraph of G and T contains all vertices of G. For example, a spanning tree of the graph in Figure 8.21 is given by dark lines. An edge in a spanning tree T is called *branch* of T. An edge of G that is not in a given spanning tree T is called a *chord*.

In Figure 8.21, x_2, x_7, x_3, x_8 and x_4 are branches and x_1, x_6 and x_5 are chords.

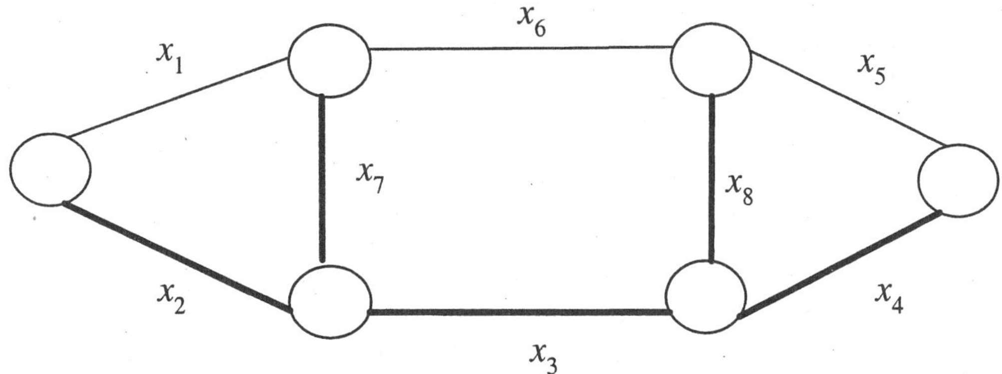

Figure 8.21 Graph and its spanning trees

8.6.1 Minimum Spanning Tree Algorithm

A *minimum spanning tree* is a spanning tree of a weighted graph such that the sum of the weights of edges is minimal. Given a connected weighted graph G, it is often desired to create a spanning tree T for G such that the sum of the weights of the tree edges in T is as small as possible. Such a tree is called a minimum spanning tree and represents the "efficient" way of connecting all the nodes in G.

A weighted graph is a graph in which each edge is assigned with a positive real number called the weight of the edge. The weight of an edge is just its value. The weight of a sub-graph of a weighted graph is the sum of the weights of the edges in the subgraph. For example, an airline may be interested in not only the existence of an air route between 2 cities but also the shortest air route. The distance between the 2 cities is the weight of the edge connecting the 2 cities. A graph with weighted edge such as the one in Figure 8.22 is called a *network*. Given a network, we must connect all the nodes in he network so that the total edge weight is minimized.

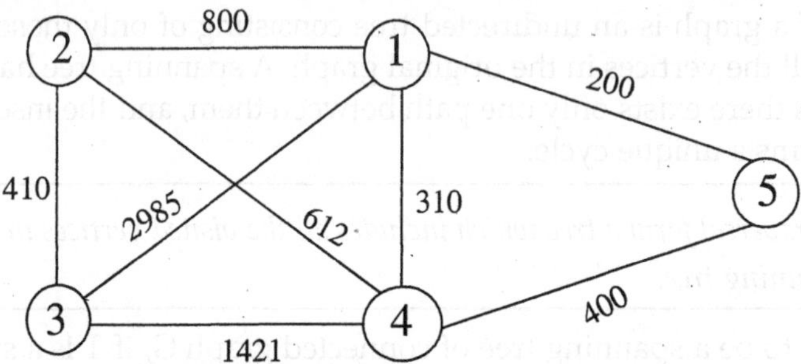

Figure 8.22 A network with weighted edges representing the distance between nodes

If graph G is a weighted graph, then the weight of a spanning tree T of G is defined as the sum of the weights of all the branches (edges) in T. In general, different spanning tree of G will have different weights. Among all the spanning tree of G, one with the smallest weight is of practical significance. A spanning tree with the smallest weight in a weighted graph is called a *shortest spanning tree* or *shortest distance spanning tree* or *minimal spanning tree.* For example, in Figure 8.23(b). T_1, T_2, T_3 and T_4 are the spanning tree, of graph of Figure 8.23(a). $Wt(T_1) = 26.8$, $Wt(T_2) = 22.8$; $Wt(T_3) = 20.6$; $Wt(T_4) = 24.8$

The tree T_3 has minimum weight (wt), hence it is an *optimal spanning tree*.

The minimum spanning tree results in a tree that contains branches chosen from the edges in the original network. Given an original network in which there is a path between any 2 nodes, the edges for the minimum spanning tree are chosen in such a way that:

1. Every node in the network must be included in the spanning tree.
2. The overall edge weight of the spanning tree is the minimum possible that will allow the existence of path between any 2 nodes in the tree.

There are several methods to find an optimal spanning tree in a connected weighted graph. Here, we consider two important algorithms for generating such an optimal tree.

Kruskal's Algorithm

Algorithm given by *Kruskal* is as follows:

List all edges of the graph G are in the order of increasing weight. Next, select the smallest edge of G.

Then for each successive step select (from all remaining edges of G) another smallest edge that makes no circuit with the previously selected edges.

Continue until *n-1* edges have been selected, and these edges will constitute the desired shortest spanning tree.

Let G be a connected weighted graph on *n* vertices. We construct an optimal tree in G by selecting the edges for the tree as follows:

Step 1: Arrange the edges of G in the increasing order of their weights. Select the edge with minimum weight.

Step 2: Then from each successive step select (from all remaining edges of G) another smallest edge that makes no circuit with previously selected edges.

Step 3: Stop when n-1 edges have been selected otherwise go to step 2

We apply these steps to the graph of Figure 8.23(a). Edges in the increasing order of weights are:

x_3, x_6, x_2, x_4, x_1 and x_5

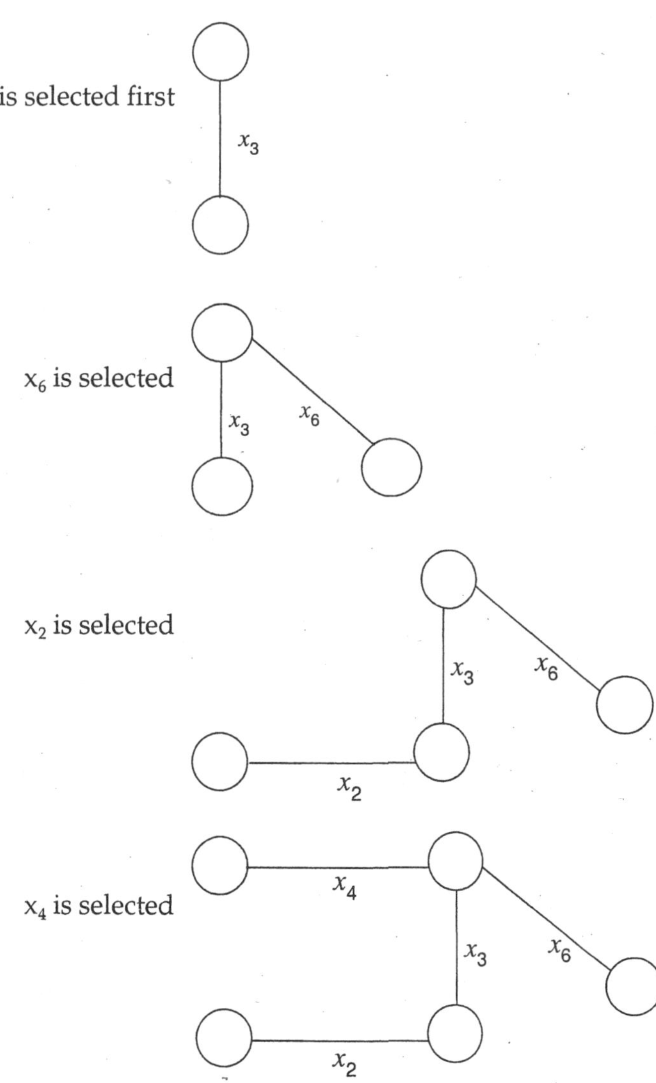

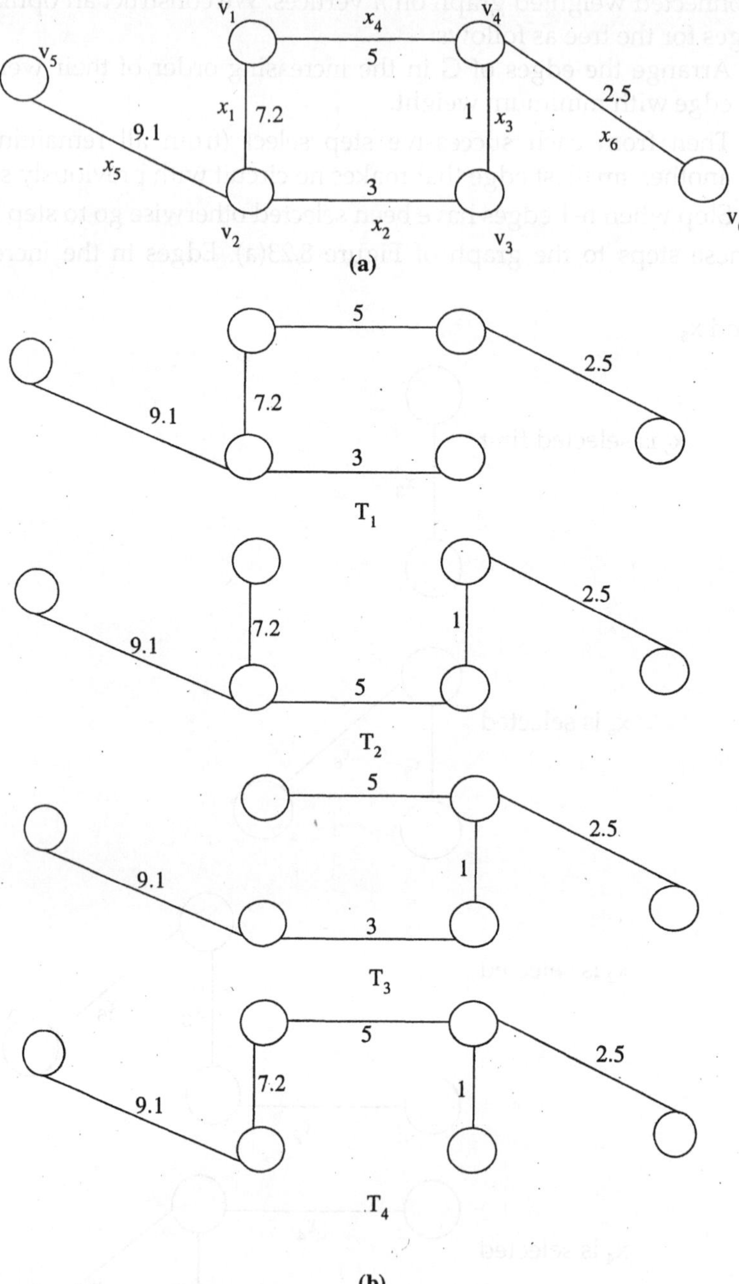

Figure 8.23 A graph with different spanning trees

Inclusion of the next edge x_1 creates a cycles. Therefore x_1 is not included. Next edge x_5 is included (See Figure 8.24).

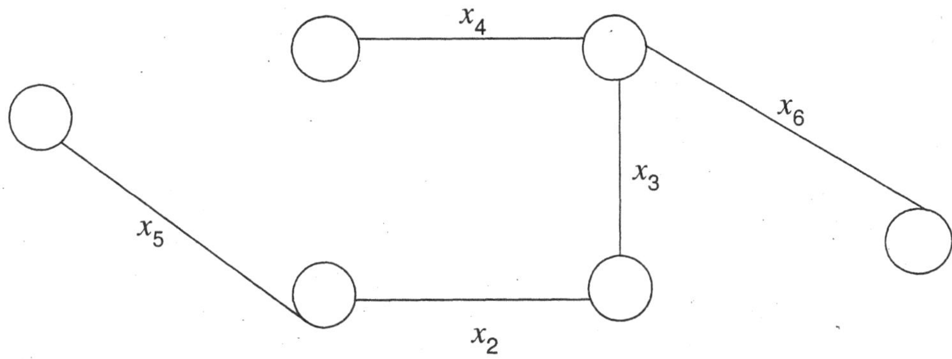

Figure 8.24 Kruskal's algorithm steps

As (n-1) = 5 i.e (6-1) = 5 edges have been selected we stop and we have obtained an optimal tree.

Prim's Algorithm

Prim's algorithm is also used for creating minimum spanning tree. Prim's algorithm, discovered independently by Prim and Dijkstra, is very much like Dijkstra's algorithm for finding shortest paths. In this algorithm, an arbitary node is chosen initially as the tree root. The nodes of the graph are then appended to the tree one at a time until all nodes of the graph are included.

☞ *Unlike Kruskal's algorithm, Prim's algorithm does not start with a list of edges sorted in increasing order of their weights.*

Step 1: Select an arbitrary vertex v_1 and the edge x_1 with minimum weight incident with v_1.

Step 2: Having selected the vertices of v_1, v_2 ..... v_k and edges x_1, x_2, ...x_{k-1}, select an edge x_k such that x_k connects a vertex of $\{v_1, v_2, v_k\}$ and a vertex of V – $\{v_1, v_2.... v_k\}$ and of all such edges x_k has minimum weight.

Step 3: Stop if n-1 edges have been selected. Otherwise go to step 2

We apply these steps to the graph of Figure 8.23(a). Start with vertex v_3; x_3 is the edge having minimum weight incident with v_3.

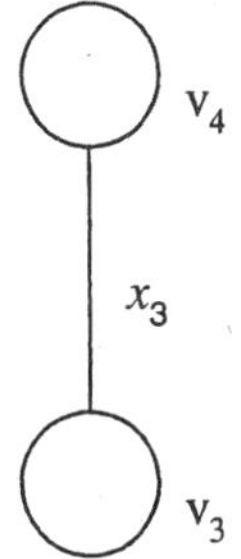

Of the edges connecting a vertex of $\{v_3, v_4\}$ with a vertex of $\{v_1, v_2, v_5, v_6\}$, x_6 has minimum weight.

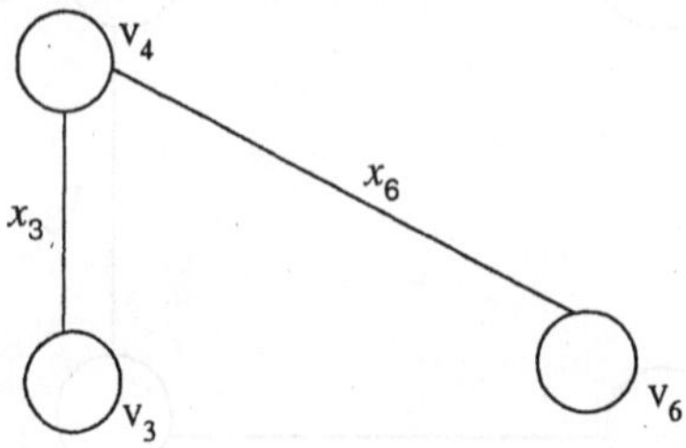

Of the edges connecting $\{v_3, v_4, v_6\}$ and $\{v_1, v_2, v_5\}$, x_2 has minimum weight.

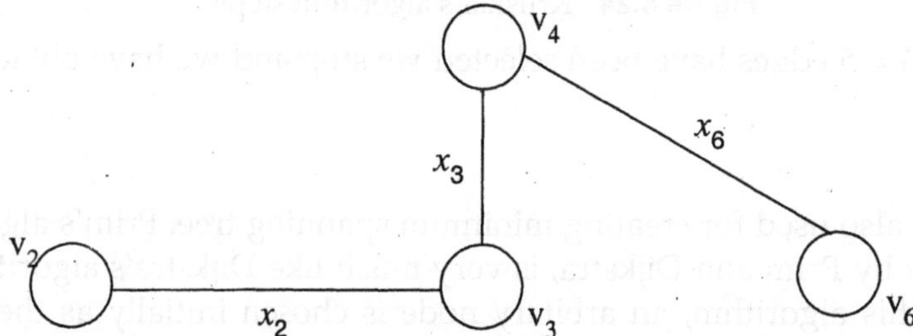

Of the edges connecting $\{v_2, v_3, v_4, v_6\}$ and $\{v_1, v_5\}$, x_4 has minimum weight.

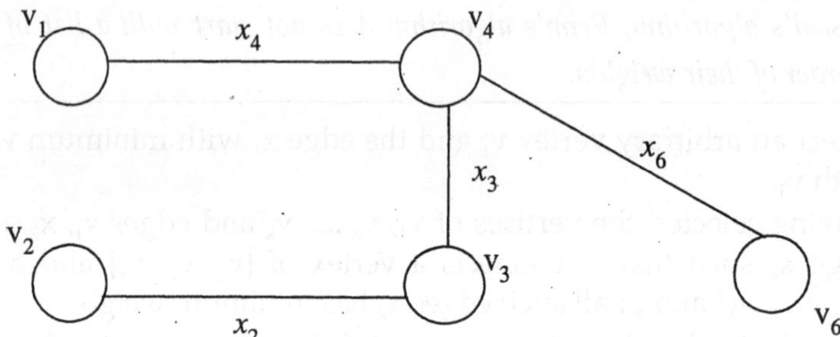

x_5 is the only edge connecting $\{v_1, v_2, v_3, v_4, v_5, v_6\}$ and $\{v_5\}$. Therefore, we select x_5.

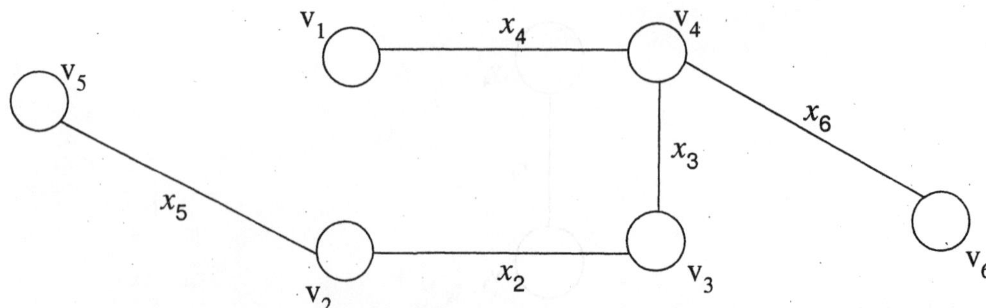

As $n-1 = 5$ edges have been selected we stop and we have obtained an optimal tree.

8.7 APPLICATIONS OF GRAPHS

- Graphs can be used to model many physical and logical situations. We might transpose a map to a graph; each vertex could represent a city, and each edge a road between cities.
- Many factories can be represented as graphs, each stage in a manufacturing process correspond to a vertex and the edges show how partially finished products pass through stages.
- A graph can be used to represent electrical circuit, with each vertex an active element and each edge a wire between elements.
- A computer program can also be represented as a graph, the vertices correspond to elementary pieces of the program, and the edges represent the flow of control among the pieces.
- Minimum spanning trees and shortest path algorithms are extensively used for applications such as electrical circuit analysis, communication networks, transportation systems, and the efficient scheduling of modules in a large project.
- There are a number of management techniques such as PERT (Program evaluation and review technique) and CPM (Critical Path Method), which use graphs as the structure on which analysis is based.

DESCRIPTIVE QUESTIONS

Q. No. 1 Explain the graph traversal methods.

Ans to Q. 1 *Depth-first traversal*

Depth-first traversal of a graph is roughly analogous to preorder traversal of an ordered tree. Suppose that the traversal has just visited a vertex V and let $w_0, w_1, \ldots, w_k$ be the vertices adjacent to V. Then we shall next visit w_0 and keep $w_1 \ldots, w_k$ waiting. After visiting w_0 we traverse all the vertices to which it is adjacent before returning to traverse $w_1, \ldots w_k$

Breadth-first traversal

Breadth-first traversal of a graph is roughly analogues to level by level traversal of an ordered tree. If the traversal has just visited a vertex V, then it next visits all the vertices adjacent to V, putting the vertices adjacent to these in a waiting list to be traversed after all vertices adjacent to V have been visited.

Q. No. 2 Explain connected graph and non-connected graph with example.

Ans to Q. 2 A graph is said to be connected if there is at least one path from every vertex to every other vertex, as in graph of Figure 8.25(a)

A non connected graph consists of several connected components. In Figure 8.25(b) A and B are one connected component, and C and D are another.

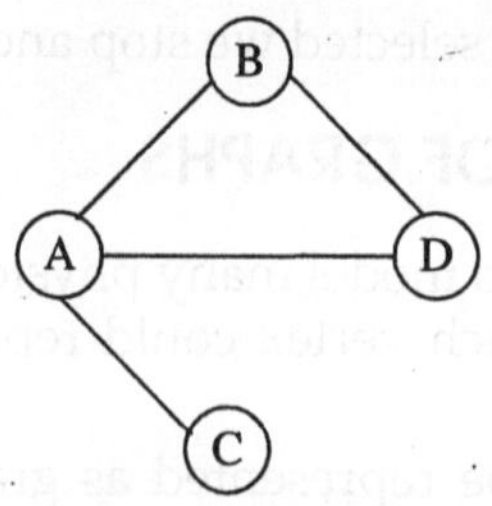

Figure 8.25(a) Connected graph

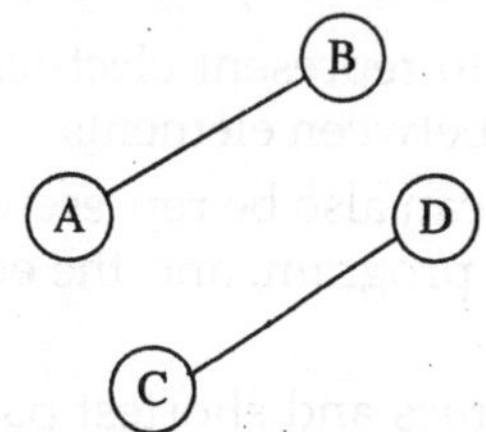

Figure 8.25(b) Non-Connected graph

Q. No. 3 Write Kruskal's Algorithm for finding a shortest spanning tree in a graph.

Ans to Q. 3 *[Refer section 8.6.1]*

Q. No. 4 Write steps to accomplish depth-first search recursively.

Ans to Q. 4 *[Refer section 8.3.2]*

Q. No. 5 What is spanning tree? Why it is so useful?

Ans to Q. 5 A spanning tree of a graph is an undirected tree consisting of only those edges that are necessary to connect all the vertices in the original graph. A

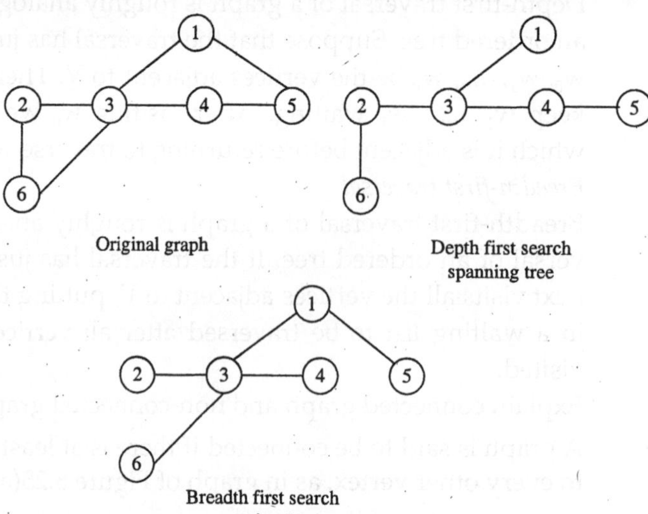

Figure 8.26

spanning tree has the property that for any pair of vertices there exists only one path between them, and the insertion of any edge to a spanning tree form a unique cycle. The particular spanning tree for a graph depends on the criteria used for generating it. The spanning tree resulting from a call to depth-first tree is known as depth-first spanning tree. Similarly, a spanning tree resulting from a call to breadth-first tree is known as a breadth-first spanning tree. Graph and depth and breadth-first search of spanning tree are given in the Figure 8.26.

The spanning tree is useful for:

- Analysis of electrical circuits
- Shortest route problems

EXERCISE

Multiple Choice

1. A vertex with degree one in a graph is called-
   (a) Leaf (b) Pendant vertex
   (c) End vertex (d) None of these
2. Which one is not a representation of a graph?
   (a) Adjacency matrix (b) Edge listing
   (c) Adjacency list (d) All represent graphs
3. In an adjacency matrix parallel edges are given by-
   (a) Similar columns (b) Similar rows
   (c) Not representable (d) None of these
4. Breadth-first search-
   (a) scans all incident edges before moving to other vertex
   (b) scans adjacent unvisited vertex as soon as possible
   (c) is same as backtracking
   (d) None of these
5. Name the sort for which time is not proportional to n^2
   (a) Selection sort (b) Bubble sort
   (c) Quick sort (d) None of these
6. In which case adjacency list representation of graph is not useful?
   (a) When no of edges is small
   (b) When no of vertices are changing due to insertion and deletion
   (c) In breadth-first traversal
   (d) It is useful in all above cases

7. Which method of traversal uses queue to hold nodes that are waiting to be processed?
   (a) Breadth-first (b) Depth-first
   (c) D-search (d) None of these
8. Which method of traversal does not use stack to hold nodes
   (a) Breadth-first (b) Depth-first
   (c) D-search (d) None of these
9. Back tracking is another name for this method of traversal
   (a) Depth-first (b) Breadth-first
   (c) D-search (d) None of these
10. Knuth-Morris-Pratt string matching algorithm, for finding an instance of a string of length p, in another string of length m runs, in an amount of time at worst proportional to-
   (a) m (b) m+p
   (c) p (d) m*p

Key to Multiple Choice Questions

1. b	2. d	3. c	4. a	5. c
6. d	7. a	8. a	9. a	10. a

TEST PAPER

Note: Answer all questions.

1. Find out the adjacency matrix and adjacency list for the graph given below:

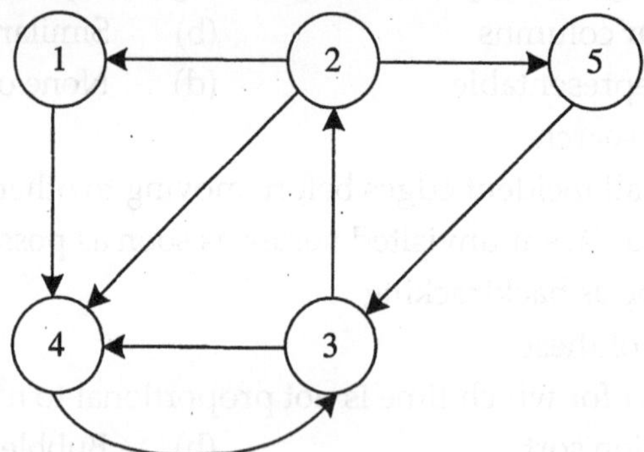

2. Find out the minimum spanning tree of the following graph by Prim's and Kruskal's algorithms.

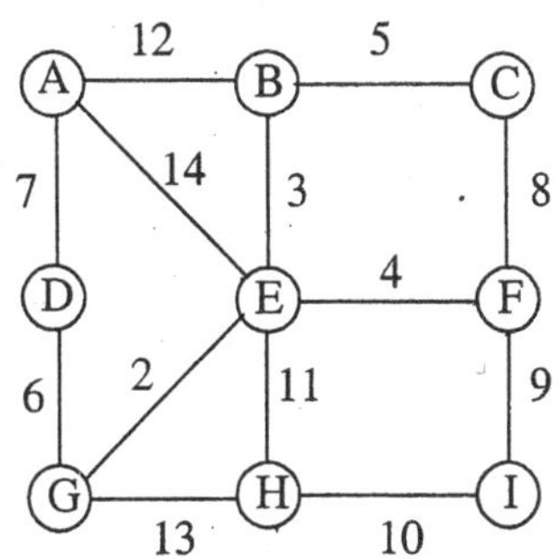

3. What is a spanning tree? Why is it useful?
4. (a) What is the indegree and outdegree of each node in the following graph?

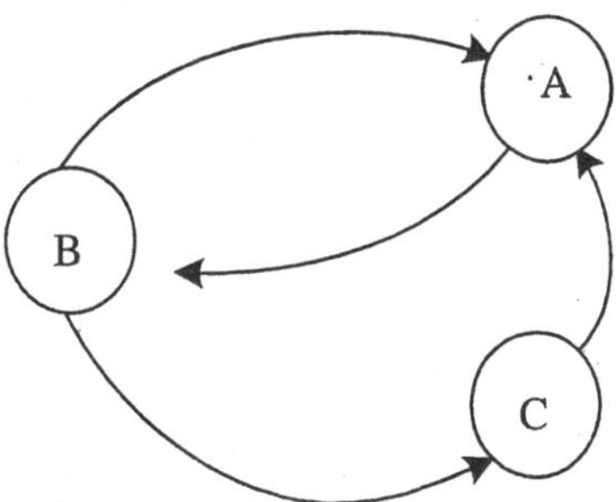

   (b) Draw a graph that has cycles in it.
5. Define the following:
   (a) Graph (b) Node (c) Edge
   (d) Digraph (e) Graph
6. What is a topological order? For what kind of graphs is topological sorting defined.
7. Explain the difference between *depth-first* and *breadth-first* traversal of a graph.
8. What is topological sorting? Explain with an example.
9. Describe graphs as both mathematical structures and data structures.
10. What do you mean by strongly connected and weakly connected directed graphs?

APPENDIX A

2–3–4 Trees

A.1 INTRODUCTION

It is a special case of B-Tree. The 2, 3, and 4 in the 2-3-4 tree refer to how many links to child nodes can potentially exist in a given node. For non leaf nodes, the following three arrangements are possible.

- A node with one data item always has two children.
- A node with two data items always has three children.
- A node with three data items always has four children.

In otherwords, a non leaf node must always have one more child than it has data items.

☞ A 2-3-4 tree can have nodes with up to four children, so it is called a multiway tree of order 4.

Figure A.1 shows a 2-3-4 tree, where each node can hold one, two or three data items.

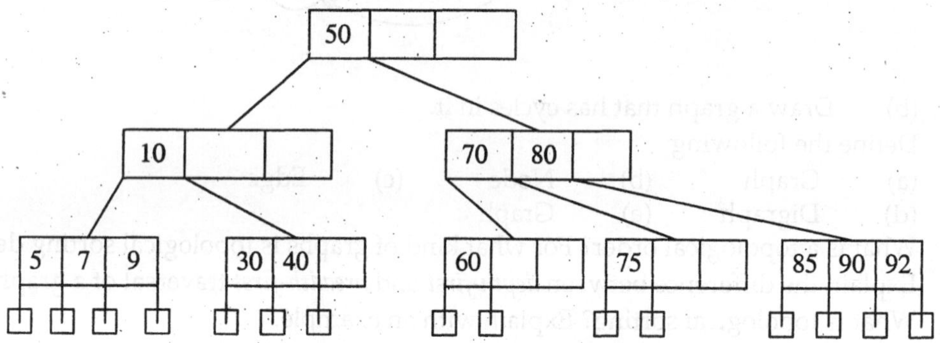

Figure A.1 A typical 2-3-4 tree

Here the top three nodes have children, and six nodes on the bottom row are all leaf nodes, have no children. In a 2-3-4 tree all the leaf nodes are always on the same level.

In a 2-3-4 tree, nodes with a single link are not permitted. A node with one data item must always have two links, unless it is a leaf. A node with two links is called a 2-node, a node with three links is a 3-node, and a node with 4 links is a 4-node, but there is no such thing as a 1-node.

A 2-3-4 tree is a search tree that is either empty or satisfies the following properties:

- Each internal node is a 2, 3 or 4 node. A 2-node has one element, a 3 node has two elements and a 4-node has three elements.
- All children in the subtree rooted at child 0 have key values less than key 0.

- All children in the subtree rooted at child 1 have key value greater than key 0 but less than key 1.
- All children in the subtree rooted at child 2 have key values greater than key 1 but less than key 2.
- All children in the subtree rooted at child 3 have key values greater than key 2.
- All external nodes are at the same level.

A.1.1 Red-Black Trees

A Reb-Black tree is a binary search tree with some special features. If data is inserted in a non-random sequence, the tree becomes unbalanced, degrading its performance. A Red-Black tree can fix this by ensuring that the tree remains balanced all times.

Red-Black tree is an extension of 2-3-4 trees. In the Red-Black balancing scheme, each node is given a new characteristic: a colour that can be either red or a black i.e the child pointers of a node of a Red-Black tree are of 2 types: Red or Black. If the child pointer was present in the original 2-3-4 tree, it is black pointer otherwise, it is red pointer.

A set of rules, called Red-Black rules, specifies permissible ways that nodes of different colour can be arranged. These rules are applied while inserting or deleting nodes.

1. In Red-Black tree, every node is either red or black.
2. The root is always black.
3. If the node is red, its children must be black.
4. Every path from the root to a leaf, or to a null, must contain the same numbers of black nodes. The Red-Black tree representation of the 2-3-4 tree is shown in Figure A.2.

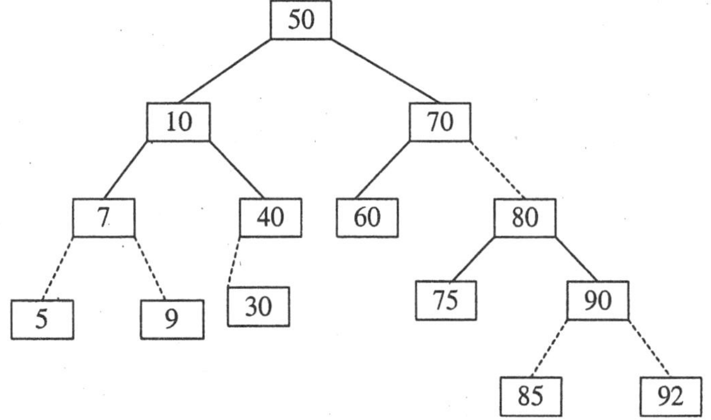

Figure A.2 Red-Black representation of the 2-3-4 tree of figure A.1

APPENDIX B

File Organization

B.1 INTRODUCTION

File Organization, is the arrangement of data in the form of a file. It deals with the arrangement of data items in a secondary storage device like magnetic disk.

☞ *The arrangement of records or data items in a file is known as **file organization**.*

Computer files are similar to ordinary files (containing papers belonging to the same subject). Both types of files store information at a central location and both contains the basic unit of information as a record. A single record contains information about a single entity. For example, the record of one employee, one inventory part number or one current account. A typical file structure stored in a secondary storage device say hard disk is shown in Figure B.1.

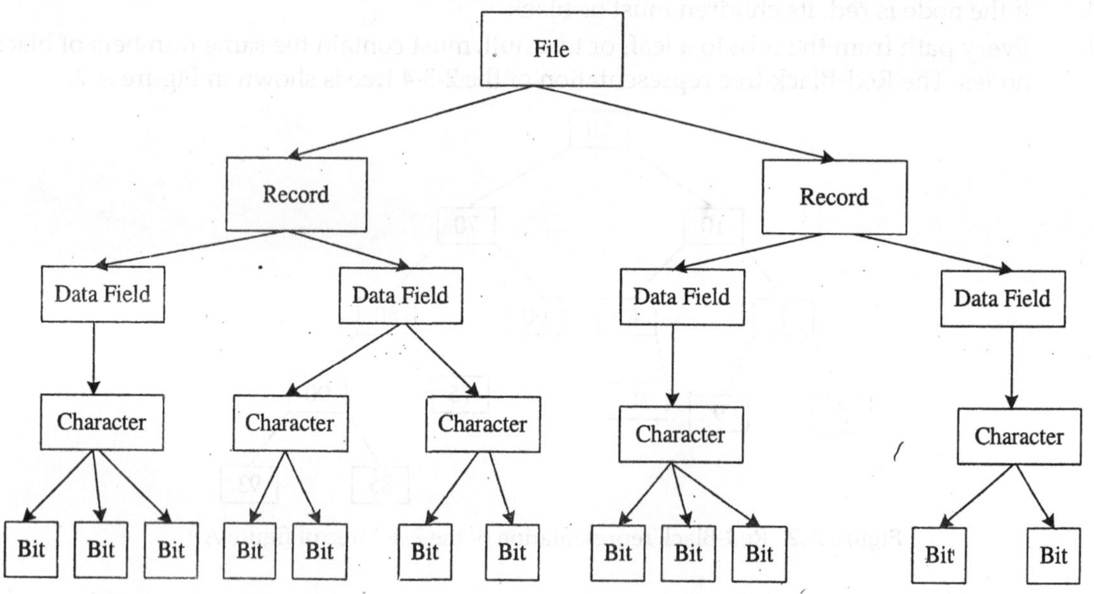

Figure B.1 A file stored on a secondary storage device contains an hierarchy of data

As seen in Figure B.1, data in the secondary storage device is stored in an hierarchical structure, starting with bits that form characters, and these in turn form data fields. Data fields when grouped together form records. The records grouped together would form a file.

B.1.1 Objectives of File Organization

The main objectives of file organization are as follows:

(a) To provide an efficient method to locate records needed for processing.

(b) To facilitate file creation and its updation in future.

For organizing records efficiently in the form of a computer file, following three objectives are important:

(a) A logical method should be observed to organize records in a file.

(b) File structure should be so designed that it would allow quick access to needed data items.

(c) Means of adding or deleting data items or records from files must be present.

Depending on the above considerations, a file may be organized as:

(a) Serial file or

(b) Sequential file or

(c) Direct or random access file or

(d) Indexed–sequential file

B.1.2 Serial File

In a serial file, the records are placed one after the other. However, there is no specific order in the arrangement of these records. On a magnetic tape storage device, the records of a serial file are written along the length of the tape (See Figure B.2). And on a magnetic disk, records are stored along the tracks, one after the other.

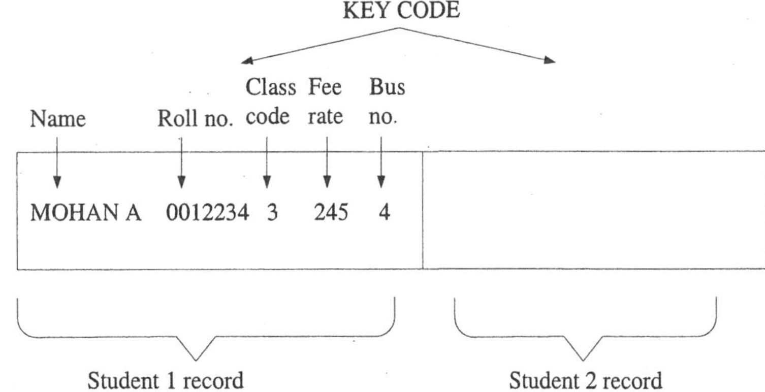

Figure B.2 Serial file organization

Serial files are ill-suited for many applications. They are usually created as temporary files and then sorted in some sequence before being processed. For example, in a batch processing application, transactions of the batch period are entered and created as a serial file without manually sorting them. This serial file can then be sorted by the computer on the required key field to produce the sequential file for processing.

The main advantage of a serial file organization is that the space on the storage medium can be utilized to the maximum possible extent.

B.1.3 Sequential Files

A sequential file is a file in which the records are stored in an order. For example, student file contains records of students in the ascending order of roll number of students. It is not necessary that all the records of a sequential file should be in physical adjacent positions. On a magnetic tape, the records are written one after the other along the length of the tape. In case of magnetic disks, the records of a sequential file may not be in contiguous locations. The sequential order may be given with the help of pointers on each record as shown in Figure B.3.

☞ *Sequential files are preferable when they are to be stored on sequential access devices such as Magnetic tapes.*

1001 Rec.1	1002 Rec.2	1003 Rec.3	1004 Rec.4	1005 Rec.5	1006 Rec.6

A sequential file on tape

1001 Rec.1	1002 Rec.2		1004 Rec.3	1005 Rec.4

1015 Rec.1	1017 Rec.2

A sequential file on disk

Figure B.3 Sequential file organization

Advantages of Sequential File

The main advantages of sequential file organization are:

(a) File design is simple.

(b) Location of records requires only the record key.

(c) When the activity rate is high, simplicity of the accessing method makes processing efficient.

(d) Low-cost file media such as magnetic tapes can be used for storing data.

Drawbacks of Sequential File

The main drawbacks of sequential file organization are:

(a) Updating requires that all transaction records are sorted in the record key sequence.

(b) A new master file, physically separate and exclusive, is always created as a result of sequential updating.

(c) Addition and deletion of records is not simple.

B.1.4 Direct Access Files

Suppose a customer at a bank wishes to know the balance amount in his savings account. If the customer file is organized sequentially, the record of this customer has to be obtained by searching sequentially from the beginning. There is no way of picking out the particular record without traversing the file from the beginning and this may take a long time. Hence, in such situations, random access or direct access file organization provides a means of accessing records speedily.

In random access or direct access method of file organization, each record has its own address on the file. With the help of this physical address, the record can be directly accessed for reading or writing. The records need not be in any sequence within the file and also need not be in adjacent locations on the storage medium. Such a file cannot be created on a magnetic tape medium. Random (or direct) files are created only on magnetic disks. Since every record can be independently accessed, every transaction can be manipulated individually.

☞ *Random access file organization is best suited for on-line processing systems where current information is the one that is always required.*

How Direct Accessing is done?

It is not necessary for the user to know where the record is kept on the disk. He identifies the record only by its key (say the account number of the customer at the bank). The operating system finds the address of the record from this key using some address-generating functions. The same address is generated while writing the record whenever it is accessed. The address-generator should not only generate unique addresses for each record but also reserve enough space for the records that may be added in future. This leads to wastage of space on the disk. There are many ways of minimizing this wastage and optimizing the available space on the disk.

Advantages of Direct Access Files

The advantages of Direct Access File Organization are:

a. Immediate access to records is possible.
b. Up-to-date information will always be available on the file.
c. Several files can be simultaneously updated.
d. Addition and deletion of records is not very complex.
e. No new master file is created for updating a random access file.

Disadvantages of Direct Access Files

The disadvantages of Direct Access File Organization are:

a. Less efficient in the use of storage space.
b. Uses a relatively expensive medium.
c. Not well suited for batch processing.
d. Data security is less due to direct access facility.

B.1.5 Indexed Sequential Files

Some files may be required to support both batch and on-line activities. For example, a share or equity stock file may be updated periodically by batch processing and at the same time may have to provide current information about stock's availability on-line. They can be thus, organized as indexed sequential files. Indexed Sequential file combines the advantages of sequential and direct file organizations.

An indexed sequential file is basically a sequential file organized serially on key fields. In addition, an index is maintained which speeds up the access of isolated records. Just as you may use indexes to locate information in a book, similarly an index is provided for the file. The file is divided into a number of blocks and the highest key in each block is indexed (Refer Table B.1).

Table B.1

Key	Starting address of the block
125	12
860	19
1420	24
1600	42
1829	49
2225	159
2890	165
3200	807

☞ *Indexed sequential files are also known as Indexed Sequential Access Method (ISAM) files.*

Within each block the record is searched sequentially. This method is much faster than searching the entire file sequentially. It is also possible to have more than one level of indexing to make the search process faster.

Applications involving sequential file processing can thus be carried out speedily and easily.

Advantages of ISAM files

The main advantage of indexed sequential file organization is that it is suitable for both sequential and on-line or direct access processing.

Disadvantages of ISAM files

The main disadvantages of this organization are:

a. Less efficient in the use of storage space.

b. Additions and deletions of records are more complex as they affect both the index and the record number in the file.

Implicit Indexes

The index file can be simplified if instead of <key, address> pair we only store the address part. But then we have to store the addresses of every possible key in the key range, including addresses of records not present in the file. The addresses of non–existent records can be set to an impossibly high or low value to indicate their absence from the file.

☞ *When <key, address> pairs are stored in an index file, it is called Explicit Index. When only addresses of every possible keys are stored in the index file, it is called Implicit Index.*

Figure B.4(a) shows explicit indexing and B.4(b) shows implicit indexing. Note that in the explicit indexing, record E is not present. In the implicit index at this position the address given is -5000 which is an impossible address. Rest of the addresses (for which records are present) are given as in explicit indexing.

Keys	Address
A	12
B	19
C	24
D	42
F	49
G	159
H	165
J	807

(a) Explicit Index

Index Entries
12
19
24
42
-5000
49
159
165
-5000
807

(b) Implicit Index

Figure B.4 (a) Explicit Index (b) Implicit Index

Glossary

Acyclic graph A directed graph in which there are no paths from any one node back to itself.

Adjacency list It is a way to represent graphs using linked lists. There is one link list for each node of a graph that contains the names of the nodes to which each node is connected.

Adjacency matrix A way to represent the physical structure of a graph by a matrix that holds locational information about the graph.

Algorithm A sequence of precise and unambiguous instructions for solving a problem in a finite number of operations.

Arc A directed path between two nodes of a graph.

Array An array represents named list of finite number of similar data elements.

Assignment The method of copying of one variable into another.

Available list A linked list containing nodes that are presently not in use for active data storage.

AVL-rotation A process by which a tree is maintained in a form close to full, thereby ensuring rapid insertions and searches.

B-tree A generalized tree that can dynamically handle insertions and deletions without a deterioration in search efficiency.

Base address The starting address of a data structure.

Binary search A method used to search an ordered list. The search begins in the middle of a table and determines whether the argument is in the upper or lower half of the table, and it continues to divide that portion of the table in which the argument being sought is located until the argument is found.

Binary tree If every node in a tree can have at most two children, the tree is called a binary tree.

Binary tree search Implements the binary search method through use of a binary tree structure.

Block factor Number of records per block

Blocking The positioning of records into contiguous regions on a track of a disk so that a fixed number are brought into main memory when a record in that block is requested.

boundary folding When producing a hash position, every other number in a key is reversed before being added into the total.

boundary tag buddy system A garbage collection scheme that allows arbitrary selection of block sizes, thereby saving memory from being wasted.

Breadth first search Searching strategy for visiting nodes of a graph. All the nodes at the same level are traversed at a time before traversing the nodes at the next level.

Bubble sort Compares the top element of an array with its successor, swapping the two if they are not in the proper order.

Bucket hashing Transforms a key to a position representing a physically contiguous region of locations. After having hashed to the bucket, records are accessed sequentially.

Child Any node may have one or more lines running downward to other nodes. The nodes below a given node is called its children.

Circular linked list A linked list in which the last node of the list points to the first node in the list, eliminating the need for null pointers.

Clustering A problem arising when a hashing function is biased toward placement of keys into a single region within a storage space.

Collision The hashing of a key to an already filled array cell is called a collision.

Column major A method by which multidimensional arrays are stored in a linear sequence in memory by columns.

Compaction A process by which character strings are relocated in memory resulting in a shift of available free space to one larger contiguous memory region.

Complete binary tree Binary tree which is either full or full through the next to last level having the leaves on the last level as far as possible.

Complete graph A graph in which every node is connected to every other node.

Concatenation Joining of two character strings.

Cross arc Uses the depth-first search to connect various nodes on different trees within the spanning forest of a graph.

Cycle A path is a directed graph of length at least 1 that originates and terminates at the same node in the graph.

Data A collection of facts in raw form that become information after proper processing or arranging.

Data structure A way of organizing data that considers not only the items stored but also their relationships to each other.

Depth of a tree The maximum level of any node in a tree.

Digraph A graph in which an edge between two nodes is directionally oriented.

Diminishing return sort A synonym for shell sort.

Direct (random) access The ability to access any location in a storage medium without first having to access prior locations.

Directed graph In a directed graph, edges have a direction.

Directory The index that stores file locations.

Double hashing A collision resolution technique which applies a second hash function to the key value.

Doubly linked list A linked list containing two pointers, one to its predecessor and another to its successor, thus allowing traversal of the list both backward and forward.

D-queue A double ended queue in which we can insert items at either end and delete them from either end.

Dummy header A node in a linked list that points to the first node that contains valid data.

Dynamic memory allocation The means by which data objects can be created as they are needed during the program execution. Such data objects remains in existence until they are explicitly destroyed.

Edge A directed path between two nodes of a graph.

Execution error An error detected during execution of a program.

Execution time The total time required to execute a program on a particular system is called its execution time for that computer system.

Exit A standard library routine that causes program to terminate normally.

External sorting The sorting of data that resides on secondary storage device.

Fibonnaci numbers Numbers that are the sum of the preceding two numbers in a sequence. For example, 1, 1, 2, 3, 5.

Field A subdivision of a record that contains an elementary data item.

Fixed length method String variables that are allocated to handle the maximum possible string length and that is envisioned for an application.

Folding A hashing method by which noninteger keys are transformed into integers suitable for further hashing action.

Forest A collection of trees with root in data structure.

Fragmentation A problem that occurs when allocation and deallocation of memory breaks free space up into smaller, less useful portions.

Front The next element to be removed from a queue.

Function A function is a named part of program that can be invoked from the other parts of the program.

Function prototype A function declaration.

Fundamental data type The data types that are not composed of any other data type.

Garbage collection The effective recovery of memory that is no longer in use.

General tree A data tree structure in which each node may have any number of descendant nodes.

Generalized dope vector method A method of efficiently representing sparse band matrices.

Goto statement Goto statement transfers the program control any where in the program.

Graph traversal An algorithm that determines the possible ways of visiting the nodes of a graph.

Hashing function Function applied to a key value of a record to obtain an address.

Heap sort A two-phase sort procedure that uses a full binary tree structure.

Height-balanced tree Maximizes the speed with which insertions and searches are handled by decreasing the depth to which one must search for an item in a data tree structure.

Incidence matrix A way the physical structure of a graph can be represented by a matrix that holds locational information about the nodes in the graph.

Indegree The number of arcs entering a node.

Index A list of keys and locational information around which a file is organized.

Indexed sequential access method A partial index is built that leads to an appropriate region, where a sequential search is then undertaken.

Infix notation The operator is written inside the operands. For example A+B, A/B etc.

Information The result of data manipulation or processing which can be used to help people make decisions.

Inorder predecessor The node that, in an ordered list, comes before a node being examined.

Inorder successor The node that, in an ordered list, follows a node being examined.

Inorder traversal An algorithm that moves through a data tree structure in such a fashion that an ordered list results.

Insertion The procedure by which a given string is added into the middle of another string.

Insertion sort Inserts in the ith pass the element in its correct place.

Internal sorting Retains all the data to be sorted in main memory.

Interpreter A language processor that translates a statement of a high level language and immediately executes it before translating the next source language statement.

ISAM Indexed sequential access method.

Key A data item that identifies a record.

Key-to-address transformation An algorithm that acts on a given key in such a way as to return a position in a list where the key can be placed. A synonym for hashing.

Leaf A node in a tree data structure that has no children is called a leaf node.

Level The level of a particular node refers to how many generations the node is from the root.

Linear hashing When a collision occurs while hashing, proceeds down a list in sequential order until a vacant position is found.

Linked list A structure that contains not only a data field but also one pointer to other nodes in the list.

Logical AND (&&) The logical AND (&&) operator evaluates to true i.e 1 if both of its operands evaluate is true.

Logical Not (!) The logical NOT(!) operator negates that truth value of its operand. If original value is true, then NOT(true) is false.

Logical OR The logical OR operator evaluates to true i.e 1 if either of its operands evaluate to true.

Loop A sequence of instructions that is executed repeatedly until a terminal condition occurs.

Looping Looping is also iteration. It is the ability to perform the same set of operations repeatedly till a specific condition is met when control comes out from the loop.

Many-to-many relationships Each node or record in a database may be related to many other nodes or records without any limitation on the type of relationship. The relationship need not be hierarchical.

Matrix A two-dimensional array in which the position of a data element must be specified by giving two coordinates.

Merge sort Most commonly used in external sorting. In this, a file is divided into two subfiles. These files are compared, one pair of records at a time, and merged by writing them to other files for further comparisons.

Minimal spanning tree A subcollection of the nodes and edges of a network that results in a tree of minimum edge weight.

Mod The remainder of dividing two numbers P and Q. For example, 5 mod 2 = 1. The remainder value is 1.

Multidimensional array An array of rank higher than one. Each data element must be specified by giving one coordinate for each dimension.

Multilink files A database relationship in which the use of a secondary key is handled by linking together all those records that share a given value for a secondary key.

Multilinked list A linked list structure that has links for each of several orders in which the list is to be traversed.

Null Pointer A pointer that does not point to any data object. In C, the null pointer can be represented by the constant 0.

O-notation A way to express the efficiency of an algorithm in terms of number of comparisons.

One-dimensional array A specific number of consecutive memory locations. This number is the size of the vector.

Outdegree The number of arcs exiting a node of a digraph.

Parent Any node (except the root) has exactly one edge running upward to another node. The node above it is called the parent of the node.

Parsing The process of collapsing different expressions into one unique form, which simplifies its evaluation.

Path A sequence of arcs connecting two nodes of a digraph.

Pattern matching The procedure by which one can search a given string for an occurrence of another string.

Pivot value The value that determines into which group an item will go during partitioning, item smaller than the pivot value go in the left group, larger items go in the right group.

Pointer A pointer is a variable that holds a memory address of another variable.

Pop Removing the top entry from a stack.

Postfix In the determination of an arithmetic expression the need for parentheses is eliminated because the operator is placed directly after the two operands to which it applies. Also called reverse Polish notation.

Postfix notation The operator follows the two operands. For example AB+, AB/ etc.

Postorder traversal A recursive tree traversal in which the root is processed after its children.

Prefix In the determination of an arithmetic statement, the operator is placed directly before the two operands to which it applies.

Prefix notation The operator is written before the operands. For example +AB.

Preorder traversal A recursive tree traversal in which the root is processed before its children.

Primary key The field on which a file is most commonly accessed. Usually primary keys are unique.

Program A set of sequenced instructions used to direct and control the operations of the computer in order to solve a problem or to perform a particular task.

Programmer One who designs, writes, tests and maintains computer programs.

Programming Language A language used to express algorithms in computer understandable form.

Push Adding a new entry onto a stack.

Queue A first-in-first-out (FIFO) list structure in which insertions are limited to the end of the list, whereas deletions may occur only at the other end.

Quick sort A pivotal item near the middle of the array is chosen, then moves are made such that items on one side of the pivot are smaller than the pivot and those on the other side are larger. This procedure is applied recursively until the whole array is sorted.

Record A group of related data items.

Recursion The ability of a procedure or function to call itself.

Reverse polish notation See postfix.

Root The node at the top of the tree is called the root.

Row major A method by which multidimensional arrays are stored in a linear sequence in memory by allocating consecutive positions in a list for each new row.

Search key A database can be searched for all records whose key field has a certain value. This value is called a search key.

Secondary key A key other than the primary key on which one may sort a file or search for an item.

Selection sort Successive elements are selected from a file or array and placed in their proper position.

Sequential search Involves beginning with the first record in a list and examining each subsequent record until the records being sought is found.

Shell sort An array is divided into smaller segments that are then separately sorted using insertion sort.

Shift folding A hashing method by which noninteger keys are broken up and added into a total, which is used as the hash key.

Shortest path An algorithm used in graph structures that proceeds by obtaining from nodes not yet selected that node closest to the source node and keeping track of these in an array. On completion of the algorithm, the data in the array determine the shortest path from a given node to all other nodes.

Singly linked list A linked list in which each node contains only one link field pointing to the next node in the list.

Sink node A node that has no arcs exiting from it.

Sort The process of arranging data in a desired sequence.

Source node A node that has no arcs entering it.

Spanning forest A set of trees obtained by decomposing a graph with a depth-first search.

Sparse matrix An array with a low percentage of nonzero entries.

Stack A last-in-first-out (LIFO) list structure in which both insertions and deletions occur at only one end of the list.

Static allocation Creation of storage space in memory for a variable at compile time.

Static Data Structure A data structure fixed in size at compile time.

String length The length of a string is the number of characters in the string with all trailing blanks removed. For example, "BOOT " takes up 6 spaces. Its actual length is 4 and two blank places.

Strongly connected A digraph in which there exists, for any two nodes, a bidirectional path between them.

Substring operations A procedure that allows a user to examine a portion of a string.

Subtree A subset of a tree that is itself a tree.

Swapping Storing programs on disk and then transferring these programs into main storage as and when they are needed. The technique is used to process large programs or several programs with limited memory.

Symmetric matrix A matrix in which the ith row and i^{th} column always are identical. An incidence matrix for an undirected graph is an example.

Synonyms Describes two keys that hash to the same position.

Syntax The set of rules of a programming language that define the pattern or structure of the word order and punctuation of an instruction. It is analogus to the rules of grammar in a language like English.

Syntax Errors Errors in computer programs that typically involve incorrect punctuation, incorrect word sequence, undefined terms, or misuse of terms. These errors are automatically detected and pointed out by language processors.

Threaded tree A tree which includes additional links to the nodes according to a tree traversal ordering.

Topological sort An algorithm to establish an ordered relationship among the nodes of graph that ensures that its adjacency matrix has only zeros below the main diagonal.

Track One of the concentric circles of storage into which a magnetic disk is divided.

Traverse To traverse a tree means to visit all the nodes in some specified order.

Tree A data structure that represents a hierarchical order of precedence between two related items.

Type conversion The process of converting one predefined type into another is called type conversion.

Unbalanced tree An unbalanced tree is one whose root has many more left descendents than right descendents, or vice versa.

Underflow A condition which results when a deletion from a data structure is attempted which is empty.

Upper triangular matrix A matrix in which all entries below the main diagonal are zeros.

Vector A one-dimensional array.

Vertex A node of a graph.

Volatile file A file that undergoes frequent insertions and deletions.

Weakly connected A digraph in which there exists between any two nodes a unidirectional path.

Weighted graph Graph in which each edge carries a value.

Achievement is not measured by what you think but by what you have done.

– UNKNOWN

Index

A

I

K

L

M

S

T

U

V

W